Fascist Interactions

FASCIST INTERACTIONS

*Proposals for a New Approach to Fascism
and Its Era, 1919–1945*

DAVID D. ROBERTS

berghahn
NEW YORK · OXFORD
www.berghahnbooks.com

Published in 2016 by

Berghahn Books

www.berghahnbooks.com

© 2016, 2018 David D. Roberts
First paperback edition published in 2018

Library of Congress Cataloging-in-Publication Data

Names: Roberts, David D., 1943–
Title: Fascist interactions : proposals for a new approach to fascism and its era, 1919–1945 / David D. Roberts.
Description: New York : Berghahn Books, 2016. | Includes bibliographical references and index.
Identifiers: LCCN 2015041753 (print) | LCCN 2015048753 (ebook) | ISBN 9781785331305 (hbk) | ISBN 9781785338199 (pbk) | ISBN 9781785331312 (ebook)
Subjects: LCSH: Fascism—History. | Fascism—Historiography. | Fascism—Study and teaching (Higher) | Right and left (Political science)—Europe—History—20th century. | Europe—Politics and government—1918–1945. | Europe—Politics and government—1918–1945—Historiography.
Classification: LCC D726.5 .R56 2016 (print) | LCC D726.5 (ebook) | DDC 320.53/309041—dc23
LC record available at http://lccn.loc.gov/2015041753

British Library Cataloguing in Publication Data

A catalogue record for this book is available from the British Library.

ISBN 978-1-78533-130-5 hardback
ISBN 978-1-78533-819-9 paperback
ISBN 978-1-78533-131-2 ebook

For Beth

CONTENTS

PREFACE

The present book is an effort to assess the current state of "fascist studies" in light of calls for a new or expanded agenda. I do not hide my foundations as an Italianist, but my concern is not with Italy or any one country but with the aggregate, the totality of new responses on the Right in Europe during the era of the two world wars. The value of the long-controversial category "generic fascism" is thus centrally at issue, but so are questions about the degree to which fascism can be demarcated or isolated. After setting the stage in part 1, I consider examples, trying out some odd angles and juxtaposition, in part 2, then hazard some tentative prescriptions in part 3.

Because the book is primarily an effort at reconceptualization, I provide no overall narrative frame, discussing, for example, the rise of fascism in Italy or Germany. In seeking to extend broadly, however, I have found it necessary to adjust my approach at certain junctures, so the reader will note an occasional shift in tone. Especially to encompass the highly symptomatic Austrian, Hungarian, and Romanian cases, something of a narrative framework seemed essential, in light of the complex interweaving of domestic and supranational interaction in all three. Only by seeing how each step led to the next, yielding a particular trajectory, can we grasp the idiosyncratic places of those cases in the new universe on the Right.

I am not an expert on any of those three countries and have followed standard secondary works. I hope to have contributed by extrapolating, drawing out implications, and placing selected aspects of each case in the wider context of the present study. In seeking to establish the framework, I found myself particularly indebted to the work of Paul A. Hanebrink on Hungary and Dennis Deletant on Romania, each cited liberally in chapters 4 and 5.

I proceed primarily by means of examples, and obviously I have chosen those that seem especially challenging and illuminating. By examples I first mean particular episodes or phenomena—or juxtapositions, comparisons, and distinctions. But I also mean particular scholarly accounts, interpretations, and uses of categories. Because there is much interweaving, I repair frequently to variations on "as we have seen," which seemed necessary to keep the intersecting components of the argument clearly in focus.

I have been concerned with the problem of fascism since my first graduate colloquium at Berkeley with Richard Webster during the fall semester of 1965–66, a mere half-century ago. Indeed, it was partly that problem that led me to pursue graduate study in history in the first place. Even after treating Fascist Italy and Nazi Germany at some length in a book on totalitarianism published in 2006, I knew there were questions about generic fascism, and our efforts to get a handle on it, that I still needed to address.

But the present book was stimulated especially by three opportunities over the last several years. First, I was invited to participate in a workshop on "Fascism and Para-Fascism: Toward a Theory of the Fascist Regime," organized by António Costa Pinto and Aristotle Kallis and held in Lisbon in November 2009. I remain grateful to Professors Costa Pinto and Kallis for the occasion to participate and for including my paper, which I revised extensively in the aftermath, in the recently published volume *Rethinking Fascism and Dictatorship in Europe* (Palgrave Macmillan, 2014), which grew from the workshop.

Second, I was invited in 2011 to contribute an annotated bibliography on "The Challenge of Fascism" to Oxford Bibliographies Online. I ended up including 260 entries, now to be found in *Oxford Bibliographies in International Relations*, edited by David Armstrong (New York: Oxford University Press, posted May 2013). This enterprise enabled me considerably to extend my range.

Third, thanks to an invitation by Constantin Iordachi, I presented a lecture entitled "'Totalitarianism' and the Search for a New Agenda in Fascist Studies" at the Central European University in Budapest, in May 2013. I remain grateful to Professor Iordachi and his colleagues and students for the opportunity to discuss my work.

In the chapters that follow I have indicated "Fascism" in uppercase only when referring to Italian Fascism or Fascist Italy. Because the book is about the new Right, though to some extent in its interaction with the Left, I have rendered both Right and Left in uppercase, even when used in adjectival forms, for the sake of clarity.

The book is dedicated to Beth Louise Ellis Roberts, my wife of almost fifty years. I've persuaded myself that she never wearies of hearing me talk about fascism, but we do discuss other matters on occasion.

PART I

PROBLEMS AND PROSPECTS

Chapter 1

NEW RESTIVENESS, NEW POSSIBILITIES, AND UNFINISHED BUSINESS IN FASCIST STUDIES

The New Restiveness against a Backdrop of Uncertainty and Contest

Among students of fascism we find evidence of renewed restiveness, even calls for a new agenda. Some propose that we are entering nothing less than a new age of fascist studies.[1] More specifically, there is talk of a "transnational turn," based on all that might be learned from a deeper focus on supranational interaction within the new Right in Europe during the era of the two world wars.[2] That interaction certainly involved regimes and movements generally considered fascist, but it extended to wider reaches of the political Right and even beyond, raising questions about the significance of the embeddedness of fascism in a network of relationships.

The restiveness and assertiveness reflect new concerns, though these are interwoven with others that have been evident for decades. Indeed, before considering examples of the new restiveness, we must note that the new thinking has emerged against a backdrop of ongoing disagreement and contest that must be kept in mind. And whereas the proposed new directions surely promise to deepen the discussion, it is not clear that they adequately address all the unfinished business. Moreover, some seem to carry the potential for new modes of waywardness or overreaction. Considering together several instances of the new thinking reveals tensions that seem symptomatic and instructive.

In the present study I seek to draw out the implications of these adumbrations of a new agenda in an effort to clarify the possibilities and priorities. To some extent this is to draw out the implications for research priorities, but at this point we may need reconceptualization, even some tweaking in our sense of history, more than we need further research. Indeed, progress seems to require that we back up, rethink, shift angles, slice and dice differently.

Concern with the Aggregate

We continue to make good progress in our understanding of the several national cases at issue, and it sometimes seems that parallel histories of those cases, with comparison establishing something like an aggregate account, is all we need—or at least the best we can do. However, many are reluctant to settle for such nominalism. Yet it is especially when we seek to go beyond to address the aggregate that we find ourselves frustrated, dissatisfied. The most basic question is what the aggregate encompasses—some specifically fascist universe to be isolated, or the wider new universe on the Right? Fascism was obviously novel and came to overshadow the new Right at the time. But the circumstances bred lots of nationalist, anti-parliamentary, anti-communist departures, sometimes producing new extremes. So starting with fascism is teleological in one sense, possibly leading us to frame the novelty of the situation in an excessively dualistic way, pitting novel fascism against everything else. In thinking about the aggregate, in other words, we may pay too much attention to what we take to be specifically fascist phenomena and less to wider, more complex "fascistizing" directions. We may thereby miss essential aspects of the universe, including the place of fascism in it.

To consider the possibilities, we need first to recall something of the overall historical framework, obvious though it is in one sense. Fascism emerged from within the uncertain and largely unexpected situation that resulted in Europe from World War I, the Russian Revolution, and the revolutionary wave that followed elsewhere. The territorial settlement established by the Paris Peace Conference was itself destabilizing, though for some countries far more than others. The war had occasioned experiment with new relationships between the political and the economic spheres, but then it also brought a good deal of economic dislocation in its wake. At the same time, the war experience fostered new modes of political consciousness and mobilization. The war's immediate aftermath saw a widespread increase in trade union membership and activity that, at least for a while, seemed to mesh with the ongoing challenge from the communist Left. Whatever the scope for, or danger of, revolutionary change, new forms of mass politics seemed inevitable. For good or for ill, it was a new world.

That postwar situation was but one phase of our continuing political experiment. Still, it was unusual, extreme, perhaps unprecedented in combining a sense of challenge, risk, and vulnerability with a sense of openness and the scope for experiment and innovation. Especially where the turn to parliamentary government or to new modes of parliamentary government proved disillusioning, the new situation seemed not only to invite but to demand such experiment. Individualistic liberal democracy was not necessarily the privileged goal of history, but neither was Marxist communism, especially as apparently being implemented under unforeseen circumstances in Russia/the Soviet Union, necessarily the privileged alternative.

So there was unanticipated experiment and novelty on what is conventionally called the Right, though the Left-Right axis could itself be challenged, with Vilfredo Pareto and Georges Sorel prominent intellectual antecedents. In the present study I will follow convention and refer to the new *Right*, but we will encounter reasons to question the Left-Right axis, and we must keep in mind that taking it for granted might impede our ability to grasp the novelty, and thus the energizing excitement, the sense of what was "modern" and progressive, among at least some of the departures at issue. We would thereby miss something important about the aggregate and the whole texture of the era.

In emphasizing the conjuncture growing from World War I, I am agreeing with Geoff Eley, who insists that "rather than any longer-term societal pathologies or deep-historical structures of political backwardness, ... it was the contrasting outcomes of the war and the associated political settlements that primarily enabled the opening toward fascism."[3] In the case of Nazism, he notes that the earlier emphasis on a putative longer-term German *Sonderweg*, or special path, made it hard to grasp the impact of the war and its revolutionary aftermath in Germany as in much of Europe.[4] Extending the point, he observes that whereas the comparative developmentalism that long framed thinking about fascism has been superseded to some extent, it remains influential, though, he insists convincingly, it is teleological, based on an ideal of modernization abstracted from the post-1945 liberal democratic West. Everything out of keeping with that abstract ideal is too readily imputed to backwardness, ruling out alternative possibilities within modernity itself.[5]

Philip Morgan has been especially effective in positing two waves in the emergence of fascism, with a divide in 1929.[6] Although the degree of stabilization can be overstated, the uncertainly and volatility of the immediate postwar period seemed to have been overcome in much of Europe by the later 1920s. Then the Depression especially, but also the Stalinist turn in the Soviet Union by 1930, suggested the need and scope for further experiment. Although the effects of the Depression of course varied from country to country, it had some impact everywhere, and the Depression context obviously made parliamentary democracy even more difficult. Thus in

Hungary, for example, there was a top-down departure from parliamentary democracy in 1932, though it proved abortive in large part, as we will see.

Then the advent of the Nazi regime in Germany further changed the context. Martin Blinkhorn usefully distinguishes the spontaneous, non-imitative forms of the new Right that characterized the 1920s from those inspired by Fascist Italy or Nazi Germany, in light of their perceived successes, after the onset of the Depression.[7] Aristotle Kallis notes that the political gravitational field of fascism grew ever stronger during the late 1930s, producing the "fascistization" of large sections of the European Right.[8]

Yet even as we no doubt need to distinguish stages and periods, the cases throughout the era of the two world wars were interconnected, forming part of the same new universe. As the era progressed, in fact, further novelty kept adding to the framework, often in contingent, unintended ways. John Pollard notes how the anti-clerical violence on the Loyalist side in the Spanish Civil War led many Catholics even elsewhere in Europe to perceive that war in apocalyptic terms, prompting them to turn toward fascism.[9]

Any consideration of the aggregate points to the long debated question of temporal limits to fascism. Was fascism confined to the particular era bounded by the two world wars, or has it continued or re-emerged in new forms since 1945? Those who treat fascism as an ongoing possibility may stretch the category in ways that mislead both about "classic" fascism and about new phenomena on the Right since 1945. But those who find fascism confined to its particular epoch tend to leave vague why and in what sense it could have been so historically specific. Any new agenda could be expected to provide some fresh perspective on this set of questions.

Even insofar as we delimit fascism to the era of the two world wars, we face a comparable question about geographical limits, about fascism outside Europe, with the Japanese case no doubt the most salient. Western specialists on Japan have their own reasons for restiveness, often feeling that the Japanese case, despite its significance to the period on other grounds, is too often marginalized on the basis of inappropriate criteria.[10] Although my focus is on Europe, even assessing the place of European fascism requires asking about its impact beyond Europe and about the scope for indigenous departures outside Europe that might also be considered part of the fascist universe of the time.

Taking Seriously and Taking Too Seriously

In recent years we have heard explicitly proclaimed efforts to "take fascism seriously," which has seemed to most specialists, at least, a positive step beyond the earlier tendency to dismiss fascism, in a moralistic and triumphalist way, as a mere "historical negativity."[11] Adrian Lyttelton recently remarked that the greatest advance in fascist studies over the last forty years has come precisely from taking the fascist self-understanding seriously. Explanations in terms of social base, once de rigueur, have been discredited as we have come to accept that the character of a movement can be explained only with reference to its aims and beliefs.[12]

By now it is widely held that fascism was not some revolt against modernity but the quest for an alternative modernity.[13] This would imply that it was not merely an effort to catch up to the modern democracies through different, more extreme means—most obviously "developmental dictatorship" of some sort. And rather than merely counterrevolutionary or reactionary, fascism was in some sense "revolutionary in its own right," to paraphrase Stanley Payne.[14] Something like belief, as opposed to kleptocracy or even "power for its own sake," fueled it, no matter how much, in our cynical mood, we might seek to reduce it to various modes of banality. Taking fascism seriously in these ways is not remotely to justify it but simply better to understand it—and the epoch in which it was central.

But even as the effort to take fascism seriously seemed an advance to many, others, continuing to find debunking appropriate, charge that "taking seriously" is merely to take the fascists at face value. R.J.B. Bosworth, concerned especially with Fascist Italy, is perhaps the most prominent example.[15] Although the "face-value" accusation is surely overstated, such charges reflect a plausible sense that we may tend to an overblown conception of fascism, even if we know better than simply to accept the fascists' own overblown claims. Bosworth's skepticism also reflects his sense of the superficiality of fascism, which meant that its impact in Italy, vis-à-vis what would have been experienced there in any case, was more limited than we tend to recognize as we talk of "Fascist Italy" or "the Fascist period."[16]

In principle, fascism can be taken seriously in an overtly negative mode, but some worry that the dominant ways of taking seriously have entailed too much neglect of the dark side, including the centrality of violence or dictatorship.[17] Sticking with the Italian example, Paul Corner asks—provocatively—"Whatever happened to dictatorship?" as, taking Fascism seriously, we came to feature culture, style, liturgy, even the sacralization of politics.[18]

More specifically, connecting the dots for them to some extent, the skeptics plausibly worry that taking seriously means privileging a priori concepts that gloss over the heterogeneity and fissiparousness, the hollowness and even ephemerality, of fascism. Obviously, such ephemerality, or whatever it was, was in no sense incompatible with horrific consequences. But the skeptics plausibly worry that whatever its destructiveness, fascism can be taken too seriously, that perhaps because of its destructive outcomes, we tend to make too much of it in other respects. If we do indeed need to take it seriously yet may tend to take it too seriously, fascism seems to entail a singular combination of substance and hollowness difficult to understand in tandem. And indeed there has long seemed something odd, even anomalous, about the consistency of the novel set of phenomena we designate as "fascism," making it especially hard to place the aggregate historically.

Questioning Generic Fascism

Even the Italian case, taken on its own, seems to entail an anomalous combination of partially conflicting elements difficult to put in convincing proportion. The problem obviously deepens when we seek to address something like the aggregate, fascism as a multi-national phenomenon, seemingly in some sense characteristic of the era of the two world wars. It is clear that the term "fascism" was coined, and embraced, by a new movement in Italy in 1919, but to what extent is it appropriate to apply the term more widely, generically, to a range of novel phenomena beyond Italy? Disagreement over the issue has been ongoing, coming periodically to center stage. Doubters feel that the category is too quickly applied, based for the most part on the Italian and/or German cases, thereby obscuring both the singularity of individual instances and the richness of the universe of responses on the new Right. For some, the notion of "generic fascism" inherently entails essentialism and reification.

We may of course accent the singularity of any one instance while still finding generic fascism appropriate for the rest, or at least for some subset of the universe at issue. Students of German Nazism and Nazi Germany, with Ian Kershaw particularly insistent, have especially tended to accent German singularity.[19] Though there are prominent exceptions, German students of Nazism have tended not to treat generic fascism.[20]

Approaching the issue from the opposite direction, we note that such influential authorities as Zeev Sternhell and A. James Gregor similarly take Nazism as singular, even as they have no problem with a concept of generic fascism that treats the Italian case as archetypal while excluding the German as anomalous. In assembling a major collaborative volume purporting to be a "handbook of fascism," Bosworth pointedly delimits Nazism and Nazi Germany to two comparative articles in a volume of 626 pages. In the same way, the conferences and collaborative volumes engineered by the Portuguese political scientist António Costa Pinto tend not to include specialists on Nazi Germany. Conversely, however, Nazi Germany is something like the elephant in the room; can we even dare to talk about the generic or the aggregate in light of the all-too-obvious sense in which Nazi Germany ended up overwhelming?

In any case, the rationale for treating Nazism as a case apart is clear—and plausible. There is simply disagreement about the relative importance of the criteria. But ultimately at issue is the utility of any concept of generic fascism, however widely we cast the net.

The Canadian historian Gilbert Allardyce offered a particularly stinging critique of the concept in a well-known, if inevitably controversial article entitled "What Fascism Is Not: Thoughts on the Deflation of a Concept," published in *American Historical Review* in 1979, with comments by Stanley Payne and Ernst Nolte.[21] The use of the concept, Allardyce charged, tends to reify, objectify, and/or essentialize fascism, making it into a thing, when in fact, he insisted, "there is no such thing as fascism. There are only the men and movements we call by that name."[22] General concepts, he insisted, have not illuminated and have probably obscured the individual identities as issue.[23]

At the same time, Allardyce voiced another, partly distinguishable concern. Somewhat like Bosworth later, he sensed that fascism was being over-inflated, taken too seriously. The "era of fascism," he noted, really involved only Rome and Berlin. Elsewhere fascist movements were noisy and extravagant but weak and struggling. By 1937–38, he pointed out, most fascist organizations were foundering, and even in Italy, young people were debating the failure of fascism.[24]

In principle we might argue that our understandings of generic fascism have simply been premature, that, in the wake of further specialized research, truer to each individual case, we might eventually find the categories for a more differentiated, flexible, and thus more convincing notion. But for Allardyce, clearly, we already knew enough about fascism in 1979 to rule out even the possibility. No generic category could ever be appropriate in light of the disparate and ultimately ephemeral character of the phenomena at issue.

When Ernst Nolte commented that fascism was marked by paradoxes—that it was simultaneously nationalist and internationalist, reactionary and revolutionary, bourgeois and populist, modern and antimodern—Allardyce took obvious delight in replying that some might conclude from Nolte's paradoxes that the emperor has no clothes.[25] Nolte seemed simply to be adding fuel to Allardyce's fire; in light of such diversity and contradiction, we would surely be better off not thinking in terms of generic fascism at all.

Although his way of turning around Nolte's comment was convincing to a degree, Allardyce was so eager that he seemed to miss how Nolte's point might feed another aspect of Allardyce's own argument. Despite his skeptical stance, Allardyce, too, found something distinctive about the movements we lump together as "fascism," so by implication it was possible to say *something* about fascism in general—but in essentially a negative mode. Rather than an ideology of the sort that emerged in the nineteenth century—a thought system that provided a theoretical outlook upon experience—fascism, he argued, appeared as "a kind of 'happening,' a collection of forces in motion, at once spontaneous and imitative, committed and unprincipled, extroverted and self-absorbed."[26] Once the men and organizations we call fascist were defeated, there was nothing to carry forward; "fascism" passed into history. In that sense, again, fascism was hollow and ephemeral, destructive though it undoubtedly was.

Allardyce's argument reflected the sense, noted above, that there was something singular about the aggregate of phenomena at issue; lacking "roots" and a common unifying ideology, fascism emerged in motion, activist and opportunistic, adapting to circumstances. Thus it was especially protean, contradictory, and, again, ephemeral, so it especially eludes conceptualization, even though we can generalize about it in this negative way.

Still, even as Allardyce was making an important point about hollowness and ephemerality, he tended to neglect the innovative purposes and directions in response to modernity that later scholars, seeking to take fascism seriously, have come to emphasize. Even though we find ephemerality in one sense, we also find greater substance and staying power in some of the components than Allardyce seemed to recognize. Extending the point, in light of such substance we cannot attribute fascism's distinctive hollowness, ephemerality, and ramshackle quality simply to the ideological emptiness that Allardyce featured. Even the contradictions and paradoxes that Nolte indicated do not necessarily justify dismissal as incoherence, confusion. Nor do they warrant the notion popular later that fascism found coherence only on the level of style.[27] As a response to mainstream modernity, fascism arguably contained coherent pods or components, even if there were tensions among them.

Although Allardyce was one-sided, the deeper we get into the substance, the more fragmented and tangled it seems, suggesting that the aggregate was a messy, perhaps overloaded mixture, with disparate components pulling in different directions—feeding our sense of contradiction, hollowness, and ephemerality overall. In indicating contradictions, Nolte was surely seeking to do justice to that fragmentation and disparity, which help bridge the gulf between substance and hollowness. The challenge is to encompass both the genuine substance in certain of the components and the overall hollowness, raggedness, contingency, even ephemerality—and to make sense of the peculiar combination.

We must also note that Allardyce, with this deflating bent, was too quick to accent the weaknesses of fascism in general by 1937–38. Let us recall

Kallis's point that the strengthening gravitational field of fascism "fascis-tized" large sections of the European Right during the late 1930s. Even as we find "authentic fascism" to some extent being marginalized or even actively suppressed in Hungary and Romania, we note the wider radical-ization on the Right in those countries at the same time. Allardyce was missing the sense in which, though it proved hollow and ephemeral in one sense, fascism was not being merely marginalized but was deeply affecting the political agenda across Europe by the later 1930s. Tim Kirk extends the point to the whole era: "Fascism determined the political agenda in Europe for a quarter of a century, from its origins in the right-wing political violence that followed the First World War to the defeat of Nazi Germany in 1945."[28] In any case, our concern to avoid overinflating fascism must not lead us to underestimate it.

Commenting in 1979, Stanley Payne found Allardyce's article a wel-come deflation of excesses and reification. But an ideal type, he pointed out, does not require the procrustean and reductionist tendencies that, as Payne saw it, Allardyce had so effectively criticized. There was still scope for a fascist minimum, necessary if only to clarify differences and the uniquenesses of particular cases. The basic fact, Payne went on, was that "a series of radical nationalist movements with revolutionary aims that were at one and the same time anti-Marxian, antiliberal, and anticonser-vative (in the conventional political sense) appeared in Europe between the world wars." We simply seek to pinpoint what these new revolutionary nationalists had in common that set them off from more mainstream con-servative nationalists like Alfred Hugenberg, Heinrich Brüning, and José Maria Gil Robles.[29] And for Payne the terminology is distinctly secondary. We call it "fascism" simply for the sake of convenience.

Although it does not address all the implications of Allardyce's ephem-erality notion, Payne's minimum still has much to recommend it; it is suffi-cient to identify the problem while avoiding reification or an overemphasis on classification. To be sure, Allardyce properly pointed out in response that "revolutionary" is itself a ragged notion and that Leftists might well dispute Payne's application of the category to fascism.[30] Certainly the ques-tion of whether fascism may legitimately be considered revolutionary re-mains controversial.[31] However, that does not preclude the sort of inquiry Payne was inviting. We simply have to consider what we mean by revolu-tionary, and perhaps expand the category, as our inquiry proceeds and as new historical instances emerge.

But whereas Payne's minimum seems reasonable, once we ask what the fascists had against Marxism, liberalism, and conservatism, things seem to explode on us; the commonality proves vague, perhaps superficial. Even if we seek to pin things down by adding a common emphasis on nation or society at the expense of liberal individualism, it is not clear that we have a useful least common denominator. Once we get deeper into the aspirations fueling fascism, we note disparity, fissuring, contestedness, and a resulting open-endedness in the ensuing dynamic. Moreover, we wonder whether the sharp distinctions Payne seems to envision are really what we need. Perhaps the assumption that they are indeed the priority obscures what was actually going on—and thus also the texture and contours of the era.

Generic Accounts and Their Limits, 1991–2004

In any case, Allardyce certainly did not prevail. Despite periodic expressions of such skepticism, efforts to treat fascism generically not only did not disappear but seemed to get a new lease on life, at least in the English-speaking world, during the 1990s, especially as what seemed instances of neo-fascism came to prominence after the collapse of the European communist regimes during 1989–91. The next fifteen years saw major efforts by Roger Griffin, Walter Laqueur, Stanley Payne, Roger Eatwell, Robert Paxton, Philip Morgan, and Michael Mann to treat fascism as a whole.[32] All found a way to incorporate not only Italy and Germany but an array of cases across Europe during the era of the two world wars. All were sensitive to concerns like Allardyce's for singularity but still found it possible—and fruitful—to bring the disparate instances of fascism together. Each took fascism seriously, and each at least addressed the question of whether we have seen recurrences of fascism since 1945.

But whereas these efforts surely had considerable value, they still left reasons for doubt. Writing in 2002, Griffin suggested that a new consensus had emerged, but much remained contested even among the major students of generic fascism.[33] For example, Eatwell was critical of Griffin, and Mann was critical of both.[34] I have sought elsewhere to indicate the problems that I myself find in the accounts by Griffin, Paxton, and Mann, especially.[35] Even as each usefully goes beyond earlier modes of dismissal to take fascism more seriously, their categories delimit their questions—and thus the possible range of frequencies they are prepared to hear. For example, Griffin's way of tracing fascism to a longing for palingenetic renewal proves reductionist in tracing fascism to a common psychological weakness in the face of modern "canopy loss."[36] So whereas Lyttelton convinces up to a point in asserting that learning to take fascist values and ideology seriously has been our greatest advance over the last forty years, we arguably need further expansion and above all further reconceptualization if we are more convincingly to place fascism historically.

Few would disagree with Morgan's insistence that the study of fascism should proceed from the particular to the general, without imposing generic categories as if they provided a ready-made solution.[37] No one advocates—or confesses to—the related but distinguishable pitfalls of essentialism, homogenization, teleological thinking, and reductionism. Although we agree that some preliminary sense of the object of inquiry is at once inevitable and necessary, in principle we all embrace reflexivity and openness to learning, as opposed to conducting our researches through a prism already in place. Insofar as we seek to specify ideal types and "heuristic value," these seem self-recommending, especially when their uses are framed ecumenically, as Griffin does in suggesting that "fascism," "totalitarianism," and "political religion" all have heuristic value.[38] Used merely heuristically, they would seem to avoid the standard pitfalls by definition.

Still, Morgan's imperative implies that the premature use of concepts is a lurking danger. Meanwhile Griffin, though his definition or fascist minimum, wound around "palingenesis," has been particularly influential, has had to keep defending himself against charges of essentialism—and has even come to level counter-charges against those he deems "the real essentialists."[39]

The effort to take fascism more seriously does not in itself overcome the dangers of essentialism and teleological thinking and indeed may invite them. Even as we seek to delimit fascist minima and ideal types as merely heuristic, they may entail taking so much a priori that they excessively channel our researches and restrict the range of frequencies we are prepared to hear. Kevin Passmore nicely pinpoints the problem in summarizing an earlier response of his to Griffin: "Fascism theories sometimes slip, in spite of protestations to the contrary, from the claim to have provided a merely heuristic category to the assumption that the definitional characteristics actually constitute the core of the movement. This in turn encourages researchers to derive the meaning of historical actions from theoretical assumptions."[40] In other words, taking this or that combination as the core, we are led to privilege what fits, marginalizing as "atypical" whatever does not. We may thereby miss the diversity and even disparity among the impulses at work.

In fact, we need to expand the range of frequencies if we are to grasp the substance in the diverse range of the experimental responses to be encompassed. We also need better to encompass the overall sense of new challenge and opportunity, including the scope for a new mode of unity and action to overcome the division and dithering that some found inherent in parliamentary democracy.

But such greater openness entails the possibility of surprise and challenge to our assumptions, even our self-understanding. So it is perhaps to be expected that triumphalist assumptions enabling us to sidestep such challenge continue to lurk in the discussion. Surely, it would seem, liberal democracy proved itself superior in winning out over fascism; the question is simply how the losers could have been so deluded. Such triumphalism is essentially what Eley has in mind in insisting, as we noted above, that a developmentalist frame, based on an idealized conception of Western modernity after 1945, has restricted our approach to earlier fascism. But triumphalism may affect us only indirectly. Thus, for example, Stephen Holmes, speaking not of fascism but of totalitarianism more generally, notes a certain complacency in our contemporary liberal self-understanding, the result, he suggests, of the reluctance of anti-liberals to push their diagnoses, prescriptions, and values in the aftermath of totalitarianism.[41] Whether the reasons are direct or indirect, we feel confident that we are attuned to an adequate range of frequencies. But insofar as we work beyond triumphalism, we realize that we have tended to oversimplify, that we may have been missing something. We prepare to widen our range.

Triumphalism reinforces a distinguishable tendency toward teleological thinking, leading us to approach whatever fascist trajectory on the basis of assumptions derived from outcomes. Such thinking sometimes combines, curiously in one sense, with short-term thinking to make us quick to find dead ends and turning points at the expense of sensitivity to openness and contingency. With the obstacles mutually reinforcing, we end up subject not only to teleological thinking but also to essentialism, homogenization, and reductionism in spite of ourselves. The standard approach also shades into a quest for clear distinctions, precluding the openness to rough edges, blurring, and uncertainty that may be necessary if we are to make sense of the universe of responses on the new Right.

Ongoing Pitfalls and Blind Spots: The Italian Example

Taking as an example the particular case I know best—the Italian—will give us a better sense of the unfinished business, including some ongoing pitfalls and blind spots. Although we are indebted to much fine work that continues to advance our understanding, discussion of Italian Fascism and Fascist Italy, perhaps especially in accounts of generic fascism, is too often one-sided, essentialist, and/or teleological as scholars pick and choose to fit a priori notions, then over-generalize, marginalizing what does not fit, or miss the ongoing openness and uncertainty through excessively teleological approaches. They thereby fail to do justice to the internal divisions and to the fluid, changing dynamic of Fascism in Italy.

In his laudable effort to take Italian Fascism seriously, Emilio Gentile came to feature "the sacralization of politics," encompassing liturgy, ritual, symbol, and myth, all propagated by the Fascist Party, which, he insisted, was not reduced to a merely choreographic role during the 1930s to the extent long believed.[42] But whereas "political religion" was prominently in play in Fascist Italy, that dimension had different proportions and meanings at different times and is easily over-emphasized. Some fascists found it overblown, reflecting the frustration or degeneration of the impulses that had fueled the Fascist departure in the first place. Gentile's emphasis on sacralization not only homogenizes Italian Fascism unduly, but glosses over questions concerning institutional locus and the interface of components.[43] So we must beware taking the sacralization of politics as either the essence or the telos of Italian Fascism.

In any case, some authorities came to believe that emphases like Gentile's made Italian Fascism seem too benign. Thus there was a renewed emphasis on "the dark side," including especially the role of violence and coercion in Fascist Italy. Indeed, many impute an actual cult of violence— a common belief in the regenerative character of violence—to Italian Fascism.[44] But whereas the place of violence is not to be minimized, a closer look indicates that it was exercised differentially at different stages and that there was much conflict within Italian Fascism over the place and desirability of violence, as over so much else. And we wonder how taking violence as central, even definitional, squares with the legalistic statism that others find central to Italian Fascism, especially in seeking to differentiate it from German Nazism.[45] It is too easy to take violence as essential and to marginalize as atypical, or as less than genuinely fascist, those fascists playing it down. Even today there remains uncertainty and disagreement over who qualified as a genuine fascist—just as there was at the time.

For Goffredo Adinolfi, the philosopher Giovanni Gentile, despite a number of major cultural roles in the Fascist regime, was not a fascist but a Nationalist like Alfredo Rocco.[46] Adinolfi seems not to recognize that Gentile explicitly repudiated Rocco-style Nationalism, with its naturalistic conception of the nation and its rigid elitism, in favor of a more open-ended, democratic, and "spiritual" conception.[47] Gentile highlighted the difference even from within the Fascist regime.[48] Still, Gentile and Rocco surely had some things in common that distinguished them from other fascists—from the violent *squadristi*, for example. Adinolfi may view these latter as the real fascists, and certainly some would agree. Partly because neither Rocco nor Gentile was a fascist of the first hour, let alone a *squadrista*, some not only take them as not really fascist but conflate them. But this is too dualistic. Rocco served for seven years as the Fascist regime's minister of justice, in which capacity he was the major architect of the new Fascist state. Are we to say that because Rocco had begun as a leading light in the

Italian Nationalist Association, that state was "Nationalist" and not really fascist at all?

Some come close to arguing as much, that in Italy "genuine fascism" got compromised through fusion with the more conservative Nationalists—an argument that we can better consider in chapter 4. The key for now is that we cannot make sense of Italian Fascism, let alone its place in the wider universe of the period, without doing justice to its messy, catchall quality; only on that basis can we understand the debilitating fissiparousness that ensued. Lyttelton wisely entitled his still-valuable anthology of fascist writings *Italian Fascisms*, in the plural.[49] If we keep cutting deeper, doing greater justice to the messy mixture, we find elements in motion, coalescing and reacting against each other, making "Italian Fascism" an uncertain, unstable field of forces.

To accent contingency, the lack of some a priori logic, is not to boil it all down to mere opportunism, let alone to mere activism, whether "for its own sake," in some sense, or "to keep the masses in motion." Among the conflicting components we find genuinely revolutionary aspirations for an alternative to mainstream modernity. However, even these conflicted among themselves in significant ways. The fissuring and contest did not keep the regime from developing a policy and course of action in this or that area, but insofar as we eschew teleological thinking and attune to openness, contingency, and the changing dynamic over time, we understand that even the outcomes did not reveal some defining essence there all along.

Again and again the combination of short-term and teleological thinking has led to an overemphasis on the blunting or even the definitive defeat of "genuine" or radical fascism.[50] Such blunting there surely was, in the Italian case and elsewhere, as we will also discuss in chapter 4, but it is too easy to miss the contestedness and ongoing openness of the trajectory. Part of the problem is that the criteria of radicalism, and even Left and Right, were often not clear at the time, in light of the novel, experimental quality of Fascism, so what was at issue is easily misconstrued. Axes of overlap and division can be hard to discern and characterize. In thinking about Fascist radicalism, some point to Roberto Farinacci, envisioning a certain role for the Fascist Party, while others point to Giuseppe Bottai, envisioning a certain role for corporatism with roots in the revolutionary syndicalist tradition. Though they overlapped in certain respects, the party and corporatist currents were often at odds.

Those who posit a definitive defeat for the fascist "Left" sometimes cite the Pacification Pact of 1921, sometimes the redirection of the fascist trade-union movement in 1928, sometimes the defeat of Ugo Spirito's proposal for proprietary corporations in 1932. There are other possibilities as well. But the very fact that such disparate, chronologically separated instances are cited suggests that we are too eager to find definitive defeats. We need to be better attuned to how much remained in play, even as there was indeed narrowing by the end, as we will discuss especially in chapter 8.

As layers piled up by the later years of the regime, conflicting impulses and uncertainties had produced considerable cognitive dissonance, including inflated rhetoric and mythmaking, themselves key aspects of the Italian Fascist trajectory. Evidence of that cognitive dissonance abounds in specialized work on Italian Fascism, though its sources and its implications for the ongoing dynamic are rarely considered explicitly. Such dissonance seriously weakened the corporatist thrust so important to the Italian Fascist self-understanding by the early 1930s. But then as expansionism and foreign policy came to loom larger by the mid-1930s, cognitive dissonance came to be wound especially around the relationship with Nazi Germany.

The new emphasis on race, purity, and exclusion stood in obvious tension with the earlier valorization of the cosmopolitanism and inclusiveness that had seemed evidence of Rome's universal mission—and that, as embraced by Fascist Italy, putatively made Italy culturally superior within the Axis, whatever the inferiority in military power.[51] Yet the Fascist accent on Italian cultural primacy, based on the originality and superiority of Latin civilization, remained central until the fall of the regime in 1943. Such cognitive dissonance helped to compromise the regime's competence and even to sap its energies by the early 1940s. Ultimately, it contributed significantly to the superficiality and ephemerality that proved to characterize Italian Fascism.

In light of the internal differentiation fueling the particular open-ended dynamic in Italy, even Italian Fascism was not a "thing" but at best a process with a characteristic dynamic. But if this, the first and arguably the archetypal case of fascism is so slippery, what scope is there for encompassing the wider aggregate? Let us consider what might be learned from the new restiveness and assertiveness, which picks up on the earlier concerns regarding essentialism and other pitfalls but also reflects some further concerns. In what sense do we have the makings of a new agenda?

Notes

1. Stein U. Larsen, "Decomposition and Recomposition in Theories: How to Arrive at Useful Ideas Explaining Fascism," in *Rethinking the Nature of Fascism: Comparative Perspectives*, ed. António Costa Pinto (Basingstoke: Palgrave Macmillan, 2011), 44.

2. Note also the subtitle of Constantin Iordachi's "Fascism in Interwar East Central and Southeastern Europe: Toward a New Transnational Research Agenda," *East Central Europe* 37 (2010): 161–213.

3. Geoff Eley, *Nazism as Fascism: Violence, Ideology, and the Ground of Consent in Germany, 1930–1945* (London and New York: Routledge, 2013), 207.

4. Ibid., 205–6.

5. Ibid., 200–1, 203.

6. Philip Morgan, *Fascism in Europe, 1919–1945* (London and New York: Routledge, 2003), 29–118.

7. Martin Blinkhorn, "Introduction: Allies, Rivals, or Antagonists? Fascists and Conservatives in Modern Europe," in *Fascists and Conservatives: The Radical Right and the Establishment in Twentieth-Century Europe,* ed. Martin Blinkhorn (London: Unwin Hyman, 1990), 6.

8. Aristotle Kallis, "Neither Fascist nor Authoritarian: The 4th of August Regime in Greece (1936–1941) and the Dynamics of Fascistisation in 1930s Europe," *East Central Europe* 37 (2010): 327.

9. J.F. Pollard, "Fascism and Catholicism," in *The Oxford Handbook of Fascism,* ed. R.J.B. Bosworth (Oxford: Oxford University Press, 2009), 173.

10. See especially *Japan in the Fascist Era,* ed. E. Bruce Reynolds (New York: Palgrave Macmillan, 2004), which we will consider in chapters 3 and 5.

11. This is a long-standing interpretive tack well characterized by Emilio Gentile in "Fascism, Totalitarianism and Political Religion: Definitions and Critical Reflections on Criticisms of an Interpretation," in *Fascism, Totalitarianism and Political Religion,* ed. Roger Griffin (London and New York: Routledge, 2005), 36.

12. Adrian Lyttelton, "Concluding Remarks," in *Rethinking the Nature of Fascism: Comparative Perspectives,* ed. António Costa Pinto (Basingstoke: Palgrave Macmillan, 2011), 273, 275; António Costa Pinto, *The Nature of Fascism Revisited* (Boulder, CO: Social Science Monographs, 2012), ix.

13. Among prominent examples: Roger Griffin, *The Nature of Fascism* (London: Routledge, 1993), 47; Morgan, *Fascism in Europe,* 192; Michael Mann, *Fascists* (Cambridge: Cambridge University Press, 2004), 1; and Eley, *Nazism as Fascism,* 210–11.

14. Stanley G. Payne, *A History of Fascism, 1914–1945* (Madison: University of Wisconsin Press, 1995), 494. Morgan, *Fascism in Europe,* 197–99, is also quite good, and explicit, on the sense in which fascism was revolutionary.

15. See R.J.B. Bosworth's introduction to *Oxford Handbook,* ed. Bosworth, 3–6. See also R.J.B. Bosworth, *The Italian Dictatorship: Problems and Perspectives in the Interpretation of Mussolini and Fascism* (London: Arnold, 1998), 21, 26–27, and throughout for a more sustained debunking discussion. Explicitly following Bosworth, George Talbot similarly fastens upon the undoubted limits of the ideological penetration, sometimes to indulge in mere put-down, in *Censorship in Fascist Italy, 1922–1943: Policies, Procedures and Protagonists* (Basingstoke: Palgrave Macmillan, 2007), 7, 10, 12–13, 19, 172, 194.

16. See especially R.J.B. Bosworth, *Mussolini* (London: Arnold, 2002), which portrays Mussolini himself as the key to the Fascist regime's superficiality, its lack of clear direction, and its failure seriously to mold the Italians.

17. Talbot, *Censorship in Fascist Italy;* Michael R. Ebner, *Ordinary Violence in Mussolini's Italy* (Cambridge: Cambridge University Press, 2011).

18. Paul Corner, "Italian Fascism: Whatever Happened to Dictatorship?," *Journal of Modern History* 74, no. 2 (June 2002): 325–51.

19. Ian Kershaw, "Hitler and the Uniqueness of Nazism," *Journal of Contemporary History* 39, no. 2 (April 2004): 239–54.

20. Prominent exceptions include Arnd Bauerkämper, *Der Faschismus in Europa, 1918–1945* (Stuttgart: Philipp Reclam jun., 2006); and Wolfgang Wippermann, *Faschismus: Eine Weltgeschichte vom 19. Jahrhundert bis Heute* (Darmstadt: Primus, 2009). This latter is notably idiosyncratic in its range.

21. Gilbert Allardyce, "What Fascism Is Not: Thoughts on the Deflation of a Concept," *American Historical Review* 84, no. 2 (April 1979): 367–98 (with comments by Stanley G. Payne and Ernst Nolte and a reply by Allardyce).

22. Ibid., 368; see also 387.

23. Ibid., 369.

24. Ibid., 376.

25. Ibid., 394 for Nolte's comment, and 396 for Allardyce's reply.

26. Ibid., 385.

27. See, e.g., Jeffrey T. Schnapp, *Staging Fascism: 18 BL and the Theater of Masses for Masses* (Stanford, CA: Stanford University Press, 1996), 5–7.

28. Tim Kirk, "Fascism and Austrofascism," in *The Dollfuss/Schuschnigg Era in Austria: A Reassessment,* ed. Günter Bischof, Anton Pelinka, and Alexander Lassner (New Brunswick, NJ: Transaction, 2003), 10.

29. Payne comment on Allardyce, "What Fascism Is Not," 389–91; the quoted passage is from 389.

30. Allardyce, "What Fascism Is Not," Allardyce reply, 398.

31. For some indications, see Roger Griffin and David D. Roberts, guest co-editors, "'The Fascist Revolution': Utopia or Façade? Reconciling Marxist and Non-Marxist Approaches," special issue, *European Journal of Political Theory* 11, no. 4 (October 2012).

32. Also worthy of note from the same period are Richard Griffiths, *An Intelligent Person's Guide to Fascism* (London: Duckworth, 2000); and Kevin Passmore, *Fascism: A Very Short Introduction* (Oxford: Oxford University Press, 2002). Whereas they both offer worthy insights, they are briefer, are pitched slightly differently, and, it seems to me, have had less overall impact than the other seven studies indicated.

33. Roger Griffin, "The Primacy of Culture: The Current Growth (or Manufacture) of Consensus within Fascist Studies," *Journal of Contemporary History* 37, no. 1 (Jan. 2002): 21–43. See also the invited commentaries by David D. Roberts, Alexander DeGrand, Mark Antliff, and Thomas Linehan that appeared in the next issue, 37, no. 2 (April 2002): 259–74.

34. Roger Eatwell, "Universal Fascism? Approaches and Definitions," in *Fascism outside Europe: The European Impulse against Domestic Conditions in the Diffusion of Global Fascism,* ed. Stein Ugelvik Larsen (Boulder, CO: Social Science Monographs, 2001); 27–28; Mann, *Fascists,* 11–13.

35. On all three, see David D. Roberts, "Fascism, Para-fascism, and the Framework for Interactive Political Innovation during the Era of the Two World Wars," in *Rethinking Fascism and Dictatorship in Interwar Europe,* ed. António Costa Pinto and Aristotle Kallis (Basingstoke: Palgrave Macmillan, 2014), 45–47, 54–56.

36. David D. Roberts, "Fascism, Modernism, and the Quest for an Alternative Modernity," *Patterns of Prejudice* 43, no. 1 (February 2009): 91–95, 101–2.

37. Philip Morgan, "Studying Fascism from the Particular to the General," *East Central Europe* 37 (2010): 335.

38. Roger Griffin, "Introduction: God's Counterfeiters? Investigating the Triad of Fascism, Totalitarianism and (Political) Religion," in *Fascism, Totalitarianism and Political Religion,* ed. Roger Griffin (London and New York: Routledge, 2005), 16, 21.

39. Roger Griffin, "Uniqueness and Family Resemblances in Generic Fascism," *East Central Europe* 37 (2010): 338–39.

40. Kevin Passmore, "Theories of Fascism: A Critique from the Perspective of Women's and Gender History," in *Rethinking the Nature of Fascism,* ed. Pinto, 131. For the earlier, more complete argument, see Kevin Passmore, "The Essence of Fascism," in *Fascism Past and Present, West and East: An International Debate on Concepts and Cases in the Comparative Study of the Extreme Right,* ed. Roger Griffin, Werner Loh, and Andreas Umland (Stuttgart: Ibidem, 2006), 353–55.

41. Stephen Holmes, *The Anatomy of Antiliberalism* (Cambridge, MA: Harvard University Press, 1993), 154.

42. Emilio Gentile, *The Sacralization of Politics in Fascist Italy,* trans. Keith Botsford (Cambridge, MA: Harvard University Press, 1996).

43. For further discussion, see David D. Roberts, *The Totalitarian Experiment in Twentieth-Century Europe: Understanding the Poverty of Great Politics* (London and New York: Routledge, 2006), chapter 6, esp. 321–23, 325–29.

44. See, e.g., Federico Finchelstein, *Transatlantic Fascism: Ideology, Violence, and the Sacred in Argentina and Italy, 1919–1945* (Durham, NC: Duke University Press, 2010), 75; Mark Antliff, *Avant-Garde Fascism: The Mobilization of Myth, Art, and Culture in France, 1909–1939* (Durham, NC: Duke University Press, 2007), 1–6; and Ebner, *Ordinary Violence,* 5–11.

45. E.g., Richard Shorten, *Modernism and Totalitarianism: Rethinking the Intellectual Sources of Nazism and Stalinism, 1945 to the Present* (Basingstoke: Palgrave Macmillan, 2012), 40–43, 239–40. We will consider Shorten's argument in chapter 8.

46. See Goffredo Adinolfi, "Political Elite and Decision-Making in Mussolini's Italy," in *Ruling Elites and Decision-Making in Fascist-Era Dictatorships,* ed. António Costa Pinto (Boulder, CO: Social Science Monographs, 2009), 49.

47. Giovanni Gentile, "Nazione e Nazionalismo" (1917), republished in Giovanni Gentile, *Guerra e fede* (Florence: Le Lettere, 1989), 35–38.

48. See especially Giovanni Gentile, *Politica e cultura,* ed. Hervé A. Cavallera (Florence: Le Lettere, 1990), 1:401–6.

49. Adrian Lyttelton, ed., *Italian Fascisms from Pareto to Gentile* (New York: Harper & Row [Torchbooks]), 1975.

50. For a few examples, see Robert O. Paxton, *The Anatomy of Fascism* (New York: Random House [Vintage]: 2005), 60–64, 120–21, 152; Kershaw, "Hitler and the Uniqueness of Nazism," 248; and Blinkhorn, "Introduction," 9–10.

51. Joshua Arthurs delineates the tension well, but without drawing out its wider implications for the nature and fate of the Fascist regime. See Joshua Arthurs, *Excavating Modernity: The Roman Past in Fascist Italy* (Ithaca, NY: Cornell University Press, 2012).

Chapter 2

Assessing the New Restiveness

Six Exemplars

Let us consider six exemplars, all leading specialists, each of whom has recently dealt with fascism and fascist-era dictatorships from a perspective that is not primarily Italian or German. Four of them—Constantin Iordachi, Michel Dobry, Stein Ugelvik Larsen, and António Costa Pinto—embrace fascist studies in general in calling for a new agenda. But we can usefully add Mary Vincent and Aristotle Kallis, whose calls for new approaches to the Spanish and Greek cases, respectively, parallel the calls for a new agenda and help us assess the possibilities.

A certain clustering among these figures should be acknowledged. Dobry and Larsen have important essays in a volume edited by Pinto, published in 2011. Pinto and Kallis have jointly edited a collaborative volume, published in 2014, that includes an essay by Iordachi, among others. Both Kallis and Larsen contributed to an important special issue of *East Central Europe* that Iordachi published in 2010. But despite a measure of overlap in their restiveness, these scholars offer quite different perspectives, and it is very much worth considering all of them. Especially when considered together, their concerns seem especially symptomatic, and their proposed directions, especially promising. But comparing their diagnoses and prescriptions also indicates tensions and uncertainties that raise further questions. Let us first consider each in turn.

Constantin Iordachi

Based in Hungary, the Romanian scholar Constantin Iordachi has started from notable work on the Romanian Iron Guard, or Legion of the Archangel Michael, to argue for a broader new agenda, including a more central role for east-central and southeastern Europe. He worries that certain parameters of the wider discussion, even the prevailing notions of ideal type or fascist minimum, tend to smuggle in a standard that privileges some "center" and takes others as merely imitative or coerced. More particularly, certain delimited notions of modernity and normal development have made it too easy to marginalize east-central and southeastern Europe. As Iordachi sees it, we need to approach each case more attuned to singularity and indigenous sources. Doing so entails greater openness to the scope for multipolar originality and creativity, which, he insists, were not confined to the West or the more familiar cases. If we are to understand the new universe on the radical Right, we need to encompass the whole array of impulses, even those that remained relatively isolated and powerless. Better attuning to a variety of experiments could at once expand and deepen the discussion.[1]

But Iordachi is not calling simply for greater justice to singularity and variety. We cannot settle for mere nominalism because the individual cases constantly influenced each other, producing, as he puts it, "a trans-national cross-fertilization of illiberal political ideas and practices."[2] He notes that the multipolar creativity he had insisted upon was itself bound up with this web of interaction, as local impulses and external influences came together to produce specific forms of ideological syncretism.[3] To do better at researching this transnational interaction, he suggests, we could usefully follow wider recent innovations in interdisciplinary and comparative studies focusing on shared or entangled history, or what has come to be called, thanks especially to the work of Michael Werner and Bénédicte Zimmermann, *histoire croisée*.[4] Let us note, moreover, that as propounded by Werner and Zimmermann, *histoire croisée* entails a reflexive dimension encompassing the possibility of challenge to our assumptions, consistent with the need to attune to a wider range of frequencies discussed in the previous chapter.

To some extent Iordachi might seem to be talking out of both sides of his mouth in accenting both indigenous innovation and interaction, but his point is clear. We should not start by so privileging the Italian and/or German cases that we assume imitation or imposition—or even exaggerate the import of inspiration. Thus we can be truer to indigenous sources. But from there we cannot treat each case in isolation, as singular, all involved in merely parallel histories, or at best brought together through comparison. Each was caught up in a web of interaction, but that web, too, must be conceived in a relatively egalitarian and open-ended way.

In his concern that we be open to indigenous experiment, without assuming imitation or imposition, Iordachi is congruent with Peter Sugar, who plausibly noted in 1971 that the fascist-style groups in the successor states of the Austro-Hungarian Empire would probably have emerged even without the Italian and German models, in light of the particular dislocations and challenges that resulted from World War I.[5] But Iordachi goes beyond in his implication that we must understand not only emergence but subsequent trajectory. And that requires attention to interaction, which significantly affected the trajectories at issue.

Michel Dobry

The noted political sociologist Michel Dobry approaches the overall problem from a French angle that proves instructive in a different way. He has been particularly prominent in questioning the notion, still somewhat widely held, that France was immune to genuine fascism as found in Italy and Germany.[6] But his aim is not remotely to show that this or that movement or party on the new French Right was fascist after all—or, for that matter, that it was not fascist.[7] Preoccupation with the classification question obscures what was actually going on in France at the time. Clearly, however, Dobry's argument does not pertain to France alone but has wider implications and suggests a wider program—indeed a wider way of conceiving the universe at issue. Still, for him it was the need for a different approach to the French case in particular, in light of concerns about "the immunity thesis," that brought the wider limits and possibilities into focus.

As Dobry sees it, what was happening on the French Right has long been assessed in terms of criteria that do not bear up under scrutiny. He makes the point first on the level of specifics, rejecting the notion, which he finds implicit in the reigning approaches, that the failure of the new Right—during the crisis surrounding the Stavisky Scandal in 1934, for example, but also more generally—stemmed from a lack of ideological coherence. He agrees that, for example, Colonel François de La Rocque's program for the Croix de Feu was inconsistent, vague, bland, and devoid of originality. But whereas the dominant view seemed to impute a contrasting measure of coherence and substance to Italian Fascism and German Nazism—accounting for their success—Dobry minimizes the difference on that level, denying that the Italian and German movements had coherent programs or road maps before gaining power.[8] So the presence of those was not the key variable.

Although Dobry surely overstates the degree to which the standard view attributes to Italian Fascism and German Nazism the coherence, lacking in France, that brought success to each, it may indeed be true that our tendency to privilege the Italian and German cases compromises our understanding of what was happening in France—and, by implication, elsewhere as well. In any case, the error, as Dobry sees it, stems from a deeper problem, the reigning premium on "classificatory reasoning," which entails the two related but distinguishable pitfalls of essentialism and "historicism," in Karl Popper's idiosyncratic sense of the term. First, classificatory reason starts with aspects of the Italian and German cases and makes them definitional, entailing fixed essences or natures, which then become the basis for classification and distinction.[9] Dobry explicitly criticizes Roger Griffin and Robert Paxton for falling into this trap. Even Stanley Payne, with his claim of an inductive inventory of characteristics, takes too much for granted. The problem remains even if the definition reflects greater attention to the practical side, such as styles of action and modes of organization.[10] Yet it is on the basis of such essentialism that French movements of the radical Right during the 1930s have been opposed to "authentic fascism."

In Dobry's account, classificatory reason entails a second step, ascribing something like historicist laws of development, and thus causation and a typical, distinctive trajectory, to that essence or nature. Every outcome must result from that particular trajectory. This makes the trajectory of "authentic" fascism radically different from other political trajectories. Dobry finds this historicist illusion especially pernicious because it shapes even the selection of facts.[11] And it is this that leads proponents of the immunity thesis to a distorted conception of the processes leading to different outcomes in Italy and Germany than in France.

More particularly, the historicist illusion precludes the possibility that what tipped the course of events in a particular direction in each case might have been quite marginal. Local or minor factors could have had huge effects, even overriding underlying structural trends. Focus on outcomes blinds us to the "frequent contingency of these outcomes, to the fact these outcomes are produced by chance combinations between multiple series of determining factors, between separate and heterogeneous causal chains."[12] And in fact the key variable in France, Dobry implies, was not the relatively stable side of political movements featured in essentialist definitions; it turns out to have been much more situational and contingent.

For Dobry, the solution is to embrace a "relational perspective" as an alternative to flawed classificatory reason. Rather than conceiving those groups that either actively embraced or actively rejected the fascist label in isolation, as entities unto themselves, we must conceive them primarily in terms of their relationship to the particular competitive social spaces in which they found themselves, defined themselves, and acted on a day-to-day basis. Those spaces entailed changing situational logics, with particular constraints and conflicts, particular practical possibilities and local stakes.[13]

As Dobry sees it, the appropriation of the "fascism" category in our standard academic discourse, reflecting our propensity for classificatory reasoning, leads us to conceive fascism from the start as radically different from other phenomena. We thereby freeze something that was soft, fluid—and much contested at the time.[14] We need more attention not only to how the actors classified themselves and others but also to how they manipulated the classifications at issue. More specifically, we need to understand how the actors positioned themselves vis-à-vis the fascism label, which, Dobry reminds us, is not remotely the same as fascism as such.[15]

Thus, Dobry goes on, we should ask not whether the Action Française, for example, was authentically fascist but why, at a particular moment, it declared that it was *not* fascist, even though its leaders were deeply and durably sympathetic to Italian Fascism.[16] In the same way, we need to understand that Georges Valois defined himself and his movement, the Faisceau, *as* fascist especially in light of his bitter rivalry with the Action Française. That he did so does not indicate some qualitative difference between social conservatism and fascist radicalism. What we find on the French Right more generally, Dobry contends, is "more like a sort of action system or configuration in which each adopts a position in relation to the positions of others: a system based on interdependence that conditions and often constrains the behaviour of each participant."[17] Only by thinking in terms of their relationship to the changing competitive social spaces or fields, to the constraints in the particular conjuncture, can we grasp the refusal of so many on the new French Right to embrace the fascism label.[18]

The key constraint facing the French Right is of course familiar. Everywhere outside Italy and Germany, would-be fascists faced the dilemma of combining nationalism with admiration for formations that crystalized elsewhere, first in Italy, then in Germany. But the dilemma was particularly acute in France, with Germany, especially, seeking to undo the gains France had achieved through its victory in World War I, and with even Italy threatening French territory, and especially French colonial possessions, over the longer term. The need for ideological bricolage to cover this dilemma was bound to distinguish the new Right in France from Italian Fascism and German Nazism. And such bricolage was often strained and awkward. Dobry notes that the Action Française claimed seniority and paternity over Italian Fascism even as it eschewed the fascist label.[19]

Dobry revisits Gilbert Allardyce, largely endorsing his critique of "generic fascism," but drawing different conclusions. Insofar as we point more radically than Allardyce beyond the concern with classification, we see that we need not settle for a focus on singular individual cases. And for Dobry, contrary to Allardyce, we should simply accept the fluidity or vagueness of the term "fascism." Indeed, we must encompass the struggles over the term during the period, including the role of anti-fascists, who made their own contribution to what it was taken to mean. The conflict over the term should not be separated from the object, though viewed in terms of this fluidity or vagueness, the object itself comes to appear differently.[20]

As the antidote to historicism, Dobry insists that we back off from the assumption that the objective is to explain outcomes. That assumption rests on the deeper assumption that there is a direct causal link between intentions and outcomes, that outcomes encapsulate the processes that produced them. For Dobry, we need greater attention to openness, uncertainty, and contingency.[21]

But Dobry's relational perspective also entails relating phenomena we have taken to be "fascist" to others more widely, not limited to those customarily considered fascist or quasi-fascist. Especially because fascism had such monstrous consequences, we tend to assume that it was singular, exceptional—a case apart. But it should not, Dobry insists, be separated from other phenomena, perhaps similar in certain respects, that produced different outcomes. We need to compare even the seemingly incomparable and even across temporal borders. This might include, for example, considering charismatic domination, or the situational constraints affecting new entrants into the political arena, in various cases.[22]

All this is to suggest that we are prone to overinflate fascism, which, for Dobry, means that we miss out in two distinct ways. First, we fail to grasp that what in fact differentiated fascism was more its contingent trajectory than some a priori essence. Second, by taking fascism as exceptional a priori, we fail to take advantage of the ways the fascist experience might illuminate diverse aspects of our still-unfolding political universe.

For Dobry, theoretical confusion is a big part of the problem, so the new turn must be theoretically informed.[23] But his aim is not some new "theory of fascism"—quite the contrary, it would seem. He implies that theoretical clarification enables us better to see why such a theory is *not* what we are seeking—and what we in fact need instead.

Stein Ugelvik Larsen

For Stein Ugelvik Larsen, in contrast, decomposition and recomposition in the theory of fascism is precisely what is at issue. Still, he too finds us to be overly concerned with definitions and semantics and insists that we content ourselves with greater looseness and vagueness. Even when assessing comparability, our criteria might change in the course of research.[24]

At the same time, Larsen usefully reminds us that the complexity of the phenomena at issue defies single-factor explanations or any single theory of fascism during the period in question. German electoral statistics cannot explain the Holocaust, just as ideological tenets reflecting Germany's defeat in World War I cannot explain the polycentrism of the Nazi regime.[25] Although he, unlike Dobry, does not charge leading recent students of generic fascism with such deficiencies, Larsen clearly feels that tendencies to oversimplify continue to lurk in the discussion, in light of our excessive concern with definition, concept, and theory of a certain sort.

As an alternative, Larsen wants to turn from the "genetic" approach, privileging the Italian case, and to embrace an "emergence" approach, based on Karl Popper's adaptation of Darwinian evolutionary thinking.[26] As a latecomer, fascism was seeking its political space, necessarily in interaction with competing political forces. Its survival depended on finding, and defining, its own evolutionary niche, and doing so necessarily depended on the political situation in each country.[27] Because these situations varied considerably, we must turn from Italy as archetype and become more open to local political antecedents.

At the same time, Larsen proposes that, following Popper, we recognize the propensity for new political impulses to emerge from particular historical conjunctures, each competing to survive by establishing space for itself in light of the particulars of that conjuncture. The origins of any such impulse may well be indeterminate, but in light of contextual specifics, there is a determining logic when explaining what happens to that impulse, its endurance or growth.[28] So to understand the development of any one fascist movement, we must grasp that logic, which structures the competition within that particular context. In light of the centrality of such contextually specific logics of development, it is not surprising that we find much diversity and sometimes even antagonism among fascisms and fascists.

But for Larsen, as for Dobry, the aim is not simply greater justice to singularity. As Larsen sees it, the key to a new age of fascist studies is to put together a kind of map, a systematic inventory of findings, to keep us from reinventing the wheel and to clarify what we have learned and still need to learn. We might, for example, ask about generational differences in ideological emphases among fascists, or we might consider what ideological themes were simply impossible in which contexts and under what circumstances. The quest for such an inventory is obviously a multinational task and stands opposed both to starting at the top, through some new definition, and to assuming—with Angelo Tasca—that if we would understand fascism, all we can do is simply convey its history.[29] As Larsen sees it, devising such an inventory would establish a "new theoretical platform," which would have implications for a wide range of social phenomena even beyond the field of fascism, and not originally envisaged by students of fascism.[30] So Larsen converges with Dobry in finding the scope for placing fascism in a much broader comparative network.

In an essay of 2001, foreshadowing aspects of his more recent argument, Larsen makes a strong case for encompassing political innovations outside Europe in the discussion of fascism during the era of the two world wars—or in any effort to develop a general theory of fascism. Fascism was a global phenomenon at the time, not a quintessentially European phenomenon diffused from Europe, whether by imitation or imposition. So in treating global fascism we need the emergence as opposed to the genetic approach that privileges Europe and especially Italy, just because it happened to have produced the first fascism.[31]

Europe was undeniably first to experience certain modern configurations by about 1900 that, Larsen argues, made fascism possible.[32] Fascism emerged from an imbalance in the interface between modernization and early liberalism; such imbalance could entail either strong liberalism and weak modernization or strong modernization but underdeveloped liberalism. Either way, the result was an overload inviting new political departures.[33] Although Larsen does not comparably feature the modernization-liberalism matrix in the later essay considered above, he relies on it in his recent contribution to Iordachi's special issue of *East Central Europe,* though with reference to Italy and Germany as opposed to the non-European world.[34]

But Larsen's wider point is that non-European countries were undergoing the same processes and could encounter those same configurations, though obviously in their own way. So he insists that though non-Europeans certainly sought to learn from European fascism, fascism need not require foreign models. It could and did arise in a diversity of national contexts, yielding distinctive contextual features outside Europe.[35] And we need to be more attuned to indigenous manifestations in their distinctiveness and thus, by implication, their variety and avoid measuring them according to some European and essentialist standard. Still, for Larsen we can compare and even rank individual cases heuristically on a scale or continuum with many variables, as long as we specify and analyze their joint effects, and as long as we are prepared to work with a more or less vague, implicit definition of fascism overall.[36]

Up to a point, Larsen's call to encompass the non-European world anticipates Iordachi's argument for encompassing east-central and southeastern Europe. In each case, privileging the "center" leads us to fail to learn from what has seemed the periphery—and even to miss what it is we are seeking to understand. Thus, again, the need to become more "egalitarian."

António Costa Pinto and Mary Vincent

We note a comparable, if instructively different, mode of restiveness and prescription in the Iberianists António Costa Pinto and Mary Vincent, who complain of too much either/or thinking, too much preoccupation with whether this or that was "fascist" or not, and too great a tendency to force the totalitarian-authoritarian binomial in treating, respectively, the Salazar regime in Portugal and the Franco regime in Spain. We are too prone to assume that if they were not fascist and/or totalitarian, they were merely authoritarian, conservative, and/or traditionalist. In forcing either/or categories based on experiences elsewhere, we miss innovation in the departures at issue, misconstrue their place in the wider universe of responses at the time, and unduly delimit the range of that universe itself.

Drawing especially on the work of Ismael Saz Campos, Vincent charges that the long-standing distinction between fascism and authoritarianism in approaching the Franco regime reflected a failure to grasp the radicalizing interaction with wider European fascism on the part of all sectors of the Spanish anti-Republican Right during the 1930s. As the result of that radicalization, she concludes, the emerging Franco regime was neither fascist nor merely authoritarian but, rather, a hybrid, a "fascistized" state.[37] Vincent's implication is that even Stanley Payne's way of distinguishing "fascism" from José Maria Gil Robles's conservative nationalism is iffier than Payne seemed to recognize.

Even as he casts his net well beyond Portugal, Pinto takes a parallel tack, at least up to a point. Seeking to get away from rigid, dichotomous interpretations of the interwar Right, he contends that the relationship between dictators and their parties, especially if those parties existed prior to the seizure of power, was more complex than the standard fascism-authoritarianism dichotomy suggests.[38] With respect to the Salazar regime specifically, whereas he accepts the widespread view that it was not fascist but deeply conservative, relying primarily on the Catholic Church and provincial elites, he denies that it can be understood as merely authoritarian or dictatorial. Its involvement in the wider web of interaction on the Right made it something new, entailing novel mechanisms of socialization and institutionalization, even if it was not specifically fascist or totalitarian. As it evolved, moreover, the Salazar regime was taken as a valuable new model by some on the new Right elsewhere precisely because it seemed to avoid the more aggressive and radical aspects of fascism.[39] In light of these considerations, Pinto has been particularly explicit in challenging the totalitarian-authoritarian binomial.[40]

Pinto also challenges conventional lines in focusing not simply on fascism but on "fascist-era dictatorships."[41] To be sure, this mode of expansion still means focus on governments or regimes, whereas Iordachi advocates encompassing movements that did not come to power and even, by implication, impulses articulated as something like "ideology" that did not fully coalesce to fuel a movement. Still, in principle, at least, these imperatives are not mutually exclusive; expansion in both directions is possible.

Pinto and Vincent reflect the current tendency to depart from the fascism/para-fascism distinction popularized by Roger Griffin twenty years ago.[42] Using "para" in its dictionary sense as an alteration, perversion, or simulation of the real thing, Griffin suggested that Rightists elsewhere tended merely to exploit the trappings of Italian Fascism and German Nazism for defensive or authoritarian purposes. Even before Griffin popularized the term, Franco's regime in Spain seemed the archetypal example of para-fascism, and the Spanish case is still widely viewed in some such way. To be sure, "para-fascism" was in principle a mere ideal type to aid research, but Pinto and Vincent imply that it has outlived its usefulness, that we must ask some new questions and better attune to what may be unfamiliar aspirations and combinations. We noted Vincent's use of the terms "hybrid" and "'fascistized' state" as alternatives for characterizing the Franco regime.[43]

In his foreword to the new Pinto and Kallis collaborative volume, Roger Griffin holds to the term "para-fascism" but seems implicitly to admit that his earlier postulation was too rigidly dichotomous. So he recasts it in light of new research and reconceptualization. Para-fascism was not a watered-down, pale imitation of fascism but a genus in its own right, to be distinguished from *both* merely reactionary or authoritarian conservative regimes and from "real fascism." Like fascism, it was seeking an alternative modernity, seeking to address the problems of modernization without the problems of liberalism and the excesses of the Soviet experiment. But the para-fascist regimes also sought to proceed without the revolutionary totalitarianism of Italian Fascism and Nazism. In that sense para-fascism was a "fourth way," with its own distinctive solution to the problems of modernity. Although it attempted to fuse tradition and modernity, it included a genuinely regenerative aim distinguishing it from reactionary regimes or military or personal dictatorships lacking any such futural, utopian, modernist dimension. Moreover, para-fascist regimes were more numerous than "real fascist" regimes and displayed considerably greater longevity.[44]

Yet whereas Griffin hoped that the Pinto-Kallis volume would encourage seeing these regimes in that light, it is striking that whereas "para-fascism" figured prominently in the title of the workshop from which the volume grew, Pinto and Kallis, as the editors, decided against using it for the volume and instead emphasize "hybridization," understood as a dynamic, volatile, and unpredictable process with multiple possible outcomes. This process is congruent with the interaction that Iordachi emphasizes. They go on to argue that whereas there was surely a "demonstration effect," it entailed not merely passive appropriation or imitation of fascism; rather we must grasp the role of recontextualization to understand the hybrid outcomes. And each outcome opened the way to further recontextualizations and to further hybrid outcomes.[45]

Up to a point, these emphases are not incompatible with Griffin's recast notion of para-fascism. The key, however, is the greater emphasis Pinto and Kallis place on dynamic interaction, making for recontextualization and hybridization. From this perspective, Griffin, even in trying to recast and thereby save his term, is too caught up in static classification. Simply adding another category to the *new* Right is not in itself sufficiently attuned to dynamic interplay.

Whereas neither Pinto, Kallis, nor Vincent contends that lines should not be drawn, they imply that the lines need to be blurrier, less rigidly either/or, if we are to make sense of the innovations on the Right during the period. Like Iordachi, they suggest that the aggregate can be better understood through focus on the web of interaction itself. And that interaction was more open and fluid than we tend to recognize if we privilege Italy and Germany or rely on the totalitarian-authoritarian dichotomy.

In treating the interaction, Pinto has recently insisted on the centrality of corporatist ideas and experiments.[46] A sense that we are missing something in neglecting corporatism is clearly an aspect of his restiveness. Although Italy was central to corporatist discussion, Germany was not, so better encompassing the interchange over corporatism can help us place the range of experiment on the new Right in better proportion. By implication, it has been teleological thinking, including privileging Nazi Germany excessively, that has kept us from doing so. Corporatism has been neglected both because Nazism, racism, expansionism, and war have come to seem quintessential and because, despite a great deal of interest and hype at the time, it never amounted to much practice. Yet Pinto insists that the widespread diffusion of corporatist ideas challenges rigid, dichotomous interpretations of the interwar Right, with fascism on one side, authoritarianism on the other.[47]

Aristotle Kallis on the Metaxas Regime in Greece

Aristotle Kallis launched his career with an important comparative study of expansionism in the German and Italian cases. But though based in England, he is Greek, and he has remained interested in Right-wing departures in Greece. And it is partly his recent call to encompass the short-lived regime of Ioannis Metaxas (1936–41) that warrants including him among our restives.[48] But his restiveness is not merely parochial; he contends that we are missing something not just about Greece but the wider universe insofar as we approach the Greek case through the delimiting criteria we have.

Kallis acknowledges that the Metaxas regime is generally taken as peripheral to fascist studies. Because it lacked a genuinely fascist social constituency, an ideology of revolutionary rupture, and a truly charismatic leader with a revolutionary program, it has been confined to a gray analytical zone inaccessible via either generic fascism or conventional authoritarianism.[49] As Kallis sees it, the Metaxas regime was not fascist, but it bore some relationship with fascism; yet neither was it a species of para-fascism, merely using the trappings for conservative defense.[50] But precisely in defying conventional categories and expectations, the Metaxas experiment can illuminate the wider universe if we can manage the necessary reconceptualization.

The key, Kallis implies, is to understand the relationship of the Greek regime with the wider universe of the new Right, getting a handle on the proportions. On the one hand, we cannot appreciate the break Metaxas envisioned apart from "the rapidly changing political landscape of interwar Europe in the wake of 'fascist' consolidation and—in the late 1930s at least—its aura of novelty and invincibility."[51] With the political gravitational field of fascism ever-strengthening, large sectors of the European Right were being caught up in complex, often partial and inconsistent processes of "fascistization." Such fascistization did not necessarily mean, nor did it require, actually establishing a fascist regime.[52] Like Vincent, Kallis supplements "fascistization" with the term "hybrid," though he is careful to nuance it, making clear that in the Greek case it does not refer to exploiting and thereby taming or blunting a fascist movement emerging from below.[53] But of course Vincent's point was that whereas some have associated that syndrome with the Franco regime, that regime was a hybrid in a more synergistic sense.

However, although Metaxas was being drawn into that gravitational field, Kallis contends that his way of shaping his regime reflected an astute, personal reading of the fascist paradigm that was neither opportunistic nor subservient to any particular model. From within a framework of genuine political and ideological convergence, the Greek regime, like other new Right formations by the later 1930s, developed its own radicalizing momentum as it did not merely ape but adapted stylistic, organizational, and ideological facets from elsewhere. So we must avoid reading the Greek experiment in terms of the Italian or German cases if we are to do justice to its autonomous quality and place in the wider interaction. Conversely,

Kallis implies that it is especially our tendency to take Italy and Germany as benchmarks that has led us into unwarranted either/or thinking as we seek to conceive the overall universe.[54]

Common Concerns and Directions— ## and Some Symptomatic Tensions and Uncertainties

In these recent expressions of restiveness, we find echoes of long-standing concerns, but also some new accents that help us better to formulate the limits of the reigning approaches—and that might indeed help us forge a more fruitful alternative. Especially as taken together, however, these diagnoses and prescriptions raise new questions, so we must draw out some of their implications and pinpoint certain tensions as we consider how best to proceed.

Pulling back from essentialism and teleological thinking seems to entail an expanded focus, encompassing a wider universe of experiment. Indeed, all of our exemplars, though some more explicitly than others, suggest that we must de-privilege the Italian and German cases, making that universe more "egalitarian." Although Dobry and Larsen, in making their arguments, sometimes go overboard, misconstruing the place of the Italian and German cases in the discussion, their call for reassessment convinces for the most part, and the concerns of Iordachi, Pinto, Vincent, and Kallis point in the same direction.[55] The overall restiveness stems from a sense that definitions, fascist minima, or ideal types derived from either or both the Italian and German cases skew our understanding of the others and even rigidify unduly the distinction between fascist and non-fascist modes of innovation on the Right, between fascism and traditionalist conservatism, or possibly even between fascism and political phenomena not usually viewed as either Right-wing or conservative.

Unless we back up to the wider universe, encompassing more cases and treating each more openly, we miss not only aspects of those other cases in their singularity, but also the richness and complexity of the new universe of political responses—and thus the texture of the epoch itself. From this more egalitarian perspective, impulses coming from every corner of Europe, and even beyond, may be symptomatic, whether or not they fueled movements that came to power, creating novel regimes. This notion is especially congruent with Larsen's accent on the scope for experiment, as open-ended, with the results not foreordained, though a similar notion is central to Dobry and, if less explicitly, to the others as well. The openness to experiment led to varied forms of innovation and creativity, all part of the novel universe to be understood.

Kallis's point about a wider process of "fascistization" by the later 1930s is surely convincing, and both he and Vincent have good reason to adopt that term. But though it is no doubt indispensable, we must beware making it too pat, as if "fascism" was a given, rather than itself an uncertain, open-ended trajectory. In each case fascistization resulted from the particular interaction, including selective borrowing, from within a fluid, dynamic, unstable universe. In the same way, even as Kallis nuances the notion, "hybrid" may imply the juxtaposition of stable categories as opposed to the synergistic generation of something more radically new. Moreover, Kallis seems to take for granted that it is theories of generic fascism that are at issue, when we might need to start with the wider fluid, unstable universe itself and seek better to understand fascism and the process of fascistization from within it. We will return to these issues in chapter 8.

While the call for a more encompassing and egalitarian approach is persuasive, we must take care to avoid overreaction, in light of the undeniable centrality of Italy and Germany in certain respects. To de-privilege them as models does not have to entail playing down the evident asymmetry, in both ideological precedence and power relations. We can recognize the asymmetries without falling into the traps Iordachi and Dobry identify, approaching the Iron Guard or the Croix de Feu, for example, in terms of our understanding of what happened in Italy and Germany. As Iordachi and Kallis especially emphasize, the asymmetries do not mean that Romania, Greece, or the others were merely imitative or coerced. Those moving in new directions in those countries could borrow selectively to serve their own experimental departures. But we must ponder how to balance the need for an expanded and more egalitarian universe with appropriate attention to the centrality of Italy and Germany.

Our exemplars point beyond earlier objections to the most influential generic accounts to better indicate, first, *how* we tend to get hung up on definition and classification and trapped in teleological thinking and, second, what we miss in doing so. Drawing out the implications, such expansion and egalitarianism suggest the need, discussed in the preceding chapter, to attune to a wider range of frequencies with respect to ideological content. In insisting on better encompassing corporatism, Pinto has in mind precisely such an expansion. But the place of corporatism in the debates of the time is especially hard to pin down, partly because of its role in Catholic tradition, as brought up to date with Pope Pius XI's encyclical *Quadragesimo anno* of 1931. That encyclical bore a complex relationship with the corporatist thrust of Fascist Italy. Whereas Pinto's attention to corporatism is especially welcome, aspects of his approach can be questioned, a matter we can best consider in chapters 3 and 5.

More generally at issue in expanding the range of frequencies are reactions against liberal democracy and mainstream modernity that might defy our expectations. Eschewing any single model or developmental escalator means there is no one normal, healthy, rational way to deal with the modern world. It may even mean, again, the scope for challenging the Left-Right axis. So we may need to approach corporatism and other challenges to "normal" liberal democratic relationships and procedures with a more open mind.

But here we encounter an especially symptomatic tension and divergence among our exemplars. In explicitly addressing the tendency toward teleological thinking, Dobry and Larsen, albeit from somewhat different angles, suggest how we might better do justice to openness and contingency. Larsen is especially promising in linking the special challenges of latecomer status to Popper's evolutionary notion, which entails not telos but rather experiment, with the outcomes indeterminate.

Up to a point, Iordachi is congruent as he insists, convincingly, on the need to be open to more varied sources of originality and experiment. But we are bound to ask: Originality and experiment about what? According to what criteria are we to assess originality and creativity? Moreover, whereas in criticizing essentialist tendencies, Dobry explicitly and Larsen implicitly question Griffin's notion of palingenesis, Iordachi seems to take palingenesis for granted as the essence of fascism, which is precisely to settle for a delimited range of frequencies, in tension with his call to encompass a wider range of creativity and experiment.[56] So not only does Iordachi fail to indicate explicitly the need for a wider range of frequencies, he falls into essentialism in taking palingenesis so much for granted. As a result, his call for expansion falls somewhat flat.

Vincent is even more explicit, referring to "the palingenetic vision that lay at the heart of fascism," even as she too implies that fascism must be placed within the wider universe of innovation.[57] Such use of palingenesis even among restive skeptics is striking evidence that the essentialist tendencies we noted earlier, in light of the dangers of heuristic categories and ideal types, still lurk in the discussion. Although palingenesis has remained especially prominent, some feature political religion instead. For example, Kallis, in a book published in 2009, refers to "fascism's own nature as millenarian political religion."[58]

Although they illuminate up to a point, these categories can restrict, keeping us from understanding the multiple creativity and experiment that Iordachi, most explicitly, wants us better to encompass. The universe of new response may have entailed impulses more fruitfully understood in other terms, impulses that watching for palingenesis or political religion keeps us from understanding. Even when we find palingenesis, political religion, or both, we need a better sense of what else, not reducible to either, might have been at work in order to place the palingenetic and political-religious impulses in proportion.

We note not only calls to encompass a wider universe but also suggestions that we need greater attention to the web of interaction within the overall universe. Whereas aspects of the *histoire croisée* in the case of fascism have long been noted, the call is for a deeper, more sustained focus on that dimension. We have already observed some of the particulars in connection with Vincent, Pinto, and Kallis, especially. Insofar as, when focusing on the web of interaction, we also de-privilege Italy and Germany to some extent, we become more open to the uncertainty, fluidity, and crisscrossing at the time, involving various patterns of influence, pressure, challenge, competition, and selective borrowing. The interaction thus would encompass but would not be limited to the imitation and imposition usually featured. In light of the prominence of the new emphasis on interaction, however, it is especially important to make certain distinctions, to draw out certain implications, to pinpoint some open questions, and to clarify the stakes—while also indicating certain pitfalls. We will seek to do so in the chapters that follow, in which the role of interaction will be central.

In advocating *histoire croisée*, Werner and Zimmermann point explicitly "beyond comparison," too often taken as the be-all and end-all.[59] Indeed, comparison sometimes seems not only self-recommending but the ultimate aim, even if only as a kind of default setting. We note, for example, Iordachi's accents both in the title of his recent anthology *Comparative Fascist Studies* (2010) and at some points in his recent article on east-central and southeastern Europe, where he worries, for example, that without attention to the wider universe, "comparative research results remain partial and incomplete."[60] In the same vein, we note the subtitle of Pinto's recent collaborative volume *Rethinking the Nature of Fascism: Comparative Perspectives* (2011), which certainly includes a comparative dimension but which is considerably more wide-ranging.

We may think first of comparison as the key as we seek not only to encompass the whole universe on the new Right but to flesh it out, to understand its texture and consistency. In his response to Allardyce, noted in the preceding chapter, Stanley Payne stressed the value of having *some* generic concept as the basis both for demonstrating individual features and for making comparisons.[61] And Allardyce, for all his skepticism, could surely allow for such comparisons, which might, just as Payne indicated, clarify differences and singularities.

Comparison and *histoire croisée* are certainly not mutually exclusive, and comparison remains one desideratum, necessary to get beyond nominalism and ghettoization. Moreover, it is indeed partly to provide wider bases for comparison that we need an expanded range with greater openness. But we may tend to default to comparison too quickly, without considering what emphasis on comparison might lead us to gloss over or underplay. And certain of the discontents and prescriptions of our restive exemplars suggest that something more than simply wider bases of comparison is at issue. In noting the limits of treating the various cases in isolation, or even in parallel, and in calling for more attention to multinational interaction, they seem to have in mind a deeper way of conceiving the aggregate. But insofar as *histoire croisée*, in pointing beyond comparison, might give us a better handle on the macro or aggregate level, we face a new set of questions about how to do it and about what that better handle might entail.

Even as our exemplars see new possibilities, they differ in symptomatic ways over the range of interaction to be encompassed. In calling for *histoire croisée*, Iordachi seems to have in mind a specifically *fascist* universe, which, even as expanded, can apparently be demarcated relatively cleanly, with not only palingenesis but also totalitarianism as criteria. We need to be sensitive to a wider range of interplay within that fascist web. In contrast, Pinto, Vincent, and Kallis point to still wider interaction, necessary, again, not just for comparison but to grasp the novelty and the place of their respective cases in the wider universe of innovative response. As we noted near the outset of the preceding chapter, fascism, central though it was, did not exhaust that universe.

Larsen proposes a third axis or level of interaction in insisting that fascism, competing as a newcomer for political space, can be understood only in terms of the wider political competition within some particular national context. Any new fascist movement could endure and grow only in interaction with others competing for that political space. Dobry similarly features such internal interaction as new, Right-leaning movements and parties competed with the more established forces but also with each other. Indeed, he stresses that such competitive interaction was often more local than national within a particular country.

Although Larsen's evolutionary-experiment angle is promising, his emphasis on evolutionary competition and the special challenges of latecomer status tends to reduce the responses at issue to merely instrumental terms and so deflects from consideration of their content or substance, considered in light of the problematics of modernity. If anything, this is the opposite of attuning to a wider range of frequencies. The political newcomers in question obviously had to find a competitive niche, but as Larsen and even Dobry have it, such space is too close to an end in itself, like power, as what political actors necessarily seek. The question is power for what, space as the base from which to do what—and why? So whereas in assessing the responses at issue we must of course weigh their potential for success, we must also consider the deeper purposes fueling them and how those purposes responded to the wider historical moment, starting with the reasons for reacting against both the liberal democratic mainstream and the mainstream communist alternative. Only on that basis can we assess the alternative directions they claimed to offer.

And in any case, what does "success" mean under the circumstances? In Italy and Germany, fascist movements found their niche, so why did they not just settle in and endure? Fascism was not simply about competitive survival on the domestic level.

Dobry's argument that labels, and thus the meaning of categories, were centrally at issue in the interaction is especially promising. It entails at least the implication that we must expect fluidity, blurring, and various modes of tension and overlap as opposed to clean lines and clear distinctions. But in making the point, Dobry seems, like Larsen, to minimize concern with content. More particularly, his emphasis directs us away from the struggles within and among fascist movements over priorities and, ultimately, over what "fascism" was to mean. It was not just about labels to position one's own movement vis-à-vis competitors. Dobry's call for a relational perspective is surely promising, but he would seem to settle for something too loose and flexible.

At the same time, whereas both Dobry and Larsen are especially good at undercutting teleological tendencies, in doing so each drifts into problematic territory, deflecting from the sort of attention to the actual history of the epoch that each otherwise implies is necessary. We must note, first, that in seeking to ward off teleological thinking, Dobry tends to overstate the argument as he accuses the mainstream approach of "historicism," taken as positing a direct causal link between intentions and outcomes, which encapsulate the processes that produced them. This leads to his insistence that we should not try to explain outcomes. We indeed need more attention to openness, uncertainty, and contingency, and to the extent possible we need to bracket outcomes in considering originating aspirations and the contingencies of the trajectory that followed. But open-ended though the processes were up to a point, the contingent concatenations of each trajectory did yield certain outcomes, and understanding how they did so remains essential to the overall inquiry.

This leads to questions about focus and the role of theory vis-à-vis the actual history through which fascism, and the wider universe surrounding it, turned out as it did. We are bound to have a "theory" or conceptual framework of some sort, and Dobry and Larsen are surely right to insist that something like theoretical confusion has been at work. Moreover, Larsen convinces in denying that what we need is a new or better "theory of fascism," based on isolating fascism, even though for some that is precisely what we mean by theory—and it remains the priority. In his 2001 piece, Larsen himself seems to have assumed that some such theory of fascism is the self-evident aim, but in his later article he seems to back off.[62] He shares the doubts of our other restives about the extent to which "fascism" can be isolated and about whether that sort of theory is what we need in any case. However, insofar as fascism cannot or need not be isolated, to what extent are we to submerge it within a wider universe—and how is its place in that universe to be conceived?

We noted that Larsen's call to encompass non-European forms of fascism recalls Iordachi's argument for encompassing east-central and southeastern Europe. And up to a point, Larsen's emphasis on the overload inviting new departures seems to mesh nicely with Iordachi's on open-ended experiment. But Larsen comes to seem more restrictive, less open-ended, in insisting on a particular substratum involving imbalances between modernization and liberalism. Of course fascism presupposes some experience of both modernization and liberalism and entails a quest not only for a radical alternative to liberalism but also, most have come to agree, for an alternative modernity. But in insisting on his a priori triggering mechanism of imbalance, Larsen's approach may restrict the scope for response, even prove reductionist. To assume that a reaction against liberalism and parliamentary government stemmed from imbalance reflects a priori assumptions about normal development. The notion even tends to circularity: if there was a substantial reaction, there must have been imbalance. In the same way, Larsen's scale based on standard variables like charisma seems too pat, too predictable. Again, a new agenda demands more fresh reading, open to a wider range of frequencies. And this is especially true if we are to treat fascism or at least the new Right as a global phenomenon, as Larsen convincingly insists we must.

Even as they advocate a focus on national or even local interaction and competition, Dobry and Larsen carry beyond the others, and overlap, in envisioning links beyond "fascist studies" and even the universe of the new Right during the era of the two world wars. But though relating phenomena we have taken to be "fascist" to others even across temporal borders is self-recommending in one sense, treating fascism in such a way as to maximize possibilities in this direction might compromise our effort better to understand what happened, the actual particular history, the universe of political departures during the era of the two world wars. There is room for both emphases, no doubt, but we need a better sense of the trade-offs, of what might be lost or diluted by leveling out fascism to this extent.

In particular, Larsen's renewed theory encompasses his call for an inventory and map, which, however, seems incongruent with his promising emphasis on continuing experiment. His evolutionary approach would seem to entail a greater premium on the history, in its naked particularity, as opposed to isolating factors for some static inventory.

Dobry and Larsen explicitly suggest that we cease worrying about precise distinctions and classifications and settle for greater blurring. Pinto and Kallis point in the same direction, usefully insisting that at the time perceptions of fascism as a changing force mattered far more than definitions.[63] Still, the need to countenance greater blurring seems to refer mostly to how we conceive what was happening at the time. What it says about the scope for rigor and criteria of differentiation in our own use of categories after the fact is less clear. Even if we agree with Pinto and Kallis that perceptions at the time mattered more than definitions elaborated later, we surely need not choose one at the expense of the other. Does opening to blurring based on perceptions at the time entail a danger of overreaction? What scope remains for rigor, and on what basis might we pursue it, from within the looser framework envisioned?

Dobry and Larsen are particularly valuable both in deflating fascism and in stressing, as the reverse side of their emphasis on contingency, the possibility of different outcomes. Yet a deeper understanding of the actual event, the particular history, the historically specific epoch constituted by the innovation and interaction on the new Right, is also crucial. The challenge is to make better sense of that aggregate event while encompassing the reasons for deflating fascism and accenting contingency.

Notes

1. Constantin Iordachi, "Fascism in Interwar East Central and Southeastern Europe: Toward a New Transnational Research Agenda," *East Central Europe* 37 (2010): 64, 176, 196. See also Maria Bucur, "Remapping the Historiography of Modernization and State-Building in Southeastern Europe through Health, Hygiene and Eugenics," under the rubric of "new research agendas," in *Health, Hygiene, and Eugenics in Southeastern Europe to 1945*, ed. Christian Promitzer, Sevastri Trubeta, and Marius Turda (Budapest: Central European University Press, 2011), 427–45. In proposing a "new research agenda" for the region, Bucur implicitly buttresses Iordachi's more general point about what we might learn about the aggregate from taking east-central and southeastern Europe as full partners, for better or for worse.

2. Iordachi, "Fascism in Interwar East Central and Southeastern Europe," 195.

3. Ibid., 196.

4. Ibid., 195.

5. Peter F. Sugar, "Conclusion," in *Native Fascism in the Successor States, 1918–1945*, ed. Peter F. Sugar (Santa Barbara, CA: ABC-Clio, 1971), 147–56, esp. 156.

6. Michel Dobry, ed., *Le mythe de l'allergie française au fascisme* (Paris: Albin Michel, 2003). The editor's introduction suggests how to deepen the discussion, getting beyond the stale and sterile terms of the "immunity" debate. See also Michel Dobry, "February 1934

and the Discovery of French Society's Allergy to the 'Fascist Revolution,'" in *France in the Era of Fascism: Essays on the French Authoritarian Right*, ed. Brian Jenkins (New York and Oxford: Berghahn, 2005), 129–50.

7. Michel Dobry, "Desperately Seeking 'Generic Fascism': Some Discordant Thoughts on the Academic Recycling of Indigenous Categories," in *Rethinking the Nature of Fascism: Comparative Perspectives*, ed. António Costa Pinto (Basingstoke: Palgrave Macmillan, 2011), 82n13.

8. Ibid., 62–63.

9. Ibid., 53, 56, 67–68.

10. Ibid., 58–59, 68–69.

11. Ibid., 65, 67–68.

12. Ibid., pp. 64–65. The quotation is from 64.

13. Ibid., 54, 72–74, 77.

14. Ibid., 60.

15. Ibid., 71.

16. Ibid., 71–72.

17. Ibid., 74.

18. Ibid., 72.

19. Ibid., 72–73.

20. Ibid., 76–77.

21. Ibid., 57, 64–65, 78.

22. Ibid., 79–80.

23. Ibid., 79.

24. Stein U. Larsen, "Decomposition and Recomposition in Theories: How to Arrive at Useful Ideas Explaining Fascism," in *Rethinking the Nature of Fascism*, ed. Pinto, 14–15, 17.

25. Ibid., 25, 29–30, 36, 43.

26. Ibid., 38–40.

27. Ibid., 39

28. Ibid., 40.

29. Ibid., 40–41, 43–44.

30. Ibid., 44.

31. Stein Ugelvik Larsen, "Was There Fascism outside Europe? Diffusion from Europe and Domestic Impulses," in *Fascism outside Europe: The European Impulse against Domestic Conditions in the Diffusion of Global Fascism*, ed. Stein Ugelvik Larsen (Boulder, CO: Social Science Monographs, 2001), 718–22, 732.

32. Ibid., 723, 726–27.

33. Ibid., 722–23, 726, 815.

34. Stein Ugelvik Larsen, "De-Linking as an Explanation of International Fascism," *East Central Europe* 37 (2010): 362–66.

35. Larsen, "Was There Fascism outside Europe?," 730, 732.

36. Ibid., 714, 729, 732, 818.

37. Mary Vincent, "Spain," in *The Oxford Handbook of Fascism*, ed. R.J.B. Bosworth (Oxford: Oxford University Press, 2009), 365, 375, 378–79.

38. António Costa Pinto, *The Nature of Fascism Revisited* (Boulder, CO: Social Science Monographs, 2012), 148.

39. Aristotle Kallis and António Costa Pinto, "Conclusion: Embracing Complexity and Transnational Dynamics; The Diffusion of Fascism and the Hybridization of Dictatorships in Inter-War Europe," in *Rethinking Fascism and Dictatorship in Interwar Europe*, ed. António Costa Pinto and Aristotle Kallis (Basingstoke: Palgrave Macmillan, 2014), 275. See also *Salazar's Dictatorship and European Fascism: Problems of Interpretation*, ed. António Costa Pinto (Boulder, CO: Social Science Monographs, 2009).

40. Pinto made the argument convincingly against me in a response to my invited comment on an article of his. Although I continue to hold to some of the points I made in my critique, Pinto was right that I was taking the totalitarian-authoritarian binomial too much for granted, and I have sought to be more careful and nuanced in using both categories ever since. See António Costa Pinto, "Reply: State, Dictators and Single Parties— Where Are the Fascist Regimes?," *Contemporary European History* 11, no. 3 (2002): 462–66. This was a reply to David D. Roberts, "Comment: Fascism, Single-Party Dictatorships, and the Search for a Comparative Framework," *Contemporary European History* 11, no. 3 (2002): 455–61, which was a response to António Costa Pinto, "Elites, Single Parties and Political Decision-Making in Fascist Era Dictatorships," *Contemporary European History* 11, no. 3 (2002): 429–54.

41. *Ruling Elites and Decision-Making in Fascist-Era Dictatorships,* ed. António Costa Pinto (Boulder, CO: Social Science Monographs, 1995).

42. Roger Griffin, *The Nature of Fascism* (London: Routledge, 1993), 121.

43. Miguel Jerez Mir and Javier Luque also embrace Saz's notion of a fascistized regime. See their "State and Regime in Early Francoism, 1936–45: Power Structures, Main Actors and Repression Policy," in *Rethinking Fascism and Dictatorship,* ed. Pinto and Kallis, 192.

44. Roger Griffin, "Foreword: Il ventennio parafascista? The Past and Future of a Neologism in Comparative Fascist Studies," in *Rethinking Fascism and Dictatorship,* ed. Pinto and Kallis, xv–xvi, xviii.

45. Kallis and Pinto, "Conclusion: Embracing Complexity," in *Rethinking Fascism and Dictatorship,* ed. Pinto and Kallis, 275, 278. See also 3 and 5 in their foreword to the volume.

46. Pinto, *The Nature of Fascism Revisited,* 119–49. See esp. 121 and 146 for explicit reference to the centrality of corporatism to interaction and transfers.

47. Ibid., 148.

48. Aristotle Kallis, *Fascist Ideology* (London: Routledge, 2000); Aristotle Kallis, "Neither Fascist nor Authoritarian: The 4th of August Regime in Greece (1936–1941) and the Dynamics of Fascistisation in 1930s Europe," *East Central Europe* 37 (2010): 303–30.

49. Kallis, "Neither Fascist nor Authoritarian," 325.

50. Ibid., 311.

51. Ibid., 326.

52. Ibid., 325, 327.

53. Ibid., 312, 327.

54. Ibid., 312, 325–26.

55. Whereas Dobry is surely right to criticize any insistence on a sharp distinction between "authentic" (Italian and/or German) fascism and the several French nominees on the basis of the putative ideological coherence of the former, in his determination to blur such differences he tends to overstatement or settles for stereotypes. He most obviously goes overboard in characterizing Italian Fascism as lacking ideology even up to 1925. See Dobry, "Desperately Seeking 'Generic Fascism,'" 62, 81n11. See also 69, where his plausible effort to use the Italian case to show that Robert Paxton's "five stages" schema is overstated leads him further to oversimplify the dynamic in Fascist Italy. Larsen, too, sets up something of a straw man in his plausible effort to get away from the Italian case as archetypal. See esp. Larsen, "Decomposition and Recomposition in Theories," 39.

56. See, e.g., Iordachi, "Fascism in Interwar East Central and Southeastern Europe," 197.

57. Vincent, "Spain," 376.

58. Aristotle Kallis, *Genocide and Fascism: The Eliminationist Drive in Fascist Europe* (London and New York: Routledge, 2009), 321.

59. Michael Werner and Bénédicte Zimmermann, "Beyond Comparison: *Histoire Croisée* and the Challenge of Reflexivity," *History and Theory* 45, no. 1 (Feb. 2006): 30–50. See also Michael Werner and Bénédicte Zimmermann, eds, *De la comparaison à l'histoire croisée* (Paris: Editions du Seuil, 2004).

60. Iordachi, "Fascism in Interwar East Central and Southeastern Europe," 164.

61. Stanley G. Payne, comment on Gilbert Allardyce, "What Fascism Is Not: Thoughts on the Deflation of a Concept," *American Historical Review* 84, no. 2 (April 1979): 389.

62. For indications in the earlier article, see Larsen, "Was There Fascism outside Europe?" 712, 714.

63. Pinto and Kallis, foreword, 3–4; and Kallis and Pinto, "Conclusion: Embracing Complexity," in *Rethinking Fascism and Dictatorship,* ed. Pinto and Kallis, 281.

Chapter 3

Transnational Turn, Further Unfinished Business, and Some Preliminary Categories and Distinctions

Symptomatic Problems with Some Existing Accounts of the Interaction on the New Right

Those envisioning a new agenda find great promise in a deeper focus on the web of interaction that developed, both domestically and internationally, as a new Right began to emerge in the wake of World War I. Such a focus might seem to point us beyond even our worthy studies of generic fascism to a more fruitful, if possibly still more complex way of conceiving the whole thing, the aggregate.

Quite apart from Constantin Iordachi, with his explicit reference to *histoire croisée*, we find evidence of increasing interest in the sort of interaction at issue in a number of recent works. Attention to interaction includes the role of emigrant communities, which could be conduits of influence and pressure in their venues of immigration.[1] As for Italian-German interaction, Arnd Bauerkämper makes it clear that we have at last worked beyond the diplomatic-military level in probing the implications of that interaction for the self-understanding and internal dynamics of each regime. Indeed, the relationship "was shaped," as Bauerkämper rightly puts it, "not only by mutual ideological affinity, and even friendship, but also by competition and rivalry in the fascist universe."[2] Yet Stefan Ihrig, though primarily concerned to get Mustafa Kemal Atatürk's Turkey into the mix, has recently deemed it "quite remarkable" that though the Nazis continued openly to revere their Italian role models, we know little about how Italian successes and failures were discussed in the Nazi media and about how developments in Fascist Italy actually influenced Nazism. Ihrig's becomes an argument for entangled history, of Germany and more generally, during the period. A more transnational approach, he insists, can offer insights into each national history, as well as into the entanglements themselves.[3]

But better encompassing *histoire croisée* in the case of fascism is not as straightforward as it might seem. In some existing efforts we find, alongside some promising indications of what we need, symptomatic inadequacies that indicate the danger of focusing on the interaction "prematurely," without an adequate grasp of the cases involved, the questions to be asked, and the stakes of the inquiry. Too often such inquiries indicate just how unfinished some of the earlier business has remained.

The place of Fascist Italy in the interaction is central for Mark Antliff, focused on France, and Federico Finchelstein, focused on Argentina. Up to a point, each study proves innovative and illuminating, showing how fruitful probing the interaction can be. But on closer examination, each is hampered by a too-limited sense of what Italian fascism entailed—its internal divisions, the proportions of its various dimensions, the thrust of such basics as totalitarianism and corporatism, the place of violence and myth, and the dynamic that resulted from the interplay of these and other factors.[4] This limitation reflects an overreliance, on the part of each, on an abstract, a priori notion of what fascism entailed. To be fruitful, focus on the interaction must be better braided with the fascist trajectory, encompassing both openness and a wider range of frequencies. Neither Antliff nor Finchelstein seems to notice the extent to which his own findings suggest the need and the scope for a more flexible framework.

Antliff cannot do justice to the complex and uncertain trajectory of Italian Fascism partly because he relies so heavily on Zeev Sternhell, who posits a single, largely unified and homogeneous fascist ideology. For example, Antliff uses such categories as "the aestheticization of violence" in an undifferentiated way, as if "fascist philosophy" was stable and unified. He similarly uses myth in a simplistic, single-valenced way that obscures its complex role within Italian Fascism and that thus muddies its place in the interaction between Italy and France. To place either violence or myth requires sensitive distinctions about the stage or stages at issue, the relationship between rhetoric and reality, and the manifest factional differences within Italian Fascism over the significance of violence and myth.

Again and again Antliff's account betrays the need for a deeper understanding of the rationale for Italian Fascist corporatism, including the ideas about association, ethics, and initiative that were to some extent derived from Georges Sorel but that did not rest on Sorel's ideas about myth and violence.[5] But relying on Sternhell, whose treatment of the bases of

Italian Fascist corporatism is particularly ill-informed, Antliff has little grasp of the corporatist direction within Italian Fascism, so he cannot convincingly assess French responses to it, especially in light of the overarching questions about modernity and the Enlightenment legacy at issue.

In treating Argentina in its interaction with Fascist Italy, Finchelstein seems on the right track in claiming to eschew essentialism and to treat fascism as a work in progress, a new political ideology in the making. This would suggest that for outside observers, fascism presented a moving, unstable pole of attraction so that varied and changing modes of interaction were possible. And Finchelstein provides a good sense of the complexities of the interchange in the Italo-Argentine case, including the scope, on both sides, not only for mutual inspiration and support but also for resentment and rivalry, for selective borrowing, misreading, and wishful thinking. He notes, for example, that differences between radicals and conservatives within Italian Fascism were reflected in Argentine discussions, and he observes that those looking across the Atlantic had to deal with the tensions between ideals and strategic considerations that frequently arose in the practice of the Fascist regime. He usefully observes at the same time that whereas most Argentinian *nacionalistas* lumped fascism, *nacionalismo,* and Catholicism, they were misrepresenting Italian Fascism in doing so, though only a few of them noticed.[6] Finchelstein's account makes especially clear the scope for seeing in Fascism, and taking from it, almost whatever one wanted.

In concluding that "Argentine nacionalismo reformulated fascism until it was almost unrecognizable while nevertheless adopting some specific aspects of fascist propaganda," Finchelstein implies that the modes of borrowing in the Argentine case transcended mere para-fascism.[7] And in illuminating the particular interaction at issue, he helps us see how we can begin attuning to a wider range of aspirations and cross-national relationships as we seek to understand the new radical Right.

But because he consistently repairs to a reading of generic fascism that is at once conventional, one-sided, abstract, and teleological, Finchelstein falls into precisely the sort of essentialism he claims to avoid. Thus he cannot do justice to the complexities of the interaction. Relying especially on Hannah Arendt, Enzo Traverso, and Dominick LaCapra, he features a familiar syndrome encompassing irrationality, ideological blinders, a belief in violence as regenerative, and a conception of the internal enemy as an object to be exterminated. On that basis he claims that the *nacionalistas,* like the Italian Fascists, wanted to impose a culture of terror; Auschwitz was the controlled lab of fascism.[8] As a result of this abstract, ahistorical understanding, Finchelstein has little sense of the internal dynamics or the axes of division in the Italian case, so he largely misses the internal contest over, for example, the interface between totalitarianism and Catholicism.

The flaws in these efforts indicate the problems of trying to treat interaction without a better grasp of the individual cases at issue. Insofar as we remain subject to essentializing or teleological assumptions, we miss the changing trajectory and thus much of what a deeper focus on interaction could reveal about selective borrowing, about who knew what when. In reading both Antliff and Finchelstein, we wonder what the outside observers actually knew of Italian Fascism at each point, as it was evolving, and how much they really cared to know. Was "fascism" itself becoming a myth for them by some point? But none of this can be adequately assessed if we do not better grasp the components in play and the actual dynamic in Fascist Italy itself.

Although the promise of focus on transnational interaction is bound up with the promise of expansion to encompass the wider universe on the new Right, we noted that the interaction between Fascist Italy and Nazi Germany has also attracted increasing attention, beyond the diplomatic-military level. That interaction is crucial to the larger picture because the two major fascist powers competed to influence others. And precisely because, as Iordachi, especially, reminds us, the others were *not* merely imitative or coerced, the Italian-German competition played into the wider interaction in complex ways that need to be better understood.

Bauerkämper's examination of Italo-German relations certainly avoids the sorts of limitation we find in Antliff and Finchelstein, but his analysis leaves us with another layer of questions. In treating the competitive side of the relationship, he usefully features the import of the Italian Fascist claim to cultural superiority, bound up with repudiation of Nazi biological racism and anti-Semitism, which the Italians generally viewed as crude and materialistic. But he also shows how questions about relations with Germany at once reflected and affected the wider dynamic of the Italian regime.[9] This suggests the need to consider the internal trajectories and the transnational interaction in tandem, as something like interweaving strands in a single process.

Fascist Italy's interaction with Germany by the later 1930s especially intersected with calls for comprehensive renewal, to transcend all the regime's compromises. For some discontented Fascists, renewal required adapting aspects of Nazism, seemingly more dynamic and successful. For others, the key was better to differentiate Italian Fascism from Nazism. But whereas it is widely agreed that the Italians tended to trumpet their fascism as cultural, "spiritual," and thus superior to the crude biological racism of the Nazis, we must ask whether that emphasis entailed merely vacuous rhetoric and wishful thinking, as we might tend to assume, or whether—perhaps by attuning to a wider range of frequencies—we can grant it at least some measure of plausibility and depth, in light of originating aspirations reflecting the wider scope for experiment.

Bauerkämper mentions the "spiritualist" accents and propagandistic dimension of Mussolini's well-known article on fascism of 1932 for the Treccani *Italian Encyclopedia,* but not the role of the philosopher Giovanni Gentile in the preparation of this article—and more generally in trumpeting the spiritualist conception of fascism. What are we to make of Gentile's vision, which was not only spiritualist but also in a sense "activist," as well as explicitly "totalitarian"? Certainly Gentile's prominent role was bitterly contested from several sides even within Italian Fascism.[10] And some observers find merely vacuous bombast in his Fascist writings and speeches.[11]

In treating Gentile and the "spiritual" claim, I have found a measure of substance, but I have also sought to show how rivalry with the Nazis tended to make the claim ever more overblown and mythical.[12] More generally, the accumulated impulses fueling Fascism in Italy meshed ever more uneasily as the dynamic continued and the wider context changed. The result was a major instance of the "cognitive dissonance" that, as we noted in chapter 1, was coming ever more to the fore by the late years of the regime.

It cannot be our purpose here to assess Gentile's plausibility. But without going deeper than Bauerkämper and raising this set of questions about the "spiritual" or "cultural" accent, we cannot adequately treat the interaction of Fascist Italy first with Nazi Germany, but then with others as well. Although we would not, like Antliff and Finchelstein, be merely reinforcing stereotypes, we would be simply skimming the surface.

We find a comparable combination of promise and limitation in works devoted to interaction along other axes, not involving Italy. For example, a too-conventional understanding of fascism in general mars the otherwise promising researches of Dietrich Orlow, treating the interaction between Nazi Germany and Dutch fascists, on the one hand, and French fascists, on the other.[13] The same problem compromises the effort of E. Bruce Reynolds, also promising otherwise, to place Japan more centrally in what he portrays precisely as a web of interaction involving European fascism.[14]

The problem in discussions of the Japanese case is especially symptomatic because, as we will see in more detail in chapter 5, Reynolds is among those who plausibly worry that the Japanese regime emerging by the late 1930s has been too readily marginalized by Western students of fascism, even as it has been widely considered fascist from within the Marxist-inflected discussion in Japan itself. But like Reynolds, such scholars as Joseph P. Sottile and Rikki Kersten seek to encompass Japan in terms of an a priori, sometimes teleological, and in any case somewhat monolithic and arbitrary conception of what counts as fascism.[15] This is bound to compromise their efforts to understand the relative importance of interaction with Europe, on the one hand, and proto-fascist indigenous factors, on the other.

Sottile is teleological in assuming that because they came together in the Axis alliance, Germany, Italy, and Japan were the quintessential fascist nations. Comparative study of them is thus the key to understanding the fascist era.[16] Growing from World War I, fascism was all about "proletarian nations" and imperialism. Spain does not belong largely because it was a declining power incapable of the imperialistic aspirations at issue. It is undeniable that the elements Sottile features were part of the mix, but his teleological approach leads him to privilege them unduly. It is not hard to imagine how Iordachi and other proponents of a new agenda would respond. Still, even if starting with the Axis powers is too teleological as an overall approach, Sottile's way of conceiving World War II as the culmination, and end, of the fascist era has its uses—and may trump the thinking of our restives in some respects. We will return to the question of ending and the contours of the era in the three concluding chapters.

Turning from Japan back to the overall issue, whereas all these studies show the scope for selective borrowing, misreading, and wishful thinking, they tend to take too much about fascism for granted, so their sense of what could have been at issue at the time, what could have been involved in the interchange, is too limited. Often the framework seems obviously inadequate to make sense of the challenging evidence presented. Conversely, that evidence seems to suggest precisely the need for a more flexible, fluid, open-ended framework for understanding transnational interaction during the period.

Approaching the Role of Corporatism in the Interaction

At this point, we can usefully return to corporatism, which, as we noted, Antliff shows was important to French perceptions of Fascist Italy, and which António Costa Pinto insists must be more central to the overall discussion. We should note, first, that corporatism has long been marginalized in that discussion, partly because, despite a modicum of institutional innovation, it nowhere lived up to the considerable hype that came to surround it. Although it was widely seen as the centerpiece of Italian Fascism during the key period of institution building from 1926 to 1934, and thus before the turn to overt imperialism in 1935, even discussions of Fascist Italy often disregard or dismiss the corporatist thrust. Such treatment further reflects the teleological thinking and arbitrary privileging of this or that that we have noted as ongoing pitfalls.[17]

Not only was corporatism central to institutional innovation in Fascist Italy, but Italian corporatism was widely discussed, especially during the 1930s, with the Stalinist turn in the Soviet Union and the onset of the Great Depression in the capitalist democracies.[18] Corporatist departures elsewhere, especially in Portugal and Austria, also attracted considerable attention. Indeed, an interest in corporatism became almost de rigueur for those seeking innovation on the new anti-parliamentary Right. Yet even accounts encompassing corporatism beyond Italy often betray a teleological dimension in their seeming eagerness to conclude "sham" or "fraud," with insufficient attention to the range of frequencies in the aspirations and to the openness of the resulting trajectories. Even insofar as corporatism ended up largely a myth, such sidestepping or dismissal threatens not only to misconstrue originating aspirations and the composition of the mix but also to impede understanding of the wider interaction at the time.

In recent studies Pinto and Didier Musiedlak not only take corporatism seriously but feature precisely its importance to that multinational interaction. In their different ways, each makes it clear that disparate, to some extent competing modes of corporatism were at issue as new Right experiments developed, partly, at least, in search of a "third way" alternative to parliamentary democracy and class-based communism. And they provide a good sense of the rationale for certain strands.

Pinto's account is especially valuable in distinguishing between social and political corporatism. With the former, labor relations and the trade-union phenomenon were to be encompassed by a new, possibly even totalitarian state. With the latter, occupational groupings were to provide a more productive basis for political representation. To be sure, there was blurring in practice, and Pinto is careful not to force an either-or distinction. But the influence of Italian Fascist corporatism, he argues, was largely confined to the social side. Italy's Labor Charter of 1927 was widely influential, even as a putatively "totalitarian" measure, and was replicated across the European dictatorships, but Italy was slow to develop corporatist representation, reforming its Chamber of Deputies on a corporatist basis only in 1939.

So the impact of the Italian model on Portugal, for example, was fluid and complex, allowing much scope for Portuguese innovation. Although tempered by Catholic ideals, the corporatist foundation of Portugal's National Labor Statute of 1933 owed much to the Italian charter, and the mode of social corporatism it specified was strongly institutionalized thereafter. But the corporatist direction of Portuguese politics by 1933 had other sources, and Portugal and Austria proved more important than Italy to the spread of corporatist legislatures.[19] So whereas Pinto is especially good in differentiating modes of influence, he also notes, at least implicitly, how important it is to understand at what point in each trajectory the inter-change was taking place.

Pinto expresses a debt to Musiedlak, especially Musiedlak's collabora-tive volume on corporatism, limited to the Latin world, including Latin America, that grew out of a 2006 conference. In addition to contribut-ing an article on the Italian case, Musiedlak provides an introduction and conclusion congruent with Pinto on the importance of corporatism to the interaction on the new Right. And like Pinto, Musiedlak features the im-pact of Fascist Italy's Labor charter, which, as he puts it, gave the other European dictatorships the first concrete example of a corporatism ordered by the state within a dictatorship nourishing a totalitarian project.[20]

But Musiedlak points even beyond Pinto in accenting the ambiguity and malleability of the corporatist idea, seen by some as a specifically mod-ern response to industrial society, but by others as a means to restore a lost social harmony.[21] Extending the point a bit, we can say that as modern, it entailed working through the rise of Marxist socialism and the experience with trade unionism, both linked to industrialization. Corporatism could even be a vehicle for modernization. Even as specifically modern, however, trade unionism might seem to combine positive aspects—nurturing disci-pline, collaboration, and solidarity—with negative—threating particular-ism and disruption. By integrating what began as working-class formations into a wider corporatist structure, it might be possible to maximize the positive and minimize the negative.

Because of these multiple cultural and political inflections, however, the embrace of corporatism entailed the scope for friction even within partic-ular national contexts. In France, Musiedlak notes, the tensions between traditionalist and modernizing corporatists carried into the Vichy period.[22] When turning to Fascist Italy, he has a far better sense than most analysts of the tensions and ideological divisions that inevitably blunted the corpo-ratist thrust in practice.[23] By implication, this meant that the Italian cor-poratist ideas finding their way into supranational interaction were being contested on the domestic level, so that, again, the intersection of the two levels produced the complex interweaving of two open-ended trajectories.

At the same time, Musiedlak emphasizes that the corporatist thrust in Europe tended to get bogged down, so that corporatism ended up serving mostly as a façade. It was taken over by dictators seeing it simply as an in-strument for reestablishing social peace.[24] But unlike many authorities, he makes clear that in light of the centrality of corporatism at the time, this outcome is no warrant for neglect or dismissal.

Although both Pinto and Musiedlak have usefully demonstrated that centrality, each betrays tensions and uncertainties indicating the need—and the direction—for further questioning. Pinto essentially assumes that the purpose of corporatism was authoritarian, to legitimize dictatorship; thus he provides little sense of openness, uncertainty, the scope for experiment.[25] Merely authoritarian purposes would hardly account, for example, for the interest in corporatism that Antliff noted in France. Under the circumstances, corporatism could be attractive as a potentially more effective mode of economic coordination and involvement, as opposed to a mode of top-down regimentation.

Because Musiedlak is more attuned than Pinto to the malleability of corporatism, he is in some ways more open to disparate purposes—and thus is better on why it was so widely embraced. This better sense of the variety of purposes invites precisely the wider range of frequencies we need in order to understand originating aspirations, whatever the outcomes in practice. Conversely, Musiedlak's sense of the heterogeneity enables him to provide a better sense than Pinto of the fissuring even among those insisting on a corporatist direction. And thus Musiedlak has more room to conceive the interaction as an open-ended trajectory.

But in the last analysis Musiedlak betrays essentially the same limitations as Pinto—restricted frequencies and elements of teleological thinking, precluding openness. In Musiedlak's case, the relationship between corporatism and "totalitarianism" proves particularly problematic. And whereas his emphasis on how the corporatist thrust got bogged down, serving mostly as façade, is surely convincing, we still need greater openness, based on a wider range of frequencies, to the corporatist experiment as it was unfolding.

So though both Pinto and Musiedlak, in focusing on corporatism, have contributed significantly to our understanding of the interaction, their limitations keep us from understanding the trajectories, and the stakes of the interaction, as well as we might. But we must wait for our fuller consideration of international interaction in chapter 5 to suggest how we might probe the place of corporatism more fruitfully.

Trajectory, Interaction, and a Braided Dynamic

Before considering modes of interaction in more detail in the next four chapters, we need to establish a kind of road map in the abstract and to introduce a couple of key categories and distinctions. We must start with the point, obvious in one sense, but hard to encompass adequately, that "fascism" was not always part of the political universe. And it is not to privilege the Italian case, in ways that our restives warn against, but simply to do justice to the contingency, as Michel Dobry especially advocates, to note that fascism emerged in highly contingent fashion under very particular circumstances in Italy in 1919. To be sure, its origins can be traced back to the interventionist struggles of 1914–15, themselves highly contingent, but the contingencies intersected, perhaps decisively. It is well known that the Italian situation in 1919 was so volatile partly because of resentments over the Treaty of Versailles, and it was partly because of the emotions, visions, and aspirations called forth by the interventionist struggles, and because of the nature of the ensuing Italian war experience itself, that Versailles was so resented, as was the enduring antiwar posture of the pro-communist Italian Left.

The word "fascism" was new in 1919, and no one knew what it meant; no one knew how whatever it denoted would develop. So even to say that "they"—the Italians, the Fascists—"invented" fascism is misleading. It was not something that could be invented. It simply emerged contingently from its contingent birth. It was through that contingent process that what came to be called fascism, first just in Italy, but then gradually more widely, came into the world.

Although we must posit a distinguishable fascism, isolable in some sense, it was not implicit at the outset in some "seed" or "germ" that we might pinpoint in whatever combination of such impulses as paramilitarism, violence, and palingenetic nationalism. In dealing with the Italian example in the first chapter, we noted precisely the need to think in terms of an uncertain, open-ended trajectory, partly because of the messiness of the Fascist mixture, the heterogeneity of the fueling aspirations, and the resulting fissiparousness and contest. And certainly the calls for a new agenda suggest that any instance of fascism is to be approached less in terms of some a priori essence, or some determinate direction in light of outcomes, and correspondingly more in terms of an uncertain, contingent, open-ended trajectory. Again, it was through its particular, contingent trajectory that fascism came to be as it was. And thus it is difficult, if not impossible, to conceive any element of fascism apart from its place in that particular trajectory.

Thinking in terms of an open-ended trajectory is a corollary of the greater openness to innovation and experiment that the new agenda advocates. The sense of the need and scope for new political departures bred diverse formations on the new Right and considerable overloading even in the formations we take as fascist. And thus we also note a messy, catchall quality in every fascist formation. Kevin Passmore notes that among those who joined fascist movements, "there was no essential idea that united them, for even where fascists used the same language they meant different things, both to themselves and to those they addressed."[26] Although the attendant fissuring was more salient in some cases than others, everywhere contest over priorities and direction helped produce the uncertain, contingent, open-ended trajectory. That could entail something like narrowing and a kind of hollowing out by the end, but it was not over until it was over.

At the same time, doing greater justice to the disparity, fissuring, and contestedness is a corollary of attention to the open-ended trajectory. And deeper attention to open-ended trajectory enables us to incorporate both substance and ephemerality, an imperative that we noted in chapter 1. Indeed, the disparity, fissuring, and contestedness constitute a kind of bridge between substance and ephemerality.

Although proponents of a new agenda clearly envision a greater emphasis on contingent trajectory, it is hard to avoid backsliding into essentialism. Even as Dobry and Stein Ugelvik Larsen criticize starting with Italy and Germany, and even as Aristotle Kallis seeks to encompass generally marginalized cases like Greece, they tend to take the Italian and German cases as known, given, stable. What *were* the Italian Fascism and German Nazism that Kallis takes as having expanded the space on the Right by the later 1930s? They did not simply expand the space once and for all but remained in motion, their trajectories uncertain.

Even as caught up in an internal trajectory, every fascist formation found itself caught up, virtually from day one, in wider interaction as well, first with existing elites and institutions on the domestic level, then on the wider supranational level, within the new Right and beyond. And of course those interactions entailed contingencies of their own. Moreover, the interaction itself made the categories unstable and fluid because the nature of each innovative departure was affected by the proximity of others. Despite the asymmetries to be addressed in chapter 5, even Italy and Germany were deeply intertwined with the others.

Feeding into the web of interaction, fascism was already contested, fissured, fluid, unstable. The interaction complicated the dynamic further, magnifying the openness and uncertainty that would have resulted in any case from the messiness of the fascist mixture. The interweaving of the open-ended internal trajectory and the wider interaction yielded something like a braided dynamic. That interweaving, too, had its contingencies. Indeed, adapting Richard Rorty's way of emphasizing the import of contingency, we note how significantly the braided dynamic depended on "who happened to bump into whom," on what happened to bump into what, as it developed.[27]

Even recognizing that the contingent, open-ended trajectory led to particular outcomes, to emphasize such trajectory is not to fall into either of the two fallacies that Dobry, especially, warns against. First, it does not in itself entail privileging the Italian and/or German trajectories in approaching other cases. Second, because it eschews teleological thinking, it does not entail what Dobry calls the "historicist" illusion—positing a direct causal link between intentions and outcomes, assuming that outcomes encapsulate the processes that produced them. Insofar as we do justice to the contingencies, reduction to trajectory is not to preclude but precisely to open the way to the possibility of different outcomes. To think in terms of an open-ended trajectory is to avoid, for example, the combination of myopic and teleological thinking that has led to the excessive imputation of definitive defeats in treatments of Italian Fascism.

We are thinking in terms of a braided *dynamic,* so it is a given that the interaction must be conceived diachronically, in its chronological dimension, as well as synchronically, across whatever geographical span. In considering any aspect of fascism, we must always be sensitive to its place in that dynamic trajectory. We will consider an array of examples in the four chapters that follow, but we can usefully draw out certain implications of the diachronic dimension in a preliminary way here.

Dobry and Larsen especially insist upon something like that dimension but leave questions about how we are to conceive it. To do justice to it carries us well beyond questions of borrowing, influence, and originality to encompass changing concerns, emphases, and possibilities. For example, changing relationships with the churches meant changing modes of interaction. Only through attention to that changing interaction can we do justice to the fluidity of the forces in play. It mattered at what point in the trajectory of each participant the interaction took place. At every stage the results of the interaction themselves affected the basis for subsequent interaction.

In treating those looking to the Italian example, Bauerkämper usefully emphasizes the scope for borrowing selectively to suit perceived needs.[28] But it is important to draw out two implications, in light of the fascist trajectory in Italy. The uncertainty and contestedness in Fascist Italy enhanced the scope for wishful thinking, for seeing what one wanted to see, on the part of those elsewhere. And in light of the internal dynamic of the Italian regime, it mattered, again, at what point in the trajectory such interaction took place. This was partly because of the cognitive dissonance that, as we noted earlier, became ever more salient in the Italian case, necessarily intersecting with the diachronic interaction as it did so.

In his widely cited collaborative volume on fascist-conservative interaction, Martin Blinkhorn nicely characterizes the wider confusion and uncertainty at the time. After noting that to the Left it all seemed simple, because all political formations that opposed the Left were objectively serving capitalism and were thus "fascist," whether or not they used the label, he observes that "for those seeking a more rigorous understanding of 'fascism,' confusion reigned, since the differences among a whole host of Rightist movements and parties, and an increasing number of Rightist regimes, tended to be subtly nuanced and constantly shifting."[29] If we are to understand the aggregate, however, we must note that what resulted was not merely continuing oscillation but a particular braided dynamic.

Categories, Then and Now

In the four chapters that follow we will see how a more sustained focus on interaction might deepen our understanding of categories at the time, above all by restoring the uncertainly and fluidity that tend to harden in retrospect, making it difficult to understand responses then and the overall texture of the era. In doing so, we become less concerned with precise distinctions and classifications, a notion congruent with the arguments of Dobry and Larsen especially.

But this desideratum points us to the complex relationship between the uses of categories at the time and our own uses of categories, whether the same or alternative. On the one hand, we must keep the distinction between the two uses in mind. In light of the uncertainty and openness at the time, we should be prepared for disparity, fluidity, and blurred lines as we probe the place of categories like "totalitarianism" and even "fascism" itself in the interaction. Coming later, however, we need not limit ourselves to these uses; we need not simply accept *their* meanings, which necessarily reflected their uncertainties and disagreements.

On the other hand, the distinction between "at the time" and "for us" is not neat, especially as, recalling Michael Werner and Bénédicte Zimmermann on *histoire croisée*, we note the need for reflexive interplay. We have to understand and encompass the meanings, uncertainties, and disagreements at the time if we are to avoid imposing our own understanding, based to whatever extent on hindsight and teleological thinking. Our own notion of totalitarianism, for example, needs to be better informed by usages at the time, though it need not be limited to them—a notion we will discuss in chapters 7 and 8.

Understanding the web of interaction not only demands that we reflexively integrate the uncertainty and openness at the time; it helps us to do so. But interaction gave rise to novel forms that can be difficult to characterize and place in the new Right universe, especially because their relationship with fascism itself was often complex. Although we will be primarily concerned with *their* meanings in the four chapters that follow, we are bound to use our own categories—categories that were not widely used at the time—in our effort to make sense of the interaction and the novel directions that resulted. We have noted doubts about "para-fascism"; we may or may not find such categories as hybrid, "fascistizing," or *"fascisant"* more appropriate. We will try them out, especially in the next two chapters, holding more systematic consideration of their utility for chapter 8. Although integrating categories "at the time" suggests the need to countenance a modicum of blurring and uncertainty, we noted in chapter 2 that what this says about the scope for rigor, and criteria of differentiation, after the fact is not so clear. The challenge is to specify the special combination of flexibility and rigor that seems to be demanded if we are to understand the *histoire croisée* in the particular universe at issue. After considering categories at the time as we probe the four modes of interaction, we will be prepared, also in chapter 8, to draw out the implications for our own categories in a more systematic way—ultimately to seek an appropriate combination of blurring and rigor.

Notes

1. See, e.g., Luca de Caprariis, "Fascism for Export? The Rise and Eclipse of the Fasci Italiani all'Estero," *Journal of Contemporary History* 35, no. 2 (April 2000): 151–83; Claudia Baldoli, *Exporting Fascism: Italian Fascists and Britain's Italians in the 1930s* (Oxford: Berg, 2003); and Emilio Franzina and Matteo Sanfilippo, eds, *Il fascismo e gli emigrati: La parabola dei Fasci italiani all'estero (1920–1943)* (Rome and Bari: Laterza, 2003). See also Stein Ugelvik Larsen, "Was There Fascism outside Europe? Diffusion from Europe and Domestic Impulses," in *Fascism outside Europe: The European Impulse against Domestic Conditions in the Diffusion of Global Fascism*, ed. Stein Ugelvik Larsen (Boulder, CO: Social Science Monographs, 2001), 734, on the overall effort to work through émigrés.

2. Arnd Bauerkämper, "Transnational Fascism: Cross-Border Relations between Regimes and Movements in Europe, 1922–1939," *East Central Europe* 37 (2010): 216. In addition, see, e.g., Sven Reichardt and Armin Nolzen, eds, *Faschismus in Italien und Deutschland: Studien zu Transfer und Vergleich* (Göttingen: Wallstein Verlag, 2005).

3. Stefan Ihrig, *Atatürk in the Nazi Imagination* (Cambridge, MA: Harvard University Press, 2014), 226–27, 229.

4. Mark Antliff, *Avant-Garde Fascism: The Mobilization of Myth, Art, and Culture in France, 1909–1939* (Durham, NC: Duke University Press, 2007); Federico Finchelstein, *Transatlantic Fascism: Ideology, Violence, and the Sacred in Argentina and Italy, 1919–1945* (Durham, NC: Duke University Press, 2010).

5. For some of the most important passages betraying a lack of depth on corporatism, see Antliff, *Avant-Garde Fascism*, 7–8, 50–51, 140–43, 149, 167, 208–209, 211, 213, 243–44.

6. Finchelstein, *Transatlantic Fascism*, 138.

7. Ibid., 165.

8. Ibid., 75.

9. Bauerkämper, "Transnational Fascism," 226–28.

10. On the complexity of Gentile's role in the regime, including the objections among other fascists to his influence, see Alessandra Tarquini, *Il Gentile dei fascisti: Gentiliani e antigentiliani nel regime fascista* (Bologna: Il Mulino, 2009).

11. For example, Michael Burleigh notes that like other expressions of Fascist doctrine, Gentile's portions of the 1932 encyclopedia entry on fascism were "characterized by a pretentiously woolly religiosity, whose opacity (in any language) faithfully reflected the phil-

osophical tone of the times." Michael Burleigh, *Sacred Causes: The Clash of Religion and Politics from the Great War to the War on Terror* (New York: HarperCollins, 2007), 62.

12. I discuss Giovanni Gentile especially in David D. Roberts, *The Totalitarian Experiment in Twentieth-Century Europe: Understanding the Poverty of Great Politics* (London and New York: Routledge, 2006), 130–42, 184–87, 299–305.

13. Dietrich Orlow, *The Lure of Fascism in Western Europe: German Nazis, Dutch and French Fascists, 1933–1939* (New York: Palgrave Macmillan, 2009).

14. E. Bruce Reynolds, "Peculiar Characteristics: The Japanese Political System in the Fascist Era," in *Japan in the Fascist Era*, ed. E. Bruce Reynolds (New York: Palgrave Macmillan, 2004); see, e.g., 161, 183, 186–87.

15. Joseph P. Sottile, "The Fascist Era: Imperial Japan and the Axis Alliance in Historical Perspective," in *Japan in the Fascist Era*, ed. Reynolds, 1–48; Rikki Kersten, "Japan," in *The Oxford Handbook of Fascism*, ed. R.J.B. Bosworth (Oxford: Oxford University Press, 2009), 526–44.

16. Sottile, "The Fascist Era," 3, 29–33.

17. Even Emilio Gentile, arguably the most prominent Italianist, neglects corporatism in his determination to feature the ongoing revolutionary role of the Fascist Party, as opposed to those pushing for a corporate state.

18. Alessio Gagliardi, *Il corporativismo fascista* (Rome: Laterza, 2010), accents the plausibility of such interest at the time, while fully recognizing, in analyzing how the system actually worked, its undoubted one-sidedness and failure overall. Among the myriad examples of international interest, see G. Lowell Field, *The Syndical and Corporative Institutions of Italian Fascism* (New York: Columbia University Press, 1938). Other examples will come up in chapters 5 and 6.

19. António Costa Pinto, *The Nature of Fascism Revisited* (Boulder, CO: Social Science Monographs, 2012), 131–32, 146–47.

20. Didier Musiedlak, ed., *Les Expériences Corporatives dans l'aire Latine* (Berne: Peter Lang, 2010), introduction, 5.

21. Ibid., 3–4, and conclusion, 472.

22. Ibid., conclusion, 473.

23. Ibid.

24. Ibid., 473, 476.

25. Pinto, *The Nature of Fascism Revisited*, 121.

26. Kevin Passmore, "Theories of Fascism: A Critique from the Perspective of Women's and Gender History," in *Rethinking the Nature of Fascism: Comparative Perspectives*, ed. António Costa Pinto (Basingstoke: Palgrave Macmillan, 2011), 137.

27. Richard Rorty, *Contingency, Irony, and Solidarity* (Cambridge: Cambridge University Press, 1989), 107–8.

28. Bauerkämper, "Transnational Fascism," 221.

29. Martin Blinkhorn, "Introduction: Allies, Rivals, or Antagonists? Fascists and Conservatives in Modern Europe," in *Fascists and Conservatives: The Radical Right and the Establishment in Twentieth-Century Europe*, ed. Martin Blinkhorn (London: Unwin Hyman, 1990), 9.

PART II

MODES OF
EPOCHAL INTERACTION

Chapter 4

INTERNAL INTERACTION
Fascists, Conservatives, and the Establishment

Varieties of Interaction on the Domestic Level

The Dobry-Larsen emphasis on the local/national points to one key level of interaction. Virtually from birth every fascist formation became caught up in relationships with existing elites and institutions—churches and economic interest groups, for example—and even with existing social practices and everyday life. More traditional conservatives constitute a special subset because of their seeming proximity to fascism on some key issues, starting with anti-communism, but also, in most cases, nationalist sentiment and skepticism about parliamentary democracy. At the same time, however, the unanticipated emergence of fascism confronted conservatives with unruly, violent, often seemingly plebian formations with worrisome radical pretensions. Even in those places where fascism did not come to power or won power only briefly, interaction with conservatives and the establishment was also important but necessarily took different form.

At issue, most basically, is the difference fascism made in each country. Conversely, to what extent did it get blunted or neutralized by existing elites, institutions, and social practices?

Overall, much excellent work has been done on the interaction between fascists and the established conservatives. Martin Blinkhorn, having made his reputation especially through his work on Carlism in Spain, has been especially influential and helpful on this set of issues. His collaborative volume of 1990, *Fascists and Conservatives: The Radical Right and the Establishment in Twentieth-Century Europe*, is still widely cited and provides a useful baseline, especially in light of Blinkhorn's introduction, which offers ideas further elaborated in a brief subsequent study published in 2000. In his 1990 introduction, quoted in the preceding chapter, Blinkhorn characterizes especially effectively the unprecedented volatility and turbulence of the situation. And he notes that the essays constituting the volume "make abundantly clear how complex, fluid and subtle was the relationship between the radical and the conservative Right in twentieth-century Europe." Indeed, he points out, "not merely was a boundary between fascists and authoritarian conservatives never drawn with total clarity, but it became more blurred with every year that passed."[1]

From within this framework, some of the standard assumptions and approaches still have their uses as well. As we consider them, however, we begin to fidget, especially in light of the promise of a new agenda. Let us consider just three such approaches, closely related but distinguishable.

Reflecting a still widespread tendency, Blinkhorn assumed that what motivated conservative elites in their dealings with fascism was maintenance of their own power, to preserve a threatened hegemony. Their commitment to parliamentary government wavered as it no longer seemed a lasting guarantee of their position.[2] From this perspective, the question is simply why conservatives achieved whatever measure of success they did in harnessing fascism to these ends, taken as given, obvious. Any innovation on their part must have been inherently defensive. Of course, this did not mean simply keeping everything the same; new challenges called for *some* innovation, which obviously might include trying to co-opt fascism. But from this perspective the new situation demanding their response reduced to a challenge to their own position—as opposed, for example, to some irreducible challenge facing their country. However, such self-serving was not the only reason to question parliamentary government and to ponder experiment in new directions. Reductive readings obviously keep us from engaging such thinking.

Along the same lines, Blinkhorn subscribes to the fairly widespread notion that the single party in these new anti-democratic regimes tended to be a fusion of radical fascists and conservatives. His major Spanish example is incontrovertible. Although the role of the Falange remained contested at least into the early 1940s, it is clear that in April 1937 Franco fused the Falange with the Carlists, monarchists, and the rest of the Right to form the single party of his emerging regime. And Blinkhorn goes on to suggest that the process was similar, if differently conducted, to the fusion of the Fascist Party with the Nationalist Association and clerico-fascism that had taken place in Italy after 1922. As he sees it, the outcome in both cases was a compromise between radical fascism and conservative authoritarianism, though one that left radicals marginalized and somewhat discontented in both.[3] But is this sort of bifurcation adequate to characterize what was going on?

It is also widely held that fascism was able to come to power more fully in Italy and Germany than in, say, Spain and Portugal, or Hungary and Romania, at least partly because democracy had developed further in Italy and Germany, more fully eroding traditional conservative bastions, thereby giving new fascist movements a greater opening. Under such conditions, fascism could more easily bend conservatives to its will, even if not completely. Elsewhere the conservative establishment remained strong enough to keep the real fascists out, to limit them to secondary roles, as in Spain, or, when necessary, simply to suppress them, as twice in Romania. But though the strength of the conservative establishment has been widely taken as a key differentiating factor, we wonder, again, if such a distinction helps us encompass the array of relationships between conservatives and fascists across Europe. For one thing, fascist initiatives might emerge from the top down or the bottom up, which might at least add a complicating factor in areas where traditional conservatism seemingly remained strong.

So whereas much about fascist-conservative interaction is widely known and agreed upon, pondering these three standard approaches suggests that each is possibly too rigidly either/or and thus insufficiently open to the array of relationships that may have developed through the interaction between fascists and conservatives. And the new agenda, with its particular emphasis on interaction and its calls for openness to a wider range of experiment, seems especially to suggest the need and scope for some fresh questioning.

Let us recall, for example, Mary Vincent's central point about Spain, considered in chapter 2. While most explicitly concerned to counter the notion that fascism in the Spanish case was simply tamed, neutered, and exploited by a traditionalist authoritarian regime, she also implicitly charges that approaches like Blinkhorn's, suggesting a compromise fusion, lead us to miss the dynamism of the relationship and how it led to something new, transcending any such compromise. It was not just that the conservative traditionalist Right managed to keep things the same by co-opting, absorbing, and even, when necessary, repressing genuine fascism, but that the traditionalist Right was itself transformed through the interaction with fascism, no doubt partly the indigenous Falange strand, though especially, Vincent implies, across national borders. We need to be open to some measure of such transformation in every case of fascist-conservative interaction, recognizing that the interaction itself may have changed either or both sides and thus the nature of the relationship, thereby yielding unforeseen syntheses that were themselves part of the new universe.

Blinkhorn, we noted, was especially good on the fluidity and uncertainty of relationships at the time. But what degree of fluidity and uncertainty are we prepared to encompass? The answer obviously has implications for our sense of what could seem to have been happening and what could have seemed the possibilities. But it also has implications, to be developed in later chapters, for how we now might now conceive the aggregate on the new Right.

In pondering some of the possibilities in this chapter, we must keep in mind the larger braided dynamic at work. Though in some cases more than others, interaction between the new radical Right and the conservative Right cannot ultimately be disentangled from supranational interaction, especially when either of both of the two major fascist powers was involved. Indeed, we will periodically bump up against the supranational strand in this chapter, thereby getting a preliminary sense of the interweaving of strands.

Winning, Losing, and Other Modes of Relationship

In assessing fascist-conservative interaction, we must first consider what each saw in, expected of, feared in, or wanted from the other. But even on this basic level, interaction was of course complicated because neither side was monolithic or stable. On the one hand, the fissiparousness of fascism meant that an Italian conservative might welcome Alfredo Rocco as minister of justice in Mussolini's regime but dislike the seemingly more radical directions that Edmondo Rossoni, Giuseppe Bottai, or Roberto Farinacci seemed to represent. On the other hand, the establishment was not monolithic either, nor, of course, was it necessarily wedded to the status quo. "Conservatives," too, could be out to undermine existing political institutions and practices.

At issue, however, is not simply what each side wanted from the relationship but especially what effect each side had on the other. Even if conservatives initially envisioned merely exploiting fascism for defensive purposes, the conservatives' sense of possibilities and priorities could be affected by the advent of fascism and the new radical Right. Moreover, the relationship was necessarily dynamic, changing to at least some extent in light of what actually happened through the interaction.

To consider the possibilities, it helps to start by recognizing that in principle either side might have been winning at the expense of the other. Indeed, we find a continuum of possibilities, from "positive" to "negative," with the value signs of course dependent on whether the continuum is viewed from the fascist or the conservative perspective. At one end, fascism could have been gaining the upper hand, penetrating or "fascistizing" conservatives and establishment types, drawing them closer or winning them over, and genuinely transforming existing social practices and everyday life. Conversely, fascists could have been losing out as they were tamed, subordinated, or supplanted by conservative elites and institutions. At the extreme of the losing end, fascism was not merely precluded from power but actively suppressed as unruly, plebian, and dangerously radical—and as a rival for the Right side of the political spectrum. But losing could also mean that fascist impulses were being more subtly absorbed, blunted, or exploited by traditional conservatives or diluted, neutered, or deflected by the strength of traditional practices and everyday life.

Still, winning and losing, as if in a zero-sum game, do not exhaust the possibilities. Modes of relationship unforeseen at the outset could develop once the interaction was under way. We may find something like synthesis or symbiosis insofar as the purposes of the two sides proved to mesh to some extent. Especially under the volatile circumstances, however, the interaction could be more dynamic, even synergistic, radicalizing both sides, and actualizing further unforeseen possibilities. Even if conservatives initially envisioned merely exploiting fascism for defensive purposes, the process of interaction could transform their aspirations, yielding novel outcomes.

Especially in light of the scope for transformation and even synergy, in treating conservative purposes we need to get beyond the tendency toward a reductionist default setting and to prepare for novel juxtapositions transcending mere conservative defense. In repairing to such reductionism, Blinkhorn seemed to have little room for any such transformation, yet his assumption about simply maintaining hegemony stood in some tension with his accent on the uncertainty and blurring at the time.

Although differential conservative strength vis-à-vis democracy remains pertinent for certain questions, the distinction can become too neat, leading us to gloss over the import of interaction and interpenetration even in countries like Hungary where the conservatives seemed to have maintained their strength. In seeking to maintain their position, conservatives could be pushed or pulled in a fascist direction by the fascist challenge itself. Especially in pondering what seems conservative suppression of fascism, we may be too quick to view the two sides as stable, missing the possibility that either or both was being transformed by the interaction. So in treating countries with seemingly strong conservative establishments, we may not want to insist on either/or to the extent we generally have, thereby possibly missing the symptomatic importance of the outcomes even in those cases.

The novel outcomes of synthesis, symbiosis, or synergy can be hard to characterize even today. For those at the time it was obviously still harder to grasp what was happening, what was resulting from the interaction, because the situation was so fluid, partly as a result of the interaction itself. Even the extent of winning or losing was often not clear. Sometimes this or that aspect of the interaction could be read in contrasting, even diametrically opposed, terms. What looked like a definitive defeat or repression sometimes proved not so definitive down the road.

When establishment conservatives moved in what might be called a fascistizing direction, it could be difficult to tell whether they had been genuinely transformed by the interaction or simply were seeking to head off fascism by co-opting aspects of the fascist program. Even today, the proportions often seem undecidable once we get down to cases. Whatever the conservative aim, insofar as the outcome was a fascistizing direction, it was—and still is—difficult if not impossible to specify which side was winning and which was losing.

Moreover, how do we know the extent to which limits, blunting, or failure, in whatever degree, stemmed from the strength and resiliency of conservatives, the establishment, and existing social practices, as opposed to the weaknesses, divisions, and confusions in the fascist thrust itself? That, too, is surely to some extent undecidable, but the question must be kept in mind. At the same time, insofar as fascist impulses were being blunted or transformed in whatever degree, we wonder about the implications for any effort to specify what "fascism" ultimately consisted of. To what degree can we continue to isolate something specifically fascist once transformation, in whatever degree, was under way through the domestic interaction?

Relative Respectability and Modes of Innovation

To grasp in more concrete terms the scope for one mode of synergy and the tendencies that lead us to miss or misconstrue it, let us return to Blinkhorn's treatment of the Italian Nationalist Association. Although they formally merged with the Italian Fascist Party in 1923, the Nationalists are often seen as authoritarian conservative as opposed to authentically fascist. We noted that for Blinkhorn the single party in the new anti-democratic regimes tended to be a fusion of radical fascists and conservatives—a compromise in one sense, yet with conservatives gaining the upper hand. But while his Spanish example is convincing, to portray the fusion in Italy as comparable misses too much about the nature of the fascist-conservative interaction at issue.

Blinkhorn's implication was that in each case the fusion, creating the single party, entailed taming and to some extent co-opting genuine, potentially innovative and potentially threatening fascism. In principle the fusion in Italy might be understood in something like the opposite way, as a victory for Fascism, which now encompassed what had been to some extent a rival on the new Right. In fact, however, the situation in Italy transcended any such dualistic understanding in an especially symptomatic way.

As Blinkhorn implies, the fusion with the Nationalists surely reassured wider conservative circles in Italy, including the monarchy, about Mussolini and Fascism. The Nationalist Luigi Federzoni, who among other significant roles in the regime served as minister of the interior during a particularly sensitive period from 1924 to 1926, especially provided a strong bridge between the regime and monarchist circles. And he was indeed close to being a conservative authoritarian—and as such, a moderating force within Fascism.

But let us return to his fellow Nationalist Alfredo Rocco, who first came up in chapter 1. Rocco had been the leading ideologue of the Nationalist Association and as minister of justice from 1925 to 1932 was central in giving the regime its totalitarian and corporatist direction. No mere conservative authoritarian, Rocco was more radically innovative than Federzoni because he was more deeply affected by the political challenges and opportunities that had seemed to open in Italy in light of the war, the postwar challenge from the Left, including the trade-union movement, and the seeming weaknesses of Italy's liberal regime. But in insisting on the need to go beyond parliamentary democracy, which, he argued, experience had shown to be anti-historical, ineffective, and corrupting, Rocco in a sense spoke for many across Europe who, in the face of political instability and the performance of parliamentary government, began turning to the new Right during the interwar period.[4]

To be sure, conservatives were quick to turn against parliamentary democracy, even to seize chances to undermine it, but its performance could have seemed problematic in any case. And in light of, first, the challenge posed by communism and labor militancy and, second, the new uncertainties and opportunities, at least for some countries, in light of the breakup of empires, conservatives were bound to ask some new questions.

Thus especially the scope for synergy in the fascist-conservative interaction. Whereas fascism to a considerable extent involved those newly politicized, it also attracted and broke off part of what had been the constituency for more traditional, authoritarian-leaning conservatism. Rocco had something in common with such disillusioned conservatives as Gaetano Mosca and José Ortega y Gasset, who clung to liberalism even as they pinpointed what they took to be the drawbacks of democracy. But whereas these two figures remained in a sense suspended on the liberal tightrope, Rocco broke off to move in a new Right direction. The Nationalist Association had begun that move before the war, but especially as the war was ending, and then as Italy seemed to face a particular threat from a militant trade-union movement in the wake of the Bolshevik Revolution, Rocco departed further. And thus he is usefully contrasted with Mosca on the nature of the trade-union threat and how to deal with it.[5] His ideas were not coming from Fascism at that point, but precisely because Fascism seemed to afford the possibility for the new mode of action that seemed necessary, the advent of the Fascist regime and the chance to act within it drew out his ideas and gave them a practical direction. Here was the synergy at work.

Because Fascism was emerging, though still largely unformed, Rocco did not have to settle for laments of the sort he had offered in 1920 about the weakness of the liberal state in the face of the threat, and the opportunity, constituted by the modern trade-union movement.[6] He could envision acting through Fascism to build a new kind of state, channeling that phenomenon into what he believed to be more productive purposes. As minister of justice, he was able to act on that basis, helping give the Fascist regime a certain totalitarian and corporatist direction, though his role was contested, including by those with a different understanding of the rationale for both corporatism and totalitarianism. And other forces remained at work in the Fascist mix at the same time.

Still, Rocco provides a classic case of new fascists and more traditionalist, authoritarian-leaning conservatives coming together. The outcome was a synergistic synthesis that was itself "fascist," as "fascist" as any of the experiments during the period, and not, as for Blinkhorn and others, a matter of conservatives taming "authentic" fascism. The convergence between Rocco and *some* of the Nationalists, on the one hand, with Fascism, on the other, paved the way for a radically new direction, not merely a conservative check on radical fascism. Even insofar as the interaction blunted other aspects of the fascist thrust, it was the emergence of fascism, as novel if unformed, and potentially subject to shaping, that induced that departure.

In the same vein, we might observe that also in 1923 the noted philosopher Giovanni Gentile adhered to Fascism from an angle quite different from Rocco's, becoming minister of education in Mussolini's government and joining the Fascist Party. Gentile's involvement, too, made Mussolini and Fascism seem more respectable in conservative eyes. But whereas Rocco and Gentile played roles that helped to blunt certain radical fascist impulses, they were themselves, in their own quite different ways, radicals and totalitarians, and they became two of the regime's leading ideologues and functionaries.

As we noted in connection with these two figures in chapter 1, there was disagreement at the time, and there remains disagreement, over who was a *real* fascist. But surely they were all Fascists, part of the messy mixture, and what the adherence of Rocco and Gentile to Mussolini's regime meant at the time was not obvious—certainly not as obvious as Blinkhorn takes it to be for Rocco and the Nationalists. The adherence of both Rocco and Gentile fed into the open-ended trajectory. And the fact that the prominence of each was indeed resented by some other Fascists contributed not only to the messiness and contestedness of the mixture but also to the openness and uncertainty of that trajectory. Though in retrospect we see Rocco as the chief architect of the distinctively Fascist Italian state, even he did not have the last word. As part of a shake-up in the Fascist hierarchy, he left the Ministry of Justice in 1932.

To consider another aspect of possibly energizing, synergistic interaction between fascism and conservatism, complicating the story, let us turn to women and gender, the subject of much notable work in fascist studies in recent decades. The restive authorities we considered in chapter 2 do not call for greater attention to these dimensions, but a new agenda might be expected to make further sense of the insights those researches have opened up. That fascism, in some of its manifestations, entailed emphases on masculinity, virility, and a reaffirmation of traditional gender roles is well established, but so is the tension that resulted as fascism both preached domesticity and mobilized women outside the home. The deeper interest in gender in the 1980s and 1990s led to notable works by such scholars as Claudia Koonz, Victoria De Grazia, and Perry Willson showing that the unanticipated advent of fascism opened up various modes of female agency, so that, at least in certain spheres, women felt not marginalized but empowered, even influential within fascism. At the same time, however, such new modes of agency sometimes occasioned new axes of division among women themselves.

Building on that earlier work, such scholars as Julie Gottlieb and Kevin Passmore show that women not only came to fascism with agendas of their own but were able to contest and help shape the direction of their respective movements or regimes. While deeply critical of fascism overall, Gottlieb challenges prevailing assumptions in stressing the prominence of women in Oswald Mosley's British Union of Fascists, showing that for the most part women freely bought into the fascist program, though they related in their own way to male constructs of gender and masculinity. In identifying with the movement, women were rebelliously asserting their independence, even reacting against orthodox feminism, though in the name of something other than traditional female roles.[7] Extending the point, the advent of fascism and the frustrations of such women came together synergistically, opening the way to a female self-understanding not among the possibilities before.

Passmore offers his recent case study of women in the French Croix de Feu as part of a wider challenge, largely congruent with the calls for a new agenda, to our ways of thinking about fascism more generally. Appealing especially to war veterans, Colonel François de La Rocque launched the

Croix de Feu in 1928, converting the movement into a political party, the Parti social français (PSF), when the new Popular Front government dissolved the movement in 1936. In the situation of polarization surrounding the Popular Front, the party attracted even more followers. Whether or not the Croix de Feu/PSF should be considered "fascist" has been much debated and will be addressed in chapter 8. Here it is sufficient to view it as more or less fascist in order to take advantage of Passmore's insights.

The movement included significant numbers of women, who, Passmore shows, came to the Croix de Feu/PSF with specific assumptions, agendas, and social and cultural capital of their own. They could not openly contest the status of the veterans who had been at the core of the movement, but they doubted that the veteran spirit could regenerate the nation. And they redefined the political in social, moral, and religious terms. The leader, La Rocque, increasingly favored the women's perspective, and women gradually became more influential. And thus a gradual decline in paramilitary display in favor of a more social orientation accompanied the turn from the Croix de Feu to the PSF. In effect, Passmore notes, the women competed with male activists to define the movement. And their behavior was not reducible to some mindless internalization of simple images in a condition of disorientation.[8]

Passmore astutely draws out wider implications for our thinking about fascism overall. Both the Croix de Feu/PSF discourse on women's roles and the actual roles of women were tension-ridden agglomerations of pre-existing notions and behaviors. Even as they preached domesticity, male leaders mobilized women for social pacification, especially reintegrating the working class into the nation. The Croix de Feu/PSF disparaged women who remained at home and called especially for volunteer work contributing to social peace. As Passmore sees it, this was unintentionally to mobilize a form of activism shaped by religious and professional discourses, reflecting women's experience in such spheres as education and social work, that did not wholly accord with the official discourse of the movement. And he finds this indicative of the fissuring that, as we noted in the previous chapter, he finds characteristic of fascist movements overall.[9]

Passmore's example, like Gottlieb's, seems to suggest the synergizing effect of interaction. The very availability of a novel fascist movement, expanding the reach of politics, attempting more, drew conservative women beyond not only traditional roles but also mainstream modern modes of public involvement. The scope for these more active roles energized them, as did, surely, the recognition that they were affecting the direction of the movement. But a measure of blunting resulted as conflicting impulses in the Croix de Feu/PSF occasioned not only contestedness but to some extent contradictory directions, tending to cancel each other out.

Interaction with Business, the Churches, and Existing Social Practices in Italy and Germany

With the possibility of various modes of synergy in mind, let us consider the wider interaction between fascists and conservatives in the Italian and German cases. Although the centrality of these two cases to the overall discussion is in question, and although much about the degree of fascist penetration is well known in each case, we can usefully get them on the table before casting the net more widely.

Emerging very much from below, fascism in both Italy and Germany got a foothold especially because conservatives saw sufficient common interests for a measure of immediate symbiosis. For most this entailed the possibility of exploiting fascism over the longer term while boxing out what seemed the more dangerous and distasteful fascist impulses. And certainly some measure of such blunting took place in both countries. But in each case it soon became clear that fascism was strong enough, or the conservative establishment weak enough, that fascism could pursue at least some of its radicalizing aims.

Most obviously, fascism in power transformed the political process, creating a one-party state, with a monopoly of this and that. In doing so, fascists were to some extent turning the tables, co-opting or marginalizing conservatives. The penetration was more rapid and thoroughgoing in Germany, though even in Germany the outcome was a mode of party-state dyarchy, entailing ongoing overlapping, ambiguity, and infighting. Parallel, specifically Nazi institutions were often in the ascendancy, but in ways not always obvious at the time. However, this was not an either/or matter, insofar as the personnel in the pre-existing state institutions were being Nazified, diminishing whatever conservative check on Nazism they might have provided.

Radically different though they were, the Nationalist-Fascist fusion in Italy in 1923 and the purge of the SA, including the murder of its leader, Ernst Röhm, in Germany in 1934, make clear that what looked at the time, and might still look, simply like a blunting of real fascism, reassuring to conservatives, proved more complex, even a prelude to unanticipated modes of radicalization. At the time, the death of Röhm and the purge of the SA were widely construed as cutting off the potential for a more radical brand of Nazism. Certainly the army welcomed the new situation. But the meaning of what had happened would depend on what would develop subsequently. Although the purge proved a definitive defeat for certain radical impulses that had helped fuel Nazism to that point, other radical impulses remained, and if anything, clipping the wings of the SA helped bring some of them to the fore. It is generally agreed that the SS now became more central, playing a role in crucial respects more radical than might have been expected from the SA, despite its earlier prominence and pretensions.

Certainly the Nazis proceeded with their revolution, though the process raises more specific questions about the modes of relationship with conservatives and the establishment that developed. In both the Italian and the German cases, interaction with big business, the churches, and everyday life was at once central and especially symptomatic.

Fascism in Italy produced a one-party state and some energetic action and achievement, but a number of originating Fascist impulses were blunted or absorbed by traditional institutions at the same time. The resulting frustration among many Fascists occasioned periodic calls for, and even some actual efforts at, revitalization. The existing bureaucracy proved a brake to some extent, as the continuing struggle between the Fascist Party and the state makes clear. The party claimed the mantle of the ongoing fascist revolution, including its totalitarian vision, and, as we have seen, Emilio Gentile has insisted that the party's role during the 1930s was more seriously educational and less merely choreographic than had long been believed.[10]

But the party did not embody all the innovative, specifically fascist impulses within the regime, so fascism-conservative interaction was not simply a matter of the radical, innovative party confronting a conservative state bureaucracy. For many committed Fascists, the aim was a new kind of state, at once corporatist and totalitarian. The party could promote and educate, but the institutional locus had to be the state, not the party. The question then, however, was whether those with such a fascist vision were supplanting traditional bureaucrats in the state apparatus. Moreover, corporatism was to be a way of bypassing or even replacing sectors of the existing bureaucracy, so it was particularly bound to provoke opposition—specifically *conservative* opposition insofar as the bureaucracy remained in traditional hands, as it largely did.[11] But corporatism also provoked considerable opposition from the business community.

It is by now widely agreed that whatever the context, fascism was not the mere handmaiden of economic interests but rather was seeking, among other things, to reconceive the liberal understanding of the relationship between the political and the economic spheres in light of modern experience. Although we will need a wider framework, later in this chapter, to address the Fascist relationship with business in Italy, it makes sense to start with corporatism, which was central to the Fascist self-understanding as innovative and even hyper-modern. Referring especially to the 1930s, Philip Morgan notes that "corporatism became the 'revolutionary' myth of the regime, and functioned as such in raising both the international and internal profile of fascism, convincing many foreign observers and commentators of the seriousness of its universal mission to change the world, and persuading many university-educated young Italians that the regime, after a decade in power, had not lost its 'revolutionary' élan."[12] But the corporatist thrust particularly led to friction and contest with business elites. The struggle over corporatism proves the first of three levels to be considered in the relationship between Fascism and business in Italy.

We will consider the rationale for corporatism more deeply in the next chapter, in light of international interaction, but Morgan usefully notes that the function of corporatism was to be as much educational as economic.[13] Yet his account suffers from certain of the standard teleological pitfalls, which not only obscure the place of corporatism in the Fascist interchange with business elites but even provides a misleading sense of the overall texture of the regime. On the basis of three distinguishable if overlapping arguments, he seems to write off corporatism as hopeless. First, "Fascist Italy was a dictatorship, and it is hardly surprising that corporatist organs were deliberately deprived of any capacity for independent initiative and self-regulation."[14] Second, "the corporations were unlikely to be genuinely educational, class-collaborative organs of economic planning and management, when their rationale and composition simply formalized Fascism's initial and lasting anti-worker-class orientation."[15] On that basis the corporatist system ended up, unsurprisingly, compressing wages. Third, Morgan deems corporatism too cumbersome to have been compatible with what the regime needed for autarky, imperialism, and war, which, he assumes, had been the aims driving Fascism all along.[16]

Especially in combination, Morgan's formulations entail too much homogenizing, essentializing, and question-begging—or putting the cart before the horse. The net effect is to gloss over the sometimes debilitating tensions and contradictions among Fascist impulses and, conversely, to miss the openness, contestedness, and uncertainty of the actual dynamic at the time. And thus it is also to misconstrue the stakes of the internal interaction over corporatism.

That Fascism had gathered force in reaction against socialist-oriented working-class formations is undeniable, but to claim that Fascism was inherently and abidingly anti-worker is surely one-sided overall and does not remotely do justice to the aspirations of corporatists like Giuseppe Bottai, most obviously, not to mention older Fascists like Sergio Panunzio and A.O. Olivetti who had come from the syndicalist Left. That the composition and functioning of the corporatist bodies ended up unbalanced in favor of employers is also undeniable, but Morgan's characterization makes it seem that the employers were bound to win, that there was no drama to the history unfolding.[17] If the system so obviously served business interests—by compressing wages, for example—why did business so actively resist or seek to undercut it? Conversely, dictatorial power was not so obviously antithetical; it might prove the best hope for galvanizing corporatism in the face of business opposition.

The notion that corporatism was incompatible with the thrust toward autarky, imperialism, and war would suggest that it was the internal contest over priorities within Fascism, more than business opposition, that compromised the corporatist experiment. But why did corporatists fail to recognize that incompatibility? In fact, they had different priorities in the first place, but a teleological approach like Morgan's makes it impossible to do justice to them and to the potential challenge they continued to pose. And unless we do justice to that dimension too, we cannot understand the stakes of the interaction with business over corporatism.

Italian business leaders, acting especially through the Confindustria, the major industrial trade association, did not particularly welcome the Fascist regime, but especially after the Matteotti crisis of 1924, they seemed to have no choice but to work within it. As Franklin Hugh Adler has shown, the Confindustria did not affect the regime's overarching policies, which were increasingly political and irrational from an economic perspective—and which the Confindustria did not hesitate to criticize. But there was little or no scope for business initiative on that level; business could only react.[18]

Still, without the Confindustria's relatively effective moderating strategy, Fascist Italy might have developed in ways more threatening to capitalism.[19] Rather than try to exploit fascism, big business primarily sought autonomy, which entailed a minimalist conception of corporatism. Throughout much of the 1930s, the Confindustria successfully exerted pressure to blunt the development of the corporatist system or to channel it in directions favorable to business.[20]

Even in its compromised form, however, the system had more substance than is often recognized. Analyzing, as few have, how the system actually worked, Alessio Gagliardi treats it as a serious experiment, not a mere sham or myth. Moreover, he contends that despite its failure overall, to some extent the system genuinely represented economic interests and fostered participation in decision making during the 1930s, though employers were better positioned than workers to exploit the system.[21] Even as Morgan insists that decisions were being made at the top, then endorsed by the corporate bodies, he concedes that those bodies discussed important issues having to do with their respective branches of the economy and with the relationships among them. Corporatist organs thus developed a sense of real importance and exercised some powers of control and supervision in the autarkic economy of the 1930s.[22]

Despite periodic signs of life, however, the system was evidently bogging down, disappointing its adherents. Even as Didier Musiedlak stresses that corporatism in practice was emptied of revolutionary content, he is more open than Morgan to the possibility of more meaningful corporatist development in Italy, and his evidence suggests that despite frustrations and tactical defeats, committed corporatists thought it worthwhile to keep pushing.[23] They criticized the system's performance and, after even the constitution of actual corporations in 1934 proved disappointing, sought to revitalize the system by making corporatism the basis for political representation through the Chamber of Fasces and Corporations, which finally replaced the old Chamber of Deputies in 1939. Where it was all leading could not have been clear at the time, though the ultimate failure of the Fascist corporatist system is beyond dispute. Corporatism ended up a myth, surrounding by inflated rhetoric.[24]

But apportioning the reasons for that outcome is difficult. On the one hand, the fate of the Italian corporatist experiment seems a classic example of a potentially innovative fascist thrust, initially a particular source of energizing confidence, being neutered by conservative elites and institutions—especially business but also the traditional bureaucracy. On the other hand, the corporatist experiment bogged down partly because of the debilitating fissuring within Fascism itself. We have noted that Fascist Party and corporatist currents were to a considerable extent rivals, leading the party to interfere with the corporatist apparatus or to exercise on its own economic functions that were supposed to be corporative.[25] Moreover, as we will see in more detail in the next chapter, there were debilitating differences even among Fascist corporatists over priorities and the basic rationale for the corporatist direction.

But to understand the role of fascist-conservative interaction in this instance, we must back up to consider the wider frame of business's role in blunting the corporatist thrust. In light of the uncertain, changing overall dynamic, it is hard to characterize the situation overall; we find the regime co-opting business but also business restraining Fascist radicalism. But once the possibility of synergy is on the table, a symptomatic difference in accent between Morgan's and Marcello De Cecco's treatments of the regime's relationship with business proves especially illuminating. Although he overlaps with De Cecco up to a point, Morgan, as we noted, tends to force autarky, imperialism, and war as the basic thrust of Fascism all along. That direction certainly came to dominate the relationship between the regime and business by the later 1930s, but the relationship began on a different basis—which De Cecco features and which Morgan glosses over. Again we note how important it is to grasp the contingent, step-by-step trajectory.

After briefly flirting with a return to laissez-faire, Mussolini's regime began moving in a new economic direction in 1925 as it at last committed itself to building a decisively post-liberal order. In doing so, it sought the support of, and collaborated with, major industrialists like Giuseppe Volpi and especially Alberto Beneduce, industrial establishment types with ties to the highest levels of the Italian economy. And this, De Cecco makes clear, was an effort to make permanent and more thoroughgoing the statist dirigisme and technocratic management that had emerged in Italy during World War I.[26]

Italian Fascism, despite its overloaded confusion early on, was very much a product of the war, and the Fascist sense of challenge and possibility reflected a determination to draw out the wider lessons of the war experience, taken as positive, even revelatory. And those lessons would of course be hyper-modern. A statist direction in the economy would not only develop that key aspect of the wartime legacy but would also serve the regime's projects, starting with simple matters of prestige, though, more fundamentally, helping to provide legitimation as post-liberal by moving beyond the liberal relationship between the political sphere and the economy. Although autarkic tendencies were already important in the later 1920s—as with, most notably, the "battle for grain"—convergence between the regime and business elites was not yet focused as single-mindedly on imperialism and war as Morgan implies.

But the Depression upped the ante, as big business, including the banking sector, more obviously needed the state for survival. So especially under Beneduce, the regime moved more wholeheartedly in innovative statist directions, most notably with the Istituto per la ricostruzione industriale (IRI), established in 1933, essentially a giant state holding company intended to rescue failing large businesses by buying up shares, paid for through an innovative sale of bonds to the public. The IRI was initially seen as a temporary emergency measure, and some of its companies were eventually reprivatized. But it proved anything but temporary, even surviving the fall of Fascism and the return to democracy after 1945.

It was certainly symptomatic that the discussions leading to the IRI pointedly left out the capstone corporatist institution to that point, the National Council of Corporations. And the IRI, while especially innovative, has often been seen as a pragmatic response to the Depression, akin to those found all over the capitalist world, rather than an instance of Fascist or corporatist ideological fulfillment. But any such either/or assessment misses the sense in which, up to a point, the IRI was part of a novel, distinctively fascist departure beyond liberalism, even if that departure was not corporatist. Though their accents differ, both De Cecco and Morgan usefully push beyond the notion that the IRI was merely a pragmatic response, as each links the IRI to a wider, specifically Fascist project.

The IRI's ownership of a substantial chunk of Italian industry and banking was very much congruent with the wider statist direction in course, and Morgan notes that the IRI's potential utility to the regime's projects was clear even before it was institutionalized in 1937.[27] In 1935, for example, the government blocked the reprivatization of Terni, a major steel firm. Moreover, the IRI was but one of a series of innovations that reshaped the relationship between the political sphere and Italian business during the period. There was mandatory cartelization, which, though nominally under the Ministry of Corporations, was welcomed by many in the business sector, partly as preferable to real corporatism.[28] A new banking law in 1936 crowned the operation, which shifted the balance of big business ownership and governance heavily toward the state.[29]

De Cecco and Morgan essentially agree about the outcome, but because they conceive the purpose somewhat differently, they end up differing about what that outcome meant for the nature of the relationship between business and the regime. For De Cecco, because technocratic public managers were now running most of the big commercial banks and a major chunk of large, capital-intensive industry, they were free to plan Italian economic development at the micro-economic level. As he sees it, "it was their ambition to show that they could do a better job of it than their private equivalents had been able to do, and in all honesty it must be recognized that until the early 1970s they succeeded in putting Italian capital-intensive industry on a more efficient footing."[30] Morgan's conclusion is congruent: with those like Beneduce, straddling the public-private divide, calling the shots, Italy ended up with a plethora of public-private bodies running the economy at the micro-level, "an almost perfect, mutually beneficial congruence of business and state interests."[31]

But the regime's definitive turn, by the mid-1930s, toward aggressive expansionism further upped the ante. When the IRI was formally institutionalized in 1937, its charge was clearly bound up with autarky and war preparation. And in characterizing the relationship by that point, Morgan certainly convinces in part in referring to co-optation: "In IRI, its subsidiaries, and in compulsory cartels, the Fascist regime successfully co-opted and paid for the technical, managerial, and entrepreneurial expertise of the country's business managers, in the pursuit of an autarkic war economy."[32]

There seemed plenty of reason for business to go along at first. But as Italian policy vacillated between seeming recklessness and seeming restraint, and then as the prospect of European war loomed, Italian business became ever more nervous and foot-dragging. Although there is controversy about the extent, comparison with Germany especially makes this tendency clear. But whatever such hesitation or active opposition, it was not sufficient to blunt the particular radical departure—toward conquest and war—that had become predominant from within the Italian Fascist experiment.

To grasp the overall relationship between Fascism and business in the Italian case, it is important to uncouple the statist thrust from the more specific thrust toward imperialism and war and to foreground the more general point about the World War I experience and the determination to transcend liberalism. Morgan makes an unassailable point in noting that whereas the emergency economic measures adapted all over were basically similar, in Italy these were not abandoned as the Depression eased but were rather institutionalized and given explicit autarkic and warmongering functions. However, teleological thinking leads him to elide the key distinction and thereby to miss the more general statist direction already in course, as well as its wider post-liberal rationale.[33] To assess the Fascist-conservative relationship, the extent of blunting and co-option, we must grasp that more general statist thrust apart from imperialism and war.

In characterizing the overall relationship between the regime and business elites, both Morgan and De Cecco suggest synergy—evident in the quotations from each above. To posit such synergy is not to propose that Fascism was the handmaiden of big business after all; the relationship was at once more uncertain and more dynamic than any such notion suggests. As with Rocco and his thinking about how to handle the challenge of trade unionism, Mussolini's regime gave would-be innovators in the business establishment the opportunity to move in the new economic direction they had begun to envision, though the advent of Fascism surely enhanced their sense of possibility. And business eagerness and support then further galvanized the regime, though first simply in this particular statist direction, not yet obviously toward imperialism and war. What turned out to be Fascist economic policy was the outcome of that synergistic interaction; that outcome was decisively and innovatively post-liberal, congruent with the regime's wider post-liberal, statist, and even totalist direction. And Beneduce, Volpi, and their collaborators surely count as "fascists," just as Rocco does.

However, business elites did not know what they were buying into, though neither did the regime know what might come of the willingness, even eagerness, of business to collaborate. The two sides had come together, however, and as it happened, in light of the contingencies, especially the unforeseen possibilities stemming from the wider international situation, the regime ended up moving toward imperialism and war. The sense of possibilities for Italy in that direction surely opened to some extent precisely because of the mating between regime and business that had taken place on the basis of the far less grandiose stakes to that point. But in that sense the synergy, and dynamic, pointed in a radical Fascist direction that led well beyond what many in the business community had wanted or anticipated. So business ended up being sucked into one mode of Fascist radicalism, even though business had been able to blunt other modes, including corporatism, at the same time. From the business perspective, in fact, the more neutral statist direction was intended partly to, and certainly served to, undermine the possibility of different radical Fascist directions more threatening to business interests. But because business got caught up in one mode of Fascist radicalism while marginalizing others, the overall relationship between business and Fascism is especially difficult to characterize.

Not surprisingly, the direction that in fact ensued, entailing the ties to the business establishment that it did, displeased many Fascists, who envisioned some different mode of statism, some different post-liberal relationship between the political sphere and the economy. That obviously included corporatists like Bottai but also more determinedly anti-establishment—and to some extent anti-capitalist—radicals like Roberto Farinacci, who has been compared to Gregor Strasser in his effort to resist accommodation with the capitalist bourgeoisie.[34]

But it is by no means clear what a more radical Fascist alternative would have looked like. Some point to Ugo Spirito's proposal for proprietary corporations, which attracted much discussion at a major conference on corporatism in Ferrara in 1932.[35] But the place—and the fate—of Spirito's proposal has been widely misread. It certainly would have been a radical departure, but corporatist critics like Bottai and Panunzio were right to argue that not only did the different sort of radical corporatist departure they advocated not require such proprietary corporations, but the proposal missed the specifically political, as opposed to economic, rationale for the corporatist direction.[36] However, that did not remotely mean that Bottai and Panunzio would fall in behind Beneduce and the IRI.

The relationship between the regime and business that developed in Nazi Germany paralleled the Italian case in some respects but also entailed some instructive differences. In Germany, too, there was a dramatic intrusion of state power into the economy, partly for pragmatic and partly for ideological reasons. The new regulation regime that developed almost immediately under Hjalmar Schacht, as head of the Reich Ministry of Economic Affairs, included cartelization and banking measures anticipating those in Italy. Measures changing labor relations to a considerable extent paralleled those in Italy but without any pretense of corporatist collaboration. In a sense, the German case was more straightforward, partly because the Nazis came to power at the height of the Depression and thus faced challenges demanding immediate response. Autarky had become more tempting, if not a necessity. Moreover, the Nazi regime had a briefer trajectory and embarked on rearmament and war preparation more single-mindedly from the start. On the other hand, once the Italian regime, too, embarked on aggressive expansionism, it could more readily co-opt big business as a whole, in light of the state's powerful role in the economy through the IRI. In Germany the regime was more constrained to co-opt sector by sector or firm by firm.

In his widely admired treatment of the German economy under Hitler, Adam Tooze asks explicitly why the German business lobby tolerated the dramatic intrusion of state power into the economy during the Nazi period. To be sure, there was the shared opposition to communism and even parliamentary government, but there was no wholesale ideological convergence. With few exceptions, big business was not enthusiastic about Hitler coming to power. Some of the most high-profile businesses, like the chemicals and pharmaceuticals giant IG Farben, had earlier been prominent in the liberal wing of German big business, yet IG Farben ended up with particularly strong ties to the regime.[37] Conversely, Fritz Thyssen, one of the few leading industrialists who was indeed enthusiastic about Hitler from the early 1930s, took as his model Italian Fascist corporatism, unpopular both with other industrialists and with government economic leaders like Schacht.[38]

Tooze provides four reasons why big business was willing to go along. First, the business lobby had been seriously weakened by the Depression. Second, business could profit, even if the regime's autarkic turn was incongruent with the internationalist preferences of most of big business. Third, the regime coerced business only very selectively; it mostly harnessed the initiatives of business managers and technicians. Fourth, the interests of German business were not unified, and the regime proved adept at exploiting difference and making tactical alliances.[39]

In any case, the regime found big business willing to partner in many key aspects of the Nazi revolution by the mid-1930s. The initiative came from the political authorities: sometimes Schacht, as head of the Reich Ministry of Economic Affairs; sometimes from Hermann Goering's air ministry or other branches of the military; sometimes from Wilhelm Keppler and his special staff for raw materials questions; sometimes from the Reichsbank. Even when resistance might have been expected, the regime almost always found active collaboration. As Tooze puts it, "The autarchy programme, rearmament, even the mass of new regulatory authorities were all backed up and energized by managerial expertise supplied courtesy of German industry."[40]

Despite the shift in power relations, business was not merely the passive object of the new relationship. Rapidly rising profits enabled business to accumulate the capital for the large-scale investment necessary to pursue the regime's objectives of autarky and rearmament.[41] But more fundamentally, as in Italy, an element of radicalizing synergy developed in Germany, though, also as in Italy, it entailed marginalizing or going around militants who favored various more radical changes in political-economic relationships. German managerial elites were energized by the regime's concerted action beyond old-fashioned politics, and the degree of enthusiastic managerial participation surely further energized the regime. In other words, it was not only the enhanced opportunities for profit but also the seductions of the new mode of action—post-liberal, hyper-modern—that cemented the partnership. Tooze noted the sense among the new techno-bureaucrats that they were at last truly in charge, doing it right, getting it done, without parliamentary chatter or political obstacles to doing what made sense in technical terms.[42] We noted a comparable sense among public-private technocrats in the Italian case.

On occasion, however, the synergy that developed in Germany clearly transcended anything in Italy, though the mechanisms are hard to pin down. The most telling case was surely IG Farben itself, which, in the words of Peter Hayes, "more powerfully than any other industrial combine … put its talents and capacities to the service of the Nazi program of armament, autarky, aggression, and annihilation."[43] Hayes himself, in a widely admired work first published in 1987, updated in 2001, featured pragmatic accommodation as opposed to ideology in accounting for the collaboration that developed. Subject to tunnel vision, the firm's leaders at every step acted on the basis of short-term, "rational" calculations of the firm's advantage as they sought to operate a profit-making business from within the new Nazi framework.[44]

But Hayes was willing to revise his thinking in light of the researches of Stephan H. Lindner into Hoechst, one of IG Farben's key constituent companies.[45] Lindner featured the degree of ideological convergence, as opposed to such micro-economic calculation. Or rather, what emerges from Lindner's study is precisely the need to transcend that dichotomy in light of the dynamic in course. The effort to run a profit-making business under the circumstances led to the Nazification of Hoechst's leaders, even of the firm itself. But those leaders did not begin with a desire to serve radical Nazi aims. Submitting and adapting to the regime, they were drawn into a radicalizing synergistic relationship—with deeply negative consequences.

Overall, business obviously contributed to marginalizing certain radical possibilities in both Italy and Germany, but not to blunting the radical direction of each regime overall. If anything, on the contrary, the measure of synergy that developed may have reinforced those radical directions.

Fascism's relationship with the churches and existing religious practices was particularly central to its wider interaction with conservatives and established institutions in both Italy and Germany. John Pollard, considering only relations with the Catholic Church, has recently reaffirmed the baseline notion that both instances of fascism began as anticlerical and even anti-Christian, then came to terms with the church for opportunistic reasons, though the accommodation was only temporary.[46] But revisionist works by Richard Steigmann-Gall, on Nazi relations with Protestants in Germany, and Walter Adamson, on Fascist relations with Catholics in Italy, challenge the conventional wisdom in ways that seem congruent, up to a point, with the quest for a new agenda. Each suggests that we have been missing a beat insofar as we start by assuming antagonism and, on that basis, ask about winning and losing, transforming and blunting. Each suggests the scope for a deeper accommodation essentially from the outset because of a deeper convergence of aims between the two regimes and the respective churches than we have tended to recognize. So do we find further instances of synergy?

Obviously secular authority had often seen itself as the protector of religion, just as churches had often looked to secular authority for protection. And there were some evident sources of agreement between fascists and the churches—anti-communism, most obviously—but also, perhaps especially for Catholics, opposition to liberalism, associated with secularization and restrictions on the church.[47] But new modes of relationship were perhaps possible in Germany and Italy, first from the sense of new challenges to religion, most dramatically from communism. In light of what had happened in the Soviet Union, no one could doubt that the communists were serious about marginalizing or eliminating the traditional churches. And then the anticlerical atrocities during the Spanish Civil War seemed further to suggest an existential threat to the churches. Given what seemed the particular challenges of the era, a religious identity might seem to *demand* a fascist identity. At the same time, the emergence of the new mode of politics on the Right suggested the possibility of more concerted action to serve religion and the churches. In any case, the situation suggested the scope at least for symbiosis: fascism could protect the churches, which, in turn, could offer fascism active sympathy, support, even legitimation.

But of course there were also reasons for tension and rivalry, especially insofar as fascism seemed to entail totalitarian aims or even competing religious, or "pseudo-religious," claims of its own. The sense that fascism might entail some mode of "political religion" is not just an *ex post* notion but was suggested at the time, by proponents but also by outside observers, some deeply critical.[48] To serve those religious aims, fascists might borrow from religious liturgies, rituals, or symbols. Up to a point, that would seem an instance of fascism exploiting existing religious practices for its own ends. But it could also seem evidence of genuine accommodation, on the one hand, or of the dilution of fascism, on the other. At the time people on both sides disagreed, were of two minds, or saw what they wanted to see.

Interaction between the regimes and the churches obviously rested on the perceptions and expectations that each side had of the other. Neither side was monolithic; indeed, each was divided over how to relate to the other. So the relationship between each fascist regime and the dominant church was bound to be fluid, unstable, as each stage meant a new and to some extent unforeseen situation to which each side had to respond.

Even insofar as fascism saw itself, and could be seen, as pursuing Christian aims and protecting church interests, the effort could seem to require new political modes, with fascism calling the shots in ways threatening to the autonomy of church auxiliary organizations and even to the churches themselves. The implication was that that under the new circumstances it could not be left to the churches to lead the way in pursuing those aims. So there was bound to be institutional rivalry whatever the degree of doctrinal or ideological convergence. Even insofar as the churches sought symbiosis, they worried about threats to their autonomy in light of fascist totalizing claims. In principle, church nervousness or opposition stemming from such concerns for autonomy can be distinguished from nervousness or opposition in response to aspects of fascist ideology or practice that seemed to violate church teaching. But the distinction was bound to blur.

Under Pope Pius XI (r. 1922–39), the Catholic Church was quite critical of fascism and the new Right on occasion. Although Charles Maurras and the Action Française claimed to embrace Catholic tradition as essential to order and hierarchy, Pius XI condemned the movement in 1926 for its merely instrumental embrace of the church. He went on to condemn eugenics, including sterilization, in his encyclical *Casti connubi* of 1930; the putative worship of the state in Fascist Italy in his encyclical *Non abbiamo bisogno* of 1931; and central aspects of Nazi German doctrine and practice in his encyclical *Mit brennender Sorge* of 1937. Pollard notes that even as Pius XI's encyclicals moderated Italian racial and eugenic measures, Italian Catholic response to the Fascist regime's racial laws of 1938 was ambiguous.[49] Pius XI himself opposed the racial laws and commissioned an encyclical intended to condemn racism in both Italy and Germany, but he died in February 1939. His successor, Pius XII, seeking better relations with the two fascist powers, decided not to publish it when he became pope early the next month. He was hoping to moderate and head off war.[50]

In some respects, tensions between the Catholic Church and the various fascisms intensified even after the accession of the more cautious Pius XII. In noting that the relationship between the church and fascist regimes had become increasingly difficult during the 1930s, Pollard stresses the friction that developed even with regimes widely viewed as "clerical-fascist," such as that of Msgr Josef Tiso in Slovakia beginning March 1939 and Ante Pavelić's Ustasha regime inaugurated in Croatia after it became independent in 1941.[51]

In Italy, after a measure of dissension and mutual suspicion following Mussolini's appointment as prime minister in 1922, the new regime and the Catholic Church came to a seeming accommodation with the Concordat and the Lateran Treaty of 1929. And this apparent solution to the church-state problem that had plagued the new Italy since 1870 greatly enhanced the regime's legitimacy at home and stature abroad.

The Concordat gave the church a say in education and in marriage law that it had not had under the liberal regime, but thus it greatly displeased many Fascists. Such measures were certainly inconsistent with the regime's totalitarian aspirations or pretensions. But whether Fascism was being blunted or absorbed was impossible to say at that point. Fascist discontents helped push Mussolini to limit the reach of the Catholic youth organization, Catholic Action, in 1931. And those totalitarian pretensions seemed sufficiently menacing to prompt Pius XI, also in 1931, to issue the encyclical *Non abbiamo bisogno*, noted above, condemning the Fascist regime's promotion of a seemingly idolatrous state worship. This was just weeks after his encyclical *Quadragesimo anno* (Fortieth year), issued on the fortieth anniversary of Pope Leo XIII's encyclical *Rerum novarum* of 1891 and renewing the call for social harmony based on corporatism. Although some read it as further evidence of convergence between Fascism and the church, the encyclical sought to reclaim corporatism, so central to Fascist Italy's claim to novelty and modernity, for Catholic tradition.[52] So there was accommodation as well as friction and rivalry.

The German case was more complex because of the country's confessional divide. The Nazi regime agreed to a Concordat with the Catholic Church in 1933, shortly after coming to power. As in Italy, it served to reassure the church and to help legitimize the regime. But that hardly made for a stable relationship. The church welcomed aspects of Nazi population policy—the natalist measures, most obviously—while deploring others, especially forced sterilization and "euthanasia." Pius XI's *Mit brennender Sorge* of 1937 strongly condemned as idolatrous the Nazi accent on "race and blood," the conflation of the secular and the religious in such notions as "immortality," the effort of some Nazis to sever the Old Testament from Christianity, and especially the regime's interference with religious freedom in education and in associational life, clearly violating the Concordat of 1933.

Further complicating the German case was the fragmentation of the Protestant community, with the split between the German Christians and the Confessing Church (Bekennende Kirche) the most politically salient factor. The sources of the split went back to the nineteenth century, but the advent of the Nazi regime exacerbated it considerably.

In light of the preceding backdrop we can assess the revisionist accounts of Steigmann-Gall and Adamson, which, as we noted briefly above, suggest new ways of conceiving the regime-church relationships. But though each might seem to anticipate, or even to serve, the search for a new agenda, they introduce new sources of confusion or waywardness precisely in their effort to say something new. So each is worth considering in some detail.

Both Steigmann-Gall and Adamson challenge the baseline notion that fascism was secular, even anti-Christian, and suggest not only that many fascists believed in Christianity but that such belief was part, at least, of what fueled the fascist departure in each of the two countries. At the same time, each is particularly attentive to the dynamic on both sides, showing that just as fascism was not static, neither was the putatively conservative, religious side in the encounter. On that basis, each shows the import of viewing the interaction as a diachronic trajectory. And for each, up to point at least, it was not a matter of one dominating, absorbing, or blunting the other. Rather, the encounter led, at least for a while, to a novel symbiosis. And though neither pinpoints the dimension as explicitly as he might have, the two accounts both suggest novel modes of energizing synergy. It is especially in doing so, however, that each misses or misconstrues aspects of what seems to have been at work.

We will find it useful to treat Steigmann-Gall first because his book was published earlier than Adamson's essay; Adamson cites the book and seems to have been influenced by it to some extent. This order proves more illuminating even though the Italian regime came first and seemed to have established a certain baseline in dealing with the churches, or at least the Catholic Church, before Hitler had come to power.

The friction between the Nazi regime and the Catholic Church is well known, and Steigmann-Gall takes Nazi hostility to the church as a given, not bothering to mention Pius XI's encyclicals, for example. He is concerned almost exclusively with the relationship between the Nazis (some of them Catholic, to be sure) and the Protestant churches. In light of our concerns we can usefully engage four aspects of his argument, the first of which will take several paragraphs to consider.

We can best get into that first point by noting that one of Steigmann-Gall's aims all along becomes explicit in the final chapter. Christianity and the Protestant churches did not constitute a brake on or barrier to Nazism. On the contrary, a common sense that Christianity was under assault bound the two sides together. Each was responding most immediately to the decline in church membership and participation during the Weimar period, attributed to the rise of secular liberalism and atheistic socialism. So, as Steigmann-Gall sees it, whereas the Nazis surely transgressed the previous bounds of Christian practice, they were convinced not of the death of God but of the need to preserve God through a war in the name of Christianity. Nazism saw itself, and could be perceived by others, as spearheading a Christian revival.[53] Many, though by no means all, German Protestants found Nazism the appropriate Christian response to harsh new realities.[54]

Disputing earlier authorities, Steigmann-Gall shows that Hitler, convinced that symbiosis was desirable and possible, devoted much effort until 1937 to fostering a unified national Protestant Church. Common interaction among the various Protestant churches with his new regime seemed to make unity possible, and conversely, such unity would make possible the desired symbiosis between the new church and the regime. For Steigmann-Gall, the purpose was genuine mutual accommodation, not remotely to render the Protestant churches innocuous or subservient.[55]

It is here that we seem to discern not merely symbiosis but a mode of radicalizing synergy up to a point, even though Steigmann-Gall does not note the fact explicitly. The potential for some such synergy between Protestantism and a new politics was already present in Germany before the rise of Nazism, in light of an idiosyncratic mix of notions that developed especially from discussions within nineteenth-century Protestantism—even *liberal* Protestantism. Protestantism and especially Lutheranism were taken as quintessentially German, and anti-Semitism was taken as essential to Christianity. But the advent of the Nazi regime, with its promise of a more determined mode of action, drew the Protestants more radically in that direction and made them eager to accommodate up to a point. Conversely, that radicalization of the church surely emboldened the Nazis, deepening their sense of Christian mission and making genuine symbiosis seem possible.

But our three subsequent points rest on what happened from there. Hitler first left it to the churches to come together, then relied on a new state ministry to promote unity, then left it to the churches again, but nothing worked. On the contrary, the effort provoked bitter internal church struggle, deepening existing schisms. And, extending Steigmann-Gall's argument, this was surely partly because, with Nazism seeming to promise a new mode of *action* on the basis of the principles at issue, the stakes for Protestants were now much higher.

In 1937, Hitler gave up on institutional Protestantism, abandoning the idea of a unified Reich church. Now Nazi leaders began dropping their own church memberships. Protestant pastors were excluded from party membership, while party members could no longer play roles in church organizations. Anticlerical and even anti-Christian rhetoric increased among Nazi leaders. But Steigmann-Gall insists convincingly—our second key point—that all this friction, now even with Protestants, was not intended from the start but arose contingently, in light of the disappointing outcome of the interaction to that point. Nor, Steigmann-Gall contends, did it indicate increasing ideological enmity, as some have claimed.[56] The end of Hitler's effort to promote unity merely reflected a change in his sense of the relationship with the Protestants that was possible and desirable on the institutional level. As Steigmann-Gall sees it, the ideological convergence remained.

But if we accept Steigmann-Gall's argument to this point, we begin to encounter questions on essentially two levels. The first—our third overall point—concerns the practical level of interaction between the regime and the Protestant Church, with its various ancillary organizations. Although the Nazis and the Protestants still saw themselves as pulling in the same direction—promoting *völkisch* welfare, unity, and goodwill, opposing both liberal individualism and Marxist class struggle—organizational rivalry between the two sides increased markedly. The key Protestant and Catholic welfare organizations sought to retain their autonomy but found themselves, though not eliminated altogether, increasingly marginalized.[57]

Steigmann-Gall makes much of Hitler's disappointment over the churches' failure to unify. Had the Protestants unified and fallen in, as Hitler expected, perhaps church entities would have been allotted a greater autonomous role in the organization of women, youth, welfare, and leisure, on the grounds that the Nazis and the Protestant Church were indeed pushing in the same direction. However, it might be argued that, on the contrary, the totalitarian thrust of Nazism, already clear, was bound to produce friction over organizations, and thus increasing anticlericalism among Nazis, so that in terms of the overall trajectory, the churches' failure to unify was secondary at best.

In other words, it might be argued that in light of Nazi aspirations and self-understanding, this was simply the chickens inevitably coming home to roost, whatever the outcome of the effort to unify the Protestant churches. Still, Steigmann-Gall makes a plausible argument, the corollary of the contingency he emphasizes, that the Protestant failure to unify changed Nazi thinking and affected practice. But then we must draw out the implications for our questions concerning the import of the interaction for the overall trajectory. If Steigmann-Gall is right, it helped radicalize the Nazis in ways that need to be drawn out explicitly.

Steigmann-Gall certainly recognizes the totalitarian thrust of Nazism, noting that whereas the Nazi coordination of religious social organizations is generally seen as evidence of anti-Christianity, it simply reflected the exclusivism to be expected in a totalitarian state. He goes on to note that the Nazis claimed credit for protecting the *Volk* and its religiosity from the inroads of liberalism, communism, and Judaism, so despite the increasing anticlericalism, the ideological convergence remained, fueling the Nazi move to encompass the church-led social organizations.[58]

The key, however, is that the interaction seems to have made it even clearer to the Nazis, overcoming any ambiguity, that it was up to *them* to decide how what *they* took to be Christian aims were to be pursued. Only the Nazis, not the churches and their ancillary organizations, could do what needed to be done. In that sense, interaction with the Protestant Church ended up, though contingently, radicalizing, intensifying the totalitarian thrust.

But, now reaching our fourth point, organizational rivalry was only the tip of the iceberg. In his determination to insist on the continuing Christianity of the Nazis even in the face of institutional friction, Steigmann-Gall settles for a too-conventional dualism, attributing tensions or Nazi departures to anticlericalism *as opposed to* anti-Christianity, thereby missing a key aspect of the radicalization resulting from the interaction. Not only did that radicalization intensify the totalitarian coordination of organizations, but it made the Nazis understand their mission, as somehow pursuing a Christian agenda, more radically—in ways that elude Steigmann-Gall's categories and distinctions.

Steigmann-Gall recognizes that Hitler's own position changed, especially after the failure of his effort to promote Protestant unity. Now he began making anti-Christian statements. Had the German churches fallen into line, Steigmann-Gall finds it likely that Hitler would not have been so hostile to Christianity itself on occasion. So even insofar as Hitler ended up somewhat anti-Christian, this was a contingent as opposed to a teleological outcome, as if we at last get "Hitler unleashed."

In treating Hitler's musings in the wartime *Table Talk*, Steigmann-Gall finds the evidence conflicting overall, yet in the last analysis, as he sees it, Hitler's sense of doing the work of Christianity remained undiminished.[59] But we find grounds for suspicion. At one point the author asks what Hitler's religion *was* by this point if not Christianity. Had he been converted to Himmler's paganism?[60] Steigmann-Gall then concludes that Hitler probably tended toward theism by the end of his life.[61] But why must we pigeonhole Hitler in terms of some pre-existing category, as opposed to opening to the scope for novelty?

Hitler, certainly by the time of *Table Talk*, but arguably from at least the time of *Mein Kampf* in 1924, experienced his movement as facing an unprecedented challenge and opportunity, demanding grandiose action that he alone could spearhead. Steigmann-Gall helps us see how the particular sense of mission could be experienced as Christian in some sense. But the abiding Christian elements became secondary as pursuing a putatively Christian agenda seemed to depend on a radically new mode of politics. The totalitarian mode of action could not be simply a means to implement a Christian vision—even a somewhat heterodox Christian vision. Rather, it could only entail a new, post-Christian sense of human agency. In light of the challenge and opportunity of the historical moment, it seemed necessary to reconceive the human relationship with history, with the divine, with something providential, and thus to reconceive what needed to be done, what ought to be done. Although the new action could be construed and even experienced as preserving Christianity against novel existential threats, the departure was not simply a new way, necessary under the hard circumstances, of pursuing Christian aims but a qualitative departure into a post-Christian self-understanding.

Steigmann-Gall's conventionally dualistic insistence that the Nazis "were convinced that their movement did not mean the death of God, but the preservation of God" misses the complexity and novelty at work.[62] More specifically, this formulation is almost willfully to sidestep the overtly anti-Christian Nietzschean dimension in Nazism, the dimension entailing "hardness," "beyond good and evil," well delineated by Steven E. Aschheim, and central to the sense of making history in the unprecedented way necessary.[63] Steigmann-Gall seems to claim license to neglect the Nietzschean dimension because even the leading Nazi Nietzschean, Alfred Bäumler, left openings for his own thinking to be read in Christian terms.[64]

In fact, however, the sense of unprecedented history-making "beyond good and evil" through a Nietzschean mode of "great politics" points toward the elation (*Rausch*) of going beyond conventional norms that Saul Friedlander has featured, but that we also find in the experience of ordinary Nazis and even ordinary Germans buying into the Nazi experiment. Whatever the remnants of Christian rhetoric, in the last analysis the sense of common participation in something unprecedented trumped mere preservation. This is not remotely to suggest that Christianity and the churches constituted a moderating force after all but simply that Nazism came to be fueled on its own in post-Christian terms, which Steigmann-Gall's insistence on abiding Christianity leads us to miss.

Walter Adamson's starting point, in treating the Italian case, differs from Steigmann-Gall's in one key sense. On the ideological level, as Adamson sees it, the sacralization of politics in Fascist Italy may indeed have been congruent with John Pollard's baseline—anti-Christian, derogatory toward religious thinking and practice.[65] Such a difference would seem to suggest that, in principle at least, there was considerably greater scope in Italy than in Germany either for fascism to threaten Christian interests or for interaction with Christians to blunt, divert, or transform the originating fascist aims.

Seeking to be pluralistic, Adamson concedes that the secular, post-Christian, totalitarian thrust remained within the Italian Fascist mix, but he senses that we have overdone that strand and thereby missed much about Fascist interaction with the Catholic Church.[66] We need greater attention to the basis, functioning, and outcomes of that interaction. Most basically, Adamson suggests that each side came to believe not only that it could profit from working with the other but that genuine accommodation was possible. So despite the difference in initial premise, Adamson ends up paralleling Steigmann-Gall in positing, up to a point, a mode of symbiosis, perhaps even synergy, transcending mere opportunism or exploitation on either side.

Adamson shows that not only was the Catholic Church, in its interaction with the Fascist regime, not on the defensive, but it was engaged in an aggressive, self-confident social offensive, bound up with re-totalizing pretensions of its own. It was gaining a new lease on life on the popular level and renewing its aspirations on the institutional level. And ordinary Italian Catholics seem to have been responsive. Adamson notes that there was a significant Catholic revival especially during the 1930s as, for example, the cult of saints was renewed, membership in Catholic mass organizations expanded, and church-sponsored celebrations attracted large numbers of participants.[67]

In featuring convergence between the church and the regime, Adamson makes two distinguishable points. First, clearly differentiating, from within the Fascist effort to sacralize politics, an ideological side, derogatory toward religion, and a "ritualistic-symbolic" side, he argues, plausibly enough, that the latter was parasitical upon Catholicism, even impossible without it, and that such parasitism may well have made possible whatever success the Fascist effort had.[68] In other words, even though the effort may have been secular and even anti-Christian in intent, it proved very attractive to Christians—and specifically to Catholics—because of this ritualistic-symbolic dimension.

Up to a point Adamson's argument is congruent with Pollard's that even as Italian Catholics mostly tended to be "a-fascist," going their own way, not really committing to the regime, there was some measure of attraction because the Fascists were seeking to sacralize politics in a country with a living religious culture. Pollard cites evidence of Fascism's subordination to Catholicism on this level, including, for example, seeking the church's blessing for the cult of the dead.[69] The Spanish Falange and the Romanian Legion of the Archangel Michael similarly sought church blessing for comparable rituals. But whereas Adamson is congruent with Pollard up to a point, he posits a stronger link between the regime and the church in Italy.

Here we reach Adamson's second, more general point about the relationship between Fascists and Catholics. While noting that there were of course tensions, he contends that the regime "understood that it needed the support of institutional Catholicism and its mass base and spent much political capital courting an alliance with it."[70] But this courting was not merely instrumental. Adamson plays up the "'substantial collaboration' or 'cohabitation' that Fascism and the Catholic Church enjoyed."[71] The growing assertiveness on both sides suggested shared ambitions and a convergence in underlying aims. Each side came to view the other as a genuine ally.[72]

Indeed, the interaction seems to have emboldened both sides, so in this case, too, the outcome was a mode of synergy transcending mere symbiosis. As Adamson puts it, the church and the regime

> saw in the 1929 reconciliation a shared recognition that Catholicism could be conjoined with fascism to undergird a new, "healthy" modernity based on religious faith rooted in the family, the local community, and the fascist corporation (which Catholics tended to link with the corporatism advocated by Pope Leo XIII in *Rerum novarum*). Such a modernity could lead Italy to "national greatness," to an "alliance of patriotism with religion," and thus to a reversal of the concepts of secular modernity promoted by the common enemies of Catholicism and fascism.[73]

Adamson goes on to suggest that "fascism appears to have been understood by an overwhelming number of Catholics, and thus an overwhelming number of Italians, as sharing the agenda of the promotion of what we might call a counter-secular society—a society aiming 'to preserve God *against* a secular society.'"[74] Here Adamson quotes Steigmann-Gall and implicitly suggests that despite the initial difference in aims, the interaction in Italy made for a substantial parallel between the German and Italian cases, as both regimes sought a counter-secular society.[75]

Adamson himself comes close to suggesting synergy: Catholic hopes for what might come of a Catholic-Fascist alliance "should remind us ... just how much Italian Catholics felt emboldened by the political reconciliation they had achieved with the Italian state." But he goes on, in a helpful way congruent with calls for a new agenda, to emphasize that those hopes should also remind us "that Italian fascism was indeed an 'experiment' whose future trajectory seemed quite unpredictable in the early 1930s, and thus quite open to being creatively shaped."[76] In other words, we can understand the interaction only in terms of an uncertain, open-ended trajectory entailing experiment, the scope for—even the inevitability of—selective readings, and what seemed the opportunity for each side to influence the other.

Although Catholic hopes would prove illusory, Adamson shows that they persisted well into the 1930s.[77] And his wider point—that "the courtship was mutual"—continued to hold.[78] In showing how enduring the mutual attraction was from within the uncertain, open-ended trajectory, he helps us avoid teleological thinking and to grasp the contingency of the disillusioning outcome for Catholics.

Calling for pluralism in concluding, Adamson is quite clear that the alternative to overdoing the "secular" strand is not to privilege the Fascist-Catholic alliance instead. We simply need "a sharper sense of the weight of and balance among all of these elements."[79] Moreover, he usefully offers a nod to the fissuring over matters of religion within Fascism itself.[80]

Adamson surely points us toward a more differentiated understanding of the relationship between the Fascist regime and Catholicism. But though he covers himself to some extent with his call for pluralism, he skews our sense of the balance in one sense, even as he no doubt improves it in another. And his inquiry suggests further questions and possibilities that could usefully have been considered.

Adamson takes the periodic friction between the two sides as a given. But can the scope for an accommodation be assessed apart from attention to the basis for the friction, including the aims of the conflicting "secular" side? It is partly Adamson's use of Emilio Gentile's conception of the Fascist sacralization of politics as a foil that leads to a delimited sense of the forces in play. Conversely, the sort of balance Adamson calls for requires a sense of the Fascist side in the interaction that does not afford such privilege to Gentile's terms. Gentile's secular-oriented sacralization and Adamson's religiously oriented cohabitation were not the only alternatives at issue in the Fascist struggle over the appropriate relationship with Catholicism and the church.

As for the immediate friction, we might expect some mention of Pius XI's 1931 encyclical *Non abbiamo bisogno,* overtly critical of Fascism for its totalitarian tendencies toward state worship. And what of Giovanni Gentile, the "chief theologian" in the Fascist sacralization of politics, whose treatment of Catholicism in education was of particular importance to his totalitarian vision and program?[81] It helped get Gentile's works placed on the church's Index of proscribed writings in 1934. Even these examples suffice to indicate a deeper shadow over the quest for cohabitation than Adamson acknowledges.

In a passage quoted above, Adamson invokes the Catholic attraction to Fascist corporatism, an aspect of Fascism that Emilio Gentile almost willfully neglects. If corporatism is to be adduced as evidence for convergence or the scope for convergence, we need a better sense of corporatist thinking on both sides, as well as a better sense of the overall contest over the rationale for corporatism. Above all, we must grasp the non-Catholic and even anti-Catholic dimensions of the secular Fascist rationale for a corporatist direction. As for the Catholic side, Adamson notes Leo XIII's encyclical of 1891, *Rerum novarum,* in linking Catholicism to Fascist corporatism, but curiously does not mention Pius XI's 1931 encyclical *Quadragesimo anno,* issued, pointedly, on the fortieth anniversary of *Rerum novarum. Quadragesimo anno* might have further persuaded some Catholics of the scope for symbiosis, but as we noted above, the encyclical can be read as competition over the "ownership" of corporatism, as opposed to evidence of a convergence of aims.

Quite apart from the problems of one-sidedness, how did the interaction affect Fascist aims and actions over the course of the trajectory? Because Fascism was fissured over relations with the church, there can be no simple answer. For a start, however, let us note that whereas some Fascists saw the scope for genuine alliance with the church, those in Adamson's secular strand also needed to woo Catholics. In adapting Catholic ritual, however, or in currying Catholic favor to legitimize a more novel, totalitarian politicization, their purposes were more strictly instrumental. To that extent there was no genuine convergence of aims, though even if doing so was merely instrumental, adapting ritual and currying favor could seem to Catholics to be advancing the Catholic agenda. There can only be ambiguity over the degree of instrumentalism, but we need to keep the slipperiness in mind as we ponder the interaction.

We also need to ask whether the interaction, even if it began in instrumental terms, may have ended up actually blunting, absorbing, or redirecting the more secular Fascist purposes, so that the degree of instrumentalism diminished, perhaps approaching zero. In considering the possibility of conservative blunting of fascism in this chapter, we have already noted that conservative strength and fascist weakness could both have been at work, often in undecidable proportion. In the case at hand, the energizing synergy that seems to have resulted from the regime's move toward the church could have led even more secular Fascists to believe that success in this uncertain experiment entailed winning over Catholics, thereby cementing a certain mode of unity around the Fascist regime. From this perspective, the originating, post-Christian thrust was not so important after all, and a genuine convergence of aims could seem to be developing over time. But even if there was no such convergence, the merely instrumental approaches surely siphoned off energies and thus diluted the impulses that fueled Fascism in the first place.

So even as we recognize that secular Fascist approaches to the Catholics may have remained instrumental, we need to consider, as Adamson does not, that secular Fascism was possibly being blunted or transformed through the interaction. Again, proportions are surely undecidable, and the combination makes it difficult to isolate the specifically fascist element on the Italian new Right. But in glossing over instrumentality and transformation, Adamson leaves a misleading picture of the interaction, even as he deepens our understanding of its import in other ways.

Finally, it is not clear how to square the cohabitation Adamson features with his contention that "in general, commitment on the part of Catholics to fascism appears to have been superficial," or with John Pollard's point, which Adamson cites with approval, that what Catholics were seeking was not the radical extremism of Fascism but the kind of Catholic, conservative, corporatist, and authoritarian state championed by Charles Maurras and the Action Française in France, and perhaps best expressed by the military dictatorship of Miguel Primo de Rivera in Spain.[82] (Pollard also mentions Vichy France as a comparably "best" expression.) How does the "superficiality" at issue mesh with the quest for cohabitation?

In invoking both superficiality and this more moderate, "Maurrasian" vision of political change, Adamson seems to lose sight of the implications of his valuable point that Fascism was an open-ended experiment, one that Italian Catholics could both read selectively and view as subject to shaping. In that light, they surely must have thought that Fascism was on its way to producing, or could be made to produce, precisely the kind of "Maurrasian" state at issue. In that light, they did not experience their commitments as superficial. Perhaps they seem superficial now, in light of our sense that Fascism aimed precisely at a more radical, extreme transformation. But we must take particular care at this point. The notion of "superficiality" in this context suggests some "real," essential Fascism that the Catholic perception misconstrued or at best reflected dimly. Insofar as we take seriously the notion that Fascism was an open-ended experiment, with no built-in telos, it might indeed have been channeled in the direction Catholics desired. Only the history would tell—and tell what proved superficial.

Conversely, to accept Pollard's point about Catholic aims is implicitly to recognize the depth of the challenge faced by those Fascists who were trying to do something more deeply novel and totalitarian, and more threatening to Catholic interests, than anything Maurras or Miguel Primo de Rivera envisioned. How were they to produce such a transformation in the face of those more "moderate" desires and expectations on the part of so much of the Italian population? Insofar as their aspirations were simply unrealistic, the result, first, of all the grandiose myth-making growing from Italy's experience of World War I, they were unrealizable. But they might also have gotten bogged down, neutered, deflected through co-habitation with the church. Yet again, we encounter undecidable proportions. In any case, as it happened, partly from exogenous contingencies changing the framework, the Fascist trajectory took a particular radical direction, culminating in Italian intervention in the war in 1940. That direction largely alienated the church and its members, who had envisioned something else. Thus, in part, the ultimate hollowness and ephemerality of Fascism in Italy.

Both Adamson and Steigmann-Gall usefully show the way to a more differentiated understanding of fascism's interaction with the churches. Each is attentive to the openness and contingency of the process that resulted. As a corollary, each implies that fascism is not easily disembedded from its relationship with Christian conservatives. Their new ways of thinking about interaction and embeddedness point us deeper into what actually happened, into the actual trajectory, without the commonplaces that still lurk in the discussion.

But ultimately Adamson and Steigmann-Gall betray pitfalls to be avoided as we pursue a new agenda. In their welcome determination to ask new questions, each tends to force his argument, going overboard in featuring the hitherto neglected mode of interaction and embeddedness. The eagerness to blend fascism with the churches leads both to gloss over or play down the distinctive, novel fascist element, which was above all totalitarian, as we will discuss in chapter 8. But the result is not only misleading proportions. In forcing the argument, each misses even some of what his own evidence suggests about the effects of the interaction on the trajectory of each regime.

Adamson's argument provides a good transition to the question of the impact of fascism in Italy and Germany on existing social practices and everyday life. Insofar as Italian Fascism had to piggyback onto Catholic ritual and liturgy, its transformative power was clearly blunted. Conversely, insofar as it went beyond cohabitation in a radical direction, it tended to alienate Catholics and leave ordinary Italians behind.

The extent of transformation or absorption resulting from the interaction of fascism with existing social practices has occasioned much scrutiny in both the Italian and the German cases. In arguing for the singularity of Nazi Germany, Ian Kershaw contended that after fascism came to power in Italy, "its élan rapidly waned," and a normalizing phase began in 1925.[83] In one sense this claim seriously misleads. It was precisely in 1925 that Mussolini's regime began attempting to build a new, specifically fascist state. Still, by implication, at least, Kershaw was suggesting that it was especially the effort to act in earnest that created new, unforeseen modes of interaction with existing elites, institutions, and practices that, in turn, came deeply to affect what fascism became in Italy. In retrospect, that interaction did not merely reveal but actually engendered certain limitations of "Italian Fascism" as a historical phenomenon.

The uncertainty and open-endedness of the Fascist trajectory of course meant that those limitations were not obvious at the time. But they became ever more obvious, and thus the soul-searching and internal criticism to which the regime became subject during the 1930s. But the very fact of such soul-searching and criticism suggests that until the whole thing came to an end, the substance was never altogether diluted, absorbed, or reduced to mere myth.

In chapter 1 we noted R.J.B. Bosworth's accent on the limits of the Fascist regime in Italy. Despite its bluster and despite the undoubted measure of consensus it achieved by the mid-1930s, the regime was insecure. Against that backdrop, Bosworth shows, ordinary Italians got on with their lives, often defying the regime's control, and often on the basis of factors such as family, locality, and religion that were not specifically Fascist.[84] Insofar as life simply went on, the specifically fascist thrust was compromised and diluted. Yet no one would suggest that Fascism made no difference. The question Victoria De Grazia once asked—"What was 'Fascist' about Fascist Italy?"—nicely encapsulates the overall problem we are left with.[85] In the same vein, Philip Morgan later asked "what was 'Fascist' about the running of the Italian economy during the Fascist era."[86]

De Grazia herself stressed limits, but also ambiguities, in her pioneering study of the Dopolavoro, or Fascist leisure-time organization, which she portrayed as the popular or "low" culture of Fascism. Although it reflected what she considers to have been the paternalistic condescension of the leadership toward ordinary people, the organization developed a depoliticized underside that made possible a kind of passive support, furthering the regime's ability to continue.[87]

But the effectiveness of the Dopolavoro has been contested in symptomatic ways. Writing well after De Grazia, Emilio Gentile, reconsidering the whole Fascist totalitarian project, especially during the 1930s, denied that it was merely depoliticizing and insisted that it had some genuine educational impact as part of the wider effort, spearheaded by the Fascist Party, to remake the Italians.[88] However, some found Gentile to be going overboard. Dismissing his argument, Robert Paxton invoked De Grazia as he stressed the superficiality of the Dopolavoro, as well as the Fascist youth organizations, *even as* the party was extending its control.[89]

But these are disputes over degrees. Even Gentile was not remotely claiming that Fascism pulled off its "anthropological revolution," actually creating a "new man." For John Pollard the resilient presence of the Catholic Church was the chief reason the Fascist regime failed to remake Italians.[90] But to what degree are we to attribute the limits to the strength of traditional institutions and practices, and to what degree to the weaknesses and confusions of Fascism itself? Again, we cannot say. But whereas we need to maintain openness, avoiding "premature" teleological or reductionist denigration, in treating such Fascist initiatives as corporatism and the Dopolavoro, we must also recognize the degree of superficiality, with its implications of hollowness and ephemerality.

The Nazi regime, too, remained embedded within a network of prior elites, institutions, and social practices—far more so than the Soviet regime, for example. Still, there is a broad consensus that it more fully bent established German institutions to its will and penetrated German society more deeply, more fully creating a new frame of mind, than did the Fascist regime in Italy. For example, the German Kraft durch Freude (Strength through Joy) was surely more effective than its Italian equivalent, the Dopolavoro, in conforming the outlook of its participants to Nazism. Shelley Baranowski has highlighted its symptomatically paradoxical blend of belt-tightening measures with foretastes of improved living standards and the good life. But she goes on to show how the notion of "living standards" was made to encompass not merely commodities but also personal satisfaction in contributing to collective ends—and in receiving nonmaterial recognition in return.[91]

A variety of studies suggest something like a "conceptual revolution" leading to a realignment of loyalties and a genuine experience of *Volksgemeinschaft* (people's community), wound around racial homogeneity, in Nazi Germany. This was bound up with a deeper marginalization of outsiders. Thus, for example, anti-Semitism, while not central for most Germans at the outset of the Nazi regime, gradually became part of the consensus. Common qualms and common complicity also cemented a sense of belonging and community.[92]

Insofar as the impact of fascism was greater in Germany than in Italy, probing interaction on the internal level suggests a principle of differentiation to be considered in chapter 8. But even recognizing that greater impact, there was something hollow and ephemeral about the German case as well, even as Nazism wrought something like a conceptual revolution at the time, and even as it resulted in horrific consequences. But here we begin to encounter the question of the singularity of Nazi Germany, to be considered in the concluding chapter.

Top-Down Shading into In-Between

Outside Italy and Germany, fascism achieved power only briefly, at most, and we must consider whether this relative lack of success resulted from conservatives blunting, absorbing, or suppressing fascism. Mary Vincent's point about Spain, first noted in chapter 2, has already suggested something more complex—a "hybrid," in her terms. And we have seen that António Costa Pinto and Aristotle Kallis call for greater attention to such processes of hybridization across Europe. Looking beyond Italy and Germany we do find further complex modes of interaction, even, again, modes of symbiosis or synergy, yielding departures that were part of the new Right universe even if the specifically fascist formation was marginalized or actively suppressed along the way.

We can usefully begin sorting out conservative-fascist relationships in these cases by returning to the distinction between top-down and bottom-up fascism within the new Right. The distinction is a mere ideal type, of course, but it can help us conceive fascist-conservative interaction along a kind of continuum. Although the extent to which the top-down moves of Gyula Gömbös in Hungary in 1932, Engelbert Dollfuss in Austria in 1933, Ioannis Metaxas in Greece in 1936, and King Carol II in Romania in 1937 were in fact fascist challenges remains in dispute, each was a departure from established parliamentary procedures in the direction of fascism, and each is certainly part of the new universe of experiment on the Right. But such fascist or quasi-fascist challenges were obviously likely to be far less threatening to the conservative establishment than a fascist challenge from below. They were also less likely to be weakened by internal fissuring. Yet even such efforts from above could encounter blunting and failure from conservative resistance.

Gömbös and Metaxas each moved in a fascist direction from above without being pushed or threatened by a fascist movement from below. But the fortunes of their respective experiments differed, showing the scope for being repulsed by conservatives in the case of Gömbös, for going around the conservative establishment in the case of Metaxas. The departures in Romania and Austria, in contrast, were partly responses to a more specifically fascist challenge, and each produced something new on the Right as a result. Are we to read them not as a fascist challenge but as a conservative effort to blunt or neuter a fascist challenge? Or does the distinction begin to break down? If so, how do we understand the fascist-conservative relationship in each case?

Under its regent, Admiral Miklós Horthy, Hungary achieved relative political stability by the later 1920s, but the Depression opened the way to at least some measure of political experiment. By the time he was appointed prime minister in 1932, Gömbös had joined the governing party, but he had come to prominence as a paramilitary leader just after the war. By the early 1930s he was Hungary's most important advocate of radical Right politics and well known to be an admirer of Mussolini.[93]

Gömbös sought to move to toward a top-down, dictatorial, single-party system. Shortly after taking office, he transformed the governing party into a mass-based National Unity Party, giving his own radical Right supporters key positions. But his new order was to be based above all on mandatory corporate involvement based largely on the Italian model. The Depression especially seemed to warrant a turn toward autarky, protectionism, and a more interventionist state role in the economy, both to overcome unemployment and to foster modernization. Hungary was to become an organized, planned, disciplined society with no place for carping political parties.[94]

However, Gömbös repeatedly encountered opposition, from big business and large landowners, but also from most of his own governing party. Prominent in the business leadership were Jews, suspicious of any fascist direction in light of the 1935 anti-Semitic legislation in Nazi Germany. Gömbös's proposal for Italian-style compulsory corporatist involvement especially provoked opposition. By 1936 Horthy seems to have been prepared to dump the prime minister, but Gömbös's death late that year ended the experiment.[95]

Up to a point, the fate of this top-down, statist departure is a classic example of a fascist thrust being blunted by establishment conservatives. But the outcome of the fascist-conservative interaction in this case is easily misread if we fail to recognize the openness of the Hungarian trajectory. Although Gömbös was not strong enough to engineer a radical change in policy, he managed changes in personnel that helped fuel a wider turn to the Right after his death.

First, we noted that Gömbös gave his own radical Right supporters key positions in the new National Unity Party (NEP). This brought new sectors to political involvement, sectors able even to stand up to established elites on the local level.[96] Second, though partly through intimidation, bribery, and forgery, Gömbös managed a considerable victory in the parliamentary elections of March–April 1935, which, though still from within the governing party, brought a substantial new contingent from the extreme Right into parliament. That stratum would get ever more posts in the public administration thereafter. For Maria Ormos, the election of this cohort in 1935 proved "a caesura in Hungarian power relations between the two world wars."[97] Third, Gömbös's purge of senior army officers, also in 1935, similarly had important effects several years later, especially as the new officers he appointed joined with new, more radical fascist formations.[98] So it was not as if heading off the Gömbös experiment meant the definitive taming of "fascism" in Hungary. If anything, aspects of the outcome radicalized the possibilities for subsequent stages, to be considered below.

Like Gömbös, Metaxas in Greece spearheaded a departure in a fascist direction essentially on his own, without some push by a fascist movement, though at first he was simply the sitting prime minister backing the recently restored king, George II, in a royal coup. In 1936 the king suspended the constitution and declared a dictatorship in the face of parliamentary stalemate. But it was Metaxas, with his own ideologues around him, who sought to give the new regime its particular content, making it very much a part of the new Right. In seeking an alternative to both communism and liberalism, in light of what could have seemed a genuine impasse of parliamentary government, it was not merely defensive and conservative but drew from contemporary fascism, of course adapting foreign models in its own way.[99] And though this experiment, too, proved short-lived, it was more successful than Gömbös's. But how did the interaction between the fascist thrust and conservatives affect the trajectory in Greece?

To win working-class support, Metaxas took a number of steps, especially involving labor legislation, not likely to please the business community. Mogens Pelt notes that such legislation was seriously enforced, with no hesitation to fine employers. Metaxas also managed a considerable reduction in unemployment. But even as Pelt recognizes Metaxas's ideological commitments, especially to corporatism, he seems quick to attribute this direction to an effort merely to project an anti-plutocratic image.[100] In the same way, even as he admits that the experiment was cut short by the war, he is quick to judge as "ersatz" the new top-down organizations for the workers and peasants the regime devised, at least partly to replace independent unions.[101] Aristotle Kallis, more attuned to the quest for a new agenda, seems more open to the scope for genuine experiment in the Greek case.

At the same time, Metaxas gave the Orthodox Church a more central role in politics and popular culture. This reflected his insistence that his new regime was not a mere imitation of the two fascist regimes but was rooted in Greek history and tradition. More particularly, it was to combine the iron discipline of Sparta with the profound religiosity of medieval Byzantium.[102] And the church welcomed the opportunities that the new political direction seemed to entail. However, we seem to need further research, or at least more translations of Greek-language works, to consider whether symbiosis or synergy resulted, whether church support helped legitimize the regime, and whether the church provided any kind of brake or buffer.

But in monarchist circles and other reaches of the conservative establishment there was clearly unease with the more radical of Metaxas's goals. His institutional centerpiece, the National Youth Organization, was a particular flash point because it forced the dissolution of long-established, highly regarded groups such as the internationalist Christian Brotherhoods and the scout movement. Kallis shows that the king's entourage, church elites, and the military were highly skeptical about Metaxas's National

Youth Organization, though for somewhat different reasons. Monarchist circles particularly admired and sought to protect the scout movement. A compromise was reached in December 1938, but essentially on Metaxas's terms.[103]

Indeed, Metaxas's self-confidence vis-à-vis both the monarchy and the Orthodox Church was increasing by 1938–39.[104] He replaced royalists with his own trusted associates, who were the most oriented toward fascism, and increasingly marginalized the king.[105] To strengthen ties with Nazi Germany, he simply went around the monarchy, as we will see in more detail in the next chapter. This suggests that insofar as a fascistizing initiative from the top failed to subordinate or draw in the conservative establishment, it might simply proceed on its own.

Metaxas's firm stand against Fascist Italy's designs on Greece won him considerable popularity among the Greeks. Although he died in January 1941, he was at the helm during the first part of the successful resistance against Italian aggression in 1940–41. The Greeks subsequently took considerable pride in what seemed the first Allied victory against fascism.[106] But the ironic and tragic outcome for Greece at the time was bound up with the Italian-German relationship and is best held for the next chapter on international interaction.

So we have the Gömbös and Metaxas experiments as essentially top-down, and it is useful to keep them on the table as we move to more complex, ambiguous interaction involving both top-down and bottom-up initiatives in Austria, Hungary, and Romania. These three cases constitute particularly striking examples of the braided dynamic, including international interaction, but we will limit ourselves to the extent possible in this chapter to fascist-conservative interaction on the domestic level. Complex though it is, the Austrian case was short-lived and is best treated as intermediate, before we move on, in the next section, to the still more complex Hungarian and Romanian cases.

Although the Austrian case entailed a concerted top-down effort to create a new regime, the experiment included a greater from-below dimension than Gömbös's or Metaxas's, in light of the role of a movement that claimed to be and is generally considered to have been fascist, the Heimwehr (Home Guard), which had emerged, first in a highly fragmented, regional way, in the immediate aftermath of World War I. It was in some sense the interaction between the Heimwehr and establishment conservatives that yielded this additional short-lived new Right experiment, from 1933 to 1938, but the relationship in the Austrian case is especially difficult to pin down. Do we find symbiosis or synergy, or were conservatives heading off fascists, being pushed by fascists, or moving in a fascist direction on their own?

Even during the 1920s, the politically dominant Christian Social Party, representing the conservative establishment, was to some extent turning against parliamentary democracy and party politics and moving in a new Right, largely Catholic corporatist direction on its own. Still, the dominant Right-leaning portion of the party was also being prodded by the Heimwehr, rivals of the Austrian National Socialists, or Nazis. The Heimwehr was especially heterogeneous, but it looked to Fascist Italy as a model and received much support, financial and otherwise, from the Italian Fascists. Still, it tilted more unambiguously toward the Catholic Church and Catholic corporatist thinking than did Italian Fascism. Whereas the rival Nazis looked forward to an Anschluss with Nazi Germany, the Heimwehr sought to maintain an independent Austria and remained concerned, at least to some extent, with Catholic Austria's traditional leading role in a multinational region.[107]

As Tim Kirk has shown, the critique of parliamentary democracy grew shriller toward the end of the 1920s, when the Heimwehr emerged as a significant force and the Left within the Christian Social Party lost ground. The Heimwehr was prominent in increasing calls for constitutional revision, establishing a corporatist state to replace the parliamentary system.[108] And the Heimwehr was clearly emboldening conservatives, drawing them further to the Right. In 1932 the Heimwehr was brought into a new government under Engelbert Dollfuss in an effort to shore up the shaky Christian Social majority. But this antagonized the Left, helped produce paralysis in parliament, and thus proved part of a chain of events that prompted Dollfuss to suspend the democratic constitution in 1933. Unrest on the Left had fueled an abortive Social Democratic Party uprising, which in turn prompted a public backlash and lent a modicum of legitimacy to Dollfuss's coup from above. Although the parliamentary system was genuinely in crisis, Dollfuss was eager to exploit the situation to replace parliamentary government permanently with a new kind of state—authoritarian, corporatist, and Catholic.

After establishing a mass organization, the Fatherland Front, and engineering a new, explicitly corporatist constitution, Dollfuss was assassinated in a botched Nazi coup attempt in July 1934. It was left to his successor as chancellor, Kurt von Schuschnigg, to build the new corporatist order. As it happened, however, he had little time. The Anschluss of March 1938 ended the experiment, satisfying the Austrian Nazis, who had remained opposed to the new regime.

The Austrian corporatist regime is sometimes considered fascist, sometimes characterized as "Austro-fascism," sometimes deemed an instance of "clerico-fascism" because of its close ties to the Catholic Church.[109] Thus, again, its symptomatic ambiguity. Even the Fatherland Front, which Dollfuss established in 1933 as the mobilizing arm of the new order, is hard to characterize. In addition to articulating the regime's ideology, it intervened in labor disputes and organized demonstrations and social programs, from tourism to welfare. Its organization was highly hierarchical, with Dollfuss as führer, and it adopted much of the external paraphernalia of a fascist movement—uniforms, parades, and the like. Although it was the only permitted political organization, the Fatherland Front was not a party and claimed to be nonpartisan, open to all. It eschewed any fascist claim to a monopoly of authority, claiming full freedom of thought within the framework of loyalty to authoritarian German Austria.[110]

However the Austrian departure is to be characterized, its source matters for our immediate question concerning fascist-conservative interaction and degrees and modes of symbiosis or synergy. But assessment of its source also has implications for the place of the Austrian case in the wider universe. In an argument congruent with wider calls for a new agenda, Corinna Peniston-Bird insists convincingly that we must seek indigenous foundations and appeal and avoid overdoing the Italian and German models in our approach to the Austrian case.[111] Thus, for example, whereas Fascist Italy's corporatist direction was undeniably influential, there were indigenous sources as well, especially Othmar Spann's much-discussed *Der wahre Staat* of 1921.[112] The proportions are largely undecidable, but the more we focus on indigenous sources, the more important domestic interaction looms.

The extent to which the Christian Socials' turn to the Right, culminating in Dollfuss's coup from above in 1933, stemmed from Heimwehr pressure is also undecidable. Even during the 1920s the political instability in Austria raised questions about parliamentary government and the party system; it would perhaps itself have been sufficient to push the Christian Socials in a fascist direction. And though the Heimwehr was one vehicle of Spann's influence, he also influenced conservatives directly. At the same time, the Heimwehr had intellectuals of its own, including a close collaborator of Spann's, Walter Heinrich, who wrote the Korneuburger Oath of 1930 in an unsuccessful effort to give the movement greater cohesiveness. But his *Staat und Wirtschaft* (1929) helped provide theoretical underpinnings for the new corporate state.

The relationship between the Heimwehr and the new Dollfuss regime was tricky indeed. Gerhard Botz, the dean of Austrian historians of the Austrian case, nicely sums it up in characterizing the Heimwehr as at once Dollfuss's main ally and chief rival. And he goes on to convey some of the ongoing cat-and-mouse game between the Dollfuss-Schuschnigg regime and the more radical Heimwehr.[113] But Schuschnigg dissolved the organization, incorporating its paramilitary units into the Fatherland Front's

Frontmiliz, once corporatist development was under way in 1936. However, the dissolution of the Heimwehr does not seem an instance of conservative authoritarians co-opting part of the fascist program, then dispensing with the organization, seen as a threat to the conservatives themselves. Botz notes that whereas the Heimwehr had been in decline, it temporarily gained strong influence in the new corporate state.[114] And its renewed decline in influence thereafter was determined more by the changing, increasingly cordial relationship between Italy and Germany than by internal developments.[115] With Italy decreasingly concerned to counter German influence in Austria, Italian political and financial support for the Heimwehr waned, and the Heimwehr lost influence as a result.

Peniston-Bird adds that in dissolving the Heimwehr, the chancellor was seeking to placate both the Germans, long sympathetic to the Austrian Nazis as opposed to the Heimwehr, and the democracies.[116] So seemingly it was not a sense that the Heimwehr had outlived its usefulness, let alone that it constituted a potential "fascist" threat to authoritarian conservative dominance, that produced its dissolution.

But whatever it sources, did dissolving the Heimwehr blunt the fascist thrust in Austria? The novel corporatist experiment, with its Austrian Catholic resonances, continued, but Botz finds the fate of the Heimwehr part of the de-fascistization of the regime, which left it a traditional authoritarian dictatorship, comparable to those in Portugal, Greece, and Spain. Relying on the police and the bureaucracy, as well as its political monopoly, the Austrian dictatorship did not mobilize but rather demobilized the crisis-driven middle classes.[117] But that sort of dichotomizing is now being called into question, and it may especially preclude an adequate consideration of the possibilities in this complex case.

To better conceive the possibilities—and the ambiguities—we need to consider the place of the Catholic Church, which supported and helped legitimize the new regime, but which also exerted direct influence on it. We have noted that much about the Austrian reading of corporatism could be traced to Catholic social thought and tradition. The most recent inspiration was Pius XI's 1931 encyclical *Quadragesimo anno*, which, as we have also noted, was issued partly to reclaim corporatism for Catholic tradition as opposed to modern fascism.

However, even as the Catholic Church supported the new Austrian regime, the church of course remained autonomous, and this had conflicting implications. On the one hand, the church's influence provided something of a brake, impeding further radicalization and thus helping to preclude features like violence and social Darwinism prominent in fascism elsewhere.[118] In that sense, one set of establishment conservatives was moderating another, even as each was feeding the other in the turn away from liberal individualism and parliamentary democracy. On the other hand, despite its embrace of Catholicism, the regime was sufficiently novel and even totalitarian in direction to threaten the church's autonomy and social role. Peniston-Bird notes that, if anything, the long-standing church-state rivalry intensified, especially as the state sought to influence areas traditionally addressed by the church. At the same time, she notes that the corporatist state did not allow the free association and the choice of government that Pius XI's *Quadragesimo anno* had called for. Thus, she concludes convincingly, it is not at all clear that the Austrian corporatist regime constituted a conservative alternative to the full-scale fascism of Italy and Germany.[119]

The ambiguity in relations between the new regime and the church was obviously important, but we must take a further step to grasp the idiosyncratic possibilities in the Austrian case. Tim Kirk offers a useful start in seeking to pinpoint what differentiated Austria from Italy and Germany. Despite totalitarian tendencies in each case, none of the three regimes managed fully to coordinate the church or churches. The difference in Austria was not only that the Catholic Church was closer to the regime, but that Catholicism was a defining ingredient in an "Austrian ideology," with Catholic identity linked to Austria's earlier supranational empire and role.[120] The new regime sought to mobilize popular support for such an Austrian Catholic identity.

Especially in light of Steigmann-Gall and Adamson, we recall that a comparable sense of mission, bound up with Christian identity, to some extent characterized the German and Italian cases as well. But in Austria the ideology suggested a more deeply symbiotic or even synergistic relationship. It was not simply that the regime was to pursue aims shared by the church, but that Catholic identity and church support were essential to the regime's raison d'être, as offering a new Right departure that was specifically Austrian, not merely consistent with but making deeper sense of Austria's continuing existence as an independent state.

For Austrians, Catholic identity could suggest the basis for an energizing great task, engineering some sort of Catholic Danubian Confederation, requiring not only the support but the active involvement of the church. Such a role for Austria might be especially relevant, even "modern," under the unforeseen circumstances—including not only a truncated Austria but also ethnic volatility in the other successor states— that had resulted from the war, the breakup of the Habsburg Empire, and the terms of the Paris peace treaties. The Catholic link made it important to give Austrian corporatism a Catholic spin, but that link was not simply about the pursuit of a conservative and harmonious social policy. It also suggested a supranational role, differentiating the Austrian regime from Nazi Germany, pan-Germanism, and *völkisch* thinking. Within the new universe on the Right, the Austrian regime was a thing unto itself, a unique combination —specifically Austrian; post-parliamentary and authoritarian, but corporatist and not merely de-mobilizing; and Catholic, but with Catholicism suggesting the possibility of a wider regional role.

However, Kirk's treatment of the Austrian "identity" theme proves symptomatically ambivalent. In suggesting that it was especially the Austrian ideology, wound around Catholic identity, that differentiated Austria from Italy and Germany, he seems to want to take that ideology seriously. But he then dismisses it, saying that the identity it sought to foster rested on nostalgia for the imperial past and on a sentimentality associated with traditional values.[121] It is surely tempting to assume as much, but if we are better to attune to experiment and unfamiliar combinations, especially in treating so short a trajectory, we must be less dismissive up front. In the same way, Kirk may be too quick to claim sham and fraud in characterizing both the corporate system and the Fatherland Front, thereby precluding openness and experiment.[122]

Yet in his imputation of nostalgia and sentimentality, Kirk convincingly suggests a lack of realism that, in turn, suggests the shallowness and ephemerality of the Austrian experiment, which was swept away with the Anschluss in March 1938. The popularity of the Austrian Nazis, growing with the successes of Nazi Germany and foreshadowing the degree of support for the Anschluss among Austrians, made it especially hard to cement the new order.[123] It was not merely fortuitous that the experiment proved so brief. The Austrian case especially indicates the need to encompass experiment and openness, on the one hand, hollowness and ephemerality, on the other.

Hungary and Romania: Repression of Fascism with Fascistizing Outcomes

We have seen that in Austria, the Heimwehr's challenge from below helped push the conservative establishment to the Right, but the eventual degree of symbiosis was such that the Heimwehr did not seem to threaten conservative dominance. As formations considered fascism go, however, the Heimwehr was not particularly virulent. In Hungary and Romania, more extreme, bottom-up forms seemed to constitute a more direct challenge, prompting conservatives to marginalize or suppress them. These outcomes have been widely attributed to the syndrome we noted above: in contrast with Italy and Germany, where democracy had more seriously eroded conservative power, conservatives in Hungary and Romania remained strong enough to put down or marginalize threatening forms of fascism.

Philip Morgan suggests the need to expand our focus when he notes that "the Romanian Iron Guard and the Hungarian Arrow Cross were two of the most important fascist movements in Europe, and we certainly need to know a lot more about … how they became mass political movements, who supported them and why, and equally important, their relationship to and relations with the authoritarian regimes of Horthy and King Carol II."[124] But even this formulation may be too dichotomizing in conceiving the interaction between fascists and conservative authoritarians.

We must consider what happened when conservatives put down or marginalized fascism. In both the Hungarian and Romanian cases the outcome was not merely conservative, preserving the status quo, but a departure into the new Right universe. So what if any role did the interaction between fascists and conservatives play in producing those outcomes? Could modes of synergy have been at work even when conservatives suppressed fascism?

We noted the fate, by 1936, of Gyula Gömbös's experiment with a top-down move in a fascist direction in Hungary. We also noted that whereas on the immediate level the experiment failed, precisely from loss of establishment support, we need a longer-term trajectory to assess its results. Gömbös's appointments and the results of the elections he engineered contributed to the further strong Rightward drift.

Controversial though he became among Hungarian conservatives, Gömbös had been the one unifying figure on the new radical Right. With his death in October 1936, movements competed to fill the vacuum.[125] Even during the first half of the 1930s, the rise of Nazism had helped foster the emergence of a number of new radical Right formations in Hungary, heterogeneous but, unlike Gömbös, oriented less toward Fascist Italy than toward Nazi Germany, which seemed to be going from one success to another by the time of Gömbös's death.

After 1935 the Arrow Cross Movement, loosely modeled on the German Nazi Party, quickly emerged as the dominant radical Right formation. Its founder was Ferenc Szálasi, who had been an important army officer, though his political activism mandated his departure from the army. He never made the Arrow Cross the sole voice of the Hungarian extreme Right, but the movement grew rapidly to a peak in 1938–40. It achieved its maximum electoral success in May 1939 when, together with several smaller Nazi-style parties, it won almost 25 percent of the vote, an imposing figure given restrictions on the electoral process favoring the governing party.[126] And there is general agreement that the Arrow Cross was the spearhead of a considerable and broad-based support for fascism in Hungary by the late 1930s.[127]

Not only did the Arrow Cross, in contrast to the Gömbös initiative, emerge from below, but it became a genuine mass movement, with a "plebian" character—or so it seemed to more respectable conservatives. And it won support especially because it seemed to promise significant social change in the interests of poorer Hungarians, especially the peasantry. Most obviously, the Arrow Cross advocated radical land reform, breaking the power of the large landowners. But it also enjoyed considerable success among younger industrial workers.[128]

In treating the interaction between this new fascism and conservatives, we must consider both the governing elite and the churches, although church leaders were sometimes part of that governing elite. As Paul Hanebrink has shown, both the radical Right, spearheaded by the Arrow Cross, and more establishment conservatives partook of a wider "National Christian" or Christian nationalist ideology, itself a new Right departure in Hungary reflecting the unsettled circumstances surrounding the end of World War I. For Hungary that included military defeat, severe territorial loss, and an abortive but serious communist revolution. Departing from the liberal assimilationism that had for the most part characterized Hungary, as it differentiated itself from Austria after the *Ausgleich* creating the Dual Monarchy in 1867, this ideology envisioned a new identity linking Hungary to the defense of Christian culture and tradition, putatively threatened especially by Jews, who had indeed played a disproportionate role in Hungary's recent modernization.[129]

Though majority Catholic (roughly 64 percent), Hungary had a strong Protestant minority, especially in the eastern part of the country, with the Calvinist Reformed Church (roughly 20 percent) the largest denomination. Although in terms of the National Christian ideology there were some Catholic-Protestant differences, they proved secondary. Each of the two churches partook of that ideology, as did the Arrow Cross, though its reading added social reform, biological racism, and a particular notion of Christian moral order. The National Christian vision afforded a kind of umbrella under which the interaction between the conservative and the radical Right took place.

Although degrees varied on both sides, there was significant interest in both the Catholic and the Reformed churches in social reform, reflecting sympathy with the plight of the peasantry, viewed as authentically Hungarian, suffering under the dominance of large landowners linked to Jewish financiers.[130] And thus the Arrow Cross's combination of reforming social activism and anti-Semitism won it some qualified support from the churches. At the same time, however, even church activists for the most part maintained some distance from the Arrow Cross, seen as rabble-rousing and too extreme in its racial thinking. Although Szálasi was a devout Catholic, the heterodoxy of some of his religious ideas worried church leaders, even though some of those ideas, most notably his denial of the Jewishness of Jesus, were widespread in German Christian circles.[131] But the key sticking point proved the proto-totalitarian statism of the Arrow Cross, though the issue was complex, producing a symptomatic tension in the interaction.

Concerns about peasant poverty were often bound up with worries about the health and even viability of the Hungarian nation. Especially in light of social and family policies in both Fascist Italy and Nazi Germany, some church activists, especially from the Reformed side, came to urge a stepped-up state role. It was argued that the latest scientific research showed that certain marriages would compromise national health, so the government had a duty to act in the national interest even at the expense of individual rights. And because national health required strong and healthy families, activists urged state intervention in family life to combat declining birthrates and to promote more prosperous families among the peasantry. They also called for tough measures against putatively family-destroying influences like prostitution, abortion, and pornography.[132]

Such statism did not mandate support for the Arrow Cross specifically, nor, conversely, was the statist thrust just from the fascist Right. But a more activist, interventionist fascist government might be expected to pursue the necessary policies. Still, from the perspective of the churches, such statist interventionism could only be a mixed blessing, since it was potentially threatening to church autonomy. Hungarian church leaders were especially troubled by the treatment of the Catholic Church and its youth organizations in Nazi Germany. Pius XI's encyclical *Mit brennender Sorge* of 1937, condemning Nazi policy, drew considerable attention in Hungary.

Especially in light of the totalitarian pretensions of the Arrow Cross, religious leaders feared for the independence of the Christian churches and religious schools in any Hungarian fascist regime. Szálasi's ideas suggested that an Arrow Cross government might reduce the churches to nationalist associations.[133] Like Hitler's Germany, in other words, such a regime might well view the challenge to be such that, even to pursue Christian aims, a new type of political regime had to call the shots, mandating a wholly new relationship between the political sphere and the churches. The Hungarian churches were not prepared to go that far.

During 1937–38 the increase in Arrow Cross membership and activism alarmed conservatives, who condemned the movement as extremist, comparable to Bolshevism in its revolutionary demagoguery. With Horthy's support, the government broke up numerous Arrow Cross rallies, closed

newspapers, and imprisoned prominent leaders.[134] But the government itself was leaning ever further to the Right at the same time, partly as a result
of Gömbös's appointments and the elections he had engineered in 1935.
The governing party began to realize some of the radical Right's demands
while suppressing its most disruptive demonstrations. As pressures from
the Right continued, the distinction between the radical Right and the
conservative Right grew blurrier.

In 1938, accompanied by further crackdown on the extreme Right, including the arrest of Szálasi himself, the government passed the first of
three anti-Semitic laws making Hungary an explicitly racist state.[135] Each
law would prove more severe than the preceding. The third, which took effect in August 1941, was modeled on Nazi Germany's Nuremberg Laws of
1935. Among other things, it prohibited marriage between Jews and non-
Jews and established the principle of racial as opposed to religious discrimination. A 1942 amendment specified the delimited modes of labor that
Jews could do—or were obliged to do. Although Horthy and other government leaders softened the harshest provisions of the third law in practice,
Hungary had taken decisive steps toward racist population engineering.[136]

Meanwhile, the government adopted other aspects of the statist population and social policy that some from the radical Right, but also from
sectors of the churches, had been advocating. Although the Nazi example
was no doubt a factor, Hungary had its own traditions of racial and eugenic
thinking going back to the eve of World War I, as Marius Turda, especially,
has made clear.[137] The novelty was in the concerted effort on the part of
the state, still in the hands of conservatives, to begin concerted action on
that basis.

The policy reflected the growing sense that national strength had to be
understood in biological terms and required new measures to improve both
the quantity and the quality of racial Hungarians. New laws expanded the
state's power to regulate marriage in the name of public health and to
provide improved pre- and postnatal care in rural areas. The new direction also included population transfers, resettling carefully selected "pure"
Magyar families into sensitive border areas of mixed ethnicity. A Hungarian National-Biological Institute was formed in May 1940 to seek ways to
produce a unitary nation of 20 million.[138] At that point Hungary's population was about 9,280,000.

We have noted that the Hungarian churches were nervous about what
government by the Arrow Cross might portend for church autonomy, but
how did they respond to the conservative government's turn to the extreme Right? Did the new direction beginning in 1938 seem sufficiently
fascist and totalitarian to provoke opposition? Again, the answer is not
clear-cut.

Although the first two anti-Semitic laws raised questions about the definition of Jewishness and thus implicitly about the scope for conversion, it was especially the third law that brought that issue to a head—and with it the sense, on the part of many church leaders, that the government was now going too far. Those objecting generally held that genuine conversion to Christianity was possible; those of Jewish origin professing Christianity should not be considered Jewish under the law. The state, in claiming to determine who was a Christian and who a Jew, seemed to be undermining the social authority of the churches.[139] The regulation of marriage under the third law especially troubled Catholic leaders, who insisted that what counts as marriage is up to the church.[140]

Yet the churches were becoming complicit in the wider direction even as they continued to worry about their own autonomy. The bottom line, from Hanebrink's convincing analysis, is that whereas the third Jewish law, especially, occasioned much opposition from the churches, that opposition was couched in terms that implicitly justified the wider definition of Hungary as Christian, with no place for Jews.[141] Even church support for converts to Christianity carried only so far. One prominent Reformed bishop argued that whereas conversion could indeed transform the soul, it was no guarantee against financial loss or other privations. If the state found anti-Semitic measures necessary for the national good, converts should suffer them with humility and patience.[142]

Meanwhile, as the government moved more radically to the Right, the Arrow Cross was to some extent marginalized and found its support waning. Maria Ormos notes that by October 1941 it had suffered a big decline that could not have been predicted in September 1940.[143] Tricky relations with Nazi Germany and Romania were partly at issue, as was the unpopularity of war once Hungary joined Nazi Germany in fighting the Soviet Union in June 1941. But clearly the Arrow Cross declined also because aspects of its program had been co-opted by the government. In moving strongly to the Right, the Horthy-led conservative government at once yielded to radical Right pressure and succeeded in undercutting support for the radical Right.[144]

Obviously, the radicalizing direction is not remotely sufficient to charge Horthy or his regime with "fascism."[145] Horthy's Hungary retained its multiparty parliamentary system, allowing genuine debate even over the third anti-Semitic law. After Germany occupied Hungary in March 1944, forcing a further move to the Right, including a cabinet more acceptable to the Germans, Horthy insisted successfully that the Arrow Cross be kept out of the new compromise government. It was only when a German-inspired coup ousted Horthy in October 1944 that Szálasi and the Arrow Cross finally came to power.

The key is that even as the "real" fascists were being marginalized, fascist-conservative interaction yielded a synthesis and a novel government departure in a clearly fascistizing direction. There was nothing conservative or traditionalist about the new direction; it was even in a sense totalitarian. To say that the direction was not fascist because the government was not as plebian as the Arrow Cross or because it precluded the unruly Arrow Cross would be beside the point. Both Mussolini and Hitler marginalized more militant sectors of their own movements or parties when it seemed necessary.

So the fact that traditional conservatives were strong and determined enough to keep the real fascists out is only half the story. On closer examination the Hungarian case indicates that fascism was helping to set the agenda even where it was in one sense marginalized. In that light, we also note the limits to Gilbert Allardyce's notion, discussed in chapter 1, that fascism peaked in 1937–38 and declined thereafter. The question of fascism during the period cannot be confined to the fortunes of the most overtly fascist movements.

Seeking to account for what seemed the characteristic differences in the fascist trajectory in the successor states, Peter Sugar suggests that the fascists did not need to come to power at once because the more established Right was moving in the desired direction.[146] Though convincing up to a point, that characterization seems slightly disingenuous, as if, in Hungary, for example, the symbiosis was so obvious that the radical Right could relax, because just being part of the mix was sufficient for the fascistizing direction chosen. On the contrary, the outcome resulted from a complex, unpredictable interaction between the radical and the conservative Right.

Still, Sugar's notion leads us to ask whether we should view the population measures and anti-Jewish legislation as a defeat for fascism, in light of the blunting and absorption, yielding a loss of popular support, or as a victory, since pressure from the radical Right had helped force an otherwise somewhat reluctant government in the desired direction. It could be read either way.

Arguably even more significantly than in Spain, the interaction in Hungary transformed establishment conservatives, though taken as a group they were moving toward a more activist, statist policy in any case. But here we encounter the difficulty of generalizing about conservatives and the conservative response. For some, the advent of the radical Right had no doubt suggested new possibilities, the scope for more radical, concerted action, but the new direction needed to be pursued more "respectably." For others, like Pál Teleki, prime minister from 1939 to 1941, and for the most part Horthy himself, the challenge was more negative, even if a fascistizing response seemed necessary to head off that challenge. In responding they were to some extent holding their noses.

Still, whereas this distinction must be kept in mind, the key is that the conservative side, taken as a whole, was not merely threatened but also influenced, and no doubt emboldened as well, by the challenge of fascism. Up to a point at least, the need to box out fascism by co-opting aspects of its program provided an excuse to do what conservatives came to realize they wanted to do in any case.

The government was moving in a fascist, totalitarian direction even in its relations with the churches, yet the churches, in what remained a pluralistic, conservative authoritarian regime in many respects, moderated this thrust only at the margins. In a sense the churches were working with the government to marginalize the radical Right, which threatened not only the constitutional sociopolitical order but also, even more than the government, the autonomy of the churches and their role in key family and marriage areas. Thus, in a sense, the churches were compromising with the government, and thus the degree of ambiguity in their relationship.

In Romania the fascist Iron Guard (earlier known as the Legion of the Archangel Michael) was violently suppressed on two quite different occasions by seemingly conservative, authoritarian leaders. Even as fascist movements went, the Iron Guard was particularly violent, unruly, power-hungry, and threatening to conservatives, though its strong religious bent, to be considered in chapter 8, won it considerable support among Orthodox clergy. But in each of the two Romanian cases a complex dialectic was at work, yielding, as in Hungary, a novel new Right departure and trajectory that did not merely reinforce the dominance of conservatives in the face of the fascist threat.

In 1937, with Romania still under a parliamentary system, King Carol II sought to box out the Iron Guard by entrusting the government to a smaller, but more moderate and respectable anti-Semitic party, the National Christian Party, which promptly made anti-Semitism state policy through measures from the suppression of certain newspapers to the revocation of the citizenship of Jews who were naturalized citizens. This latter action was intended to encourage emigration. But in February 1938 King Carol abolished the 1923 constitution, dissolved all political parties, and proclaimed a royal dictatorship. The king was acting from the top down, but this step was prompted especially by the challenge of the Iron Guard from below.

Although the Guard's leader, Corneliu Codreanu, acquiesced in the royal coup, suppression of the Iron Guard quickly followed, including the arrest and trial of Codreanu and other leading figures in the movement. The substantial remnant of the Guard fought back, but the resulting unrest prompted further repression, including the murder of the imprisoned Codreanu and thirteen other members of the Guard, shot while allegedly trying to escape in November 1938.

Still, Carol was determined to suppress the Iron Guard not simply because it challenged conservative hegemony. Its unruliness made normal government difficult, but above all he feared that it was merely a tool of Hitler's Germany and thus a threat to Romanian sovereignty. The initial crackdown in March 1938 came shortly after the Anschluss, and Codreanu and the others were killed in November shortly after Carol had met with Hitler, who urged him not only to release Codreanu and the others but to invite them to form a Guardist government.[147]

Carol remained firm, even as the violence against the Iron Guard in November prompted a widespread public backlash against him. In the aftermath of the killings, other Guardists, seeking revenge, engaged in riots, hatched various plots, and finally managed to assassinate the prime minister in September 1939, prompting another crackdown.

However, Carol became more conciliatory as early German successes in the war suggested the need for Romanian friendship with Germany. So in January 1940 he ordered the release from detention of a number of Guardists. With the fall of France in June, he established the Party of the Nation as a single party subservient to the monarch; Horia Sima, now the Iron Guard leader, ordered the Guard's members to join the new entity.

So the king's treatment of the Iron Guard, including its suppression during 1938–39, stemmed less from conservative, authoritarian defense than from the vicissitudes of Romania's supranational interaction within the new Right universe. And the result was not merely such defense but another experiment that, short-lived though it was, had its own place in that universe. As Radu Ioanid sees it, in fact, Carol had "ended up by establishing his own brand of a totalitarian right-wing movement with unmistakable fascist features."[148] Still, Carol's effort proved too-little, too-late as German military successes enhanced the Iron Guard's popularity and influence.

And thus began the complex three-way interaction between Carol, the Iron Guard, and General Ion Antonescu that would lead to another fascistizing departure bound up with another effort to suppress the Iron Guard. Although more detailed consideration of Romania's relationship with Nazi Germany must wait for the next chapter, here we must keep in mind the trajectory, which entailed ever-closer relations from 1938, when it became clear that the European order that had emerged from World War I was breaking down, to November 1940, when Romania adhered to the Tripartite Pact with Germany, Italy, and Japan, and on to June 1941, when Romania declared war on the Soviet Union alongside Nazi Germany.

By summer 1940, with the Iron Guard fomenting disorder and the mo-narchical dictatorship in crisis, eyes turned to General Antonescu as the one person who might turn the situation around. Although he had only a modicum of political experience, he was highly respected for his compe-tence and rectitude. But Carol, fearing that Antonescu's popularity might erode his own power, ordered Antonescu's arrest in July 1940. However, this dissolved any remaining popular support for the king. Early in Septem-ber, hoping to save his throne, Carol agreed to full powers for Antonescu, but at Iron Guard insistence he abdicated in favor of his son Michael, who was nineteen years old when Antonescu was installed in power on 6 Sep-tember 1940.

Especially in light of his experience in government, Antonescu had come to view the parliamentary system and political parties as ineffective and corrupting. He had particular contempt for the Iron Guard, which seemed totally incompetent even as it lusted for power. Indeed, he tended to conflate Guardists with communists.[149] Yet Antonescu knew he lacked any political base, whereas the Iron Guard enjoyed considerable and grow-ing prestige in the country by September 1940. And it had strong support from higher-ups within the Nazi Party in Germany. As a concession to the Guard as Romania's leading political force, Antonescu, just a few days after assuming power, had King Michael proclaim Romania a National Legion-ary State, with Antonescu as leader and the Guard the only recognized political movement. The Guard was given posts making it the dominant force in Antonescu's new cabinet. And Antonescu wore the Guard's green shirt on several ceremonial occasions, including when addressing meetings of the Guard itself.

In one sense Antonescu's seeming need for a political base produced only a sort of fascist façade, but the Iron Guard was initially accorded real power in his regime. Still, the relationship quickly proved disastrous, as problems led first to friction, then to outright Guard rebellion, and fi-nally, with Hitler's blessing, to another violent suppression of the Guard. Whereas Antonescu wanted discipline—as did Hitler, especially to pro-mote the economic efficiency of his Romanian ally—the Guard was given to power grabbing, mismanagement, and lawlessness, which not only chal-lenged Antonescu's authority but also antagonized the Romanian middle class.[150] Meeting with Hitler in January 1941, Antonescu discussed the role of the Iron Guard, which still had support in major circles of the Nazi regime. Without explicitly giving Antonescu a free hand, Hitler suggested that his own relationship with Antonescu trumped the relationship be-tween the Nazi Party and the Guard. When a complex sequence led to further violence and then an Iron Guard uprising, including the wanton murder of Jews, Antonescu put down the rebellion and prepared to execute the leaders. The officer class in Romania firmly supported Antonescu in the showdown.[151]

Hitler ordered his subordinates to follow Antonescu, but Germans on the scene and sympathetic to the Iron Guard managed to get a number of the remaining Guard leaders, including Sima, out of Romania and into Germany. So even after being suppressed in Romania, the Guard was able to regroup in Germany, biding its time, still with significant support from within the Nazi hierarchy, including the SS. The Guard might still be a player in Romania, depending on German demands on the Romanian government. Even the fact that it remained a potential player no doubt made some difference in Antonescu's calculations. However, suppression was followed by the official dissolution of the National Legionary State in February 1941, just five months after it had been proclaimed. Further repression ensued, including a massive effort to round up those involved in the Guard uprising. More than nine thousand, many of them Orthodox priests, were taken into custody by the end of February. Guardists accused of killing Jews were executed.[152]

But Antonescu was already embarked on a radical program congruent, up to a point, with the general direction the Iron Guard had favored. It entailed above all a program of population engineering initiated in 1940, starting with anti-Semitic measures that carried further the course initiated earlier, in 1937, prior to Romania's alliance with Germany. At that point the direction responded to increasing Iron Guard influence, though it was to some extent intended to undercut the Guard, as we have seen. Antonescu took further anti-Semitic steps almost immediately upon coming to power in September 1940, then still further steps even after cracking down on the Guard. Because it remained congruent with what the Guard had advocated, this more radical direction surely would have siphoned off support for the Guard, whether or not it could be construed as co-opting aspects of the Guard program.

The intensified anti-Semitism was part of a wider program of population engineering, including the sort of interventionist eugenics measures that the Iron Guard had called for, though it had not been alone in doing so.[153] Eugenics was bound up with efforts to "cleanse" the country of ethnic minorities and to repatriate ethnic Romanians living abroad. Although Antonescu's implementation of the policy was vacillating in some respects, the aggregate outcome was horrific. Jews were the major target, and more than 250,000 of them died, but Romania's Roma were also subject to deportation and starvation.[154]

Obviously this was not merely to preserve conservative hegemony or the status quo. Antonescu was clearly anti-Semitic, but such anti-Semitism was not new in Romania and at that point was not remotely confined to

Antonescu and those around him. What *was* new, requiring explanation, was the radical program, the determination to act as never before, including steps beyond discrimination to actual extermination of Jews from within the wider program of population engineering. What had been mere possibilities were now being drawn out, actualized.

This program, especially, suggests that the Antonescu regime was assuming a place in the new Right universe. The question of whether the program or the regime itself is usefully considered "fascist" or "totalitarian" must wait for chapter 8, where we will consider criteria of differentiation. But it is worth noting here that whereas Vladimir Solonari, in his recent study of the population program, recognizes that it might seem the regime's most "fascist" measure, he explicitly denies "fascism," especially on the grounds that the genuine fascists, the Iron Guard, played no role in implementing it.[155] We will need to assess the importance of that criterion.

At the same time, implementation of the program took place in the context of German domination of continental Europe, and Aristotle Kallis has shown the importance of Nazi Germany as a catalyst for such radical, exterminationist population engineering in much of the continent, including Romania, during World War II.[156] Certainly the trajectory of the program cannot be disentangled from Romania's relationship with Germany, as we will see in the next chapter. But though Nazi Germany offered a kind of license, that was not remotely the same as applying the sort of pressure that might mitigate Romanian responsibility. Certainly Antonescu could be quite independent in his dealings with Hitler and the Germans, and his program of population engineering was not simply an effort to ingratiate himself with the Nazis.

But if this was an indigenous policy, why did ethnic homogeneity come to seem so important in Romania at that point? Do we have, as to some extent in Hungary, conservatives moving in a radical Right direction because of the need to head off radical Right pressures from below? In fact, though the departures in both cases led into the new Right universe, the dynamic in the two cases differed in instructive ways.

In Hungary the Arrow Cross had been marginalized but was still part of the mix and could be unleashed by the Germans—as indeed it was in October 1944. In Romania, in contrast, Antonescu had unequivocally suppressed the Iron Guard, which had been widely discredited among Romanians by its months in power in any case. To be sure, Antonescu's suppression had by no means eliminated the Guard, which, as we have seen, was able to regroup in Germany. So like the Arrow Cross, it too might be unleashed if doing so would seem to suit German purposes. Still, once the Guard had been suppressed, co-opting the radical Right was less immediately a concern in Romania than in Hungary.

What especially radicalized the situation in Romania was not Iron Guard pressure but the contingent concatenation that resulted from the instabilities inherent in the new territorial situation stemming from World War I. So the fuel for the Antonescu departure cannot be understood in terms of whatever combination of domestic fascist pressure, German pressure, and German license. The particulars of that new situation must wait for the next chapter. For now we can say simply that the international interaction that followed especially from Nazi German revisionism revealed Romanian vulnerabilities that seemed to demand a new population policy in response. The sense of vulnerability galvanized the abiding anti-Semitism, actualizing what had been only the latent possibility of expulsion and even extermination. Grasping the Antonescu departure as a response to what was apparently being revealed about Romania's international situation is one way of opening to a wider range of challenges and possibilities as we seek to grasp the sources of the era's fascistizing directions.

A Brief Conclusion on Domestic Interaction between Fascists and Conservatives

In this chapter we have seen that whereas the interaction between fascists and conservatives sometimes led to the blunting, absorption, or redirection of fascist impulses—and even, on occasion, to the active suppression of fascist movements—the relationship was generally dynamic, producing transformation on both sides and instances of synthesis or synergy on occasion. Especially when we encounter synergy, it becomes difficult or even impossible to disembed "fascism." We also note the difficulty at the time of knowing what was happening—whether fascism was being blunted or was helping to produce "fascistization." There was scope for seeing what one wanted, and proportions are often undecidable even for us now.

As we move from here into international interaction, we note that what was involved from the fascist or fascistizing side was the product of the internal interaction already in progress. How Fascist Italy, for example, came across to others was partly a function of its relationship with, to maintain our examples from above, big business or the Catholic Church. And yet again we note the scope for wishful thinking, for seeing what one wanted to see, taking what one wanted to take, on the part of those looking at whatever instance of fascism from the outside. At the same time, however, external interaction reflected back on and affected the internal interaction. Thus the braided dynamic.

Notes

1. Martin Blinkhorn, "Introduction: Allies, Rivals, or Antagonists? Fascists and Conservatives in Modern Europe," in *Fascists and Conservatives: The Radical Right and the Establishment in Twentieth-Century Europe*, ed. Martin Blinkhorn (London: Unwin Hyman, 1990), 3–4, 9, 12. See also Martin Blinkhorn, *Fascism and the Right in Europe, 1919–1945* (Harlow: Longman, 2000).

2. Blinkhorn, "Introduction," 4–5.

3. Ibid., 10.

4. See, e.g., Alfredo Rocco, Manifesto of *Politica*, in *Italian Fascisms from Pareto to Gentile*, ed. Adrian Lyttelton (New York: Harper & Row [Torchbooks], 1975), 251–52, 260.

5. See David D. Roberts, *The Syndicalist Tradition and Italian Fascism* (Chapel Hill: University of North Carolina Press, 1979), 144–50, on Rocco and Nationalist thinking about the weakness of the liberal state in the face of the threat, and the opportunity, constituted by the modern trade union movement. For the contrasting liberal view, see Gaetano Mosca, *The Ruling Class*, ed. Arthur Livingston, trans. Hannah D. Kahn (New York: McGraw-Hill, 1939), 479–82.

6. Alfredo Rocco, "Crisi dello Stato e sindacati," in *Scritti e discorsi politici*, 3 vols (Milan: A. Giuffré, 1938), 2:631–45.

7. Julie V. Gottlieb, *Feminine Fascism: Women in Britain's Fascist Movement, 1923–1945* (London: I.B. Tauris, 2000).

8. Kevin Passmore, "Theories of Fascism: A Critique from the Perspective of Women's and Gender History," in *Rethinking the Nature of Fascism: Comparative Perspectives*, ed. António Costa Pinto (Basingstoke: Palgrave Macmillan, 2011), 132–36. See also Passmore's edited volume, *Women, Gender and Fascism in Europe, 1919–1945*, ed. Kevin Passmore (New Brunswick, NJ: Rutgers University Press, 2003).

9. Passmore, "Theories of Fascism," 133–34, 136–37.

10. See especially Emilio Gentile, *La via italiana al totalitarismo: Il partito e lo Stato nel regime fascista* (Rome: La Nuova Italia Scientifica, 1995).

11. Philip Morgan, "Corporatism and the Economic Order," in *Liberal and Fascist Italy*, ed. Adrian Lyttelton (Oxford: Oxford University Press, 2002), 158.

12. Ibid., 156. See also Gianpasquale Santomassimo, *La terza via fascista: Il mito del corporativismo* (Rome: Carocci, 2006), which is concerned not with actual functioning—he finds the conclusions of earlier studies still valid—but with the place of corporatism in wider Italian Fascist discussion and debate. Especially on 12–13, he takes seriously the notion that there was a leftist, radical, anti-bourgeois component to it.

13. Morgan, "Corporatism and the Economic Order," 152.

14. Ibid., 158.

15. Ibid., 156.

16. Ibid., 165.

17. Ibid., 157.

18. Franklin Hugh Adler, *Italian Industrialists from Liberalism to Fascism: The Political Development of the Industrial Bourgeoisie, 1906–1934* (Cambridge: Cambridge University Press, 1995); see 438–39 for a succinct statement of a major overall theme.

19. Ibid., 347.

20. Ibid., 133.

21. Alessio Gagliardi, *Il corporativismo fascista* (Rome: Laterza, 2010).

22. Morgan, "Corporatism and the Economic Order," 158–59.

23. Ibid., 130, 132–33, 138.

24. Again see Santomassimo, *La terza via fascista*, cited in note 12 above. See also Roberts, *The Syndicalist Tradition*, chapter 11, entitled "Critics and Myth-Makers, 1925–1943."

25. Morgan, "Corporatism and the Economic Order," 160–61.

26. Marcello De Cecco, "The Economy from Liberalism to Fascism," in *Liberal and Fascist Italy*, ed. Lyttelton, 74–75.

27. Morgan, "Corporatism and the Economic Order," 162.

28. Ibid., 162–63.

29. De Cecco, "The Economy from Liberalism to Fascism," 74–78; Morgan, "Corporatism and the Economic Order," 161–63.

30. De Cecco, "The Economy from Liberalism to Fascism," 76.

31. Morgan, "Corporatism and the Economic Order," 162–63. The quotation is from 163.

32. Ibid., 163.

33. Ibid., 155.

34. The innovative Marxist Ernesto Laclau made this comparison while portraying Farinacci as a genuine Leftist radical. See Ernesto Laclau, *Politics and Ideology in Marxist Theory: Capitalism, Fascism, Populism* (London: NLB, 1977), 122–24.

35. For the proceedings, see Ministero delle Corporazioni, *Atti del secondo convegno di studi sindacali e corporativi: Ferrara, 5–8 maggio 1932*, 3 vols (Rome: Tipografia del Senato, 1932). Ugo Spirito, *Il corporativismo* (Florence: Sansoni, 1970), includes Spirito's key writings on corporatism.

36. Giuseppe Bottai, *Esperienza corporativa (1929–1934)* (Florence: Vallecchi, 1934), 538–43.

37. Adam Tooze, *The Wages of Destruction: The Making and Breaking of the Nazi Economy* (New York: Penguin, 2006), 115.

38. Ibid., 121.

39. Ibid., 660–61.

40. Ibid., 134, summarizing the key chapter on the partnership with big business (99–134).

41. Ibid., 114.

42. Ibid., 112–13.

43. Peter Hayes, foreword to Stephan H. Lindner, *Inside IG Farben: Hoechst during the Third Reich*, trans. Helen Shoop (Cambridge: Cambridge University Press, 2008), xiii.

44. Peter Hayes, *Industry and Ideology: IG Farben in the Nazi Era* (Cambridge: Cambridge University Press, 1987; new edn, 2001). Hayes, foreword to Lindner, *Inside IG Farben*, xv, provides a good brief summary.

45. Hayes, foreword to Lindner, *Inside IG Farben*, xvi–xviii.

46. J.F. Pollard, "Fascism and Catholicism," in *The Oxford Handbook of Fascism*, ed. R.J.B. Bosworth (Oxford: Oxford University Press, 2009), 167–68.

47. Ibid., 175.

48. Eric Voegelin has perhaps become the best known. See David D. Roberts, "'Political Religion' and the Totalitarian Departures of Inter-war Europe: On the Uses and Disadvantages of an Analytical Category," *Contemporary European History* 18, no. 4 (2009): 382, 388.

49. Pollard, "Fascism and Catholicism," 180.

50. Ibid., 173–74.

51. Ibid., 167.

52. Ibid., 172–73, 178.

53. Richard Steigmann-Gall, *The Holy Reich: Nazi Conceptions of Christianity, 1919–1945* (Cambridge: Cambridge University Press, 2003), 114.

54. Ibid., 261–62; see also the concluding paragraph on 267.

55. Ibid., 155, disputing especially Richard Conway.

56. Ibid., 155, 186–88, 218.

57. Ibid., 199, 210, 213–14.

58. Ibid., 216.

59. Ibid., 252–53, 258–59.

60. Ibid., 252–53.

61. Ibid., 259.

62. Ibid., 261.

63. Steven E. Aschheim, *The Nietzsche Legacy in Germany, 1890–1990* (Berkeley: University of California Press, 1992), 232–71. See also David D. Roberts, *The Totalitarian Experiment in Twentieth-Century Europe: Understanding the Poverty of Great Politics* (London and New York: Routledge, 2006), 150–63, 349–52.

64. Steigmann-Gall, *The Holy Reich*, 105–6.

65. Walter L. Adamson, "Fascism and Political Religion in Italy: A Reassessment," *Contemporary European History* 23, no. 1 (February 2014): 54.

66. Ibid., 71.

67. Ibid., 62.

68. Ibid., 54.

69. Pollard, "Fascism and Catholicism," 181, 183.

70. Adamson, "Fascism and Political Religion in Italy," 71.

71. Ibid., 56.

72. Ibid., 71–72.

73. Ibid., 64.

74. Ibid., 65 (emphasis in the original).

75. Quoting Steigmann-Gall, *Holy Reich*, 12 (emphasis in the original).

76. Adamson, "Fascism and Political Religion in Italy," 64.

77. Ibid., 64–65.

78. Ibid., 71–72.

79. Ibid., 71.

80. Ibid., 58.

81. Emilio Gentile, *The Sacralization of Politics in Fascist Italy*, trans. Keith Botsford (Cambridge, MA: Harvard University Press, 1996), 58. There is no kinship between the earlier philosopher Giovanni Gentile and the contemporary historian Emilio Gentile.

82. Adamson, "Fascism and Political Religion in Italy," 63. Adamson draws on Pollard, "Fascism and Catholicism," 182.

83. Ian Kershaw, "Hitler and the Uniqueness of Nazism," *Journal of Contemporary History* 39, no. 2 (April 2004): 248.

84. R.J.B. Bosworth, *Mussolini's Italy: Life under the Dictatorship, 1915–1945* (New York: Penguin, 2006).

85. As I recall, this was the title of a presentation she made to the Columbia University Seminar on Modern Italy in about 1981.

86. Morgan, "Corporatism and the Economic Order," 152.

87. Victoria De Grazia, *The Culture of Consent: Mass Organization of Leisure in Fascist Italy* (Cambridge: Cambridge University Press, 1981).

88. See especially Gentile, *La via italiana.*

89. Robert O. Paxton, *The Anatomy of Fascism* (New York: Random House [Vintage]: 2005), 120–21, 123–25.

90. Pollard, "Fascism and Catholicism," 183.

91. Shelley Baranowski, *Strength through Joy: Consumerism and Mass Tourism in the Third Reich* (Cambridge: Cambridge University Press, 2004).

92. Peter Fritzsche, *Life and Death in the Third Reich* (Cambridge, MA: Belknap Press of Harvard University Press, 2008); Robert Gellately, *Backing Hitler: Consent and Coercion in Nazi Germany* (Oxford: Oxford University Press, 2001); Robert Gellately and Nathan Stoltzfus, eds, *Social Outcasts in Nazi Germany* (Princeton, NJ: Princeton University Press, 2001); Thomas Kühne, *Belonging and Genocide: Hitler's Community, 1918–1945* (New Haven, CT: Yale University Press, 2010).

93. Mark Pittaway, "Hungary," in *Oxford Handbook,* ed. Bosworth, 385–86.
94. Maria Ormos, *Hungary in the Age of the Two World Wars, 1914–1945,* trans. Brian McLean (Boulder, CO: Social Science Monographs, 2007), 236–64, esp. 236–37, 245, 252, 257–58.
95. Ibid., 252, 254, 259–60.
96. Pittaway, "Hungary," 385. See also Paul A. Hanebrink, *In Defense of Christian Hungary: Religion, Nationalism, and Anti-Semitism, 1890–1944* (Ithaca, NY: Cornell University Press, 2006), 138.
97. Ormos, *Hungary,* 256–257. The quotation is from 257.
98. Ibid., 251; Hanebrink, *In Defense of Christian Hungary,* 140–41, 166.
99. Aristotle Kallis, "Neither Fascist nor Authoritarian: The 4th of August Regime in Greece (1936–1941) and the Dynamics of Fascistisation in 1930s Europe," *East Central Europe* 37 (2010): 312, 316; Mogens Pelt, "Stages in the Development of the 'Fourth of August' Regime in Greece," in *Rethinking Fascism and Dictatorship in Interwar Europe,* ed. António Costa Pinto and Aristotle Kallis (Basingstoke: Palgrave Macmillan, 2014), 208–10.
100. Pelt, "Stages in the Development," 208–09.
101. Ibid., 211, 214.
102. Kallis, "Neither Fascist nor Authoritarian," 314–15. See also Pelt, "Stages in the Development," 211, on the embrace of Sparta and Byzantium.
103. Kallis, "Neither Fascist nor Authoritarian," 317–18.
104. Ibid., 322.
105. Pelt, "Stages in the Development, 208, 212.
106. Hagen Fleischer, "Authoritarian Rule in Greece and Its Heritage (1936–1974)," in *Totalitarian and Authoritarian Regimes in Europe: Legacies and Lessons from the Twentieth Century,* ed. Jerzy W. Borejsza and Klaus Ziemer (New York and Oxford: Berghahn, 2006), 257.
107. See Gerhard Botz, "The Coming of the Dollfuss-Schuschnigg Regime and the Stages of its Development," in *Rethinking Fascism and Dictatorship,* ed. Pinto and Kallis, 126–30, for a lucid account of the two fascist movements. See also Tim Kirk, "Fascism and Austrofascism," in *The Dollfuss/Schuschnigg Era in Austria: A Reassessment,* ed. Günter Bischof, Anton Pelinka, and Alexander Lassner (New Brunswick, NJ: Transaction, 2003), 15–16, 25; and Lothar Höbelt, "Nostalgic Agnostics: Austrian Aristocrats and Politics, 1918–1938," in *European Aristocracies and the Radical Right, 1919–1939,* ed. Karina Urbach (Oxford: Oxford University Press, 2007), 175–76, 180–81.
108. Kirk, "Fascism and Austrofascism," 17–18.
109. Ibid., 22–23.
110. Ibid., 23; Corinna Peniston-Bird, "Austria," in *Oxford Handbook,* ed. Bosworth, 448.
111. Peniston-Bird, "Austria," 444–45.
112. Ibid., 440, 447, 449.
113. Botz, "The Coming of the Dollfuss-Schuschnigg Regime," 134, 136, 138–39.
114. Gerhard Botz, "The Short- and Long-Term Effects of the Authoritarian Regime and of Nazism in Austria: The Burden of a 'Second Dictatorship,'" in *Totalitarian and Authoritarian Regimes,* ed. Borejsza and Ziemer, 189.
115. Kirk, "Fascism and Austrofascism," 25.
116. Peniston-Bird, "Austria," 449.
117. Botz, "The Short- and Long-Term Effects," 189; Botz, "The Coming of the Dollfuss-Schuschnigg Regime," 144–45; Kirk, "Fascism and Austrofascism," 25–26.
118. Peniston-Bird, "Austria," 450.
119. Ibid., 448. See also Botz, "The Coming of the Dollfuss-Schuschnigg Regime," 137, 140.
120. Kirk, "Fascism and Austrofascism," 22–23.

121. Ibid., 24.

122. Ibid., 23.

123. Ibid., 26.

124. Philip Morgan, "Studying Fascism from the Particular to the General," *East Central Europe* 37 (2010): 336–37.

125. Hanebrink, *In Defense of Christian Hungary,* 138–39.

126. Ibid., 164.

127. Pittaway, "Hungary," 381; Hanebrink, *In Defense of Christian Hungary,* 139–40.

128. Pittaway, "Hungary," 386, 388, 390.

129. Hanebrink, *In Defense of Christian Hungary,* 10–59.

130. Ibid., 150–52, 155–56, 159–60, 164.

131. Ibid., 143. On these emphases among the German Christians, see Doris L. Bergen, *The Twisted Cross: The German Christian Movement in the Third Reich* (Chapel Hill: University of North Carolina Press, 1996), 89, 148, 195, 143–54.

132. Hanebrink, *In Defense of Christian Hungary,* 182.

133. Ibid., 142, 159–60.

134. Ibid., 144, 148.

135. Pittaway, "Hungary," 388, 391–92.

136. Ormos, *Hungary,* 386–87; Hanebrink, *In Defense of Christian Hungary,* 169–70.

137. Marius Turda, "The First Debates on Eugenics in Hungary, 1910–1918," in *"Blood and Homeland": Eugenics and Racial Nationalism in Central and Southeast Europe, 1900–1940,* ed. Marius Turda and Paul J. Weindling (Budapest: Central European University Press, 2007), 185–221.

138. Hanebrink, *In Defense of Christian Hungary,* 166–68.

139. Ibid., 191.

140. Ibid., 171, 178.

141. Ibid., 179–180.

142. Ibid., 188–89.

143. Ormos, *Hungary,* 361.

144. Hanebrink, *In Defense of Christian Hungary,* 164.

145. Thomas Sakmyster offers a good first step in noting that it makes little sense to call Horthy a fascist, that, on the contrary, he was an interesting ideological hybrid, combining nineteenth-century conservatism with twentieth-century right-wing radicalism. See Thomas L. Sakmyster, *Hungary's Admiral on Horseback: Miklos Horthy, 1918–1944* (Boulder, CO: East European Monographs, 1994), vii, 399–400. We will consider the uses of the "hybrid" category in chapter 8.

146. Peter F. Sugar, "Conclusion," in *Native Fascism in the Successor States, 1918–1945,* ed. Peter F. Sugar (Santa Barbara: ABC-Clio, 1971), 149–50, 153.

147. Dennis Deletant, *Hitler's Forgotten Ally: Ion Antonescu and His Regime, Romania 1940–44* (Basingstoke: Palgrave Macmillan, 2006), 35.

148. Radu Ioanid, "Romania," in *Oxford Handbook,* ed. Bosworth, 399.

149. Deletant, *Hitler's Forgotten Ally,* 72.

150. Ibid., 58–61, 66–67.

151. Ibid., 63–67.

152. Ibid., 71.

153. See Vladimir Solonari, *Purifying the Nation: Population Exchange and Ethnic Cleansing in Nazi-Allied Romania* (Washington: Woodrow Wilson Center Press; Baltimore: Johns Hopkins University Press, 2010), 62–74, on Romanian eugenic thinking, and 268–75, on its role in Antonescu's program of systematic population engineering. For indications of the centrality of biopolitics, including eugenics, to the Iron Guard's vision of purification and renewal, see Marius Turda, "Controlling the National Body: Ideas of Racial Purification in Romania, 1918–1944," in *Health, Hygiene, and Eugenics in Southeastern Europe to 1945,*

ed. Christian Promitzer, Sevastri Trubeta, and Marius Turda (Budapest: Central European University Press, 2011), 41, 346; and Ioanid, "Romania," 405.

154. Deletant, *Hitler's Forgotten Ally*, 269; Turda, "Controlling the National Body," 347.
155. Solonari, *Purifying the Nation*, 339–40.
156. Aristotle Kallis, *Genocide and Fascism: The Eliminationist Drive in Fascist Europe* (London and New York: Routledge, 2009), esp. 250–55.

Chapter 5

SUPRANATIONAL INTERACTION WITHIN THE NEW RIGHT

Expanding the Range: Positive, Negative, Both, and Neither

When we turn to wider supranational interaction within the new Right, we find parallels with the internal level up to a point. Supranational interaction, too, could inspire or reinforce novel directions, or it could dilute, moderate, or deflect them—still, of course, affecting trajectories. And obviously there were many possibilities in between. But with so many new directions mixing together within the new Right universe, supranational interaction was more complex still, making for much uncertainty and intensifying the scope both for wishful thinking and for picking and choosing.

In pondering the range of multinational interaction in chapter 2, we noted a divergence between Constantin Iordachi, who features interaction within a specifically fascist universe, and António Costa Pinto and Mary Vincent, both of whom point to interaction between those generally considered fascists and others, sometimes considered merely "authoritarian" or "traditionalist," on the non-fascist Right. Each direction surely has its uses, but the distinction between them blurs, not least because, as Michel Dobry emphasizes, the interaction entailed considerable discussion and uncertainty over what counted as "fascism" and over what was entailed in embracing or rejecting it on the Right. What did fascism *have* to entail, and what might it be made *not* to entail? Transnational interaction could work to reassure or to scare, to make fascism seem more, or less, credible as a novel political option.

We can usefully begin with an example of supranational interaction that affected relationships between fascism and conservatism on the domestic level, possibly moderating the fascist impulse to some extent. Stressing the import of one aspect of the Italian example, Karina Urbach shows that the apparent support of the monarchy, and with it many aristocrats, for the Fascist regime seemed to lend respectability to a decision for fascism among aristocratic circles—and surely "respectable" circles more widely—elsewhere in Europe.[1]

Monarchist adherence certainly seemed to have helped box out the most extreme, unsavory aspects of Fascism in Italy. The prominence of an aristocratic monarchist like Cesare Maria de Vecchi di Val Cismon in several diverse roles in Mussolini's regime no doubt helped. Though he had been one of the "quadrumvirs" of the March on Rome in 1922, he became especially important as a bridge between the regime and the Catholic Church. Aristocratic adherence elsewhere might have been expected to have a comparably moderating effect.

But not surprisingly, many Italian Fascists, even as they differed among themselves over other matters, found aristocratic adhesion a mixed blessing indeed. Those elsewhere fastening upon Italian Fascist links to the monarchy were viewing Fascist Italy selectively, picking and choosing. Although their choices inevitably reflected a measure of wishful thinking, they were making their best guess about what the regime portended. That particular "aristocratic" choice was certainly plausible, but there were also reasons for doubt. Those sympathetic to the monarchy seemed to have won the upper hand within the regime well into the 1930s, but the German alliance and the path toward war were unpopular, or at least controversial, among many Fascists close to the monarchy. Certainly the apparent legitimizing role of the monarchy did not restrain Mussolini and his regime when it most counted. And the complexities of the ending of that regime in 1943, together with the bitter struggles that followed with the advent of the militantly antimonarchist, "neo-fascist" Repubblica di Salò during 1943–45, suggest how volatile the mixture of forces in Fascist Italy had remained under the surface.

For those picking and choosing from the outside, it could not have been clear how the internal interplay between more radical Fascists and monarchists within the Italian regime would turn out. This example suggests not only the inevitability of blindered views and selective borrowing, but also, yet again, the uncertainty and ongoing openness at the time. It also indicates the need for particular attention to the diachronic dimension in considering supranational interaction. At what point in the trajectory the interaction took place is linked to the scope for selective borrowing, for illusion and wishful thinking. At the same time, the import of the diachronic dimension suggests *our* need for a longer-term but not teleological perspective if we are to understand the import of whatever aspect of the interaction at the time.

As a first approximation in considering the range on the supranational level, we can usefully distinguish between "positive" and "negative" interaction, although we find much that transcends any such simple dichotomy. Whereas positive interaction, based on attraction, is relatively simple and familiar, negative interaction is less so and is thus all the more important to pinpoint. A step beyond diluting or moderating, such negative interaction entailed nervousness or active dislike, fueling first active avoidance, but then possibly also the quest for an alternative. Any such quest had to entail indigenous experiment and innovation, though it could also involve different, and positive, interaction with some other strand on the supranational level. In that sense even negative interaction could promote experiment and further variations on the new Right. So we sometimes find negative interaction from one side and positive interaction from another at almost the same time, mutually reinforcing. And thus interaction could be not merely bilateral but multilateral.

But before considering examples of positive and negative interaction, we must consider one further preliminary: the place of asymmetry in the supranational interaction. In his contribution to Iordachi's recent special issue of *East Central Europe*, Arnd Bauerkämper forcefully reminds us that supranational interaction could be asymmetrical along two distinguishable axes. First, because fascist movements had actually established new regimes in Italy and Germany, relations between those two countries and the various more-or-less fascist groups elsewhere "were grossly asymmetrical," as he puts it. But he also emphasizes the growing asymmetry in relations between the Italians and the Germans themselves, with the clout of Nazi Germany increasing at the expense of Fascist Italy.[2]

We recall that the new agenda suggests the need to pull back from privilege to Italy and Germany even in considering supranational interaction. Such privilege has seemed to entail a focus on imitation and imposition, so pulling back would open to wider avenues of supranational interaction. The aim would be to encompass the whole web of interaction, with greater attention to the experiment, open-endedness, and uncertainty at the time. But, as we have also noted, the centrality of Italy and Germany to the web of interaction is undeniable, so we must find a balance, de-privileging them as appropriate while also doing justice to their central role. Even as he included Bauerkämper's analysis of asymmetry, Iordachi seems so concerned with multipolar creativity that he glosses over the possible role of asymmetries in the web of interaction.

A new agenda might entail considering more deeply why such asymmetries were important and how they played out, to some degree contingently, affecting the interaction in changing ways. We might come better to understand why relationships that were initially only mildly asymmetrical became more so. And the two asymmetries seem to have become in some ways increasingly interwoven. Thus it is important to ponder asymmetry as a dynamic, not as given and stable, inevitable though it might appear to have been on each level in retrospect.

At the same time, however, we must recognize that asymmetry is a gross category encompassing an array of relationships among the phenomena to be considered. It is easily invoked in ways that seem to obviate the need for deeper analysis. Indeed, the very fact of asymmetry can lead us to overdo it at the expense of other factors. We must also note that what first looks like asymmetry might prove to be better understood in other terms. So the import of asymmetry in the complex interactions at issue must be assessed in every case.

More generally, emphasis on asymmetry may lead us to overdo power relations, compromising our effort to understand the whole universe of response on the new Right during the era. The premise behind expanding that universe is that a movement, even an impulse, can be symptomatic and worthy of inclusion even if it did not come to power.

Still, because fascist movements in Italy and Germany uniquely established themselves in power, these two countries seemed to provide a model or at least inspiration for others considering a new Right departure, though the Italians and Germans were generally eager to export their respective models at the same time. In the relationship between the two major powers and the others, we certainly find *some* of the "imitation and imposition" that we are cautioned not to overemphasize.

The eagerness to export on the part of Italy and Germany stemmed partly from ideological commitment and partly from foreign policy interests in undecidable proportion. And of course foreign policy interests could temper ideological zeal. It is well known that when immediate German interests were concerned, Hitler, especially, preferred to deal with those who seemed authoritarian conservatives—like Horthy in Hungary or Antonescu in Romania—than with those more eager to embrace variations on Nazi ideology, who seemed less reliable. But there was fissuring over the issue within Nazism, as we noted in the preceding chapter in considering the enduring support for the Romanian Iron Guard in leading Nazi circles.

Whereas asymmetry could obviously entail the stronger imposing itself on the weaker, it could also entail the weaker freely taking the more successful as a model. And it is not always possible to determine which was at work or how to apportion the two insofar as both were at work. Going along with the Italians or Germans could stem from genuine ideological attraction or from more delimited, pragmatic reasons of national self-interest, whether to serve territorial ambition or simply to preserve territorial integrity and to maximize sovereignty and autonomy. Insofar as both ideological and pragmatic considerations fueled an attraction to Italy or Germany, we again cannot hope to determine proportions.

Among other things, Fascist Italy and Nazi Germany stood for foreign policy activism and even territorial revisionism, which made them especially attractive to some, depending on geography and the territorial situations resulting from World War I. Although both ideology and geopolitical considerations prompted Italy and Germany to intervene on the Nationalist side in the Spanish Civil War, Spain, like Portugal, had kept out of World War I, so territorial concerns were not significant for either country in their relationships with Italy and Germany. But countries much changed in light of the war faced very different situations, though those situations differed among themselves, bringing these countries into contact with the fascist powers in varied ways. Whereas Hungary had revisionist aims of its own, Romania sought simply to preserve the highly favorable territorial settlement it had been awarded through the peace process. In the case of Austria, internal division made for a particularly volatile situation for a time, until a change in the Italian-German relationship fundamentally altered the equation.

Even an asymmetrical relationship could entail a kind of dialectic, drawing out unforeseen new Right departures from those on the weaker side. The interaction with Italy or Germany might serve to radicalize, but those on the receiving end might seek to distinguish their direction from that of the stronger, beyond merely asserting sovereignty or seeking to maximize autonomy. So the asymmetry between the two major powers and the others encompasses a variety of relationships.

The two modes of asymmetry were central to the most dramatic instances of interaction, which came in the later part of the trajectory as Italian and especially German territorial ambitions altered the dynamic and led into World War II. Interaction could still be positive, negative, or both, but now especially the two modes of asymmetry strongly affected relationships. Here again, however, it is important to avoid the teleological assumption that modes of asymmetry coming to the fore later were operative all along. Changes in modes of asymmetry were central to the changing overall trajectory.

In the earlier stages of that trajectory, much on the level of positive interaction is well established and agreed upon. Among the discontented looking for a model we have already encountered Gyula Gömbös looking to Fascist Italy, whereas Ioannis Metaxas, suspicious of Italian designs on Greece, took inspiration from Nazi Germany. And this level of straightforward influence surely remains fundamental. But let us recall that both Vincent and Pinto, in expressing restiveness, suggested that more complex though still "positive" modes of interaction were at work, making the

Franco and Salazar regimes, respectively, novel and distinctive and giving each its own place in the new Right universe. Neither was merely a lesser version of something else. With deeper attention to interaction and transfer, in other words, we recognize that the two Iberian regimes could not have been merely authoritarian, understood as traditionalist and conservative, in the earlier way. Nor, in either case, was the outcome of its interaction with the more fully fascist regimes merely instrumental, as Griffin's term "para-fascism" suggested in its original incarnation.

Though less familiar, negative interaction, too, could be relatively straightforward. Iordachi notes that later Legionnaire ideologues in Romania sought to differentiate the Legion from both Italian Fascism, taken as venerating the state, and German Nazism, taken as venerating race and nation.[3] These were plausible perceptions of the two exemplars, and there was indeed scope for new radical nationalist alternatives to both. These perceptions of the innovations in Italy and Germany seem to have helped Legion thinkers pin down what was most important to them instead.

Negative perceptions sometimes led those who might otherwise have supported new Right departures to pull back or resist, significantly affecting trajectories in individual cases. We noted that in Hungary business leaders, many of them Jewish, grew especially nervous about developments in Germany with the anti-Semitic legislation of fall 1935; increasingly suspicious of any fascist direction, they helped quash the Gömbös experiment then at its peak. We also noted the negative impact of the Nazi treatment of the German churches, especially the German Catholic Church, on Hungarian church leaders. Pope Pius XI's encyclical *Mit brennender Sorge* of 1937, condemning Nazi policy, intensified concern that the growing influence of the Arrow Cross threatened church autonomy, even as the new Right might be attractive on other grounds. As far as the Hungarian churches were concerned, the radical Right's claim to be pursuing a "National Christian" role, even revolution, cut both ways.

Well after World War II Oswald Mosley, leader of the British Union of Fascists, complained that just when some success for his movement seemed possible during the 1930s, it was undercut by the actions of Hitler or Mussolini. Gilbert Allardyce cited Mosley's lament as evidence that even those outside Italy and Germany who adapted the term "fascism" came to recognize the curse of its association with things foreign.[4] But in adducing this as evidence helping to undercut the notion of generic fascism, Allardyce missed the import of the interaction—important, in this instance, even in its negativity.

Especially significant for the texture of the era are the instances of positive and negative interaction in interplay. When considering Pinto's restiveness, we noted his point that the Salazar regime in Portugal was taken as a valuable new model by some elsewhere precisely because it seemed to avoid the more aggressive and radical aspects of fascism. To be sure, it might be argued that what Portugal offered were simply half measures that some found attractive in offering certain positive aspects of fascism without the excesses. But if, in line with the new agenda, we treat Salazar's Portugal less in the standard comparative terms and more in terms of its place in the supranational interaction, that comes to seem too simple. Indeed, we see both the Portuguese case and the interaction in a somewhat different light.

We note a number of instances of attraction to Salazar's Portugal in tandem with objection to this or that aspect of Italian Fascism or German Nazism. In other words, those seeking to enter the new Right universe could find negatives in Italy and/or Germany that thereby made the Portuguese case attractive, and vice versa. Moreover, the Portuguese sense of how the Salazar regime was being perceived by others surely fed an energizing perception among the regime's adherents that they were not merely settling for half measures, let alone merely seeking to catch up, but were actually creating a new and appropriate mode of modern governance.

The extent to which the positive appeal of the Salazar experiment reflected negative perceptions of other cases is of course hard to pin down. The Metaxas regime in Greece was especially interested in the constitutional and social experiments in Portugal during the 1930s. Metaxas even communicated his enthusiasm to Salazar in 1937.[5] Although Metaxas seems especially to have identified with Salazar's top-down approach, in embracing the Portuguese model he was to some extent turning from Italy, no doubt to some extent because of nervousness about Italian designs on his country.

The case of Pál Teleki in Hungary is clearer. As prime minister from February 1939 until his suicide in April 1941, he was forced into a difficult balancing act as he sought both to rein in the radical Right and to moderate the influence of Nazi Germany—while to some extent giving in to both at the same time. Teleki and the circle around him were anti-Semitic, strongly Catholic, and repelled by Nazism, though they sought to take advantage of German power to pursue their own revisionist territorial aims. On the domestic level, they wanted to move from parliamentary government toward a non-dictatorial corporate state structure inspired especially by the Portuguese model.[6] Teleki himself was so enthused about corporatist development in Portugal that he volunteered to write an introduction to the Hungarian edition of Salazar's selected speeches.[7] Interaction with Portugal seemed to point the way to a new Right alternative to the Nazification threatened by pressures from the domestic radical Right and from Nazi Germany itself.

In short, Teleki's dislike of Nazi Germany surely helped fuel his attraction to the Portuguese model, while the availability of the Portuguese alternative no doubt reinforced his dislike of Nazi Germany. This example makes it especially clear that the interaction at work was sometimes not merely bilateral but multilateral.

Salazar's Portugal was also attractive to the Austrian regime of 1933–38, which was caught up in multinational interaction in a still more complex way in light of the country's situation vis-à-vis both Fascist Italy and Nazi Germany. Even as a political departure to the Right seemed necessary for domestic reasons, the Dollfuss-Schuschnigg regime sought to preserve Austrian independence, which seemed most obviously to require differentiating the new regime from both Nazi Germany and the Austrian Nazis. So up to a point Fascist Italy with its corporatist direction seemed to provide an attractive alternative. But the new Austrian regime was also concerned not to be too closely identified with Fascist Italy. Corinna Peniston-Bird speculates that Austria's Catholic corporatist state was to some degree an effort to defend against increasing Italian influence.[8] So whereas the Austrian regime's relationship with Germany was mostly negative, its relationship with Italy was both positive and negative.

As a result, the Dollfuss-Schuschnigg regime to some extent went its own way, made its own path into the new Right. No doubt this reflected, in undecidable proportion, both the desire to preserve autonomy and some genuine distaste for aspects of the German and Italian regimes. Even as the Austrian regime moved toward anti-parliamentary corporatism and, with the Fatherland Front, toward totalitarianism in certain respects, it seemingly held off in part, in light of a sense that there was something excessive in the two foreign models, even including Fascist Italy. For that reason, but also to flaunt its autonomy, Austria needed to develop its own form of corporatism, differentiated from the Italian Fascist version. So the spin given to Austrian corporatism reflected attachment both to the Portuguese example and to Catholic teaching, especially as made current through Pius XI's *Quadragesimo anno*. And these were of course mutually reinforcing because Portuguese corporatism was considerably more indebted to Catholic teaching than was Italian Fascist corporatism.

Deeper into the Place of Corporatism in the Supranational Interaction

Although discussion of corporatism was involved in the emergence of a number of new Right experiments, how corporatism related to "fascism" was not clear then and is not clear now. Given the appropriate spin, it could seem to constitute an alternative to, even a bulwark against, fascism.

And we have already seen that it could play into both positive and negative interaction.

In chapter 3, we noted that the promising treatments by Pinto and Didier Musiedlak show, in the face of long-standing denigration and neglect, how central corporatism was to the interaction at the time, whatever its outcomes in practice. But we also noted that even their accounts betray certain limits. Here we must consider how we might probe the interaction over corporatism more fruitfully.

We need first to back up further to encompass a wider range of frequencies, to expand the possible range of purposes, as we consider the aspirations underlying the vogue of corporatism. We need a better sense of how interest in corporatism meshed with the perceived problems with parliamentary democracy and the perceived challenge, and possible opportunity, constituted by the class-based trade-union movement. Labor relations and the appropriate role of trade unions remain at issue today, though consensus seems to have been reached in some countries more than others. At the time, especially in the wake of the Russian revolution, the growth of unions, and the spread of labor unrest in much of Europe after World War I, it was not only plausible but arguably essential to try to rethink labor relations and the role of unions, to seek to imagine and even try out new institutional arrangements. Insofar as we open to experiment at the time, we need not take the preservation of the unions as private entities, playing the role they did within liberal systems as of around 1920, as the be-all and end-all up front.

But encompassing a wider array of purposes gets us deeper into the interplay among the frequencies and makes clearer the need to conceive the trajectory as open-ended, avoiding telos. In considering supranational interaction over corporatism, as in so many areas of the overall discussion, we are too prone to take both sides as stable, given, rather than "in play," involved in open and interweaving trajectories, and thus ultimately embedded in a braided dynamic.

In the supranational interaction around corporatism, Germany was not at all central, but Italy was out front and attracted considerable attention, as we have noted at several points. Italy was important primarily as an exemplar and inspiration. Although eager to export its ideas, the Italian regime did not seek to impose a corporatist direction as a corollary of its territorial aspirations, nor, conversely, were those looking at the Italian model from the outside simply seeking to ingratiate themselves with Fascist Italy, whether from fear or from a desire to curry favor in light of territorial ambitions of their own. With corporatism, then, asymmetry in power relations was only minimally at work, and those looking at the Italian model from the outside were relatively free to pick and choose.

Moreover, we have already encountered indications that Italy attracted attention partly in interaction or even in competition with other models, especially from Portugal, Austria, and the Catholic tradition, which could seem to have been brought up to date with Pius XI's *Quadragesimo anno* of 1931. We noted that the corporatist thrust in Austria, for example, had indigenous sources in the thinking of Othmar Spann and Walter Heinrich, especially. Other disparate individual thinkers, such as Georges Valois, Mihail Manoilescu, L.R. Rosenstock-Franck, and Henri de Man, were also part of the mix at various times.[9] But even those finding something preferable in whatever combination of the other models were generally bouncing off the Italian example.

In light of the diverse rationales for them, corporatist ideas were of course contested, but awareness of the issues varied among those on the borrowing or receiving end, who could see and take what they wanted. John Pollard notes whereas many in various parts of Europe saw *Quadragesimo anno* as a papal endorsement of Fascist Italy, and whereas many Catholics were attracted to Fascist Italy because of its corporatist direction, the encyclical was in fact critical, rightly noting that Fascist corporatism was not Catholic in inspiration and charging that it meant regimentation of the workforce and dependence upon the state.[10]

Pinto and Musiedlak both note the centrality of the Italian case, and each treats it usefully as a baseline while pinpointing elements of heterogeneity and malleability that played into the interaction over corporatism. As we noted in chapter 3, Pinto usefully distinguishes between social and political modes of corporatism, with Italian influence largely confined to the former. But what thinking had led to the Italian social model? What might that model be made to entail, and what did those looking from the outside think it entailed?

In treating the Italian case, Pinto features Alfredo Rocco and the Nationalists as the most systematic theorists of integral corporatism and national syndicalism. And he sees Rocco's statism as "a strategy for the passive and subordinated integration of the masses into the state," especially contrasting with Catholicism.[11] But though Rocco's corporatism contrasted with the Catholic version in highly symptomatic ways, even for Rocco this characterization is too restrictive, based on unwarranted a priori assumptions. It is crucial, first, that Rocco did not propose mere demobilization; he insisted on the great value of the trade-union phenomenon. The problem was with the liberal framework, treating the unions as private entities. In his determination to retain the unions, making them state entities, he was not seeking merely to tame them. On the contrary, though his vision certainly entailed hierarchy and regimentation, corporatism was to be the vehicle for more intense politicization, to inculcate productivist values, to make everyone feel the political implications of their economic roles, and thereby to enable the state to tap into the newly focused energy of the masses. So whereas the masses were indeed to be "subordinated," they were not to be merely "passive."

More importantly, Rocco did not remotely speak for all Italian Fascist corporatists, yet Pinto, in featuring Rocco, offers nary a mention of the contrasting, Leftist syndicalist sources of the corporatist thrust in Fascist Italy. That tradition had a key role in giving the Italian Fascist regime a corporatist direction when, in light of the Matteotti crisis of 1924, it seemed essential for the fledgling Fascist regime to commit to a definite course of institutional change.[12] Nor does Pinto consider the broader support this syndicalist vision had already garnered, even among the early *squadristi*.[13] But the vision was then developed in wider Fascist circles, most notably by Giuseppe Bottai, minister of corporations, and arguably the most important Italian Fascist corporatist, who explicitly portrayed corporatism as carrying forward the ideas of 1789, in the face of those associating fascism with the counterrevolutionary tradition.[14] Corporatism also drew the active support of those like Arnaldo Volpicelli and Ugo Spirito, disciples of Giovanni Gentile who became significant corporatist publicists, trumpeting a vision much closer to Bottai's than to Rocco's.

In short, in Fascist Italy there were divisions over the basic rationale for a corporatist direction that were never overcome. We saw in chapter 3 that Pinto stressed the international impact of Fascist Italy's Labor Charter of 1927.[15] But we must keep in mind that the charter was a compromise in which Bottai and Rocco each had a hand. In the preparation of the document, Mussolini himself was instrumental in seeking to placate veteran syndicalists and to check Rocco's influence.[16] But whereas the Labor Charter reflected a cultivated ambiguity, the differences among Italian Fascist corporatists were sometimes clear and explicit, as with the revealing exchange of articles in 1926 between Sergio Panunzio, a veteran syndicalist, and Carlo Costamagna, who was much closer to Rocco's vision.[17]

For those like Panunzio coming to Fascism from the Left, trade-union membership and activity, including but not limited to strikes, had politicized the workers in the best sense, drawing them out of their narrow, individualistic world, teaching them to combine initiative with collaboration and even self-sacrifice when necessary. Integrated within the state, the unions could be vehicles for more constant and direct participation than the liberal parliamentary system had made possible. Without understanding how corporatism, on this basis, could have seemed promising, even exciting, we cannot grasp all that might have been at issue as the Italian case became central to the multinational interaction over corporatism.

Musiedlak, a major authority on the Italian Fascist state, is more attuned than Pinto to the heterogeneity in Italian corporatism. More specifically, he does greater justice to Leftist syndicalist sources, even finding them at the root of an ongoing "revolutionary" current within Italian Fascist corporatism. He plausibly traces that current to the corporatist constitution, the *Carta del Carnaro*, that the syndicalist Alceste De Ambris, with assistance from his fellow syndicalist A.O. Olivetti, elaborated for Gabriele D'Annunzio's outlaw "Regency" in the disputed city of Fiume (now Rijeka, Croatia) in 1920.[18] Although De Ambris rejected Fascism, many syndicalists, including Olivetti, adhered, partly because it seemed potentially the vehicle for the national syndicalist or corporatist revolution they had come to advocate.

In this context it is worth recalling that Renzo De Felice, in his famous interview of 1976, insisted explicitly that "D'Annunzian" corporatism was an important aspect of Italian Fascism as "movement" and must be taken seriously, even if the regime ended up reducing corporatism to a mere administrative instrument.[19] In other words, we must avoid telos and understand the aspirations fueling Fascism in the first place, whatever the outcomes.

But even Musiedlak's sense of the possibilities is too limited to enable him to convey the basis and implications of the alternative to Rocco's reading. Although, following Ruth Ben-Ghiat, he notes that into the 1930s corporatism was still seducing intellectuals and youth with its revolutionary and antibourgeois accents, he does not probe the basis of the alternative.[20] He might have considered why the *Carta del Carnaro*, in particular, continued to enjoy mythic status within Italian Fascism, affording an ongoing basis for associating corporatism with a genuinely revolutionary transformation having populist and productivist valences.

But above all, Musiedlak betrays confusion over how corporatism interfaced with totalitarianism in Italian thinking.[21] In implicitly, but quite clearly, associating totalitarianism with Rocco, contrasted with the revolutionary current, he fails to grasp how the alternative to Rocco's reading could also have been "totalitarian," albeit in a different way than Rocco's. We will discuss the Italian Fascist understanding of totalitarianism in chapters 7 and 8, but Musiedlak seems not to grasp how corporatism, revolution, and totalitarianism came together in Italian thinking, and thus he does not adequately convey the stakes of the interaction over corporatism, both in Italy and internationally. Although he is surely right that the statist mode that emerged in Fascist Italy voided corporatism of serious content, those outcomes stemmed not from totalitarianism per se but from the overall Fascist trajectory of which totalitarianism was but one strand.[22]

In treating corporatism outside Italy, Musiedlak certainly convinces that in the emerging Franco regime in Spain, the corporations established with the 1938 charter proved mostly a vehicle for suppressing the existing unions, seen as Marxist and anarchist bastions.[23] But we tend to be too quick with that sort of default setting insofar as we lack an adequate sense of the alternative secular reasons for a corporatist response to the trade-union phenomenon.

Turning again to Pinto, we note that he follows Juan Linz in arguing that corporatism encourages apoliticism and transforms issues into technical and administrative matters.[24] While recognizing some variation overall, Pinto goes on to feature the congruence between the organic-statist core of corporatist representation and the ideology of a single national interest, typical of the apoliticism of military thinking and conservative, anti-democratic elites.[25] These characterizations convince up to a point, but they are too quick to reduce corporatism to such apoliticism. Pinto's sense of politicization is too limited to conventional democracy to grasp the case against individualistic liberal democracy at the time—the sense that it atomizes, fragments, and does not nurture genuine political capacity. Without a better sense of that case, based on what experience with parliamentary democracy seemed to have revealed, we cannot understand why corporatism, even as—especially as—embedded within a wider totalitarianism, could have seemed to promise a superior alternative. But only on that basis can we grasp the possible stakes of the interaction over corporatism.

Among those Italian Fascists who favored a corporatist direction, those coming from the Left and the Right agreed on the inadequacy of parliamentary government and the need for a totalitarian alternative, to include more intense politicization, taking advantage of the trade-union phenomenon, making mandatory membership in occupationally based groupings the basis for a new kind of state. As founded on the workplace and thus on complementary economic roles, corporatism could foster an organic, productivist society with a sense of common long-term interests in a way that liberal individualism, party politics, and representation by elected politicians could not. But those favoring a corporatist direction differed over what the more intense politicization was to entail—over the extent to which it was merely to mobilize support and the extent to which it was to make possible new modes of participation and even initiative from below.

Though the Left and Right forms of Italian corporatism conflicted, each reflected actual experience with both liberal democracy and trade unionism. Precisely in this sense each was seeking an alternative modernity, as opposed to lapsing into mere nostalgia for a putative social harmony being undermined by modern trends. De Felice usefully insisted on the "modernity" of Italian Fascist corporatism in this sense; it did not derive from medieval guilds or from the social Catholicism that Giuseppe Toniolo had advocated in the late nineteenth century.[26]

We have emphasized, however, that Italian Fascism was a messy mixture, and the syndicalist and Nationalist currents we have pinpointed did not account for all the corporatist sentiment among those considering themselves Fascists. In the previous chapter we noted that though Pius XI's *Quadragesimo anno* was primarily an effort to reclaim corporatism for Catholic tradition against fascism, it was also read as giving a Catholic spin even to Italian Fascist corporatism, appealing to those seeking to harmonize their Fascist and Catholic sentiments. So the contest over corporatism in Fascist Italy was not confined to the Left and Right currents; there was plenty of scope for Catholics to weigh in. And so, again, those elsewhere could read what they wanted into Italian corporatist development and borrow selectively.

We noted above that though Italian Fascist corporatism was particularly influential, interaction was wider, more complex, allowing even more scope for picking and choosing, especially as other experiments developed and other ideas were offered. Indeed, we find a crisscrossing web of influences. Whether or not the resulting experiments and proposals were considered fascist at the time or are to be deemed fascist now, they assumed a place in the new Right universe, overlapping to some extent.

Peniston-Bird observes that Pius XI's *Quadragesimo anno* helped inspire quests for a corporatist "third way" in Austria, Portugal, Poland, and Spain.[27] The Portuguese experiment was influential in its own right partly because, as Pinto shows, Portugal seemed for a time to be advancing with greater determination than Italy toward a corporatist basis for political representation. Musiedlak notes that whereas Salazar's corporatism was inspired especially by Italy, in the last analysis it was more Catholic than Italian.[28] Certainly Portuguese corporatism seemed to embody Catholic tradition far more obviously than the Italian did. We have already indicated debts to the Portuguese departure on the part of the Austrian corporatist regime, on the one hand, and Pál Teleki in Hungary, on the other. Pinto shows that not only the Metaxas regime in Greece but the new constitution drafted in Slovakia, upon becoming a German protectorate 1939, similarly reflected the influence of Portuguese corporatism.[29] Even as he features Portugal's role, Pinto notes that Italian corporatism also influenced Metaxas, whereas Austrian corporatism also influenced Slovakia.[30]

At the same time, however, we must recognize that especially as embraced from above, corporatism could be a kind of fad, adopted but then dropped as other challenges or opportunities came to the fore. Whereas Pinto certainly convinces in noting Metaxas's interest, Kallis goes a step further, showing that whereas Metaxas began a horizontal restructuring of economic and trade-union relations reflecting Italian corporatism, the effort did not get far. By 1939 corporatism had disappeared from the Metaxas regime's rhetoric.[31]

Because those seeking new Right alternatives had their own traditions and concerns, we find an array of purposes underlying choices for a corpo-ratist direction, as Musiedlak emphasizes to especially good effect. Even in the same country, those embracing corporatism could have very different purposes, as we noted in the Italian case. In Romania, Mihail Manoilescu, a noted economist who served as a central banker and later, in 1940, as foreign minister, sought to make the Iron Guard corporatist as part of a program, much like that of Gömbös in Hungary, linked to autarky and a quest for more rapid economic development. He opposed democracy espe-cially because it gave too much power to the seemingly anti-modernizing peasantry. But whereas Corneliu Codreanu, the leading Guard figure until his death in 1938, also embraced corporatism, his vision, while not merely traditionalist, did not feature the sort of economic modernization so im-portant to Manoilescu.[32]

In chapter 3 we saw that Musiedlak notes tensions between modernizers and traditionalists among French corporatists in the 1930s, tensions that carried into the Vichy period.[33] This example, especially, makes clear that axes of differentiation in internal disputes over corporatism could differ in symptomatic ways from one country to the next. In Italy the currents de-riving from syndicalism and Nationalism, even as they differed significantly over other matters, were both modernizing, seeking to foster productivism against the culture of parasitism putatively fostered by Italian tradition and the scope for living off the favors of the parliamentary state.

In light of outcomes, we are especially prone today to dismiss corpo-ratism as a "sham" or "fraud." Tim Kirk concludes that "the reality of the Austrian corporate state was even more of a sham than that in Italy."[34] In the same way, Musiedlak contends that Salazar's corporatism, like the Italian, ended up pure façade.[35] We have good reason for such judgments today, but in making them we easily fall into teleological thinking, missing the uncertainty, the openness and scope for other outcomes, at the time. If we are to grasp the place of corporatism in the supranational interaction, we must keep in mind that it could not have been clear what a corporatist direction portended. The place of corporatism depended on its contingent interplay with other elements in a still-open trajectory.

In stressing the seriousness of the corporatist experiment in Fascist Italy, Alessio Gagliardi's study, cited in the preceding chapter, makes it clear that those looking to Italy from elsewhere were not only being taken in by sham, myth, or wishful thinking.[36] To be sure, no one denies that the corporatist thrust seriously bogged down in Italy, but Gianpasquale Santo-massimo notes the paradox that as the actual course of Italian corporatist development was producing disillusionment among its proponents, Italian Fascist corporatism was broadly influential on the international level, its putative achievements widely credited.[37] Though all the interaction over corporatism was essential to the texture of the epoch, corporatism was becoming a myth.

Increasing Asymmetry in the Italian-German Relationship

The fact that Italy, unlike Germany, was central to the interaction over corporatism indicates an important difference between the two that affected their relationship virtually from beginning to end—and that plays into the interweaving of the two asymmetries in complex ways. Even as the Italians and Germans both sought to influence others, their emphases differed, and partly for that reason, the Italian-German relationship became competitive even in light of their common asymmetrical relationship with the others. It is obvious that Fascist Italy ended up weaker than—even subservient to—Nazi Germany, so it became less attractive as a model and less able to impose its will. But to understand the evolution of that relationship and the place of that evolution in the wider trajectory of the aggregate, we must keep in mind that whereas the relationship was clearly *becoming* asymmetrical by the later 1930s, it was not asymmetrical from the start. Mussolini's regime came first, well before Hitler's, and even after Hitler came to power in 1933, Italy seemed the senior fascist power for several more years. Upon coming to power in 1933, Hitler expressed both an explicit debt to Mussolini and a sense of welcome political-ideological kinship. In principle, such kinship could have led simply to alliance and collaboration, but it also entailed the potential for rivalry.

Especially with their embrace of corporatism, totalitarianism, and Gentilian "spirit" as opposed to crudely deterministic biological racism, the Italians felt their form of fascism superior to Nazism in transcending the limits of both mainstream liberal-positivist culture and Marxism. On that basis the Italians believed themselves to be offering something more relevant and modern than Nazism. We have seen how Italian Fascist corporatism claimed to reflect modern experience and to embrace what had proven most valuable in the trade-union phenomenon. Considering Bauerkämper's account of Italian-German interaction in chapter 3, we noted the centrality of Gentile's "spiritualist" claim. In the little-known discussion among Nazi ideologues from 1933 to 1935 over the uses of "totalitarianism" as trumpeted by the Italians, the Germans explicitly invoked Gentile in associating Italian Fascist totalitarianism with a Hegelian statism they found incompatible with Nazism.

We can best ponder the particulars of that debate in chapter 7, where we consider the place of the "totalitarianism" category in the wider interaction at the time. But the debate makes clear the sense in which Italy remained the senior fascist power in the first years after Hitler became chancellor. The Nazis were learning from but then measuring themselves against the Italians, and the interaction, the developing sense of competition and rivalry, seems to have helped draw out and perhaps magnify differences, leading the Nazis even more to understand their departure in terms of an open-ended movement based on "blood." In light of the differences that the German discussion brought to the fore, outsiders might have found either the Italian or the German side more attractive on the basis of their respective arguments over the issue.

Differences in accent came most dramatically to the fore during this early period at the Montreux conference of 1934, the peak of efforts to foster some sort of fascist international. The Italians particularly sought to use the conference to establish their priority, with Italy as the spiritual and financial center of "universal fascism," comparable to the Soviet Union in world communism.[38] But while the Italians trumpeted their "spiritual," cultural conception, the Nazis emphasized a contrasting, race-based anti-Semitism. The conference split over the Jewish question, then agreed only to vague, general principles. The Italians left disappointed and let the grandiose internationalist enterprise drop, even as they continued to try to influence movements and regimes elsewhere, and even as the rivalry with Nazi Germany continued.

But especially as German assertiveness changed the international situation, the Italo-German relationship was bound to evolve. In an earlier study, Aristotle Kallis showed that the interaction between Mussolini and Hitler helped to radicalize the expansionist policies of both regimes, beyond what either initially had envisioned. But the impact became asymmetrical as Italy's relative weakness came to light, first after the two regimes intervened in the Spanish Civil War. Kallis noted that even as Mussolini oscillated between aggressiveness and peaceful diplomacy from 1938 to 1940, his increasing sense of inferiority and jealousy produced inflating international ambitions and a concomitant determination to regain the initiative.[39]

Meanwhile, the evolution of the Italo-German relationship itself changed the wider dynamic in Europe and even beyond, adding new challenges, possibilities, and opportunities, and thereby altering the situations to which others had to respond. Thus the changing relationship between Italy and Germany interfaced with the asymmetrical relationship between them, as the major fascist powers, and the lesser movements and regimes.

As we saw in the preceding chapter, the impact of their interaction on Austria, newly a rump state wedged between an enlarged yet still ambitious Italy and an aggrieved, revisionist Germany, was especially dramatic.

Indeed, interaction with both Italy and Germany significantly affected the domestic political interaction in Austria—an archetypal example of the braided dynamic.

By 1934, with the new post-liberal regime emerging, Austria was subject to Italian-German rivalry, reflecting not only the somewhat different ideological accents of the two fascist powers but also their radically different territorial and foreign policy concerns with respect to Austria. Italy's relations with the new Austria were especially sensitive because of Italian territorial gains at the expense of Austria, including German-speaking areas in the South Tyrol (Trentino-Alto Adige), as a result of World War I. But the threat to Italy, in light of such ethnic complexities, came primarily from Germany, should Germany incorporate the rump Austria in an Anschluss, producing an enlarged Germany on Italy's northern border. While Italy aggressively opposed it, the Nazis made it clear that they intended precisely such an Anschluss, though it had been specifically precluded by the Paris peace treaties.

Still acting independently in 1934, Italy helped head off the first effort by the new Nazi regime to annex Austria. But the dramatic change in the relationship between Italy and Germany between 1934 and 1938 significantly affected Austrian politics. As we have seen, the decline of influence of the Heimwehr from 1934 until its dissolution in 1936 was arguably determined more by the increasingly cordial relationship between Italy and Germany than by internal developments in Austria.[40] Less concerned to resist Nazi pressures in Austria, Italy pulled back from its political and financial support for the Heimwehr, which lost influence as a result. And returning to Peniston-Bird's point that the chancellor, in dissolving the Heimwehr, was seeking to placate *both* the Germans and the democracies, we note that the Heimwehr had long been identified with Italian influence, and in 1936 Italy's invasion of Ethiopia was making Mussolini's regime increasingly unpopular in significant sectors of the democracies.[41]

When, in March 1938, the Anschluss ended the corporatist experiment in Austria, Italy was willing to acquiesce, in marked contrast to its stand in 1934. In one sense, Fascist Italy's readiness to ditch the Austrian regime indicated a determination to play for higher stakes, especially in the Mediterranean, where Italy had designs on Greece and the Middle East, as Nazi Germany did not. So let us consider a few further examples to assess the role of the increasingly asymmetrical relationship between Italy and Germany.

In an especially well-researched study, Manuela Williams probes Fascist Italy's propaganda effort in the Middle East, especially Palestine and Egypt, during the 1930s.[42] Drawing out certain implications of her account can help us better to grasp the complex, interpenetrating layers of interaction during the period. Seeking to portray itself as a counter to British and French imperialism, Italy was caught up first in relations with the Arabs, but then also in relations with those competitors, especially the British. The relationship with the Germans became more salient as a result of the outcome on those first two levels.[43] And the multipronged external interaction, with its unforeseen results, affected the overall internal trajectory of Italian Fascism.

Many, but not all, disaffected Arab intellectuals took a sympathetic interest in Fascism and Nazism in light of perceived problems with democracy, quite apart from their resentments of British and French colonialism. And as Williams tells it, the Italians, as revisionists who could claim, at least, to be sympathetic to revisionist nationalism in general, did reasonably well for a time at reaching out to them, through Arabic-language broadcasts, for example, and in recruiting Egyptians to attend Italian schools. Meanwhile, British perceptions of Italy were also at issue, though as late as 1939 the British response to the Italian campaign was generally cumbersome and flat-footed, surely enhancing Italian confidence. Partly because they found overt, fascist-style propaganda morally objectionable, British policymakers were reluctant to respond in kind to the Italian effort.

Despite success up to a point, however, the Italians held a dubious hand. In wooing the Arabs, Italian propagandists sought to minimize Italy's violent colonial record and to promote Mussolini as a champion of Islam. As early as 1935, that effort split Arab nationalists in Palestine, pitting pro-Italian elements against those pointing to Italy's imperialist aspirations and harsh treatment of Libya. Williams concludes that because Italian ambitions were too obvious, Italy did not profit from the decline of British prestige. Moreover, the British, becoming more aggressive by mid-1939, finally had some success in undercutting the Italian effort. And by that point, the comparison between Fascist Italy and Nazi Germany was coming into play. Many Arabs found Nazi Germany more attractive, precisely because Germany seemed to have fewer ambitions in the Arab world.

This example suggests that what initially looks like a simple instance of asymmetry may prove to entail considerably more complex interactions in dynamic relationship. It was not simply that Nazi Germany muscled Italy out or even that the Arabs ended up opting for the stronger side. In the last analysis, what compromised the Italian effort was not overt resistance on the part of the apparently weaker Arabs or the greater strength of Nazi Germany, but the cognitive dissonance we have already noted in Italian Fascism.

As Williams's study shows, the Fascist departure could be dynamic and effective up to a point, but then it encountered the contradictions, even the self-defeating quality, inherent in the overall effort. The regime was trying to do too much at once, and its efforts proved largely wasted because they ended up canceling each other out. Although Williams does not make the point explicitly, the Fascists had come to believe their own propaganda, including the myth that Italian imperialism was different. From within the new mode of action they had initiated, they were decreasingly able to assess the situation realistically, facing up to contradictions and making coherent choices. So the multiple interactions in this case proved to bring out the hollowness and ephemerality of Italian Fascism.

We find another indication of the need to look beneath seeming instances of asymmetry in the trajectory of the Organization of Ukrainian Nationalists (OUN), which changed its orientation from Fascist Italy to Nazi Germany during the later 1930s. As John-Paul Himka shows, this occurred especially because Hitler appeared to be gearing up for war against the Soviet Union, which seemed the major enemy of Ukrainian nationalism. So the change in orientation was not simply to bend to pressure or to go with the stronger of the two fascist powers.[44] And the turn to a more ferocious anti-Semitism in the OUN seems a matter of currying favor with Germany, as opposed to turning toward Germany *because* it was more obviously anti-Semitic than Fascist Italy. The overall change in orientation proves not so much an example of asymmetry but of the diachronic dimension of the overall interaction, the interface of changing trajectories.

But even if the power differential between Germany and Italy was not always as important as it may seem in retrospect, the relationship surely became more asymmetrical as Fascist Italy and Nazi Germany came together during 1936–38 and as Germany's greater clout became clear by the eve of World War II. The interplay of the relationship with the trajectory of the Metaxas experiment in Greece is especially instructive.

As in the Austrian case, both Fascist Italy and Nazi Germany had reason to interact with the Greek experiment, and Metaxas had reason to interact with each of them. But interaction with the two stronger powers came into play in different ways in different phases of the trajectory. Again as in Austria, the changing relationship between Italy and Germany affected the interface, but in Greece, in contrast to Austria, the asymmetry in that relationship came dramatically to the fore. At the same time, in Greece, too, interaction with the other powers very much affected the new Right direction on the domestic level.

Mogens Pelt argues that the establishment of the Metaxas dictatorship can be seen as a response to the increasing militarization of international relations and the incipient arms race initiated by the fascist powers. The potential Italian threat to Greece, evident even during the 1920s, became all too real with the Italian assault on Ethiopia in 1935. Whereas Greece had been linked to Britain and France, the changing power balance seemed to suggest to Metaxas and his circle that Greek interests could best be served by tilting toward Nazi Germany, which had no designs on Greece. Economic and armament considerations also came into play, as did hopes that Germany would restrain Bulgaria in its claims on Greece growing from the World War I settlement. And for complicated reasons, preventing government by either of the two major, and warring, parliamentary factions seemed necessary if such a reorientation of Greek foreign policy was to be cemented.[45] Thus, in part, it was so important for Metaxas to develop a viable, new Right alternative to the parliamentary regime.

At the same time, Metaxas had to go around the monarchy, which maintained its long-standing pro-British orientation, to develop closer relations with Germany. But increasingly self-confident by 1938–39, he did so, though he sought to avoid antagonizing Britain at the same time.[46] The fact that the British rejected a new security pact with Greece in October 1938 suggested that they could not be counted on and strengthened Metaxas's position vis-à-vis the king.[47] But after war began, Mussolini, determined to seize the initiative to the extent possible, embarked on a "parallel war" of aggression in Greece in October 1940. And ironically the disastrous failure of that effort, from the Italian perspective, prompted Germany to conquer Greece and install a particularly brutal occupation regime in June 1941.

The outcome in Greece at once reflected and reinforced the asymmetry already coming to the fore in the relationship between Italy and Germany. We have seen that differences in the military performance of the two sides as they intervened in the Spanish Civil War brought home German superiority. Beyond that, Hitler's string of foreign-policy successes by 1939 seemed to leave Italy scrambling to catch up. Yet, famously, Mussolini had to tell Hitler that Italy would not be prepared for a major war until 1943. Partly because of domestic opposition, Mussolini's Italy could only remain on the sidelines when war began in September 1939. Italy finally intervened in France only at the end, in June 1940, in time to share in the spoils, which included a role in the occupation of France.

Still, though the asymmetry had become obvious by that point and necessarily frames our understanding of the later German-Italian relationship, its implications for the Italian trajectory and for Italy's interaction with others on the new Right are not so easily pinned down. It entailed considerable Italian subservience, but awareness of the developing asymmetry fueled further efforts on the part of the Italians to differentiate themselves from the Germans at the same time. Thus in part the recklessness and overreach of Italian policy, most notably Mussolini's decision to launch the "parallel war" in Greece in October 1940.

Up to a point, the outcome in Greece not only manifested the asymmetry but also reinforced it. As in France the year before, Italy was allotted a share in the occupation of Greece and Croatia in the wake of German victory in the Balkans, but as Davide Rodogno has shown, the Germans conceded the Italians extremely narrow margins for maneuver in both areas, as they had in France. Yet if anything, the Italian Fascist self-understanding became even more unrealistic as a result. From within this framework it seemed still more important to assert Fascist Italy's cultural superiority over Nazi Germany. Though such claims seem clearly to have been at once mythmaking and nakedly self-serving, we need to understand their implications both for the Italian trajectory and for Italy's interaction with others on the new Right.

The challenge is to do justice both to the asymmetrical framework and to those more subtle implications. Rodogno's study of the Italian occupation effort during World War II is invaluable in many ways, not least in engaging, if mostly only implicitly, the double asymmetry in Italy's relations with Germany and in the relations of both with the occupied territories.[48] He nicely draws out certain implications of the Italian-German asymmetry that affected the wider dynamic. But in the last analysis he ends up so determined to accent Italian subservience, even on the ideological level, that he glosses over the scope for an alternative reading that seems to make better sense even of some of his own evidence.[49]

Let us first get onto the table some key aspects of what Rodogno has shown. Once the Italians had achieved a foothold in their occupation zones, they sought to carve out a broader role than Germany was willing to grant. They assumed that a victorious Germany would respect the Italian sphere once the war was over—an assumption that persisted into 1943, even as the tide of war turned. At the same time, Rodogno recognizes a good deal of dedication, enterprise, and adaptability among those implementing Italian policy; they were not remotely resigned to defeat.[50] But he also goes beyond to note that despite the common insistence on a new order, including *Lebensraum* for Germany and *spazio vitale* for Italy, there were significant differences both in concepts of empire and in policies in the respective occupation zones.

As we have noted, the Italians were bound to resent their subordinate status after having spearheaded fascism and started as an equal partner in the Axis. It was partly to suppress recognition of that status that the Italians deluded themselves into believing they still enjoyed autonomy in their occupation space—and into acting accordingly. At the same time, determination to maximize their autonomy led the Italians to play up their differences with the Germans, even over the meaning of the war and the nature of the new order under construction.[51]

Above all, the Italians claimed to be playing a more positive role, more attentive to the needs of local populations, than the exploitative Germans, and to some extent they genuinely sought to do so. In Greece, for example, the Italian army helped to increase crop yields and to restore public utilities and public health as they sought to display Italian concern for Greek well-being. During much of 1942, that program won the admiration of some Greeks, up to a point. But economic difficulties made it increasingly difficult for the Italians to sustain these efforts.[52]

More generally, the Fascists trumpeted a quasi-Mazzinian vision of enduring international peace that allegedly distinguished Italy both from Nazi Germany, envisioning endless Darwinian struggle, and from the capitalist powers, driven by their need for economic exploitation. This vision was bound up with a claim to value ethnic-national diversity. Whereas the Nazis stressed racial domination, the Italians sought simply to make race, nation, and state coincide. Even the effort to impose ethnic homogeneity on the new provinces was an indication that nations were to be valued, not subjugated. As long as they accepted Italian predominance, Albania and Croatia, made ethnically homogeneous, would be welcomed into the Italian imperial community.[53]

But even as Rodogno usefully gets all this onto the table, and even as he is certainly right to feature the discrepancy between Italian ambitions and accomplishments, he is quick to invoke the asymmetry to explain what happened, rather than follow the contingent play of elements in a trajectory of multiple interaction. That would entail, first, more consistently taking seriously that the difference in originating vision remained. As it is, he is quick to conflate Italian and German practices, explaining away Italian differences in instrumental or pragmatic terms. For example, although Italian efforts in Greece to help Italian Jews get to the Italian zone suggest something approaching a concerted rescue effort, he reduces them to economic considerations, the desire to keep the assets of these Jews from falling to the Germans. Elsewhere, he explains away apparently humanitarian impulses in terms of propaganda value. What looked like an Italian "rescue operation" in Croatia was but an effort to show the Balkan peoples that Italy was resisting the Germans and dealing independently with Croatian authorities.[54]

In short, Rodogno is so determined to play up subservience that he tends to explain away what seem genuine and enduring differences in vision. Despite some undoubted elements of ideological subservience, the Italians genuinely thought they were doing, and genuinely tried to do, something different. And up to a point this difference surely could have affected the relations of both Italy and Germany with others, both on the new Right and beyond, in the occupied territories. Recognizing this enables us to delineate more convincingly what happened to that vision—and the implications of what happened for Italian policy and for Italian relations with others.

It was not simply that Italy had no choice but to fall in behind Nazi Germany. The need to deny the actual degree of subservience led the Italians to play up the genuine differences, and to some extent exaggerate them, thereby compensating for relative military weakness. But thus they descended ever deeper into mythmaking and wishful thinking, glossing over the contradictions into which they had become enmeshed by this point—in their thinking about race and nationality in the Balkans, for example, but especially in their whole self-image as conquerors who were promoting national identity and a more just international order. Thus they misread their actual prospects—and how they were likely to come across to others.

Rodogno convincingly argues that the Italian combination of intransigence, vacillation, and impotence ultimately bred contempt on all sides in the occupied territories.[55] But we must better account for the mythmaking, wishful thinking, and contradiction among the Italians if we are to understand this outcome and its implications for the web of interaction—and thus for the aggregate on the new Right. To some, at least, and in some ways, the tendencies of Italian policy surely made Nazi Germany, brutal though it was, look better by comparison.

The Italian mythmaking at issue was neither a constant nor a telos but emerged in response to a contingent conjuncture within an ongoing process entailing the interaction of strands and changing proportions. But this outcome particularly made for hollowness and ephemerality. And though the proportions are undecidable, the debilitating discrepancy between Italian ambitions and accomplishments may have stemmed less from German domination than from such mythmaking and contradiction. In any case, we cannot even address the question without a more imaginative consideration of the possibilities within the asymmetrical relationship than we find in Rodogno's account, indispensable though it is.

Nazi Germany in Asymmetrical Interaction with Others over Territorial and Population Matters

Although Peter Sugar convinces on the indigenous emergence of fascist-style movements in the successor states of the Austro-Hungarian Empire, the trajectories there and elsewhere in east-central and southeastern Europe eventually proved inseparable from wider interaction, especially with Nazi Germany.[56] And that interaction took place from within the framework that had resulted contingently from World War I, which produced a vast territorial shake-up in these regions, with clear winners and losers, and with some of the losers having claims on some of the winners. These countries were caught up together in epochal interaction in the wake of the postwar settlement. Our challenge is to specify, to the extent possible, the place of the German relationship in the complex, contingent trajectories yielding fascistizing directions and horrific outcomes during World War II, even as the most overtly fascist formations—the Arrow Cross in Hungary and the Iron Guard in Romania—were actively suppressed or marginalized, at least for most of the period.

We noted that in Austria, division over the desirability of an Anschluss, as opposed to maintaining independence, based to some extent on a Catholic identity, helped fuel the rivalry between the Austrian Nazis and the Heimwehr and helps explain the contrasting appeals of Nazi Germany and Fascist Italy. But even in Austria, aspirations for territorial revision led some to look to seemingly resurgent Germany, quite apart from *völkisch*, pan-German considerations. Lothar Höbelt notes that though the Austrian aristocracy leaned toward the Heimwehr and away from the Nazis, some, mostly younger aristocrats supported the Austrian Nazis because understanding with Germany seemed to promise the chance to reacquire German-speaking lands lost as a result of World War I. He cites as a key example the Grusbach circle of Austro-Bohemian nobles who wanted Austrian-German cooperation in pressure on Czechoslovakia.[57]

So even the Austrian case indicates that relations with Germany, while asymmetrical, were not merely bilateral, quite apart from the place of Italy. The new postwar framework entailed a complex web of relationships—including Austria-Czechoslovakia in this case—and we can consider only a few especially symptomatic aspects bound up with the advent of World War II. Especially during the first years of the war, 1939–42, relationships were especially complex, and phases sometimes succeeded each other rapidly. It is crucial to keep in mind that in the wake of the Nazi-Soviet Pact of August 1939, Germany collaborated with the Soviet Union for almost two years before attacking the country in June 1941. The European war took on a very different character thereafter.

In several cases the trajectories fueled by interaction with Nazi Germany were relatively short. Germany conquered Poland and dismembered Czechoslovakia and Yugoslavia, setting up puppet states in Slovakia and the former Yugoslavia. Only Hungary and Romania fully collaborated with Nazi Germany as sovereign states. They did so especially in light of their territorial concerns, though as it happened they had the most important fascist movements in Europe outside Italy and Germany, movements actively pushing for collaboration with Nazi Germany on wider ideological grounds. Hungary and Romania present the most instructive cases and most demand our attention.

Space permitting, Bulgaria might also be considered. It, too, had territorial aspirations but had hoped to pursue them peacefully. It adhered to the Axis bloc only in March 1941, several months after Hungary and Romania, and its adherence stemmed especially from German coercion as Germany was preparing to invade Yugoslavia and Greece. Bulgaria ended up sharing in the Axis occupation of the Balkans, and its domestic and occupation policies, like those of Hungary and Romania, were fascistizing in some respects. But Bulgaria's domestic fascist movement was never as strong. Moreover, unlike Hungary and Romania, it did not join Nazi Germany in the assault on the Soviet Union that began in June 1941. So while significant, the Bulgarian case is ultimately less instructive than the Hungarian and Romanian cases.

The relationships of Hungary and Romania with Nazi Germany are usefully considered in tandem because in important measure the concerns of the two countries were diametrically opposed, yet each ended up in the German orbit, though to some extent as rivals. Whereas Hungary had been one of the great losers as a result of World War I, Romania had been a notable winner, largely, but not exclusively, at the expense of Hungary. Still, in light of geography and the results of the war, neither of their respective relationships with Nazi Germany can be disembedded from a wider web of contingent relationships with other nearby countries.

In treating the Hungarian and Romanian cases in the previous chapter, we noted how difficult it is to separate domestic considerations from interaction with Germany beginning as early as 1936. By focusing here on the other side of the equation, we can consider the extent to which the asymmetrical relationship with Nazi Germany interfaced with domestic politics to fuel the fascistization in each case.

On joining the Allied side in World War I in August 1916, Romania was promised Transylvania, which was then part of Hungary, in the event of victory. Despite making a separate peace in April 1918, Romania not only gained Transylvania but roughly doubled in area and population to encompass virtually all ethnic Romanians and several significant minority groups. Although this expansion came especially at the expense of Hungary, Bulgaria and the Soviet Union also had claims on Romania in light of the postwar territorial settlement.

Hungary was particularly subject to resentments and irredentist aspirations in light of the territorial losses imposed by the Treaty of Trianon in 1920. The country lost more than two-thirds of its prewar territory to Romania and the new states of Czechoslovakia and Yugoslavia, and those three countries would be the obvious targets of Hungarian irredentism. Hungary suffered partly from Georges Clemenceau's determination, even in violation of principles of ethnicity and self-determination, to maximize the weight of Czechoslovakia, Romania, and Yugoslavia so that they might replace Russia as an eastern bulwark against Germany.

Whereas Hungary was revisionist during the interwar period, with territorial ambitions especially at the expense of Romania, Romania sought to preserve the status quo, taken as the new normal. The Little Entente of Czechoslovakia, Romania, and Yugoslavia came together in 1921 partly as a deterrent against Hungarian revisionism. But above all, until the later 1930s, Romania thought that it could rely first on France, but also on the League of Nations, pledged to preserve the territorial integrity of its members. However, Romania found itself being sucked into the German orbit as it came to seem that it could not count on either France or the League.

For its part Hungary first sought to cultivate British support for territorial revision during the 1920s, with little success. As Nazi Germany began shaking things up by the mid-1930s, Hungarian revisionists began looking toward Germany instead. So whereas the German relationship with both Hungary and Romania was clearly asymmetrical, the interaction was multinational, and the Hungarian-Romanian antagonism complicated the relationship. Partly thus, the asymmetry would play out differently in the two cases, enabling new Right departures with some instructive differences, and different places in the new Right universe.

More specifically, these two cases especially make clear that in the wartime context territorial concerns alongside Nazi Germany could feed population engineering and even ethnic cleansing or extermination. As we have noted, Kallis has delineated persuasively the overall role of Nazi Germany as a catalyst for indigenous efforts at ethnic cleansing all over Europe during World War II, but in every case, including the Hungarian and Romanian, we encounter questions about the role of asymmetry in the complex interaction at work.[58]

To invoke asymmetry is not to deny any degree of autonomy on the weaker side, and Hungary's interaction with Nazi Germany entailed a measure of contingency, subtlety, and pulling and tugging to the bitter end. So to understand how this particular asymmetrical relationship played out, we must follow the sequence of steps and the interplay of strands, showing how they yielded a contingent trajectory, even an unforeseen synergy, enabling a fascistizing direction and a horrific outcome that could not have been anticipated beforehand.

Especially because, on the basis of ethnicity and self-determination, the peace settlement could have been considered unfair to Hungary, Hungarian revisionism was surely plausible. And revisionist aspirations were widespread across the Hungarian political spectrum.[59] In itself such revisionism was not fascist or definitive of the new Right, but it could easily feed the new Right and even fascistization, especially as it led Hungary toward Nazi Germany.

Still, it must be remembered that the new Hungarian-German relationship was not initially about "fascism" but about territorial adjustment, in light of territorial aims widely shared among Hungarians. So the quest for territorial revision did not in itself mean ideological kinship, but neither were the two strands likely to remain entirely separate in light of Hungary's need for German support. The asymmetry in the relationship stemmed not only from greater German power but also from the territorial ambitions that made Hungary so readily sucked into the German orbit.

We note the contrast between the Hungarian situation and that of Austria, which, though also defeated and dismembered, had an Anschluss, wound around pan-Germanism, as one possibility. Folding within a greater Germany, which would mean losing Austria's autonomy as a Catholic nation, might be ardently desired or ardently resisted, but the very possibility meant that Austria's relationship with Nazi Germany was bound to be very different from Hungary's.

Germany's seeming foreign policy successes, including the Anschluss, at once inspired the Hungarian extreme Right and fed support for the Arrow Cross—from within the military, among other sectors.[60] But on certain of the questions at issue, the Arrow Cross was more moderate than other revisionists who were more centrist in some respects. It claimed to envision cultural pluralism and autonomy, though under Hungarian leadership and excluding Jews and Roma, should Hungarian territory be restored.[61] In 1940, with Hungary at last achieving some of its territorial goals, two Arrow Cross members of parliament proposed a bill to realize the party's program of cultural autonomy for ethnic minorities. But the very proposal led to accusations of treason by the conservative government.[62] In this volatile, rapidly changing situation, it was often hard to tell who was the more radical or who was pushing or pulling whom.

It was surely plausible for Hungary to look to Germany for help in recovering lost territories, but the Germans were not very encouraging at first. Seeking to maintain good relations with Romania and Yugoslavia, they told Hungarian leaders that adjustments would only be at the expense of Czechoslovakia.[63] And in the wake of, first, the Munich agreement of September 1938, and then the dismemberment of Czechoslovakia in March 1939, Hungary regained two areas that had been lost to Czechoslovakia after the war. This even gave Hungary a border with Poland. But these acquisitions at the expense of the former Czechoslovakia could not have been sufficient, given Hungarian claims especially against Romania, but also against Yugoslavia. Yet, working alongside Germany, Hungary managed substantial territorial gains at the expense of Romania in 1940 and Yugoslavia early in 1941.

Still, it was only because of wider exogenous factors that Germany became willing to go further to assist Hungary. Those contingencies played into the German-Hungarian relationship in complicated ways, sometimes enhancing and sometimes diminishing the scope for Hungarian agency.

The opportunity for Hungary to advance its demands against Romania depended first on the unforeseen framework of the Nazi-Soviet Pact. Soviet demands led Romania to cede territory that Russia had lost to Romania in the postwar settlement. Hungary sought to take advantage of Romanian vulnerability to make its own demands on Romania, and the Germans were willing to go along, but only up to a point. Fearing a joint Soviet-Hungarian move against Romania, which might jeopardize German access to Romanian oil fields, Germany imposed a diplomatic solution, restoring roughly 40 percent of Transylvania to Hungary. Hungary had a chance to gain territory at the expense of Yugoslavia the next year thanks only to the fortuitous combination of Italy's military failure in Greece and the indigenous coup in Yugoslavia that ousted the pro-German government, prompting Hitler to intervene and dismember Yugoslavia. In this case, Hungary was dragged along.

It is widely agreed that the regent, Miklos Horthy, disliked Nazism and disliked working with Nazi Germany. He was certainly willing to assert Hungary's interests and sought to preserve its autonomy. When Germany was preparing to invade Poland in 1939, Hungary refused to allow German troops to pass through Hungary to get to Poland.[64] After the Germans conquered Poland, Horthy especially angered Hitler by giving asylum to many Polish officers and officials.[65] But by first exploiting Germany's dismemberment of Czechoslovakia, then taking advantage of the complexities in Germany's relations with Romania, and finally joining Germany in war against Yugoslavia, Hungary regained almost 40 percent of its lost territory.[66] And despite his ongoing nervousness about working with Germany, Horthy was willing to take credit for the initial fruits of the relationship. In the aftermath of the annexation of part of Transylvania, amid celebrations in Hungary, he entered the new Hungarian territory on a white horse.[67]

Territorial ambition overrode hesitations about Nazi Germany and even engendered wishful thinking that neutralized doubts about Germany's ability to win the war. In that regard the fate of Pál Teleki as prime minister from February 1939 to April 1941 is especially symptomatic. In the preceding chapter we encountered Teleki's dislike of Nazism and corresponding attraction to Portuguese corporatism. Because of Hungary's territorial revisionism, however, he was bound to interact more with Nazi Germany than with Salazar's Portugal. Still, as a traditionalist conservative Catholic, he was made prime minister in February 1939 in an effort both to rein in the radical Right and to moderate the influence of Nazi Germany.

Teleki was more reluctant than most in the Hungarian leadership to go along with Germany, not only because he disliked Nazism but also because he doubted the scope for a durable German victory.[68] Here we have another indication of the importance, at the time, of differential perceptions, of the need for best guesses, easily tempered by selective readings and wishful thinking. When Germany demanded that Hungary participate in the attack on Yugoslavia, Teleki, doubting that Germany could prevail over the long term, sought to minimize Hungarian responsibility in the eyes of the Western powers. It was apparently the unfavorable reply from London that prompted his suicide on 3 April 1941.[69]

But Teleki was becoming isolated in any case, as German successes seemed to belie his perceptions. Horthy, supported by the cabinet and the majority in parliament, agreed to Hungarian participation in the assault on Yugoslavia in exchange for the promise of further territorial gains—which, as we noted, were promptly forthcoming.[70]

On 27 June 1941, five days after the German invasion of the Soviet Union, Hungary joined Germany, declaring war on the Soviet Union and quickly occupying large areas of Ruthenia (now in Ukraine) that had been part of pre-1918 Hungary. In its treatment of Jews in these new territories, the Hungarian government, facing calls from the extreme Right for a radical solution, maintained a semblance of law and even sought to foster relatively humane treatment in organizing forced labor companies. Isolated atrocities were punished.[71] Horthy dragged his feet even in implementing the third anti-Semitic law, and he resisted the increasing German pressures, beginning in 1942, to deport Hungarian Jews to Nazi extermination camps.

Meanwhile, Horthy and the governing party maintained their effort to confine the Arrow Cross and the extreme Right to a marginal role. To be sure, as the war in the Soviet Union began clearly to go badly by early 1943, it became increasingly unpopular in Hungary, and that in itself contributed to the dramatic decline in support for the Arrow Cross.[72] However, the Arrow Cross might still threaten the Hungarian establishment insofar as it enjoyed German support, which varied, though it never exceeded certain bounds until fall 1944. The Nazis were ambivalent about Arrow Cross leader Ferenc Szálasi, and some saw Horthy as the key to preserving order in Hungary in any case.[73] As we have noted, Hitler preferred working with relatively predictable conservatives like Horthy to promoting untried firebrands like Szálasi, even if they were more clearly "fascist" in some sense. Not all Nazis agreed, but insofar as the Germans got what they wanted from Horthy and the governing party, they were not likely to elevate Szálasi and the Arrow Cross. Conversely, Horthy and the governing party could keep Szálasi and the Arrow Cross marginalized by continuing to work with Germany, though obviously there were other reasons for working with Germany as well.

In principle, the Arrow Cross might have become more aggressive, stepped up the pressure, more obviously competing with the government.

But the fate of the Romanian Iron Guard gave pause—an especially dramatic instance of negative interaction. As we noted in the previous chapter, the Romanian leader Ion Antonescu, with Hitler's acquiescence, violently suppressed the Guard in January 1941, though it still enjoyed significant support from within the Nazi hierarchy. Worried that the Arrow Cross might suffer a comparable fate, Szálasi became very cautious. Maria Ormos surmises that such concerns dictated his behavior up to September 1944, when a change in regime was on the horizon.[74] But such caution surely contributed to the marginalization of the Arrow Cross, even as the overall direction of Hungarian policy remained "fascistizing" in important respects. Conversely, it is important to note that the fascistizing direction continued despite the decline in support for the Arrow Cross.

In keeping the Arrow Cross at bay, and in consciously *not* doing what the Germans would have preferred on occasion, Hungarian leaders could feel not just autonomous but still respectably conservative as opposed to fascist, whatever the fascistizing direction of significant governmental policies. Such moderating no doubt served as a kind of safety valve, helping to make not only the relationship with Germany but also the fascistizing domestic policy more acceptable in their own eyes. And in that indirect, paradoxical sense, the moderating helped fuel the radicalizing, fascistizing direction.

By later 1943, the Soviets were rapidly advancing westward, prompting Horthy to explore switching sides. To head off the possibility, Germany occupied Hungary on 19 March 1944. Still, the Germans, facing manpower and other constraints, wanted a constitutional outcome without the use of force. So they were willing to compromise, keeping Horthy as head of state and engaging in genuine negotiations over the composition of the new government. Horthy insisted successfully that a fellow military officer, General Döme Sztójay, who had been ambassador to Germany, be installed as prime minister and that the Arrow Cross remain precluded from the government.

Still, the new Sztójay government immediately began implementing much of the program of the radical Right, dissolving the Social Democratic Party and the agrarian reformist Independent Smallholders Party. But above all, the government moved more radically in the anti-Semitic direction we discussed in the preceding chapter. As we noted, the first steps in that direction stemmed primarily from domestic pressures as opposed to direct pressure from Germany. We also noted just above that Horthy had moderated Hungarian Jewish policy and, above all, had resisted German pressures for the deportation of Hungary's Jews. But after the German occupation the Sztójay government not only began closing and expropriating all Jewish stores but began deporting Hungarian Jews, almost exclusively to Auschwitz. Jews were rounded up by zone, with those from Budapest to be deported last. At first the Jews of Budapest were simply forced to move to houses marked with yellow stars.

The relative importance of German pressure and domestic initiative in the Hungarian deportations has long been controversial and obviously cannot be determined definitively. But clearly the Hungarians were not simply doing the Germans' bidding, let alone being coerced. Indeed, only full-scale Hungarian involvement made the deportations possible.[75] Adolf Eichmann planned the deportations in concert with Hungarian officials, leaving it to the Hungarians to carry out the policy. And the government proved quite zealous in stripping Jews of their last remaining liberties and in organizing the deportations.[76] The German occupation simply removed barriers to what the extreme Right had wanted.

But the context of Hungarian Jewish policy continued to change, in some ways contingently, making evaluation ever more difficult and the place of the Hungarian trajectory in the new Right universe ever harder to specify. After 437,000 Jews had been deported, Horthy ordered a halt on 7 July 1944, and he resisted German efforts to enforce a resumption of the deportations thereafter. Responding to worldwide protests, he was especially trying to curry favor with the democracies prior to changing sides or simply leaving the war. Resistance to German demands seemed the key to convincing the Allies that Hungary had been coerced by the Germans—and thus to obtaining lenient treatment. Conversely, German pressure on Hungary to deport its Jews to the Nazi extermination camps had been increasingly fueled by a concern to keep Hungary on the German side.[77] Insofar as the Hungarians could be forced to hand over the Hungarian Jews, they could no longer claim resistance in their discussions with the Allies and would more likely remain bound to Germany.

Meanwhile, Romania switched sides on 23 August, under circumstances that we will consider below, and for Peter Longerich that decisively deepened Horthy's determination to check the anti-Semitic direction. Horthy specified that Jews were not to be deported but confined to camps. He then gave prime minister Géza Lakatos, with whom he had recently replaced Sztójay, an explicit order, kept secret from the Germans, to end the persecution of the Jews. By late August, however, the Germans seem to have given up the expulsion effort in any case; Longerich surmises that it had come to seem counterproductive as an effort to bind Hungary to Germany.[78]

Meanwhile, Horthy was indeed seeking to negotiate Hungary's exit from the war. Although he had at first hoped simply to get out, prompting the Germans to leave Hungary, as they had done in Finland, the rivalry with Romania seemed to mandate switching sides instead. Romania, in joining the Soviet side, had sought to reopen the question of Transylvania, and though the Soviets seemed sympathetic, they avoided definite commitments. As Horthy took his turn in secret negotiations with the Soviet Union, he got nothing on Transylvania. But the fact that Transylvania was back on the table meant that Hungary was now competing with Romania for favor with the Allies. Greater leniency in treating the Jews could be expected to help Hungary's case. So in another contingency, the Hungarian-Romanian relationship seems even to have affected Hungarian policy toward the Jews at this key moment.

In late September, Soviet forces reached the eastern border of Hungary, and on 15 October Horthy announced that Hungary was leaving the war. The Germans knew this was coming, however, and quickly launched a well-prepared coup, toppling Horthy and installing an Arrow Cross government, with Szálasi at last in power as both head of state and head of government. To give the governmental transition a pretense of legality, the Germans forced Horthy into a face-saving signature and sent him to Germany under German protection. The coup kept Hungary in the war, so the Soviets invaded.[79]

And the arrival of the Soviets produced a radically new framework in which the fascistizing direction, under Szálasi's regime, turned into something else—one of the most brutal episodes of the era, actualizing some of the most extreme possibilities in fascism. The potential was realized only through the contingent, unforeseeable trajectory that produced the particular play of forces in this late stage. But the fascistizing direction in Hungary to that point was essential to the mix, helping to make the ultimate outcome possible.

Whereas Horthy, to the end of his tenure, had continued to resist Szálasi's party, the threat of Soviet invasion won the Arrow Cross new support. Then the actual Soviet invasion and the advent of the new Arrow Cross regime galvanized further support among those who believed that the Bolshevik menace required heroic efforts to secure the survival of Christian Hungary. It is not remotely to exonerate the Arrow Cross to note that through the contingencies of the trajectory, it came to power under genuinely extraordinary circumstances that helped shape its response. Although the Arrow Cross was what it became under these circumstances, what it became cannot be taken as a revelation of what it had been all along. The point is simply the embeddedness of fascism in its contingent history.

Even as the Soviets advanced rapidly into western Hungary, Szálasi remained determined to fight to the end. His regime terrorized political opponents and anyone resisting the army call-up to fight the Soviets. And the regime sought to rid Hungary of its remaining Jews, assumed to be communist sympathizers—surely in fact more likely in light of the treatment already meted out to Hungary's Jews. The gas chambers at Auschwitz-

Birkenau having been closed down, 76,000 Budapest Jews were force-marched to Hungary's western border to meet German demands for slave labor. The 15,000 Jews remaining in Budapest were killed, many of them drowned in the Danube, between October 1944 and February 1945, when Budapest capitulated. Once the Soviet victory in Hungary was complete in April 1945, Szálasi and other Arrow Cross leaders were tried and executed. Something like 564,000 Hungarian Jews had died.

As Ormos sees it, the death of Teleki in April 1941 overcame the last barrier to Hungary falling into the Nazi trap.[80] But Ormos had already concluded that Hungary lost its freedom of maneuver earlier, in November 1940, when it adhered to the Tripartite Pact that had brought together Germany, Italy, and Japan in September.[81] This bit of uncertainty indicates that we need better to put together the pieces of what *did* happen, as opposed to speculating about what did not.

In light of Hungarian territorial aspirations and German successes, the relationship with Germany was not obviously a trap for Hungary until early 1943, and even thereafter, even until the very end, Hungary retained at least some freedom of maneuver. The fascistizing direction and the extreme outcome would not have emerged without the interaction with Germany, but the asymmetrical nature of that interaction did not in itself determine that trajectory. And whereas "fascism" was surely part of the mix, fascism did not determine that trajectory either. Nor was that trajectory the trajectory *of* fascism in some sense. The trajectory and the outcomes resulted from a contingent intertwining of strands, involving both domestic and multinational interaction, from within the unforeseen framework that had resulted from World War I. That concatenation proved to nurture a kind of synergy that, in turn, actualized possibilities that would not otherwise have come to the fore, thereby giving the Hungarian case its particular idiosyncratic configuration—and place in the wider new Right universe of the era.

We have noted that because of the antagonism between Hungary and Romania, Romania's relationship with Nazi Germany was diametrically opposed to Hungary's up to a point. And partly for that reason, whereas the Romanian-German relationship was comparably asymmetrical, the asymmetrical relationship played out differently in Romania than it did in Hungary. As a result, though the outcome in Romania, too, was horrific, the Romanian case had a somewhat different place in the new Right universe.

For obvious reasons, Romania, seeking to preserve its gains in the wake of World War I and tied to both France and Britain, did not immediately identify with Nazi German revisionism. We saw in the previous chapter that King Carol II was determined to suppress the Iron Guard in 1938 partly because it seemed a tool of Hitler's.[82] This was a particularly dramatic indication that the interaction between conservatives and fascists on the domestic level could become intertwined with the wider, sometimes asymmetrical supranational interaction on the new Right.

But Romania's international situation was increasingly unstable by the late 1930s, in light of the apparent weakening of France and the growing assertiveness of Nazi Germany. These were accompanied by Soviet noises regarding Bessarabia and Northern Bukovina, territories that Russia had lost to Romania as a result of the war. Then Hungary began winning German support for its revisionist aims, first in the wake of the Munich agreement, as we have seen. And Hungary's aspirations at the expense of Romania were clear. So Romania seemed compelled to do its own lobbying with the Nazis. In November 1938, shortly after Munich, Carol met with Hitler, who realized that the possibility of German support for either Hungary or Romania gave him leverage over both.[83] He was evasive about Transylvania, but the Hungarian threat prompted Romania to accept closer economic ties with Nazi Germany.

Although the Germans welcomed these closer relations and especially access to Romania's oil fields, they offered little help with what most mattered to Romania—preserving its territorial integrity. Romania, still under King Carol, remained neutral with the outbreak of war in September 1939. Germany's successes in the west by June 1940 prompted still closer ties to Germany, though Germany offered Romania no help regarding Soviet claims to Bessarabia and Northern Bukovina. Having already agreed to such a Soviet claim as part of the secret annex to the Nazi-Soviet agreement, the Germans advised Romania to accept the Soviet demands. Romania ceded Bessarabia and Northern Bukovina in June 1940.

This humiliation was much exacerbated by the treatment suffered by Romanians, especially the army and government officials, retreating from those territories in the aftermath. They endured abuse and injury at the hands of the Russian population and especially, it seemed, the Jews, settling scores over earlier anti-Semitic legislation. The retreat from the two provinces discredited Carol, inflamed anti-Semitic feeling, and strengthened the Iron Guard.[84]

Fearing further Soviet claims and seeing German support as its only hope, Romania joined the Axis in July 1940. But Hitler specified that Romania could expect German protection only if it settled its territorial disputes with Hungary and Bulgaria. Thus, eventually, the mediation leading to the award of 40 percent of Transylvania to Hungary late in August 1940. Transylvania was considerably more important to Romanian identity than Bessarabia and Northern Bukovina, so this outcome was a particular shock to Romania. But Carol and his ministers feared that rejecting the agreement would provoke a Hungarian attack, a German occupation of

Romania's oil fields, and even a Soviet invasion of eastern Romania. Bulgaria's claim was settled without controversy, but Romania lost roughly one-third of its territory in 1940, with a population loss from 19.9 to 13.3 million. The economic consequences were severe. In exchange Hitler gave his guarantees of protection.[85]

It was from within this context, so deeply troubled on both the international and domestic levels, that General Ion Antonescu was installed in power on 6 September 1940, just days after the enforced settlement over Transylvania. Let us recall the circumstances noted in the previous chapter. Antonescu was granted full powers as King Carol abdicated in favor of his nineteen-year-old son Michael. The Iron Guard had been rapidly gaining support, and Antonescu initially felt he had no choice but to work with them. But, with Hitler's blessing, he soon suppressed the Guard, which, however, regrouped in Germany, biding its time, with significant support from within the Nazi hierarchy.

Antonescu was among those Romanians who had concluded from the combination of German successes and British and French hesitance that Romania had no choice but to work with Germany, and he adhered to the Tripartite Pact on 23 November 1940. As in the Hungarian case, however, asymmetry did not preclude a good deal of Romanian autonomy and initiative. The fact that Antonescu quickly won Hitler's particular confidence did not hurt, but Antonescu was proud, stubborn, and more than capable of independence in any case.[86] Indeed, in Romania as elsewhere, the very fact of asymmetry may have produced a kind of feedback, reinforcing the determination of the weaker power to go its own way. The resulting effort to differentiate could even moderate the new Right departure.

So though Antonescu developed a strong personal relationship with Hitler, his policies produced lots of friction with the Nazi regime. We noted that even after he had violently suppressed the Iron Guard, it continued to enjoy significant support in Nazi circles. Conversely, Antonescu's toleration of the two opposition parties, the National Peasant Party and the National Liberal Party, angered the Germans.[87] And there was friction in the sensitive area of Jewish policy, as we will soon see.

What Antonescu wanted from the relationship with Germany was not remotely open-ended territorial conquest; his aim was simply to restore and secure, especially against Hungary and the Soviet Union, the greater Romania that had emerged with the World War I settlement. That aim was not specifically fascist and would not in itself warrant placing Antonescu's regime within the new Right universe. And it could produce friction with Germany in any case.

While the Nazi-Soviet Pact remained in force, the Romanians could only hope for German pressure against further Soviet designs on Romania after the cession of Bessarabia and Northern Bukovina. But once, with the German attack in June 1941, the Soviet Union was suddenly Germany's enemy, Romania and Germany were more clearly pulling in the same direction. Antonescu was eager to participate in Operation Barbarossa when the plans were finally revealed to him. Not only could Romania win back Bessarabia and Northern Bukovina—which were indeed recovered by late July 1941—but the definitive defeat of the Soviet Union seemed the best long-term guarantee of Romanian security to the east. However, Antonescu was fueled by a quasi-religious anti-communist fervor at the same time.[88]

Still, whereas Romania's interests came to converge with Germany's regarding the Soviet Union, Romania's rivalry with Hungary over Transylvania could only complicate the Romanian-German relationship. In adhering to the Tripartite Pact on November 23, Romania followed Hungary by just three days, and in the meeting in which he adhered to the pact—his first meeting with Hitler—Antonescu brought up Transylvania and urged that the award to Hungary be overturned. Hitler's response was vague, but he admired Antonescu's determination. Antonescu, for his part, found ongoing collaboration with Germany essential not only because of concerns about the Soviet Union but also because of longer-term hopes regarding Transylvania.[89]

After the initial successes in the assault on the Soviet Union, Romania was entrusted to administer the restored Bessarabia and Northern Bukovina as well as the adjacent eastward slice, Transnistria. In February 1942 Hitler suggested to Antonescu that Romania might permanently expand eastward in exchange for leaving Hungary its part of Transylvania. But Antonescu, seeking the restoration of Romania's 1939 borders, did not like either part of the deal. Transnistria was not historically Romanian; incorporating it over the long term could only antagonize the Soviets. For Romania the war against the Soviet Union was ultimately defensive. But neither was Antonescu prepared to give up permanently the part of Transylvania ceded to Hungary. When Hitler raised the possibility of the exchange, Antonescu replied that whatever the German position, he intended to overturn the Transylvania settlement that Romania had been forced to accept in 1940.[90]

But though Antonescu's war aims would not in themselves warrant placing his regime within the new Right universe, we saw in the preceding chapter that some of his policies and programs, especially the population engineering initiated in 1940, do suggest such a place. Indeed, Romania is numbered a major participant in the Holocaust. And not only Vladimir Solonari, treating the overall population program, but also Jean Ancel and Radu Ioanid, treating the Holocaust specifically, emphasize that the killing of Jews, especially, stemmed from indigenous concerns as opposed to German pressure or even German license. All three authorities are concerned to demonstrate Antonescu's responsibility in the face of efforts, especially after the fall of the Romanian communist regime, to rehabilitate him by claiming he was indeed subject to Nazi pressures or by featuring all he did to resist them, thereby helping to limit the toll on Romanian Jews.[91] But in light of our concerns about interaction and the role of asymmetry, we might be able to go beyond that either/or problematic to better understand the place of Antonescu's population program, and thus his regime itself, in the new Right universe.

Even if the population program did not result from German pressure, we still must ask what difference it made that Romania carried it out while in direct, if asymmetrical, interaction with Nazi Germany. Most basically, Nazi population engineering possibly provided a stimulus and model, each of which must be distinguished from sheer pressure. Even as Ancel plays down German pressures in emphasizing Romanian responsibility, he recognizes that "although the 'evil' was of Romanian origin, without Germany's domination of Europe and help in freeing its Romanian allies from their complexes, it would not have amounted to much."[92] In energizing the Romanians, the relationship with Germany helped to actualize certain possibilities, though, in light of the asymmetry, the relationship was not precisely synergistic. Ancel's notion seems congruent with Kallis's argument that Nazi Germany constituted something like a catalyst, though, as always, it is crucial that the interaction was producing a particular dynamic, not simply making possible the realization of a stable vision or aspiration already in place. What could be imagined or desired was itself changing as the intertwining trajectory proceeded.

But why would the Romanians have been stimulated by or attracted to the Nazi example at that point? Whatever the degree of inspiration from the Nazis, they had reasons of their own for the program, in light of their immediate experience. In the previous chapter we concluded that domestic fascist pressure was not the decisive impetus for Antonescu's program. And we went on to propose, in a preliminary way, that even if German pressures were not decisive either, Romania's multinational interaction *was* decisive. In light of the postwar settlement and thus the historically specific challenges the country faced, that multinational interaction bred a particular sense of vulnerability that we are now prepared to contemplate.

Romania's postwar expansion at the expense of Hungary, Russia, and Bulgaria inherently entailed potential threats both from resentful neighbors and from ethnic minorities within. The resulting sense of vulnerability fed the deepening concern with eugenics, social hygiene, and public health, in the face of a perceived threat of "degeneration."[93] Such concerns were found throughout the Western world, of course, but Romania's sudden expansion seemed to constitute a special challenge. By the late 1930s, moreover, that challenge had come to seem greatly magnified.

The stakes of German revisionism for Romania had not been clear in 1937, but they rapidly became clear by 1939–40, even before Romania's formal alliance with Nazi Germany, as that revisionism brought Soviet and Hungarian demands against Romania to the fore. Now the Soviet and Hungarian threats became frighteningly real. What transpired beginning in 1940 enhanced not only concerns for Romania's territorial integrity but also the sense of long-term vulnerability, which seemingly could be countered only through radical population engineering. Though the program was merely defensive in one sense, the new situation resulting from the dynamic international interplay to that point seemed to demand a radical new response. National health, even survival, was at stake.

After Bessarabia and Northern Bukovina were reacquired from the Soviet Union in 1941, Antonescu was especially determined to "cleanse" them of Jews. Obsession with these Jews in particular stemmed from the humiliation that had surrounded the Romanian withdrawal from the two provinces in 1940. Jews were taken to be especially pro-communist—and thus likely to be spies and saboteurs. So these Jews were forced into Transnistria, initially controlled by Germans, who refused to accept them. But as the Romanians persisted, the province was soon entrusted to Romania to administer.[94] It is estimated that 60 percent of the Jews deported to Transnistria died or were killed along the way. And under the Romanian administration of Transnistria, 220,000–260,000 Jews and 20,000 Roma died, largely from inhumane treatment, but also by shooting.[95]

Precisely insofar as the fuel was indigenous, Romania's way of carrying out the program could easily engender friction with the Germans. And such friction, a form of negative interaction, provoked Antonescu to resist German pressures, to insist on doing things his way. Thus there were fits and starts. At this point, especially, such friction might have served to moderate the radicalization to some extent.

Especially when Germany, during summer 1942, began organizing its program of mass extermination and became more demanding with respect to Romanian Jewish policy, Antonescu resisted, becoming, if anything, even more determined to pursue his own course. He reversed the policy of deporting Jews to Transnistria and rebuffed German calls to deport Jews in the region for extermination. A plan to deport the Romanian Jews to Belzec was put on hold early in October 1942—*before* Stalingrad, as Ancel emphasizes.[96] But Antonescu continued with the autonomous, often chaotic Romanian program at the same time.

What had happened in Bessarabia and Northern Bukovina had lowered the threshold of paranoia. The notion that Jews especially, but also other minorities, were likely to be spies and saboteurs seemed also to apply else-where in Romania, though the resulting deportations were never as viru-lent or systematic as they had been in Bessarabia and Northern Bukovina. Genuine vulnerabilities and dangers were exaggerated, then attributed especially to the Jews, who were conflated with communists, though An-tonescu had also conflated the fanatically anti-Semitic Iron Guard with communism.

Even as the interaction with Germany produced fits and starts, other factors also came into play. Concern about perceptions abroad was appar-ently one reason for reversing the policy of deporting Jews to Transnistria in the summer of 1942. The Queen Mother's opposition to the policy may also have influenced the reversal.[97] By early 1943, with defeat coming to seem possible after the defeat at Stalingrad, where Romanian forces, fight-ing alongside the Germans, also suffered heavy losses, Antonescu became even more determined to pull back, hedging his bets. Much like Horthy in Hungary, in the event of defeat he wanted to be able to present himself as having helped save Jews.[98] After the German occupation of Hungary in March 1944, the Antonescu regime defied the Germans by admitting flee-ing Hungarian Jews and allowing them to leave via the Black Sea.[99]

But even as Antonescu's determination to preserve a measure of au-tonomy and initiative may have moderated the effects to some extent, his anti-Semitic policy led to the deaths of more than 250,000 Jews. Although that policy was only one aspect of the program of radical population en-gineering, it produced the most horrific results. Antonescu was executed for war crimes by the new Soviet-supported regime in Romania in 1946, although Dennis Deletant argues convincingly that a Western court would have convicted him in the same way.[100]

Despite his concern for Romanian sovereignty and his periodic friction with the Germans, Antonescu stuck with Germany until King Michael finally dismissed and arrested him on 23 August 1944. The ending of An-tonescu's regime reflected the changing fortunes of war, though Roma-nia's relations with the Soviet Union, on the one hand, and Hungary, on the other, remained central. During 1943–44, Romania faced the difficult question of whether sticking with Germany or abandoning the German alliance, possibly switching sides, seemed more promising with respect to Romania's territorial integrity. When Michael finally dismissed Antonescu, Soviet troops were in Romanian territory, yet Antonescu had refused to request an armistice. The fact that he stuck with Nazi Germany for so long might seem to suggest a particular ideological attachment to the Nazi regime.

Certainly the Nazi claim to be leading an anti-communist crusade—a claim increasingly prominent as the Soviets were turning the tide—had some resonance, but Antonescu seems to have remained primarily concerned with Romanian independence and territorial integrity. He had begun considering an understanding with the Allies as the Romanian military situation deteriorated after Stalingrad. Hitler confronted Antonescu about these peace feelers in April 1943. But now another contingency came into play. At the Casablanca Conference in January 1943, Roosevelt proposed and Churchill agreed that the Axis powers would be subject to unconditional surrender, and this, from Antonescu's perspective, was the chief obstacle to a separate peace. Unconditional surrender seemed incompatible with Antonescu's concern to guarantee Romania's postwar independence from the Soviet Union.[101]

Although Antonescu's fear of the Soviets was ideological as well as geopolitical, it was surely partly the dynamic in course, with the actual Soviet geopolitical threat it entailed, that actualized his hatred and fear of Bolshevism, fueled his conflation of communists and Jews, and furthered his determination to act in a new way. In any case, Antonescu held out for terms that would guarantee the independence of Romania vis-à-vis the conquering Soviet side. But he also felt an obligation to Germany, now on the defensive and especially dependent on Romanian oil. He wanted to break with Germany in a decent way.[102] Still, this was clearly more a matter of military-style honor than ideological commitment.

King Michael and those around him, including the long-standing opposition leaders Iuliu Maniu of the National Peasant Party and Constantin Brătianu of the National Liberal Party, were more sanguine about the possibility of working with the Soviets. The two countries signed an armistice in Moscow on 12 September 1944, with British and American agreement. So Romania not only left the alliance with Nazi Germany but promptly joined the Allied side, participating with the Soviets in the invasion of Hungary. Michael had felt that switching sides meant the right to be treated as a co-belligerent, not as a defeated enemy. But Stalin proved unwilling to forgive Romania for its role in the German invasion of the Soviet Union.[103]

Although Antonescu's overriding concerns with Romanian sovereignty and territorial integrity were not remotely "fascist," the framework of multinational interaction, encompassing not only the asymmetrical relationship with Germany but also the relationships with Hungary and the Soviet Union, enabled a fascistizing departure giving the Antonescu regime its own distinctive place in the new Right universe. It does not merely constitute a footnote alongside Germany. But for understanding the overall web of interaction at the time, it is crucial that it was not so much the asymmetrical German relationship as Romania's multinational territorial situation, and the sense of vulnerability it engendered, that fueled the Romanian trajectory and produced the tragic outcome.

Vichy France offers another complex but illuminating instance of asymmetrical interaction over wartime population engineering. Indeed, the changing context of Jewish policy in France by the onset of the Vichy Regime in July 1940 provides an especially telling indication of why attention to the fluidity, the changing dynamic at the time, points us away from essentialist, reified categories. Without in any sense minimizing Vichy complicity, Michael Marrus and Robert Paxton, in their classic study of Vichy Jewish policy, stress the import of the Jewish refugee crisis in France by 1938–41. Occasioned by Nazi treatment of Jews in Germany and beyond, that crisis significantly changed the situation in France, including perceptions and the meaning of choices.[104] Paxton has recently reaffirmed the importance of the refugee crisis, despite its relative neglect in the ongoing discussion of Vichy complicity in the Holocaust.[105]

In Marrus and Paxton's account, it was especially that crisis that prompted the new Vichy government to introduce anti-Semitic measures, distinguishing between native and non-native Jews, almost immediately upon assuming power. The Vichy government took this step on its own initiative, and with considerable popular support, though foreign-born Jewish refugees had initially encountered relative tolerance among the French. Not only was the new departure not imposed by the Germans, but it defied the Germans, who still wanted France as a dumping ground for German Jews.

Even as they actively participated when the Germans began deporting Jews to death camps in 1942, Vichy leaders tended to see the deportations as merely the next phase in dealing with the refugee crisis. They were prepared to accept official German explanations, which, Marrus and Paxton stress, could have seemed credible in context. In light of the refugee crisis, there seemed grounds to believe the forced labor narrative or that some international Jewish resettlement project was in the offing. To some extent the Germans were simply taking back Jews they had previously forced to emigrate into France. To be sure, Marrus and Paxton make clear, there were increasing grounds for doubt, especially in light of the nature of the transports out of France, but uncertainty persisted even into 1943.

This situation affords an especially telling, if also especially unsettling, example of the braided dynamic. Probing the interweaving of the domestic strand with multinational interaction, we better understand why the direction and the outcomes could only have resulted from within this unprecedented new universe. We become less prone to assume that it was all intended, that what was happening was understood at the time, or that we can readily explain it all in terms of abiding anti-Semitism.

Anti-Semitism there surely was, as a necessary but not sufficient condition. The question is how the asymmetrical relationship affected the particular mode of acting on that anti-Semitism in the early stages of the Vichy regime. It surely turned out, as Paxton has recently insisted, that "Vichy made it worse," but the agents did not know what proved the larger contours of the event in which they were involved. They did not know what it was they were making worse, let alone *that* they were making it worse or how they were doing so. And whereas our *ex post* judgment is of course indispensable, we also need to see it from their point of view to understand how it could have happened. Together with anti-Semitism we find illusion and wishful thinking alongside German license and pressure in an undecidable mix.[106]

When considering the impact of Nazi Germany on radical Right departures elsewhere, we find a continuum of possibilities, and in assessing any one instance, we can only hope to pinpoint a range as opposed to specifying a definite relationship or proportion. In the last analysis, the import of asymmetry, too, is undecidable. Such departures may have been essentially indigenous even in the presence of the Nazi example or of Nazi pressure. And insofar as Nazi pressure was undeniably operative, it was more direct in some instances than others, and how direct it was affected responses on the other side. Here we have a further indication that in assessing the web of interaction, we need to be alert to the scope for gradations as opposed to neat lines. And in assessing international interaction, we especially see the braiding of the aggregate dynamic, as domestic and supranational trajectories intertwined and as, on occasion, the international level entailed multilateral interaction.

Supranational Interaction beyond Europe

But what of interaction beyond Europe? As we noted in the first chapter, getting a better handle on the aggregate requires confronting the question of geographical reach. We have already encountered Federico Finchelstein on Argentina, several studies of Japan, and Didier Musiedlak's collaborative volume on corporatism in the Latin world, encompassing Latin America. And certainly we note many departures outside Europe during the period that might be considered instances of the new Right or even fascism, with Turkey and Japan the most obvious examples. In every case we ask to what extent the departure was indigenous, as opposed to imitative, and to what extent and in what ways each was caught up in the web of supranational interaction. Insofar as we play up indigenous generation as opposed to diffusion from Europe, what was it about the era, on a global level, that seemed to mandate the new Right experiment?

Diffusion from Europe would not in itself have constituted interaction of the kind we have considered so far in this chapter. But the sense that others, even beyond Europe, were impressed, were borrowing, was surely further evidence, emboldening fascists in Europe, that fascism was the modern forefront. For example, E. Bruce Reynolds, seeking primarily to have Japan more centrally encompassed, stresses the considerable impact of fascism in Asia—in a significant faction within Chiang Kai-shek's Chinese Nationalist Party, for example, but also in Burma and beyond.[107]

Conceiving European fascism broadly, Stein Ugelvik Larsen's invaluable collaborative volume of 2001, entitled precisely *Fascism outside Europe*, includes four chapters on "The Spread of Fascism from Europe," devoted to Germany, Italy, Spain, and Portugal, respectively, as well as case studies from around the world. In his substantial concluding essay, discussed in chapter 2, Larsen takes for granted that fascism was first European, so diffusion is the first question. But he concludes that the effect of direct import/export was relatively minor because of rivalries among the exporters, internal uncertainties and disagreements over how best to export fascism, and hesitations among non-Europeans about accepting direction from Europe. But Larsen recognizes the import of fascist ideas and models, perceived as succeeding in Europe; even when they were not imitated, they served as catalysts.[108] In other words, diffusion invited indigenous new Right experiments that might well not have resulted otherwise.

Although the cases of Argentina and Brazil, especially, raise questions about temporal limits that we will consider briefly in chapter 8, we must limit ourselves to what are surely two of the most salient cases, Turkey and Japan. Whereas cultural differences are of course at issue even as we ponder the disparate European cases, they are even more central when we extend our reach to Turkey and Japan. But we must take care not to overdo their importance. Having been significantly affected by the peace settlement of 1919–20, and experiencing the sense of new challenges and possibilities after the war, Turkey and Japan were in the same universe as the European countries most at issue.

In a recent study Stefan Ihrig features the impact of the new regime of Mustafa Kemal (Atatürk) on Nazism and Nazi Germany. Indeed, the Nazis openly proclaimed Kemal and his regime as role models, and as Ihrig sees it, Kemal and Turkey were at least as important as Mussolini and Italy in crystalizing Hitler's ambition. Yet the import of the Turkish-German interaction has been widely neglected.[109] Whatever the relative import of the two models, the Nazis often linked Kemal and Mussolini as pioneering a new course. At the very least, Kemal constituted further evidence of the scope for innovative departures in the new world after World War I.

Turkey seemed to exemplify an energetic and successful effort at rebuilding in the wake of catastrophic defeat. The Treaty of Sèvres, imposed by the victors on the Ottoman Empire in 1919, called for, among other things, the partition of Anatolia. But the Turks resisted, mounting a war of independence especially against Greeks in the west and Armenians in the east, both supported by Britain, France, and Italy. By 1923 the Turks had prevailed, forcing the replacement of the Treaty of Sèvres with the Treaty of Lausanne, signed in July 1923. The new Turkish Republic was declared in October 1923, as the military hero Mustafa Kemal emerged as undisputed leader from within the national resistance movement.

From there, Kemal, who would go on to be accorded the honorific surname "Atatürk" (father of the Turks) by the parliament in 1934, engaged in a concerted effort to create a homogeneous Turkish national identity along with sustained modernization. This was under genuinely difficult circumstances in a new nation, in some ways starting from zero. It could seemingly be accomplished only from the top down and with a monopoly of power in a single party. A comprehensive educational effort to instill the official worldview—republican, nationalist, and secular—was required.[110] And especially since it had led Turkey into further war, the Paris peace settlement led to demographic challenges in some ways more dramatic than those in east-central Europe. New measures of population engineering seemed essential in light of the deportations, massacres, and compulsory exchanges of populations that had depopulated large areas of Anatolia and Thrace.[111]

Ihrig notes that the Nazis' image of Turkey, based on a selective reading of Turkish realities, was settled by 1933 and remained static thereafter. Embracing the new Turkey, seen as an example of a modern führer and *völkisch* state embarked on a rapid, revolutionary transformation, enhanced the Nazis' sense of their own modernity. As Ihrig tells it, the Turkish expulsion of the Greeks and even the earlier Armenian genocide indicated an exemplary capacity for newly decisive and, when necessary, ruthless modes of action.[112]

In seeking to foster a homogeneous and unifying Turkish identity, Kemal was thinking in terms of nationality transcending ethnicity; the decisive criterion was the citizen's decision for Turkish national and cultural identity.[113] In contrast, the Nazis insisted on ethnicity, or race, but for the Nazis the difference was not decisive in viewing the Turks. Ihrig notes that for Hitler the Turks themselves were not one of the lesser races like those in India or Egypt, whose struggles were not comparable to Germany's. Racially European, the Turks had proved their worth in winning their war of independence, forcing revision of the Paris peace settlement, and in building a new Turkey.[114]

The Kemalist regime emerged and took shape at almost exactly the same time as Mussolini's regime in Italy, and it certainly borrowed from the Italians thereafter. So Kemalist Turkey was very much caught up in the energizing interaction at the time and surely must be encompassed in the new

Right universe. But might the Kemalist regime be considered an instance of fascism? And if so, how do we balance the import of imitation or borrowing as opposed to indigenous and structural factors in producing a fascist direction?

In his contribution to the Larsen volume, Fikret Adanır notes that the comparability of the Kemal regime with the two fascist regimes was much discussed at the time. Mihail Manoilescu included Turkey along with Italy, Portugal, and Germany as examples of especially successful single-party rule in Europe.[115] And the matter has been at least implicitly at issue ever since, though Turkish academics have been virtually unanimous in denying that Kemal's regime was fascist. It was seeking to promote Westernization and modernization, eventually to be based on parliamentary democracy, but the transition in a backward society required authoritarianism. However, Adanır finds in recent Western literature on Turkey a growing emphasis on at least proto-fascist and even totalitarian features. The accent is on imitation, especially of Fascist Italy, as opposed to indigenous factors based on structural parallels.[116]

Adanır's own assessment suggests the difficulties of placing the Turkish case, especially once we do deeper justice to perceptions at the time and to both positive and negative interaction. In concluding, he makes the obvious but essential point that our assessment of the Turkish regime depends on whether we understand fascism in terms of the Italian case, taken as archetypal, or as a possibility in any modern state, apart from borrowing or imitation.[117] And near the outset he says he wants to play up the indigenous aspects of the Kemalist direction.[118] The Kemalist youth movement was based on prewar Ottoman organizations, and ideologues from the prewar Young Turk movement remained influential—in fostering, for example, the notion that ordinary people, ignorant of their own interests, had to be led from above.[119]

But Adanır certainly recognizes the import of the borrowing from Italy, selective though it was. In doing so he cites the work of Çağlar Keyder, who notes that up to a point the Kemalist regime compared itself indiscriminately with Fascist Italy, the Soviet Union, and later Nazi Germany, all as spearheading a revolutionary step beyond liberalism, with its prejudicial understanding of personal liberty and its tendency to foster class conflict.[120] And Adanır notes that whereas some invoked Italian models of mass organization and education, others claimed that Soviet innovations were more pertinent for Turkey.[121] But Adanır and Keyder agree that borrowing from Italy was especially prominent and overt. Fascist Italy influenced the statist direction in the Turkish economy, even prompting some to advocate Italian-style corporatism.[122]

At the same time, the Turks embraced what was perceived as a totalitarian conception of party-state congruence, also based on Italy.[123] But this last, especially, is a good example of the blind spots, selectivity, and wishful thinking in the borrowing from European fascism. Turkish enthusiasts were missing the contestedness and uncertainty of the Italian Fascist trajectory, first over the party-state relationship but also over what counted as totalitarianism.

For their part, the Italians followed developments in Turkey closely and viewed the emerging Kemalist system as heavily indebted to Italian Fascism—a perception that surely enhanced Italian self-confidence.[124] And in concluding, despite his emphasis on indigenousness, Adanır suggests that the Kemalist regime had closer affinities with Mussolini's Italy than has been suspected.[125] On occasion he is quite willing to characterize the Kemalist regime as totalitarian as opposed to merely authoritarian: "The intention was to achieve a totalitarian system which left no room for any civil, cultural or political activity outside the control of the party-state."[126]

But negative interaction was also significantly at work. Even as the Kemalists borrowed quite openly from Fascist Italy, they distinguished their regime from fascism, taken as a new, illiberal, state-controlled mode of Western imperialism. Some linked fascism to the dictatorship of the bourgeoisie as well. The process of radical transformation that Turkey, as a new, underdeveloped country, was undergoing was radically different from anything in Europe, and Turkey needed to do it on its own, without European experts, avoiding European hegemony.[127]

Fascist imperialism was a concern partly because, especially with Italian ambitions in the eastern Mediterranean and the Balkans, it seemed to threaten Turkey's own interests. Negative reaction to the Italian conquest of Ethiopia in 1935–36 seems to have been decisive in reorienting Kemalist foreign policy.[128] Ihrig notes that the Nazis' static image of Turkey weathered not only this opposition to Italy but also Turkey's support for the Loyalist republican side in the Spanish Civil War.[129] That German steadfastness is striking, no doubt, but Adanır's point surely trumps: the turn against Italy proved the background for Turkish neutrality in World War II.

The Kemalist determination to distinguish the Turkish regime from European fascism would not in itself mean that that regime was not fascist, of course. But interaction led the Turks to distance themselves from fascism to some extent—most obviously in foreign policy. And the foreign policy divergence in itself may well have muted radicalism on the domestic level. For an instructive contrast, we need only recall how being sucked into the German orbit affected the course of domestic development in Hungary and Romania.

In any case, because the interaction, reflecting uncertain perceptions at the time, was both positive and negative, it bequeaths a good deal of undecidability to us. Although the Kemalist regime was part of the new Right universe, so that its place in the web of interaction must be encompassed, concern with whether or not it counts as fascist merely throws us off.

Whereas Turkey was neutral in World War II, Japan was of course central, having joined Germany and Italy with the Anti-Comintern Pact, first signed in 1936, then with the Tripartite Pact of September 1940. But quite apart from the obvious diplomatic-military considerations, we have encountered questions about the place of Japan, especially during the period from 1937 to 1945, in the wider new Right universe. The issue has been much contested among Western specialists on Japan, a number of whom, as we noted in chapters 1 and 3, have been restive because they feel that too often Japan is inappropriately left out of discussions of generic fascism, at least partly because of the either/or straightjacket so often applied.

E. Bruce Reynolds persuasively attacks some of the standard reasons for differentiating the Japanese case from fascism, including the notion that the Japanese monarchy was a traditional system in light of the central role of the emperor. As he sees it, the aims of those seeking a third way in Japan, Italy, and Germany were comparable. The differences merely reflected the differences in the frameworks and in the opportunities for the radical change desired.[130] Compromising with traditional elites and purging the most radical, pro-socialist elements hardly disqualifies Japan, since both took place in Fascist Italy and Nazi Germany as well.[131] More recently Rikki Kersten concludes that Japan was just as fascist as the others.[132] Also seeking to encompass Japan, Joseph Sottile assumes that a better definition of fascism would enable us better to do so.[133] But whether placing Japan is indeed a matter of definition, and either/or, is a question we will need to address.

In any case, there are symptomatic differences of emphasis even among those who agree not only that Japan merits a place but that it produced a form of fascism. And though asymmetry with Germany or Italy is not really at issue, much boils down to the import of supranational interaction in the emergence of what its proponents labeled the New Order in Japan. It is not enough simply to document borrowing from Europe; we need to see how it played into the indigenous dynamic to understand the trajectory and the outcome.

Whatever we conclude about the relative importance of indigenous factors and European models, there was no doubt *some* reciprocity, energizing and radicalizing both sides, starting with the Japanese army's aggression in Manchuria in 1931, in defiance of the League of Nations. At the same time, German aggressiveness after Hitler came to power in 1933 surely further emboldened some sectors in Japan.[134] But aggressive foreign policy does not in itself constitute fascism. The question is the wider import of the interaction in radicalizing the wider Japanese departure from parliamentary democracy.

Treating the Japanese case together with European fascism is tricky partly because the cultural aspects differentiating Japan could be read *either* as giving Japan a leg up on fascism *or* as providing a shield against it. Much obviously depends on our criteria of fascism, though we could not hope to establish proportions definitively whatever the criteria. Some argue that Japan did indeed produce a totalitarian fascism, but essentially on its own, on the basis of indigenous traditions, even though there was obviously interaction with the Europeans as well. For Masao Maruyama, long the key figure in Japanese debates over the issue, Japanese fascism was indigenous, not a creature of Europe or a poorly indigenized version of the European original.[135] In noted essays of the later 1940s, he pinpointed an array of cultural idiosyncrasies that had long differentiated Japan from Europe and that made Japan susceptible to its own form of fascism from above.[136] But for Maruyama fascist dynamics could arise anywhere at any time.[137]

Larsen's argument about Japan is largely congruent with Maruyama's; what Japan produced was a form of fascism, even if it was not "European."[138] This would give the Japanese case a place in the overall typology of fascism even if interaction with European fascism was of only secondary importance.

But some—at the time, and thereafter—go beyond merely featuring indigenousness to claim a kind of Japanese paternity over fascism. With its traditions of obedience, cooperation, and solidarity, Japan, the argument goes, already had at least a proto-fascist, proto-totalitarian spirit, so in contrast to the Italians and Germans, it could be totalitarian by the late 1930s without radical change. The European fascists were the ones trying to catch up. Not only was Japan, in acting further by the late 1930s, not merely copying Western fascism, but it was taking a step beyond.[139] This would still entail a mode of interaction, in the sense that taking the measure of the European fascists would no doubt have energized and perhaps radicalized the Japanese.

Reynolds agrees that such aspects of Japanese tradition as the State Shintō—the civic religion created after the Meiji Restoration in 1868—suppressed individualism and eventually helped transform the nation into a fully mobilized war machine; they can thus be seen as harbingers of the effort to forge a third way. But he finds the impact of European fascism significant as well.[140] Getting a sense of the proportions is tricky because of the ambivalence in Japanese perceptions of anything European. On the one hand, since 1868 many Japanese intellectuals had been especially concerned to keep abreast of the latest from the West. Miles Fletcher shows that in the 1930s European fascism afforded one more set of Western ideas to digest, like guild socialism and Marxism in the 1920s.[141] On the other hand, in Japan, as in Turkey, looking to Europe had negative as well as positive effects on those seeking new Right departures. Both Reynolds and Kersten stress that most Japanese seeking what might be considered a fascist transformation eschewed the terms "fascism" and "totalitarianism," taken as Western and thus associated with colonialism, most obviously, but also with a threat to Japaneseness itself. In his contribution to the Larsen volume, Gregory Kasza stresses that most of those in power in the 1930s did not see themselves as fascist and, as an aspect of their anti-European-ism, even wanted to be considered anti-fascist.[142]

Those moving to the Right in Japan also had misgivings over European and especially German racial views. Even as some propagated notions of Japanese superiority justifying a leading role in Asia, they generally sought to avoid doing so in racial terms. And the Japanese regime refused to co-operate in the extermination of the Jews during the war.[143] In the case of both terminology and racism, the negativity of the interaction could have moderated Japanese thinking and behavior to some degree. But, again as in the case of Turkey, just because these Japanese did not want to be con-sidered fascist for such nationalistic reasons does not in itself mean that what they were pursuing was not fascism. We have to consider other fac-tors and weigh the criteria.

In light of our emphasis on the enduring impact of World War I, we note Kersten's emphasis that whatever the import of the interaction, Japan was caught up in the same history as Europe in the wake of the war.[144] Certainly Japan, like Germany, Italy, Hungary, and what remained of the Ottoman Empire, felt humiliated by the outcome of the Paris Peace Conference. And for Geoff Eley, such humiliation in Japan, as in Italy and Germany, stoked radical-nationalist anger that proved crucial to the political mo-mentum of fascism.[145] Yet Eley also recognizes that because Japan was a relatively minor participant in the war, his accent on the war as the cru-cible of fascism makes it hard to encompass the Japanese case. As he sees it, however, the impact of the war and the peace on Italy and especially Germany far exceeded the threshold necessary to foster fascism. And when we ask about fascism outside Europe, an emphasis on the war's salience for European fascism should not rule out the other criteria that Eley had indi-cated elsewhere in his book.[146] He most assuredly wants to include Japan among the fascist regimes.

It is generally agreed that during the 1920s a violent new Right be-gan to emerge in Japan, largely from below, with little borrowing from Europe. But it was declining after about 1932, and it had failed as of 1936, when the state crushed the movement in the wake of a coup attempt by young officers. The turn to the Right after 1936 was engineered from above. Generally, the police kept the extreme Right in check throughout the 1930s.[147]

Meanwhile, Japan saw a gradual shift from party to military-bureaucratic rule after 1932, as representatives in the lower house of parliament steadily lost cabinet seats to military officers and bureaucrats.[148] But between 1933 and 1936, with Hitler in power and Nazi Germany seemingly successful, European fascism began to exert direct influence in Japan, galvanizing a *new* new Right, including intellectuals as well as political movements seeking to mimic European fascism to some extent. Kasza nicely nuances the nature of the interaction: "Fascism did not travel to Japan as a package. Japanese intellectuals, politicians, and state officials borrowed selectively from fascism, much as they had from earlier Western political tendencies. Their knowledge of European fascism was imperfect, and they modified what they took from fascism to accord with their own ideas and circumstances."[149] To characterize this new tendency, with its explicit links to European fascism, Kasza usefully adopts the untranslatable term the Japanese themselves used, "*kakushin* right"—suggesting selective revolution or something half-way between reform and revolution.[150]

The two most self-conscious efforts to mimic European fascism on the political level had minimal success, an indication of the Right's inability to organize on the grassroots level. The more important was the Eastern Way Society, led by Seigō Nakano, who traveled to Italy and Germany to meet with fascist notables and praised fascism at rallies in Japan. His movement wore black shirts and aped what had come to seem the fascist military style. Nakano advocated charismatic leadership and genuinely hated the increasingly repressive military-bureaucratic regime.[151] Yet he denied he was fascist—perhaps from tactical expediency, or perhaps from the genuine ambivalence we noted about borrowing from the West.

Although such overt aping of fascism bore little fruit, *kakushin* intellectuals sought to influence or goad the governing military-bureaucratic elite. But, as with Hungary and Romania, we encounter questions about who was using or exploiting whom.

In treating the intellectuals and the longer-term influence of the *kakushin* Right, Kasza draws on the earlier work of Fletcher, and the emphases of the two authorities run parallel up to a point. They agree that overtly fascist ideas became part of the mix largely through the agency of the Shōwa Research Association, a think tank formed in 1933. Its most prominent figures—Masamichi Rōyama, Shintarō Ryū, and Kiyoshi Miki—are the focus of Fletcher's study. These were engaged intellectuals seeking to provide the essential bridge between what seemed the latest political ideas and innovations from Europe and Japanese governmental policy. And they were the core of the New Order Movement, Fletcher's term for the intellectual side of what Kasza terms the *kakushin* Right.

Fletcher emphasizes that though these intellectuals had been attracted to European socialism in the 1920s, their turn to fascism entailed no real discontinuity, let alone apostasy. Like so many embracing the new Right in Europe, they were seeking a systematic alternative to liberalism, market capitalism, political parties, and parliamentary government. That mainstream modern package seemed to breed short-term interest-group squabbling, corruption, and inefficiency. A new framework could be at once less contentious, more just, and more effective.[152] Drawing explicitly from Alfredo Rocco and Rudolf Brinkman, Germany's economics vice-minister, Rōyama argued in 1934 that liberalism, capitalism, and parliamentary government had outlived their historical mission, that a new era, in which individuals would identify with the nation, was dawning. Kasza emphasizes that a belief in the imminence of such change was at the core of the *kakushin* outlook.[153]

Although the *kakushin* intellectuals borrowed selectively, eschewing any premium on charismatic leadership or violence, the vision of a new order they developed by 1940, based on a post-liberal conception of the nation, the state, and the individual, was certainly congruent with key aspects of European fascism.[154] They were especially attracted to state-directed corporatist programs, based on the Italian model, though Kasza notes that few were aware how poorly Italian corporatism worked in practice.[155]

Fletcher and Kasza agree that these intellectuals became the main vehicle for European fascist influence on the course of events in Japan. But they differ symptomatically over whether these intellectuals were themselves fascists, over how the influence took place, and over the nature of the outcome. Fletcher takes it for granted that the New Order Movement constituted a form of fascism in prewar Japan, differentiated from other strands advocating less systematic change, such as statist intervention in the economy.[156] But for Kasza the new *kakushin* Right was not fascist and did not think of itself as fascist. Its adherents explicitly repudiated violence, which Kasza, following Stanley Payne, takes as a defining feature of fascism. Their appeal to traditional values, and especially their particular mode of monarchism, with a role for the emperor utterly different than, most pertinently, that of the monarch in Fascist Italy, similarly kept them from crossing the line into fascism. They envisioned an orderly, legal transformation from within the Meiji constitutional system.[157]

Whereas Kasza, in denying that the *kakushin* Right was fascist, emphasizes the appeal to traditional values, Fletcher notes among his figures a striking *lack* of reference to Japan's intellectual past; their works were almost entirely concerned with European ideas and policies.[158] Yet elsewhere he observes that they glorified "those elements in Japan's past that were conducive to an ethic of national service."[159] And whereas they took pride in Japan's economic development and new power, their concern about modern social and political conflict led them to advocate "the revival of a unique Oriental *Gemeinschaft* in which political and economic relationships among Japanese would be cooperative, as in a small traditional and tightly knit community."[160]

But however the *kakushin* vision is to be characterized, it is especially when we consider its impact on Japanese governmental practice that we find illuminating differences in the accents of Fletcher and Kasza. Fletcher insists explicitly that "the prewar Japanese government was not fascist."[161] It was partly thus that the Shōwa Association intellectuals, seeking a radical restructuring of the political order, appealed to European fascist models, thereby encountering periodic friction with the governmental establishment. Still, they thought it possible that the military-bureaucratic elite could bring about the necessary fascist state from above, and they developed a close relationship with Prince Fumimaro Konoe, the dominant Japanese political personality during the late 1930s. He was certainly following the Shōwa Association blueprint to some extent when, as prime minister in 1940, he initiated a radical reform of the parliamentary system and the market economy around the New Order Movement, all bound up with mobilization for war.[162] This was the culmination of measures he had taken in an earlier stint as prime minister from 1937 to 1939.

But in the last analysis, Fletcher finds the goading of the Shōwa Association intellectuals to have been of only indirect importance. Their proposals were adopted when they "fit the needs of established leaders or political forces without threatening too many major interest groups."[163] For example, Konoe accepted cabinet councilors in 1937, further weakening parliament, simply to bolster his own authority, and the advent of a special agency for China in 1938 served the interests of the army in its rivalry with the foreign ministry. Whereas the innovations of 1940, especially, must have convinced the intellectuals that their influence was increasing, this was only an illusion. The military simply used their rhetoric, derived from European fascism, to legitimize its policy of domestic oppression and military conquest. Still, the intellectuals could believe they were directing policy to wider ends, overcoming the most nettlesome modern sociopolitical problems.[164] And this veneer helped enable wider circles of prominent intellectuals to support what Fletcher takes to have been a fascist new order in Japan.[165]

We note in passing this further instance of the importance of illusion, not knowing what was happening, in this case on the part of those most indebted to European fascism. We also note how a veneer of "fascism," appropriately recast for Japan, could seemingly enhance legitimacy, based on the appearance of being in the vanguard, despite the reasons to avoid the fascist label itself.

Kasza implies that the fascist-leaning intellectuals more deeply influenced major sectors of the military-bureaucratic elite after 1936 than Fletcher allows. And as a result they had a pronounced effect on public policy, producing a significant restructuring of state-society relations, until 1945. Within that governing elite, officials of the conservative authoritarian Right remained more numerous, but those influenced by the *kakushin* Right were more influential.[166] Conservative and *kakushin* officials were as often at odds as in agreement. Sometimes one side won; sometimes there was compromise. During the pivotal years 1940–41, the *kakushin* Right spearheaded change, with conservatives reacting, sometimes blocking and sometimes modifying *kakushin* initiatives.[167]

The elite neither relied on a mass movement from below nor sought to create a ruling party comparable to those in Germany and Italy, and major contrasts with the state structures of the two European fascist powers remained. But significant institutional changes concentrated power in the hands of *kakushin* officials. They not only eliminated labor unions and other civil associations, but dissolved the political parties, emasculated the parliament, and concentrated authority in new super-agencies like the Cabinet Planning Board, directly under the prime minister. Such measures involved military officers in all aspects of policymaking and enabled *kakushin* officials to draft policies free of the more merely conservative orientation of most ministries.[168]

The two organizational lynchpins of Japan's New Order, both borrowing heavily from fascist models, were the state-imposed and state-administered compulsory cartels established in many economic sectors and the mass organizations for labor, women, and youth. The German Labor Front influenced the creation of Japan's Industrial Patriotic Society, for which there were no domestic precedents. Youth and women's organizations had emerged earlier through bureaucratic mobilization, but fascist influence led the state to expand the system and make membership compulsory in the later 1930s. The Cabinet Information Bureau, equivalent to the German Ministry of Propaganda, was the entity most directly adapted from Germany. The aggregate result was a radical but selective transformation of society from above.[169]

In this case, too, we are confronting a trajectory, contingent and uncertain, but the outcome was surely a "new order," and it was substantially indebted to European fascism. But how do we place it in the new Right universe of the time? Does it matter whether or not we deem it fascist? Was it so bound up with interaction, with influence from Europe, that it conforms to the genetic model that Larsen dislikes as opposed to the emergence model, accenting indigenousness, that he prefers? And does that matter?

Kasza stresses that the transformation in Japan cannot be explained without reference to the impact of European fascism.[170] But, invoking the expected criteria, he also denies that the outcome can simply be labeled fascist—even on the basis of putative functional equivalence, which generally means that the departures in Italy, Germany, and Japan were comparable responses to the crisis of capitalism. But those authorities who insist that Japan became fascist would question Kasza's criteria. Indeed, uncertainty and contest over the criteria of fascism (and totalitarianism), and how those criteria are most appropriately weighed, are especially evident in considerations of the Japanese case.

To a considerable extent the differences in accent indicate the slipperiness of the criteria, especially if taken singly. For example, whereas some distinguish the Japanese case from fascism on the grounds that Nazi Germany was more unified and coherent, Reynolds stresses that internal rivalry and disorder were evident in Fascist Italy and Nazi Germany just as they were in Japan.[171] Yet it is striking that Kasza, in denying Japan was fascist, finds it necessary essentially to reverse the terms of the comparison. Whereas policymaking in Nazi Germany was personalistic, disjointed, and unpredictable, Japan continued with bureaucratic government through the cabinet, under career officials of the sort who would have held comparable positions during the 1920s.[172]

Meanwhile, Maruyama noted in 1946 that in light of the "sectional" impulse of government entities to defend their own sphere of interests, or turf, Japanese government had often been described as feudalistic. But he found the comparison inadequate because in Japan that impulse was believed to entail connection with the ultimate entity, personified in the emperor, making it far more active and aggressive than feudalism.[173] This is an aspect of Maruyama's argument that whereas Japanese idiosyncrasies certainly made for fascism, it was a form of fascism utterly different from the European varieties. His implication was that more recent comparisons based on institutional rivalries and the like are misleading because they do not adequately reflect the nature and import of the sectional infighting in Japan.

Other criteria are comparably slippery and arbitrary. Reynolds insists that because of certain aspects of Japanese institutions, and because Japan had not experienced Europe's wide-open democratic politics, a fascist third way emerged much more naturally in Japan than in Europe. He even suggests that Japan, as opposed to Italy, might be taken as the prototype of fascism.[174] But these judgments rest on an arbitrary selection of criteria. In the same way, it is arbitrary to take charismatic leadership or a cult of violence as defining features or to take orderly transformation within a legal framework as *not* fascist. We again encounter the futility of either/or thinking.

Whereas Reynolds and Kersten are determined to encompass the Japanese case as fascist, Kasza nicely specifies the deleterious effects of the either/or thinking at issue. In calling those involved fascists, Japanese scholars tend to overestimate their radicalism; Western scholars who deny fascism go too far the other way and conclude that they were merely conservative. They thereby underestimate the shuffling within the political elite that took place, the determination of those seizing the initiative to strengthen the nation to meet the perceived challenges of a new age, and the novelty of the programs that resulted. So Kasza asks, "Why persist in inconclusive debates over whether the adherents of the *kakushin* right were *really* conservative authoritarian or fascist, moderately reformist or revolutionary? In different respects, they were all these things, and that is why none of these labels fits."[175] But even as Kasza finds it important to deny fascism, in adopting "the *kakushin* right" he proposes another basis for classification, another typological layer, which he suggests has wider applicability. We will consider that claim below.

Although on a somewhat different basis, both Reynolds and Kersten argue for the inclusion of Japan partly because of their way of linking fascism to totalitarianism, whether explicitly or implicitly. Noting that indoctrination in the State Shintō religion became much more extreme from the mid-1930s, Reynolds contends that "it is hard to imagine a more fully totalitarian creed than that expounded by the State Shintō ideologues."[176] Thus of the three regimes Japan was the most effective in inculcating solidarity and strengthening society to face war. Reynolds comes close to taking as the essence of fascism such a totalitarian transformation of the nation into a fully mobilized war machine.[177] In the same way, Kersten contends that because the masses in Japan were mobilized through propaganda and fear, it was unnecessary to forge a mass movement.[178]

Certainly there can be disparate varieties of totalitarianism, as we will discuss in chapters 7 and 8. But in these characterizations Reynolds and Kersten are quick to smuggle in unexamined assumptions and stereotypical notions. The passive obedience, mechanical solidarity, and unthinking devotion to duty each seems to have in mind reflect a delimited understanding of the European cases. And such limits compromise not only characterization and classification but also our understanding of the stakes of Japanese interaction with European fascism. But the element of stereotyping in their understanding of the possible meanings of totalitarianism will not rule Reynolds and Kersten out of court when we consider the uses of totalitarianism as a category for differentiating fascism in chapter 8.

I said that it is not enough simply to document the borrowing from Europe, that we need to see how it played into the indigenous dynamic to understand the trajectory and the outcome. Fletcher and Kasza offer two approaches diverging just enough to open a potentially illuminating crease, which we are now prepared to probe.

Considering the trajectory from Fletcher's perspective, what happened to the proposals of the Shōwa Association intellectuals might be taken as evidence of how readily genuine fascism, emerging from outside the establishment, was diluted or absorbed. But subsequent work suggests a more complex interplay, though still with room for *some* of the illusion, the smoke and mirrors, that Fletcher concludes were operative, even paramount, in the relationship between the fascist intellectuals and those in power. We need to consider the possibility that the relationship entailed a kind of synergy between fascists, borrowing extensively, if selectively, from Europe, and conservatives, along the lines we have found at work elsewhere. Such synergy would have radicalized key segments in Japan, actualizing what had been only possibilities, even as it might well have entailed a measure of blunting and exploitative co-optation at the same time. The short duration of the experiment, which took place for the most part under the extreme conditions of wartime, makes it especially difficult to establish proportions.

It is that sort of synergy that Fletcher seems to rule out with his emphasis on illusion and veneer. The establishment had its interests and aims, the intellectuals theirs. But Kasza, though he does not hit the point hard, clearly implies that Japan would not have produced its New Order simply because of the indigenous elements in place, even in this situation of impending war. The input from European fascism was important not simply in helping to legitimize an oppressive militarist course—one that would have been chosen anyway—but especially in furthering the sense that in restructuring and acting as it did, Japan, like the fascist powers, was establishing a new and modern third way, beyond liberalism above all.

Kasza goes on to propose parallels between the top-down trajectory in Japan with several European cases. Especially in this context he addresses the limits of the standard terminology that invites either/or thinking. And he proposes that we use "*kakushin* right" in the wider discussion to characterize other top-down departures, including some, like those of Metaxas in Greece and King Carol in Romania, that we have encountered: "The term *kakushin* fills an awkward gap in the comparative typology of rightist (and perhaps also leftist) political tendencies, and it also fills a void in the English language."[179]

But though the Japanese example is especially rich and complex, surely potentially enhancing our understanding of the new Right universe, is an-

other typological slice what it suggests we need? We will return to the
question when we ponder the uses of such distinctions and classifications
in chapter 8. First, there are further modes of interaction to be considered.

Notes

1. Karina Urbach, ed., *European Aristocracies and the Radical Right, 1918–1939* (Oxford: Oxford University Press, 2007), 10.
2. Arnd Bauerkämper, "Transnational Fascism: Cross-Border Relations between Regimes and Movements in Europe, 1922–1939," *East Central Europe* 37 (2010): 217, 229, 232.
3. Constantin Iordachi, "God's Chosen Warriors: Romantic Palingenesis, Militarism and Fascism in Modern Romania," in *Comparative Fascist Studies: New Perspectives*, ed. Constantin Iordachi (London and New York: Routledge, 2010), 339.
4. Gilbert Allardyce, "What Fascism Is Not: Thoughts on the Deflation of a Concept," *American Historical Review* 84, no. 2 (April 1979): 370.
5. Aristotle Kallis, "Neither Fascist nor Authoritarian: The 4th of August Regime in Greece (1936–1941) and the Dynamics of Fascistisation in 1930s Europe," *East Central Europe* 37 (2010): 312–13, 321. See also Mogens Pelt, "Stages in the Development of the 'Fourth of August' Regime in Greece," in *Rethinking Fascism and Dictatorship in Interwar Europe*, ed. António Costa Pinto and Aristotle Kallis (Basingstoke: Palgrave Macmillan, 2014), 208–10, on Metaxas's sense of particular affinity with Salazar.
6. Maria Ormos, *Hungary in the Age of the Two World Wars, 1914–1945*, trans. Brian McLean (Boulder, CO: Social Science Monographs, 2007), 344.
7. Ignác Romsics, "The Hungarian Aristocracy and Its Politics," in *European Aristocracies*, ed. Urbach, 195.
8. Corinna Peniston-Bird, "Austria," in *The Oxford Handbook of Fascism*, ed. R.J.B. Bosworth (Oxford: Oxford University Press, 2009), 448.
9. For example, the Romanian economist Mihail Manoilescu, influential internationally for his theories of international trade and protectionism, was also widely known as an advocate of corporatism, especially through his *Le Siècle du corporatisme: Doctrine du corporatisme intègral et pur*, new edn (Paris: Félix Alcan, 1936). Originally published in 1934, it was again republished in 1938 and translated into Portuguese and German, among other languages.
10. J.F. Pollard, "Fascism and Catholicism," in *Oxford Handbook*, ed. Bosworth, 172–73, 178.
11. António Costa Pinto, *The Nature of Fascism Revisited* (Boulder, CO: Social Science Monographs, 2012), 127.
12. David D. Roberts, *The Syndicalist Tradition and Italian Fascism* (Chapel Hill: University of North Carolina Press, 1979), 213–41.
13. For a few indications of the interplay between the proto-corporatist syndicalist vision and the early *squadristi*, see Dino Grandi, *Giovani* (Bologna: Nicola Zanichelli, 1941), 220 (1920); Italo Balbo, *Diario, 1922* (Milan: A. Mondadori, 1932), 6; and Curzio Suckert, "La conquista dello Stato nella concezione organica di Sergio Panunzio," in Balbo's *Corriere Padano* (Ferrara), 16 December 1925, 1.
14. Giuseppe Bottai, *Esperienza corporativa (1929–1934)* (Florence: Vallecchi, 1934), 569–77, 583–85.
15. Pinto, *The Nature of Fascism Revisited*, 146.
16. See Roberts, *The Syndicalist Tradition*, 281–83, on the place of the Labor Charter in light of the pulling and tugging already much in evidence by that point.

17. This polemical exchange unfolded in *Rivista internazionale di filosofia del diritto*. See ibid., 240–44, for the context and the relevant references.

18. Didier Musiedlak, "Le corporatisme dans la structure de l'Etat fasciste," in *Les Expériences Corporatives dans l'aire Latine*, ed. Didier Musiedlak (Berne: Peter Lang, 2010), 139–40. See also Musiedlak's conclusion to the volume, 473. For the document itself and the circumstances surrounding it, see Renzo De Felice, ed., *La Carta del Carnaro nei testi di Alceste De Ambris e di Gabriele D'Annunzio* (Bologna: Il Mulino, 1973).

19. Renzo De Felice, *Fascism: An Informal Introduction to Its Theory and Practice (An Interview with Michael A. Ledeen)* (New Brunswick, NJ: Transaction, 1976), 49.

20. Musiedlak, "Le corporatisme dans la structure de l'Etat fasciste," 135–36.

21. Musiedlak, conclusion to *Les Expériences Corporatives*, 473.

22. Ibid.; Musiedlak, "Le corporatisme dans la structure de l'Etat fasciste," 152.

23. Musiedlak, conclusion to *Les Expériences Corporatives*, 473.

24. Pinto, *The Nature of Fascism Revisited*, 126.

25. Ibid., 146.

26. De Felice, *Fascism*, 49.

27. Peniston-Bird, "Austria," 447–48.

28. Musiedlak, conclusion to *Les Expériences Corporatives*, 473.

29. Pinto, *The Nature of Fascism Revisited*, 142–43.

30. Ibid.

31. Kallis, "Neither Fascist nor Authoritarian," 320.

32. Radu Ioanid, "Romania," in *Oxford Handbook*, ed. Bosworth, 401.

33. Musiedlak, conclusion to *Les Expériences Corporatives*, 473.

34. Tim Kirk, "Fascism and Austrofascism," in *The Dollfuss/Schuschnigg Era in Austria: A Reassessment*, ed. Günter Bischof, Anton Pelinka, and Alexander Lassner (New Brunswick, NJ: Transaction, 2003), 23.

35. Musiedlak, conclusion to *Les Expériences Corporatives*, 473.

36. Alessio Gagliardi, *Il corporativismo fascista* (Rome: Laterza, 2010).

37. Gianpasquale Santomassimo, *La terza via fascista: Il mito del corporativismo* (Rome: Carocci, 2006), 10–11.

38. Limited though it was in certain respects, Michael Ledeen's *Universal Fascism: The Theory and Practice of the Fascist International, 1928–1936* (New York: Howard Fertig, 1972), especially brought these issues to our attention and remains widely cited.

39. Aristotle Kallis, *Fascist Ideology* (London: Routledge, 2000), 134, 139, 148–49, 153–54, 157.

40. Kirk, "Fascism and Austrofascism," 25.

41. Peniston-Bird, "Austria," 449.

42. Manuela A. Williams, *Mussolini's Propaganda Abroad: Subversion in the Mediterranean and the Middle East, 1935–1940* (London and New York: Routledge, 2006).

43. See also Stein Ugelvik Larsen, "Was There Fascism outside Europe? Diffusion from Europe and Domestic Impulses," in *Fascism outside Europe: The European Impulse against Domestic Conditions in the Diffusion of Global Fascism*, ed. Stein Ugelvik Larsen (Boulder, CO: Social Science Monographs, 2001), 795–802, on the Italian-German competition for influence in the Middle East and North Africa.

44. John-Paul Himka, "The Importance of the Situational Element in East Central European Fascism," *East Central Europe* 37 (2010): 354–55.

45. Pelt, "Stages in the Development," 202, 205.

46. Kallis, "Neither Fascist nor Authoritarian," 313–14, 321–22.

47. Pelt, "Stages in the Development," 212.

48. Davide Rodogno, *Fascism's European Empire: Italian Occupation during the Second World War* (Cambridge: Cambridge University Press, 2006).

49. Ibid., 67, 224–25.

50. Ibid., 413.

51. Ibid., 35–36, 41.

52. Ibid., 205–9.

53. Ibid., 49, 55, 57, 59, 264–65, 298, 331, 412.

54. Ibid., 385–86, 390–93, 395–98.

55. Ibid., 317, 414.

56. Peter F. Sugar, "Conclusion," in Peter F. Sugar, ed., *Native Fascism in the Successor States, 1918–1945* (Santa Barbara: ABC-Clio, 1971), 147-56, esp. 156.

57. Lothar Höbelt, "Nostalgic Agnostics: Austrian Aristocrats and Politics, 1918–1938," in *European Aristocracies*, ed. Urbach, 183–84.

58. Aristotle Kallis, *Genocide and Fascism: The Eliminationist Drive in Fascist Europe* (London and New York: Routledge, 2009).

59. Mark Pittaway, "Hungary," in *Oxford Handbook*, ed. Bosworth, 384.

60. Paul A. Hanebrink, *In Defense of Christian Hungary: Religion, Nationalism, and Anti-Semitism, 1890–1944* (Ithaca, NY: Cornell University Press, 2006), 140–41, 166.

61. Pittaway, "Hungary," 388.

62. Ibid., 392.

63. Ormos, *Hungary,* 248.

64. Ibid., 355. Ormos notes that Hungarian-German relations were poor during the fall of 1939 and into 1940. There were plenty of reasons for mistrust on both sides, and neither seemed to have done enough to satisfy the other.

65. Thomas L. Sakmyster, *Hungary's Admiral on Horseback: Miklos Horthy, 1918–1944* (Boulder, CO: East European Monographs, 1994), 385.

66. Hanebrink, *In Defense of Christian Hungary,* 166.

67. Ormos, *Hungary,* 359–60.

68. Ibid., 343.

69. Ibid., 366–67.

70. Ibid., 368. After the German attack on Yugoslavia on 6 April, Hungary joined the war on 11 April and soon gained territory with one million inhabitants.

71. Hanebrink, *In Defense of Christian Hungary,* 194–95.

72. Pittaway, "Hungary," 381, 392.

73. Ormos, *Hungary,* 361.

74. Ibid., 361.

75. Randolph L. Braham's work on the Holocaust in Hungary has been fundamental. See especially Randolph L. Braham, *The Politics of Genocide: The Holocaust in Hungary* (Detroit: Wayne State University Press, 2000), a conveniently condensed version of the author's massive, two-volume standard treatment of the Holocaust in Hungary, first published in 1981, then published in an expanded edition in 1994. Braham stresses that even as it had become clear that the war was lost, the Nazi genocide found many willing Hungarian collaborators. See also Randolph L. Braham and Brewster S. Chamberlin, eds, *The Holocaust in Hungary: Sixty Years Later* (New York: Rosenthal Institute for Holocaust Studies, Graduate Center of the City University of New York, 2006), the latest in a series of books of essays on a wide variety of aspects of the Holocaust in Hungary.

76. Hanebrink, *In Defense of Christian Hungary,* 198, 219.

77. Peter Longerich, *Holocaust: The Nazi Persecution and Murder of the Jews* (Oxford: Oxford University Press, 2010), 406, 409.

78. Ibid., 409.

79. Ormos, *Hungary,* 422–36.

80. Ibid., 368.

81. Ibid., 363.

82. Dennis Deletant, *Hitler's Forgotten Ally: Ion Antonescu and His Regime, Romania 1940–44* (Basingstoke: Palgrave Macmillan, 2006), 35.

83. Ibid., 10.

84. Ibid., 15–16, 19.

85. Ibid., 22–25.

86. Ibid., 61.

87. Ibid., 74–75.

88. Ibid., 79–83.

89. Ibid., 61–62, 85–86.

90. Ibid., 93, 166–67.

91. Vladimir Solonari, *Purifying the Nation: Population Exchange and Ethnic Cleansing in Nazi-Allied Romania* (Washington, DC: Woodrow Wilson Center Press; Baltimore: Johns Hopkins University Press, 2010); Jean Ancel, *The History of the Holocaust in Romania*, trans. Yaffah Murciano (Lincoln: University of Nebraska Press; Jerusalem: Yad Vashem, 2011); Radu Ioanid, *The Holocaust in Romania: The Destruction of Jews and Gypsies under the Antonescu Regime, 1940–1944*, trans. Marc J. Masurovsky (Chicago: Ivan R. Dee, 2000).

92. Ancel, *The History of the Holocaust in Romania*, 3.

93. Marius Turda, "Controlling the National Body: Ideas of Racial Purification in Romania, 1918–1944," in *Health, Hygiene, and Eugenics in Southeastern Europe to 1945*, ed. Christian Promitzer, Sevastri Trubeta, and Marius Turda (Budapest: Central European University Press, 2011), 329.

94. Deletant, *Hitler's Forgotten Ally*, 150.

95. Ibid., 128, 150, 171.

96. Ancel, *The History of the Holocaust in Romania*, 2. See also Deletant, *Hitler's Forgotten Ally*, 121–22, 205, 209.

97. Deletant, *Hitler's Forgotten Ally*, 211–12.

98. Ibid., 100, 118.

99. Ibid., 225–26. But it is not clear Antonescu knew the extent of this policy, and the numbers involved were relatively low in any case.

100. Ibid., 260.

101. Ibid., 230–32.

102. Ibid., 235–36.

103. Ibid., 246.

104. Michael R. Marrus and Robert O. Paxton, *Vichy France and the Jews* (New York: Basic Books, 1981).

105. Robert Paxton, "Jews: How Vichy Made It Worse," *New York Review*, 6 March 2014, 40–43.

106. In this context, we might also note Daniel Carpi's *Between Mussolini and Hitler: The Jews and the Italian Authorities in France and Tunisia* (Hanover, NH: University Press of New England, for Brandeis University Press, 1994), which treats the complex interplay between Fascist Italy, Nazi Germany, and Vichy France as it bore on Jewish policy in French territories occupied by the Italians. It, too, shows how the presence of Jewish refugees in France complicated relations, but also why, for example, it seemed a priority to protect Italian Jews in Tunisia, in response to Vichy efforts to confiscate their property. Carpi's study, like that of Paxton and Marrus, makes especially clear that rather than relying on essence or telos, we must attend to the trajectory generated by the need at the time to respond to contingent concatenations.

107. E. Bruce Reynolds, introduction to *Japan in the Fascist Era*, ed. E. Bruce Reynolds (New York: Palgrave Macmillan, 2004), xi.

108. Larsen, "Was There Fascism outside Europe?," 732–37.

109. Stefan Ihrig, *Atatürk in the Nazi Imagination* (Cambridge, MA: Harvard University Press, 2014), 113–18, 226–27.

110. Fikret Adanır, "Kemalist Authoritarianism and Fascist Trends in Turkey during the Interwar Period," in *Fascism outside Europe*, ed. Larsen, 337–38, 343.

111. Ibid., 337.

112. Ihrig, *Atatürk*, 224–25.

113. Adanır, "Kemalist Authoritarianism," 338.

114. Ihrig, *Atatürk*, 128–29.

115. Adanır, "Kemalist Authoritarianism," 352.

116. Ibid., 313–15.

117. Ibid., 359–61.

118. Ibid., 315–16.

119. Ibid., 336, 351.

120. Çağlar Keyder, *State and Class in Turkey: A Study in Capitalist Development* (London: Verso, 1987), 99–100, 104.

121. Adanır, "Kemalist Authoritarianism," 353–54.

122. Keyder, *State and Class in Turkey*, 104, 107–8; Adanır, "Kemalist Authoritarianism," 353.

123. Keyder, *State and Class in Turkey*, 100.

124. Adanır, "Kemalist Authoritarianism," 352–53.

125. Ibid., 360–61.

126. Ibid., 341.

127. Ibid., 354–59.

128. Ibid., 358–59.

129. Ihrig, *Atatürk*, 227.

130. E. Bruce Reynolds, "Peculiar Characteristics: The Japanese Political System in the Fascist Era," in *Japan in the Fascist Era*, ed. E. Bruce Reynolds (New York: Palgrave Macmillan, 2004), 160–61, 182.

131. Ibid., 176.

132. Rikki Kersten, "Japan," in *Oxford Handbook*, ed. Bosworth, 543.

133. Joseph P. Sottile, "The Fascist Era: Imperial Japan and the Axis Alliance in Historical Perspective," in *Japan in the Fascist Era*, ed. Reynolds, 3–4.

134. Reynolds, introduction to *Japan in the Fascist Era*, xiii.

135. Kersten, "Japan," 539.

136. Masao Maruyama, *Thought and Behaviour in Modern Japanese Politics*, expanded edn, ed. Ivan Morris (London: Oxford University Press, 1969), 1–24, 33.

137. Kersten, "Japan," 539–40.

138. Larsen, "Was There Fascism outside Europe?," 741–46. See esp. 743n41.

139. Reynolds, "Peculiar Characteristics," 172–73, 182.

140. Ibid., 186.

141. William Miles Fletcher III, *The Search for a New Order: Intellectuals and Fascism in Prewar Japan* (Chapel Hill: University of North Carolina Press, 1982), 5, 161.

142. Reynolds, "Peculiar Characteristics," 172; Kersten, "Japan," 529, 538, 543; Gregory J. Kasza, "Fascism from Above? Japan's *Kakushin* Right in Comparative Perspective," in *Fascism outside Europe*, ed. Larsen, 189, 198-99, 213–14.

143. Reynolds, "Peculiar Characteristics," 159, 184–85.

144. Kersten, "Japan," 531.

145. Geoff Eley, *Nazism as Fascism: Violence, Ideology, and the Ground of Consent in Germany, 1930–1945* (London and New York: Routledge, 2013), 221–22n37.

146. Ibid., 222n39.

147. Gregory J. Kasza, "Fascism from Above? Japan's *Kakushin* Right in Comparative Perspective," in *Fascism outside Europe*, ed. Larsen, 197, 204–5.

148. Ibid., 184.

149. Ibid., 190–91.

150. Ibid., 199.

151. Ibid., 198–99.

152. Fletcher, *The Search for a New Order*, 4–5, 158–61.

153. Kasza, "Fascism from Above?," 208–9.

154. Fletcher, *The Search for a New Order*, 5–6, 155–56.

155. Kasza, "Fascism from Above?," 207, 208–209, 211; Fletcher, *The Search for a New Order*, 5, 36–39, 88.

156. Fletcher, *The Search for a New Order*, 157–58.

157. Kasza, "Fascism from Above?," 200, 205, 213–14.

158. Fletcher, *The Search for a New Order*, 5.

159. Ibid., 156.

160. Ibid., 157.

161. Ibid., 158.

162. Ibid., 3, 6.

163. Ibid., 155.

164. Ibid., 155, 160.

165. Ibid., 4.

166. Kasza, "Fascism from Above?," 199, 201, 205, 213–14.

167. Ibid., 225.

168. Ibid., 218, 223.

169. Ibid., 219, 221, 223.

170. Ibid., 224–25.

171. Reynolds, "Peculiar Characteristics," 166.

172. Kasza, "Fascism from Above?," 218.

173. Maruyama, *Thought and Behaviour*, 15.

174. Reynolds, "Peculiar Characteristics," 182–84, 186–87. See also his introduction to the volume, xii–xiii.

175. Kasza, "Fascism from Above?," 231; see also 89.

176. Reynolds, "Peculiar Characteristics," 165.

177. Ibid., 161.

178. Kersten, "Japan," 535.

179. Kasza, "Fascism from Above?," 231–32. See 223–32 for the overall discussion of the wider applicability of the category.

Chapter 6

INTERACTION WITH
THE LIBERAL DEMOCRACIES

Sizing Up the Liberal Rival

Although the web on the multinational level most obviously encompassed interaction *within* the new Right, it also encompassed interaction with the liberal democracies and the Soviet Union. From the start the fascists and others on the new Right expressed contempt for both liberal democracy and communism, and of course they drew bitter opposition from both camps. Such antagonisms reinforced hostility, but those on the new Right continued to measure themselves against both liberal democracy and communism, and a sense of their superiority—or at least potential superiority—over both emboldened them at the same time.

In terms of their perceptions of liberal democracy, fascists in Italy and Germany were bound to think first of superiority on the domestic level. In Italy the Fascists' violence and violation of liberal decorum provoked a prominent liberal opponent to label Fascism "totalitarian" as early as 1923, but the Fascists soon came to embrace the category, as we will see in more detail in the next chapter. The seemingly successful domestic innovations of both the Italian Fascist and Nazi German regimes attracted attention in the democracies, and how those in the democracies read them and responded was bound to affect the fascist self-understanding.

Some of course featured aspects that might be emulated, while others highlighted aspects that might be detested or feared. Again we note that those elsewhere could pick and choose, based on their own considerations, which might include an element of wishful thinking. Like so many at the time, the British economist Paul Einzig was no doubt too quick to credit the achievements of Italian Fascist corporatism, but his enthusiasm surely enhanced the confidence of the Italians. Moreover, his way of contrasting what he portrayed as the promising, innovative quality of Italian Fascist corporatism with the sterility of German Nazism was bound to reinforce the Italian Fascists' sense of superiority over the Germans.[1]

It is well known, even notorious, that both the Italian and German regimes attracted influential sympathizers in the democratic countries, though the importance of the fact for the fascist self-understanding is easily neglected. Even after, and in some ways especially after, Hitler came to power in 1933, Mussolini and Fascist Italy seemed particularly attractive—as Einzig's example suggests. Not only was World War I still widely traced to German militarism, but Nazi Germany seemed more obviously revisionist, potentially more powerful, and thus more dangerous than Fascist Italy. Hitler's racist anti-Semitism also seemed crudely excessive to many. But though Einzig could proclaim the superiority of Italian Fascism in 1933, it became harder to distinguish the two regimes as they came together on the diplomatic level by the later 1930s.

Still, John Patrick Diggins shows in his pioneering study of American perceptions of Fascist Italy that major figures in the Roosevelt administration continued to find reason to look with favor on Mussolini's regime.[2] More generally, Ira Katznelson's recent *Fear Itself: The New Deal and the Origins of Our Time* is especially good in foregrounding the "atmosphere of unremitting uncertainty about liberal democracy's capacity and fate" that surrounded the New Deal. The dictatorships were seemingly in the ascendant; even President Roosevelt might have to assume dictatorial powers if the United States was to surmount the Depression and meet the challenge of the dictatorships.[3] Katznelson, too, shows that that the attraction of fascism, and especially of Fascist Italy, continued well into the 1930s.[4]

The criteria of sympathizers varied but were often superficial, featuring anti-communism, strong leadership, the ineffectiveness of parliamentary government, and the like. Even so, it is clear that fascism, in Italy as elsewhere, was widely viewed as a promising experiment in progress. An interesting American sympathizer was the diplomat and eclectic writer Charles Hitchcock Sherrill, who lauded Mussolini both in *Bismarck and Mussolini*, published in 1931, and, more symptomatically, in *Kamal Roosevelt Mussolini*, published in Italian by the important publisher Nicola Zanichelli in 1936.[5] Sherrill had been American ambassador to Turkey in 1932–33, and he noted parallels in the strong leadership of his three protagonists. Though Sherrill's book seems naive today, it indicates how remote the texture of the time has become to us, how difficult to grasp what seemed the advent of new possibilities, new combinations. Grasping the uncertainty, fluidity, and blurring then suggests the need to loosen our own categories up to a point.

Of course interaction with the democracies did not entail simply the sympathetic interest of those like Einzig and Sherrill. Much of the considerable literature justifying a focus on fascism in Britain, where fascism was seemingly quite weak, insists convincingly that the impact of fascism must be considered widely because fascism so significantly affected agendas and debate even among those not embracing it.[6] The evidence that fascism was influencing the wider political and even cultural agendas in the democracies surely enhanced fascist confidence.

The Sense of Leapfrogging

Up to a point, in fact, interaction nurtured a sense among fascists that they were leapfrogging the established democracies and moving to the modern forefront. That sense stemmed first from simply measuring themselves against the others, but it was also fueled by responses in the democracies, as we noted in treating Einzig's take on Italian Fascist corporatism.

The sense of the scope for leapfrogging was bound up with the perception that the era entailed new challenges and possibilities demanding bold new forms of collective action. Insofar as fascists could claim to be spearheading the necessary innovation, they were not merely defending or trying to catch up. And rather than merely seeking domestic renewal, they were showing, as the democracies could not, the mode of action necessary. It was in that sense that they could be seen as leapfrogging rather than merely competing with the democracies. Idiosyncrasies of tradition and situation in Italy, Germany, and beyond might especially offer insight into the sources of complacency and weakness in the mainstream liberal democracies—perceived as flat-footed and anti-historical.

In the Italian and German cases, to be sure, the sense of leapfrogging developed from within a framework encompassing *some* admiration for the established democracies, even a determination to learn from them and simply to catch up with them in certain particulars. The self-congratulatory hoopla surrounding the proclamation of empire in Fascist Italy in 1936 obviously reflected the sensitivities of a latecomer feeling it had at last matched Britain and France. In thinking about *Lebensraum* and the possible need to exterminate populations in the way, Hitler was much influenced by what had happened as the United States expanded westward, pursuing its manifest destiny, seemingly wiping out indigenous populations as necessary.[7] The rise of the United States appeared to indicate that this was the way of the world. And Hitler's ongoing preoccupation that an ascendant United States would overwhelm smaller countries like Germany was evident in his "Second Book," dictated in 1928 but left unpublished in his lifetime.[8] If Germany was to remain genuinely sovereign, capable of competing with the United States on the global level, it had to act fast—and in a new way. In considering the run-up to war during the 1930s, Adam Tooze shows how salient such preoccupations remained in Hitler's calculations.[9]

But in both the Italian and German cases, even as elements of admiration, resentment, and competition remained, the fascists sensed that they had to show, and were indeed showing, how to do better than the mature democracies. Italian imperialism, as fascist, was purportedly new, different, not simply accomplishing what the democracies had before. Nazi Germany comparably saw itself as different in pursuing population engineering in the concerted, systematic way that seemed necessary. So even as interaction with the democracies worked both ways, it surely reinforced the fascist sense not only of difference but also of leapfrogging, a sense that emboldened and energized.

The notion of leapfrogging is a step beyond a quest for an alternative modernity, which many are now willing to concede to fascism, and which is itself a step beyond mere defense or catch-up, as we noted earlier. Seeking an alternative modernity could mean simply "you do it your way, we'll do it ours." But insofar as the fascists sensed the scope for leapfrogging, they were saying, "No, we'll do it a new way better than yours, better attuned to the historical moment, because we are so situated that we can see, as you cannot, the challenge and opportunity." Still, an emphasis on leapfrogging is not to be understood as an *alternative* to a quest for an alternative modernity. Leapfrogging was simply a particular, radical form of that quest.

To grasp the place of such leapfrogging, let us first note that Ian Kershaw, while arguing for the singularity of Nazism, pointed out that the Italian Fascists, unlike the Nazis, had little or no sense of being the last bulwark of Western, Christian culture against atheistic, Jewish, Asiatic Bolshevism. Indeed, he suggested, such pseudo-religious notions of national salvation were weaker in Mussolini's Italy even than in Franco's Spain.[10] This is taken as evidence that Fascist Italy was considerably less radical than Nazi Germany. But whereas Kershaw makes a useful distinction regarding the sense of mission in the Italian and Spanish cases, his comparison falls flat because he lacks sufficient sense of what else, rather than such defensiveness and sense of threat, might have fueled Italian Fascism. Indeed, here we have a good example of our tendency, when asking about the contours of the universe at issue, to impose criteria based on a delimited set of cases and a restricted range of frequencies.

In Italy, the alternative to that defensive sense of mission was precisely the energizing perception of moving out front. That feeling of leapfrogging constituted a kind of functional equivalent to the Nazi sense of mission, affording the same energizing sense of confronting challenges and seizing opportunities as the more complacent democracies could not. The Italian sense of leapfrogging had been foreshadowed in some ways by Futurism, the artistic movement launched with a clamorous manifesto by F.T. Marinetti in 1909. So heavy was the weight of the past in Italy that an Italian art movement could not settle simply for trying to catch up and participate more fully in European modernism. Italy could address its challenges only through a hyper-modernism, transcending the others. So its special challenges afforded Italy an opportunity to move to the modern forefront.

For the Italian Fascists, the sense of leapfrogging was based partly on totalitarianism and corporatism as specifically Italian innovations. In the previous two chapters we encountered indications of the Italian Fascist sense of superiority even over Nazi Germany in overcoming the limits of liberalism and Marxism—in handling labor relations, for example, or in meshing public and private initiatives to enhance economic productivity. The conferences and other activities of the International Labor Office at Geneva, created by the Versailles Treaty, were major occasions for taking the measure of the competition, both liberal and post-liberal, and for trumpeting the pioneering achievements of Fascist corporatism, taken as itself a totalitarian measure.[11]

Much recent literature on Italian Fascism brushes up against the sensibility at issue, though without considering its sources and implications. In an especially engaging study, Jeffrey Schnapp shows that after the visionary engineer Gaetano Ciocca visited the United States in 1934 to assess Americanism firsthand, he returned home with new ammunition to explain the superiorities of Fascist Italy.[12] To some extent, a sense of leapfrogging was implicit in, and helped to fuel, every Fascist achievement. The war on malaria, the restoration of medieval and Renaissance cities, and the excavation and redesign of Rome are examples of energetic initiatives that do not reflect interaction and leapfrogging specifically, but that drew fuel from an implicit sense that the democracies could not have done it.[13]

The interaction with the British we encountered in the preceding chapter, when considering Manuela Williams's study of Italian ambitions in the Middle East, surely energized the Italians, breeding a sense of superiority until the end of the 1930s. The Italian sense of competing with the more established colonial powers, but doing it better, is similarly evident in Mia Fuller's treatment of architecture and urban planning in the Italian colonial realm, especially in Eritrea and East Africa.[14] To be sure, the notion that Italian imperialism was different seems, from our perspective, an example of almost risible mythmaking, and we will consider the mythmaking potential of the overall sense of leapfrogging in concluding this chapter. But to understand what the Italians thought they were doing in their imperialist ventures, we need to keep in mind their way of reading their interaction with the democracies.

Whereas the sense of defensive mission that Kershaw pinpointed was indeed central to Nazism, in the German case we also find a feeling of leapfrogging, comparable to the Italian sense. Detlev Peukert forcefully brought it to the fore in arguing that seemingly Germany could surmount the crisis of the Weimar Republic only through a leap into a hyper-modernity, beyond anything accomplished or even attempted elsewhere.[15] That hyper-modernity revolved especially around science and social engineering, now widely taken to have been hyper-modern and hubristic, anything but merely atavistic. "Race hygiene," encompassing both eugenics and anti-Semitism, lay at the core.[16]

Stefan Kühl's analysis of German-American interaction over eugenics points even beyond the Peukert syndrome to show how interaction with the Americans helped foster, first within the German eugenics community, but then also in wider Nazi circles, a sense of the scope for a hyper-modern response through a systematic program, including forced sterilization and "euthanasia." Becoming prominent during the 1920s, that interaction with American eugenicists helped persuade the Germans of their own modernity up to a point. But it came to seem that Germany had to practice eugenics more radically and systematically—and could do so uniquely through Nazism.[17]

However, by the later 1930s, as the Nazi regime indeed began acting more radically and systematically than the Americans had, American eugenicists backed off, surely furthering the energizing German sense of pioneering, of being uniquely capable of the tough, systematic measures necessary. Because of the sanitizing of "modernity" after the fact, so well pinpointed by Mark Roseman, we have only recently come to grasp how those carrying out the policy, which we now find not only reprehensible but almost incomprehensible, could have experienced the effort precisely as hyper-modern, as uniquely responding to the challenges of both the historical moment and the modern world.[18]

In treating Nazi scientific work in areas from nutrition to cancer research to environmental protection, Robert Proctor has made clear the Nazi sense that they were doing what modernity required as the established democracies were not—and could not.[19] And in many areas they were indeed taking innovative, pioneering steps that would eventually come to seem progressive in the Western mainstream.

In both Italy and Germany, the sense of being out front not only energized the new fascist elite but, up to a point, drew in much of the wider society, excited by the sense of involvement in something new and grandiose. The energizing effects on the elite and the wider society proved reciprocal.

The sense of leapfrogging was operative especially in Italy and Germany, where the new regimes had the power actually to begin acting in the new ways and tackling the new tasks envisioned. A comparable sense was sometimes at work in other new Right formations, though it was less obviously linked to interaction with the democracies. The seeming leapfrogging success of the two fascist powers may have inspired a sense in these others that they too had something distinctive to offer, enabling them to leapfrog. But they did not necessarily need such inspiration to believe that idiosyncratic national circumstances or traditions equipped them to go beyond the democracies to offer something uniquely pertinent to the historical moment.

In the previous chapter we returned to António Costa Pinto's point that Salazar's Portugal was taken as a model by some on the new Right elsewhere precisely because it seemed to avoid the more distasteful aspects of fascism. It is worth considering this point in the present context as well, because even insofar as the Salazar regime was not interacting directly with the democracies, comparison with the democracies was bound to be implicit in the multinational interaction on the new Right, which could thereby produce an energizing sense of leapfrogging among the Portuguese regime's adherents. Whereas the Salazar regime might be taken today simply as evidence that Portugal was not yet ready for democracy, the attraction of others on the new Right suggested that, on the contrary, Portugal was creating a new and appropriate mode of modern politics, an alternative to *both* liberal democracy and full-scale fascism.

Although, as we noted in chapter 5, the turn to more radical, interventionist modes of population engineering in both Horthy's Hungary and Antonescu's Romania seem to have stemmed from the intertwining of indigenous impulses and German inspiration, the particular sense of national vulnerability in both cases surely helped fuel the sense that to meet the challenge they, too, had to get out front, become hyper-modern, responding in a systematic way to the latest scientific research on population, health, and national viability. In each case the government had to become more interventionist in family and population matters at the expense of individual rights. But doing so could be experienced as an innovative response to a wider modern problem of population health, one that the more complacent democracies were not prepared fully to confront.

Leapfrogging and Palingenesis

Up to a point, doing justice to the sense of leapfrogging indicates the limits of Roger Griffin's influential category "palingenesis." We note, first, that the sense of leapfrogging proves more congruent than palingenesis with the now-widespread notion that fascism was seeking an alternative modernity. But more importantly, "palingenesis" does not convey the role of interaction, of measuring oneself against others, the crucial sense that fascism could spearhead radical innovation as the mainstream democracies could not. What fascism claimed to offer was not simply the radical renewal of this or that nation as an antidote to internal decadence, as if that nation were on a trajectory parallel to the mainstream modern democracies. At work, rather, was leapfrogging to overcome a wider modern tendency toward decadence.

To be sure, Griffin, in his more recent work, based partly on much pioneering research on Nazi modernism, has seemed on his way to a more flexible understanding of the Nazi relationship with modernity that might seem to transcend national palingenesis and have room, at least, for a sense of leapfrogging. And it is worth drawing out certain implications of Griffin's effort, although doing so leads into especially sensitive territory. In contemplating the Nazi relationship to artistic modernism, we have long assumed simple rejection. On the one hand, we have fastened upon the Nazi dismissal of modern art as "degenerate" (*entartete Kunst*); on the other, we have emphasized what has seemed the Nazi emphasis on returning to tradition or on valorizing accessible popular forms. But on the basis of much neglected evidence, Griffin shows conclusively that this understanding, self-evident though it has come to seem, has been one-sided.[20]

Still, though he deserves much credit for providing a fruitful new perspective, Griffin leaves the framework too delimited to account convincingly for that evidence.[21] Whereas he backs up to what he considers the wider modern crisis, bound up with "canopy loss," we need to back up differently, more genuinely encompassing the scope for an alternative modernity, in order to contemplate a wider range of possibilities. Only when we attune to such a wider range can we begin to develop a more differentiated understanding of the Nazi relationship to modernist art as it had developed to that point. And that understanding can contribute to a more differentiated understanding of the Nazi relationship to the modern mainstream more generally—which, again, might further suggest the possibility of leapfrogging the modern Western mainstream.

Artistic modernism entailed multiple strands, of course, and the basis for the Nazi rejection of each was surely somewhat different. Let us pinpoint three of those strands, considering them as a kind of continuum. At one end, modernist art entailed formalist experiment, which can lead to a certain aloofness, or lack of societal engagement. And these could only have seemed deleterious to the Nazis, in light of their totalitarian direction, their denial of the public-private distinction. But much modernist art was highly engaged; yet, at the other end of the continuum, it could seem alienating and unhealthy. In between, we find a premium on self-expression, which might also entail alienation and aloofness, but which is not to be conflated with formalist experiment.

In whatever combination, engagement and self-expression fed the sometimes morbid quality of central European culture by the 1920s, evident, for example, in such operas as Alban Berg's *Wozzeck* and *Lulu* and Bertholt Brecht and Kurt Weill's *Rise and Fall of the City of Mahagonny*, as well as in some of Weimar German painting. I hasten to emphasize that I am among the particular enthusiasts of that culture. Although there are dissenters, we tend to take it all as healthy precisely as experimental, edgy, and avant-garde, but also, more precisely, as probing—and revealing—alienating aspects of modernity itself.[22] We also tend to value the ironic or sarcastic responses to power and authority that much of that art seems to entail.

The basis for the Nazi rejection of that current has seemed almost self-evident. Such art would be unsettling, threatening, and alienating especially to those most having trouble adjusting to modernity. Still, insofar as that art could indeed be somewhat morbid, sometimes tending to wallow in its own alienation, it could be considered "decadent" in some sense, reflecting something unhealthy in modern culture. And that unhealthiness is precisely what a quest for a superior modernity might seek to overcome. As an aspect of his newly expanded definition, Griffin suggests that fascism aims precisely at new cultural *health*.[23] And his evidence brings to the fore the Nazi sense of the scope to foster healthier, more affirmative modes of art that would still be modern, innovative, even experimental, and not merely a return to the traditional or familiar.

The point is not to blame Berg et al. or to say they should have done something different. But it is possible to look more deeply into the culture from within which they chose to do what they did, thought they were best exercising their talents as they did. And we can at least ponder the scope for a culture that might nurture more affirmative responses.

In this context we might note the accents of the noted musicologist Richard Taruskin, who, though speaking primarily of music and modernism in the Soviet Union, forcefully criticizes the emphasis on artistic autonomy and self-expression in the liberal West, an emphasis that left composers, perhaps especially, "sadly marginalized." He longs for art to play a more resonant role, but for this to happen, he feels, artists must become less concerned with autonomy and more fully involved in their societies. To be sure, Taruskin has been concerned especially with the complex role of Dimitri Shostakovich, with why he so deeply mattered during the Soviet period. It may seem dubious indeed to invoke Taruskin's argument in the context of Nazi artistic policy. The mode of participation he envisions is not remotely to be conflated with what the Nazis sought to foster; he was in no sense advocating governmental pressure to nudge, let alone force, artists in the direction of such fuller participation. The Nazi regime, embarked on a totalitarian direction, sought precisely to shape and channel artistic response in ways that we reject unequivocally today. As Taruskin himself notes, such earlier efforts at totalitarian control ended up reinforcing the liberal premium on individual self-expression in the arts.[24]

But precisely in questioning mainstream modern liberal ways of conceiving the artist and society, Taruskin helps us see beyond our usual dichotomies to encompass a wider range of possibilities. He suggests that the cult of individual self-expression can be excessive—and culturally deleterious. Certain modes of artistic involvement may have healthier cultural consequences, including a more resonant art, than a premium on artistic autonomy. Leaving serious art as a thing apart, irrelevant to modern society, is undesirable, even unhealthy. There must be ways of finding more productive modes of involvement, yielding the more resonant art that a healthy culture requires. The function of such art might even be understood as integrating, as opposed to alienating.

Again, Taruskin was not envisioning anything like Nazi policy, but merely to open the door slightly in this direction helps us to see the Nazi response from the broader perspective necessary. The mainstream modern liberal understanding of the role of the artist and the place of art did not exhaust the modern possibilities; there was scope to experiment with other *modern* alternatives. Our tendency to miss even the possibility of this direction is another manifestation of our long-standing tendency, noted by Roseman, to sweep challenging or inconvenient aspects of Nazi modernism under the rug.

At work, from the Nazi perspective, was another aspect of the scope for leapfrogging, for responding, as the complacent democracies could not, to modern decadence. What Griffin seems to mean by "decadence" is limited to what can be overcome by national palingenesis, but in their sense of leapfrogging, the Nazis felt themselves to be playing a far wider role, precisely in responding to that wider modern decadence. The effort to foster a healthier modern art was one manifestation of their energizing sense that they were producing not merely an alternative modernity but a superior modernity.

The case of the Romanian Iron Guard, and its forerunner the Legion of the Archangel Michael, founded by Corneliu Codreanu in 1927, indicates that the relationship between leapfrogging and palingenesis was more complex on occasion. Philip Morgan's recent characterization provides a good starting point:

> The Romanian Iron Guard was the strangest and craziest and most idiosyncratic of interwar European fascisms, largely because of its heretical religious Orthodoxy. ... But emphasising the strangeness of the Iron Guard does rather

obscure the fact that it was one of the most "international" and "internationalist" of European fascist movements, willingly sending its "martyrs" to die in the Spanish Civil War, and most insistent in its claim to be an integral part of a more general life-and-death struggle between "civilisations," or between different versions of European civilisation.[25]

The Iron Guard offers perhaps the most dramatic example, apart from Italy and Germany, of the fascist sense of being uniquely positioned, in light of idiosyncrasies in national traditions and present situation, to spearhead the appropriate response to the problems of the modern world. But as Morgan noted, and as Constantin Iordachi has shown to great effect, what was to be offered was nothing less than Christian salvation, the redemption of mankind, as the ultimate end of history.[26] And that role was not merely defensive, for this would be salvation or redemption as never before achieved. It was the divine, predestined mission of the Romanian people to respond to the historical moment in this way.

This sense of mission, Iordachi convincingly argues, was not simply a recurrence of millenarianism. And it entailed a new relationship between religious vision and political will. The Legion proclaimed its superiority over the Orthodox Church and, if anything, sought to subordinate the church to the new ideology.[27] As it became more politically influential under the Iron Guard label, it made major inroads into the Orthodox hierarchy. Indeed, thirty-three of 103 Guard candidates in the 1937 national elections were Orthodox priests.[28]

Obviously perceptions of the democracies helped fuel this sense of mission, but direct interaction seems to have had only a minimal role in indicating Romania's unique potential. Iordachi convincingly argues that whereas the ideology at issue owed something to earlier French and Italian thinkers, it drew primarily from a long-standing romantic tradition in Romania. On balance it was original and autonomous, not based on fascist movements elsewhere.[29]

At the same time, Iordachi persuasively portrays the Legionary vision, and the Romanian tradition from which it drew, as "palingenetic."[30] But the wider sense of mission it entailed could also entail the energizing sense of leapfrogging up to a point, as long as we conceive palingenesis broadly enough to encompass an ecumenical function and not simply renewal on the national level. In light of the wider new situation in the West, including the challenge of communism, the Romanian tradition was uniquely relevant and could now become the basis for action. The situation was such that in redeeming Romania, the Legion would necessarily lead the way for European civilization as the others, especially the liberal democracies, could not. The sense of ecumenical mission rested on perceptions of those others and envisioned interaction with them. So insofar as palingenesis can be ecumenical, it may be quite compatible not only with a sense of unique mission but also with some sense of leapfrogging.

Still, whatever the Legion's sense of what the modern world required, this vision seems to defy our usual notions of "alternative modernity." The Iron Guard specifically proclaimed itself antimodernist.[31] We might even question whether it is to be counted as fascist at all. There was nervousness in its ranks about the perceived atheism of Mussolini and Hitler.[32] But for Iordachi the ideology was specifically fascist, and certainly the sense of Christian mission did not exhaust its novelty.[33] Not only did the Guard stand for a new political relationship with religion and the church, but it claimed to envision building a totalitarian state. We can best wait until chapter 8 to assess the appropriateness of key categories like fascism and totalitarianism for the Iron Guard and the whole array on the new Right. But whether we consider the Iron Guard "fascist" or not, it surely had its own significant place in that universe, not least in its way of combining palingenetic thinking with a sense of leapfrogging.

Leapfrogging and Mythmaking

Our triumphalism makes it hard to grasp the measure of plausibility and force of the sense of leapfrogging that informed certain fascist enterprises, from the Nazi war on cancer to Italian urban planning in Eritrea. Grasping that energizing sense helps us understand the situation at the time, and we must incorporate the import of that sense into our own categories. But leapfrogging is not in itself a category for us. Coming later, we can see how much illusion and wishful thinking surrounded that sense, energizing though it was up to a point. The sense of leapfrogging had such force partly as myth all along, and it bred ever more mythmaking as the overall fascist trajectory continued.

Especially in the Italian case, first the leapfrogging notion itself, but then the element of competitive interaction with Germany, fed overblown claims, unreasonable expectations, and then mythmaking that seems especially overt in retrospect. We note this tendency in virtually every example we have encountered, from corporatism to the claim to a superior imperialism in the studies by Manuela Williams and Mia Fuller.

As they pursued their own imperialist ventures, the Italians persuaded themselves that the democracies were in it for resource exploitation or, with the British, simply to play some "great game." However serious the French might have been about their civilizing mission, Italy was different in more obviously seeking settlement colonies, in light of Italian population pressures. And the Italians claimed to stand for the sort of inclusiveness that had marked the imperialism of ancient Rome. That ideal sporadically affected Fascist practice, though here we encounter perhaps the most obvious example of the cognitive dissonance that increasingly characterized Italian Fascism. As we noted in chapter 1, the embrace of racist ideas, leading Italy to fall in behind the others and adopt anti-miscegenation laws, hardly meshed with Roman inclusiveness.

Not only did such inflation, mythmaking, and cognitive dissonance help produce the disastrous outcome of the Fascist departure, but the measure of undeniable achievement increasingly gave way to hollowness and ephemerality. In both the Italian and German cases, the sense of being able to act, to do it, as the democracies could not bred overconfidence, overreach, and ultimately defeat and dissolution.

Notes

1. Paul Einzig, *The Economic Foundations of Fascism* (London: Macmillan, 1933), v–ix. (This is from the preface, dated April 1933.)

2. John P. Diggins, *Mussolini and Fascism: The View from America* (Princeton, NJ: Princeton University Press, 1972), 276–83.

3. Ira Katznelson, *Fear Itself: The New Deal and the Origins of Our Time* (New York: Liveright, 2013), 7, 12, 17.

4. Ibid., 92–94, 111–14.

5. Charles H. Sherrill, *Kamal Roosevelt Mussolini* (Bologna: Nicola Zanichelli, 1936). Sherrill idiosyncratically spells Mustafa Kemal as Mustafa Kamal.

6. Prominent among works focusing to some extent on international interaction and suggesting that the impact of fascism on interwar Britain is too easily underestimated are Mike Cronin, ed., *The Failure of British Fascism: The Far Right and the Fight for Political Recognition* (Basingstoke: Macmillan, 1996); Thomas Linehan, *British Fascism, 1918–1939: Parties, Ideology and Culture* (Manchester: Manchester University Press, 2000); and Martin Pugh, *"Hurrah for the Blackshirts!": Fascists and Fascism in Britain between the Wars* (London: Jonathan Cape, 2005). See also Dan Stone, *Responses to Nazism in Britain, 1933–1939: Before War and Holocaust* (Basingstoke: Palgrave Macmillan, 2003), which nicely specifies the lurking danger of teleological thinking in assessing British responses to Nazi Germany before the war.

7. David Blackbourn, *The Conquest of Nature: Water, Landscape, and the Making of Modern Germany* (New York: W.W. Norton, 2006), 293–306.

8. Adolf Hitler, *Hitler's Second Book: The Unpublished Sequel to* Mein Kampf, ed. Gerhard L. Weinberg, trans. Krista Smith (New York: Enigma, 2003); see, e.g., 90, 107–18.

9. Adam Tooze, *The Wages of Destruction: The Making and Breaking of the Nazi Economy* (New York: Penguin, 2006), e.g., 9–12, 407–8. This theme runs throughout the book.

10. Ian Kershaw, "Hitler and the Uniqueness of Nazism," *Journal of Contemporary History* 39, no. 2 (April 2004): 247; Mary Vincent, "Spain," in *The Oxford Handbook of Fascism*, ed. R.J.B. Bosworth (Oxford: Oxford University Press, 2009) 375.

11. Giuseppe Bottai, *Esperienza corporativa (1929–1934)* (Florence: Vallecchi, 1934), 677–711; see esp. 681–87.

12. Jeffrey T. Schnapp, *Building Fascism, Communism, Liberal Democracy: Gaetano Ciocca—Architect, Inventor, Farmer, Writer, Engineer* (Stanford, CA: Stanford University Press, 2004), 48–56.

13. For just two examples, see Frank M. Snowden, *The Conquest of Malaria: Italy, 1900–1962* (New Haven, CT: Yale University Press, 2006), 142–80; and Borden W. Painter, Jr., *Mussolini's Rome: Rebuilding the Eternal City* (New York: Palgrave Macmillan, 2005).

14. Mia Fuller, *Moderns Abroad: Architecture, Cities, and Italian Imperialism* (London and New York: Routledge, 2007).

15. Detlev J.K. Peukert, *The Weimar Republic: The Crisis of Classical Modernity* (New York: Hill and Wang, 1993), 134–36, 187–88, 271–72.

16. See, e.g., Geoff Eley, *Nazism as Fascism: Violence, Ideology, and the Ground of Consent in Germany, 1930–1945* (London and New York: Routledge, 2013), 212.

17. Stefan Kühl, *The Nazi Connection: Eugenics, American Racism, and German National Socialism* (New York: Oxford University Press, 1994).

18. Mark Roseman, "National Socialism and Modernization," in *Fascist Italy and Nazi Germany: Comparisons and Contrasts*, ed. Richard Bessel (Cambridge: Cambridge University Press, 1996), 226–27.

19. Robert Proctor, *Racial Hygiene: Medicine under the Nazis* (Cambridge, MA: Harvard University Press, 1988); Robert Proctor, *The Nazi War on Cancer* (Princeton, NJ: Princeton University Press, 1999). See especially Proctor's preface to the latter volume, 3–12, for a concise and especially perspicacious statement of the implications of his pioneering researches for our understanding of Nazism and fascism more generally. But the implications extend to the overall era and how we have related to it.

20. Roger Griffin, *Modernism and Fascism: The Sense of a Beginning under Mussolini and Hitler* (Basingstoke: Palgrave Macmillan, 2007), 286–309. See also Gregory Maertz, "The Invisible Museum: Unearthing the Lost Modernist Art of the Third Reich," *Modernism/modernity* 15, no. 1 (January 2008): 63–85.

21. Though I cited my review essay in chapter 1, it seems worth citing again here. See David D. Roberts, "Fascism, Modernism, and the Quest for an Alternative Modernity," *Patterns of Prejudice* 43, no. 1 (February 2009): 91–102.

22. Wayne Andersen's *German Artists and Hitler's Mind: Avant-Garde Art in a Turbulent Era* (Boston and Geneva: Editions Fabriart, 2007) is an example of such dissent. Andersen's argument is something like the opposite of what I am proposing here. As he sees it, what matters is not that the cruel, morbid quality of the art in question provoked a Nazi reaction but that it foreshadowed the larger cruelty of Hitler's vision.

23. Griffin, *Modernism and Fascism*, 182 (my emphasis).

24. Richard Taruskin, *On Russian Music* (Berkeley: University of California Press, 2009), 299–321. This is the essay "When Serious Music Mattered." See esp. 300–2, 312.

25. Philip Morgan, "Studying Fascism from the Particular to the General," *East Central Europe* 37 (2010): 336.

26. Constantin Iordachi, "God's Chosen Warriors: Romantic Palingenesis, Militarism and Fascism in Modern Romania," in *Comparative Fascist Studies: New Perspectives*, ed. Constantin Iordachi (London and New York: Routledge, 2010), 340, 349, 353.

27. Ibid., 347, 353.

28. Radu Ioanid, "Romania," in *Oxford Handbook*, ed. Bosworth, 405.

29. Iordachi, "God's Chosen Warriors," 328, 350, 352.

30. Ibid., 328, 339–40.

31. Ioanid, "Romania," 410.

32. Ibid., 404.

33. Iordachi, "God's Chosen Warriors," 347, 353.

Chapter 7

INTERACTION ACROSS
THE LEFT-RIGHT DIVIDE AND
UNCERTAINTY OVER "TOTALITARIANISM"

Softening the Left-Right Divide

As our fourth and final mode of interaction, we must consider aspects of the Left-Right interaction at the time, focusing especially on three related but distinguishable areas: borrowing across and perceptions transcending the Left-Right divide; interaction between fascists and the communists in the Soviet Union; and the place of the "totalitarianism" category, devised in 1923. Each of the three angles illuminates the other, and treating them together dramatizes the wider openness, uncertainty, and fluidity of the era.

The boundary between what seemed "Left" and what seemed "Right" was itself sometimes more permeable than we might expect. Gerhard Botz indicates precisely that in light of their elastic meanings, the largely new anti-democratic notions swirling around Europe by the early 1930s even crossed the Left-Right axis on occasion.[1] In dealing with fascism and the business establishment, we noted that both Arturo Beneduce in Italy and IG Farben in Germany leaned to the Left prior to the advent of the fascist regimes in their respective countries, yet each ended up working comfortably within those regimes.

In the newly complex political mix, those hostile to or nervous about novel political formations were sometimes quick to conflate fascists and communists. We noted in chapter 4 that the increase in Arrow Cross membership and activism in 1937–38 alarmed Hungarian conservatives, who condemned the group as extremist, comparable to Bolshevism in its revolutionary demagoguery. In Romania Ion Antonescu similarly conflated the Iron Guard with Bolshevism.[2]

At the same time, some of those restive with liberal democracy were attracted to both the Soviet and the Italian experiments, which, as attempts at alternatives to the liberal mainstream, seemed to display intriguing common features. We noted that the Kemalist regime in Turkey indiscriminately compared itself with, and borrowed from, Fascist Italy and the Soviet Union, though there was periodic disagreement over which was the more pertinent for Turkey.

Before the advent of the Nazi regime, German Right-wing radicals like Ernst Jünger and Ernst Niekisch found such areas of convergence at once significant and attractive.[3] In a book published in 1927 the political scientist and economist Erwin von Beckerath was among the first German scholars to treat the young Fascist regime systematically, while also sympathetically. And while noting the obvious ideological differences, he, too, played up the commonalities between Fascist Italy and the Soviet Union. In each case opposition to parliamentary government had resulted in a novel conception of the state entailing productivism, new roles for elites, new modes of mass mobilization, and a premium on discipline and coordination. The author even invoked the common filiation with Georges Sorel, while noting that Sorel was unfortunately unknown in Germany.[4]

Although he neglects the ambiguous legacy of Sorel, William Irvine nicely characterizes the uncertainty of Left and Right and the fluidity of the Left-Right axis in France in a recent essay entitled precisely "Beyond Left and Right: Rethinking Political Boundaries in Interwar France."[5] From within that framework, he notes, what counted as "fascism" was particularly uncertain—and perhaps of little relevance, a notion congruent with Michel Dobry's argument discussed in chapter 2. And as Irvine makes clear, subsequent efforts to determine the applicability of the Left-Right axis to the polarizing French politics of the period have been strongly contested not only because of the disputes over the "immunity thesis," likewise considered in chapter 2, but also because of the controversies provoked by Zeev Sternhell's *Ni droite, ni gauche: L'ideologie fasciste en France*, published in 1983.[6]

Sternhell usefully challenged ongoing tendencies toward an unthinking reliance on the Left-Right dichotomy. However, he was less concerned to show the permeability of the axis than to argue that fascist sentiments were considerably more widespread in France than had been recognized—and that the Left-Right divide afforded no barrier. Echoes of "the Sternhell controversy" can still be heard, though Sternhell himself subsequently cast his net more widely, recently treating much of the Western world in delineating what he called the anti-Enlightenment tradition, encompassing, but by no means limited to, fascism.[7] Although France remained central to that negative tradition, he has plenty of abuse for non-French thinkers from Vico, Burke, and Herder to Friedrich Meinecke, Benedetto Croce, and Isaiah Berlin. In the last analysis Sternhell's framework proves dualistic, even Manichean, so despite his earlier accent on "neither Right, nor Left," he was not loosening distinctions to enable us better to understand responses at the time but, if anything, rigidifying such distinctions, thereby impeding understanding.

Despite his debt to Sternhell, Mark Antliff especially demonstrates the permeability of the Left-Right divide in France in treating such figures as Philippe Lamour, Germaine Krull, and Le Corbusier (born Charles-Edouard Jeanneret-Gris). They, too, found it possible to borrow from both the Soviet and the Italian experiments, not least because the two seemed to have much in common as alternatives to mainstream liberal democracy. There was even uncertainty concerning the Left-Right valences of Italian fascism itself.[8] This was plausible, though what one ended up emphasizing obviously depended on which part of the Italian Fascist elephant one observed, and through what lenses. But certainly Italian Fascism, as it came to play a significant role in French cultural interaction, was not taken as merely reactionary or backward-looking, let alone as a defense of the status quo.

As we noted in chapter 3, Antliff's account also makes clear how central Italian Fascist corporatism was to French discussion, even into the later 1930s, and even to those accenting the aesthetic dimension of fascism at the same time. It was partly on the basis of its corporatist thrust that Lamour and others in the later 1920s viewed fascism as a Leftist departure. Antliff also notes the claim by some Italian Fascists that Fascism was not the repudiation but the culmination of the process begun with the French Revolution, though he conveys little sense of the basis for the notion, which may seem implausible on the face of it.[9] Unless we more deeply probe the reasoning and the place of that claim in the Italian Fascist mix, our understanding of the scope for borrowing across the Left-Right axis is unnecessarily limited.

This is not the place for a systematic effort at such assessment, but we can articulate the question and consider one prominent indication of the thinking at issue. The question is whether parliamentary democracy was the privileged outcome of the Enlightenment tradition, with only Marxism specifying a possibly progressive alternative, or whether the experiment was still continuing, perhaps newly reopened in light of experience—first with parliamentary government, trade unionism, and the liberal understanding of the relationship between the political and the economic spheres, but then also with the results of the communists' putatively Marxist revolution in Russia.

In an inaugural lecture at the University of Pisa in 1930, Giuseppe Bottai admitted that in their impetuous youthfulness, he and his fellow Fascists had not always been clear enough about the relationship between Fascism and the French Revolutionary tradition, the ideas of 1789.[10] And their enemies, especially abroad, had exploited the ambiguity, portraying the Fascists as merely reactionary. In fact, insisted Bottai, Fascism was not a negation but a dialectical overcoming of the liberal democratic tradition that had issued from the French Revolution. That revolution had been one of the notable events in human history, yielding much that remained essential, including equality before the law, the freedom to hold and communicate ideas, and denial of hereditary privilege. But for Bottai, echoing the Fascist philosopher Giovanni Gentile, the underlying key was the emergence of the human spiritual self-awareness essential to modernity. With the French Revolution, spirit, or humanity, began to grasp its liberty, its creative power, its capacity to construct its own history. Yet liberalism could not realize the potential, most basically because, in its resistance to absolutism, it embraced the natural law tradition and thus developed a particular delimited conception of the individual-state relationship.

But whereas we must grasp the basis for Bottai's claim, we must also recognize that major Fascists like Alfredo Rocco and Carlo Costamagna would have dissented strongly. But thus, again, the scope for those elsewhere to see what they wanted to see, to take what they wanted to take. The relative weight of the factions could not be pinned down at the time, nor could the outcomes be foreseen as the kaleidoscope continued to turn.

Evan as Italian Fascist corporatism continued to attract interest abroad, many non-Italians viewed it merely reactionary, serving the interests of the employers. Ruth Ben-Ghiat notes that Indro Montanelli, the young editor of *L'Universale*, was irritated and surprised that some of the French at the Italian-French Conference on Corporativist Studies in Rome in May 1935 viewed Fascism as a nationalistic movement of the extreme Right.[11] Partly because they felt Fascism was being misrepresented abroad in this way, Bottai and his colleagues took every opportunity to respond to questions and spread the corporatist word.[12] As we noted in the last chapter, the International Labor Office at Geneva was a favored venue for trumpeting the superiority of Fascist corporatism, which was bringing the economic and political spheres together as neither liberalism nor communism could.[13] Still, the Fascists had encountered skepticism at Geneva from the outset. In light of the early fascist assault on the socialist labor movement, the veteran French trade-union leader Léon Jouhaux spearheaded objections even to seating the Italians—as Fascists.

Interaction between the Two Fascist Powers and the Soviet Union

Whereas the fascists and communists were mostly rivals, there is plenty of evidence of mutual attraction and borrowing between the Soviet regime, on the one hand, and the two fascist regimes, on the other. Each side measured itself against the other but also took inspiration from the other. Although most of the coauthored essays in *Beyond Totalitarianism*, the important volume coedited by Michael Geyer and Sheila Fitzpatrick, seek primarily to compare aspects of Nazi Germany and the Stalinist Soviet Union, several are explicitly concerned with reciprocity, and the sense of Nazi-Soviet competition, reinforcing tendencies toward extremes, is implicit in virtually all of them. Together they suggest that Nazi Germany and the Soviet Union under Stalin were caught up in the ultimate *histoire croisée*. Indeed, the editors note explicitly that the transfers and mimesis must be part of any comparative history of the two regimes.[14] And certainly the epochal interplay between the two, the competition, imitation, and projection, proved central to the contours of the era.

Brief mention of three of the essays will help clarify the stakes. In treating the Nazi-Soviet war, Mark Edele and Michael Geyer show how the two regimes fed on each other to produce escalating violence and novel modes of action. Thus, for example, resistance and retreat on the part of the Soviets intensified German brutalization. The Soviet Union came to seem "another place" where conventional norms had to be set aside. Yet the very sense of being caught up in something so extraordinary enhanced the sense of participation and belonging on both sides.[15]

But the reciprocal escalation of violence was not limited to wartime. Christian Gerlach and Nicholas Werth's essay on violence toward "asocials," prisoners-of-war, and victims of ethnic resettlement is of particular value in showing that we must conceive violence in both contexts not merely as top-down but as societal, "participatory," with violent initiatives welling up from below, and also yielding new modes of bonding. In accounting for such violence, the authors point to the overall acclimatization to violence in these societies, in light of the recent experience of war, revolution, and counterrevolution.[16] But they do not bring out all the implications of that new framework. It seems clear that part of what fueled the extraordinary violence was the sense of innovative political experiment on both the communist and fascist sides, entailing much mutual threat as each embarked upon grandiose, history-making projects, competing for the post-liberal space.[17]

In treating changes in the ways the Germans and the Russians viewed each other, Katerina Clark and Karl Schlögel stress that the images each regime developed were not logical outgrowths of earlier prejudices but novel, constituting a further departure, in light of the competing departures already under way. Thus, for example, though German views of Russians entailed long-standing prejudices, only in light of processes bound up with the Nazi revolution did the Russians come to seem *Untermenschen* who could be exterminated.[18]

Although it is under-studied, there was also interaction along the Italian-Soviet axis, at least for a while. We find a relatively conventional way of understanding it in Roger Markwick's recent treatment of the relationship between the political innovations in Italy and Russia. In his view, the Fascist and Soviet regimes both arose in response to the crisis unleashed by World War I, but Italian Fascism emerged only from the failure of the Italian Left to solve Italy's postwar crisis as, putatively, the Bolsheviks had done in Russia by seizing power and removing the country from the world capitalist system. Italian Fascism was fundamentally anti-communist and reactive—and remained so. With respect to fascism in both Italy and Germany, Markwick argues that if it was to win, it "had to appropriate much of communism's revolutionary mass appeal to traumatized European societies." Thus the outward similarities, the seeming symmetry. As Marwick sees it, however, Italian Fascism and Soviet communism were antithetical, mutually exclusive responses to the postwar crisis. The notion of "totalitarianism" does not illuminate but masks the fundamental antithesis between them.[19]

Markwick's analysis is largely *ex post*, but it precludes precisely the greater openness to the uncertainties at the time that a new agenda should encompass. Although he marshals the evidence well to support his relatively conventional view, in positing the world capitalist system as the baseline he delimits the range of frequencies, precluding the scope for experiment at the time. Rather than taking seriously at least the possibility of a revolutionary fascist alternative, he refers to "pseudo-revolutionary" and "populist demagoguery."[20]

The stakes of the Soviet-Italian interaction at the time were not so obviously predetermined. Whereas that interaction was of far less moment than the Nazi-Soviet interaction, it significantly affected the Italian self-understanding and, less directly, even the trajectory of the regime. The Fascists measured themselves against the Bolsheviks virtually from the beginning, recognizing a significant kinship, even borrowing certain Soviet techniques, but claiming superiority at the same time. In his first speech to the Chamber of Deputies, in June 1921, Mussolini complimented Lenin's artistry but went on to assert not only kinship with but even paternity over aspects of Russian communism.[21]

As the two regimes developed, Fascist observers generally emphasized that the Soviet experiment was proving negative, confirming the need for the Fascist third way, which opposed idealism to materialism and corporatism to bureaucratic statism. Bottai charged that the socialist idea in Soviet Russia was in the process of yielding an enormous, clumsy, bureaucratic state capitalism.[22] Even those more sympathetic suggested that Stalinism inevitably tended toward fascism, the only viable alternative to the liberal mainstream. In *Il trionfo del fascismo nell'U.R.S.S.* (The Triumph of Fascism in the U.S.S.R.), published in 1934, Renzo Bertoni stressed that the antithesis between communism and fascism, stemming from the materialist-idealist dichotomy, could only be temporary in light of the economic crisis, and especially in light of their common enemy, liberal individualism, with its attendant capitalist exploitation. But as an effort at socialism, the Soviet regime had definitively failed, producing forced collectivization and terror, thereby demonstrating the absurdity of communist principles. The Soviets could only abandon Marxism and move toward the Fascist mode of organizing production and regulating class relations.[23]

An array of Fascists traveled to the Soviet Union and interacted with the Soviets on various levels, especially during the years from 1929 to 1935.[24] Among them was the visionary engineer Gaetano Ciocca who, we noted in the preceding chapter, visited the United States in 1934 to assess Americanism firsthand. But he had already worked in the Soviet Union from 1930 to 1932, returning home to publish an influential book assessing the Soviet situation in 1933. All that surely enhanced the force of his assessment of Americanism three years later.

After the Soviets hired FIAT, the leading Italian auto maker, to build a huge ball-bearing plant, FIAT signed Ciocca to go to the Soviet Union to spearhead the plant's design and construction. Ciocca's sojourn proved complex, but he played a major role in the project, which would continue to be touted as a highlight of the Soviets' crash industrialization program.[25] Mussolini himself coauthored a preface to the book Ciocca wrote in the aftermath.[26] And again, of course, direct experience in the land of the competitor seemed to afford plenty of evidence of the superiority of the Italian Fascist system.

Uncertainty and Contest over "Totalitarianism"

Interaction across the putative Left-Right axis necessarily brings us to the question of "totalitarianism," though the applicability of the category to the new extremes of both Right and Left was contested then as it has been for the most part ever since. We noted just above that Roger Markwick finds it misleading at best as a way of bringing the Soviet and Italian Fascist experiments together. At the time, the meaning and desirability of "totalitarianism" was more widely at issue in efforts to make sense of the new political departures and the possibilities that seemed to open.

The interaction over totalitarianism included opponents as well as proponents or potential proponents, those seeking to make sense from the outside as well as those actively involved on the new Right. And even among those on the new Right, there was a great deal of uncertainty and dispute. The fact that "totalitarianism" was part of the mix affected what could be imagined or aspired to, so the category offers clues to the sense of novel challenge and opportunity. But to some it suggested the danger of excess in the experiments in progress—a new threat to be avoided, resisted. And whether the experiments being imagined, advocated, or implemented could be conceived as totalitarian was to some extent hammered out through the interaction.

As one of the novel categories and possibilities being discussed at the time, totalitarianism is not simply an *ex post* analytical category that we today can take or leave. But in seeking to grasp the place of "totalitarianism" in the interaction, we especially encounter the reflexive intermingling of "at the time" and "for us." We are bound to approach what it meant to contemporaries, whether proponents or opponents, with some sense of what it has come to mean to us, in light of the trajectories of a number of extreme regimes, beginning with, but not limited to, the era of the two world wars. But we can seek to open, to loosen, to listen so as not only better to understand those at the time but also to nuance our own *ex post* analytical category. Conversely, insofar as we are probing what they meant by the category, we are not seeking to determine whether this or that direction was *really* totalitarian or not.

We must start with the original Italian usage of "totalitarianism," a term coined for critical purposes by a leading liberal anti-Fascist, Giovanni Amendola, in 1923. It quickly came to serve anti-Fascists more widely for polemical ends, though it was used inconsistently. But in 1925, as the regime began more radically to break from the liberal tradition, the Fascists themselves began embracing the category, which quickly became central to the Fascist self-understanding. Whatever the limits to the realization of the totalitarian aspiration in Mussolini's regime, the sense of challenge and opportunity bound up with the aspiration was certainly novel, and it fueled movement in a particular direction in practice in the Italian case.

However, as Abbott Gleason has shown in his valuable survey of the uses of the category, even for the Fascists the connotations of "totalitarianism" evolved, though the philosopher Giovanni Gentile, who began using the term in March 1925, gave it some measure of consistency.[27] But we have noted that a number of Fascists disputed Gentile's role, and even within Italian Fascism "totalitarianism" was uncertain, controversial, and contested. Some, especially those closest to the monarchy and the Catholic Church, avoided the category, and self-proclaimed totalitarians were sometimes diametrically opposed on important issues. Gleason provides a preliminary sense of the changing and even conflicted meanings, but he misses important subtleties and distinctions.[28] The Fascists generally agreed on the need to forge the instrument for a new kind of sustained collective action, and thus on the need to depart from liberalism, with its emphasis on individualism, pluralism, and the public-private distinction, but they disagreed over the need for hierarchy, over the capacity for political vision among ordinary working people, and thus over the modes of participation that were appropriate.[29]

At the same time, "totalitarianism" began serving outside observers, whether sympathetic or hostile, as an analytical category. Especially during the early 1930s, with the Stalinist turn in the Soviet Union and the advent of the Nazi regime in Germany, such outside analysts, now mostly critical, began bringing the several surprising new regimes together around "totalitarianism" in an effort to make sense of them.[30] Although the texts he presents are by critics and analysts as opposed to Italian Fascist proponents, Bernard Bruneteau's recent *Le totalitarisme: Origines d'un concept, genèse d'un débat* especially make clear how central "totalitarianism" had become by the end of the 1930s, well before it became subject to political application during the Cold War.[31] Obviously at issue was whether, despite the continuing antagonisms between fascism and communism, the seeming commonalities in their departures from liberal pluralism and individualism were somehow more symptomatic and important than whatever Left-Right differences there were between them.

Some of those seeking their own new Right departures actively embraced totalitarianism from the outside. However, in light of the uncertainties and controversies surrounding the category even in Fascist Italy, it is not obvious what they thought they were getting. Totalitarian directions could be more or less indigenous, more or less imitative, but the conflicts even among Italian totalitarians meant that would-be totalitarians elsewhere had no choice but to define their own totalitarian direction. Thus, examining cases outside Italy may turn up different, unexpected totalitarian aspirations, based on a different sense of the challenges and possibilities. We must also remember that a movement could have been totalitarian in aspiration even if did not come to power. And, as we have emphasized, insofar as we seek to encompass the whole universe of novel anti-liberal and nationalistic responses during the period, we need to understand aspiration and intent as well as actual practice, with whatever combination of accomplishment, failure, and human cost.

In any case, although its meaning was fuzzy, totalitarianism was readily embraced by many on the new Right. José Antonio Primo de Rivera, leader of the Spanish Falange, referred frequently to building a totalitarian state, to include corporatism as in Fascist Italy. Before winning the Spanish Civil War, General Francisco Franco observed in a 1938 interview that his new state would be structured like the totalitarian regimes, such as those in Italy and Germany, but with specifically Spanish characteristics.[32] Miguel Jerez Mir and Javier Luque note that by 1944 many of the Franco regime's own adherents perceived it as totalitarian, but not always with approval. Some called for an end to the totalitarian regime and the reestablishment of a traditionalist Catholic monarchy.[33]

All over, there were those who found totalitarianism more appropriate than fascism itself for understanding and characterizing their own innovations, yet the relationship between the two categories was by no means clear. Aristotle Kallis notes that the leaders and ideologues of the Metaxas regime in Greece avoided using "fascist," opting instead for the more ambiguous "totalitarian." Metaxas was explicit, however, that this meant precisely that his regime, as innovative, had something in common with the Italian and German regimes, but also with the Soviet regime, as anti-democratic or, we might say, post-democratic.[34] Metaxas conceived his key institutional innovation, the National Youth Organization, as a totalitarian device for social engineering.[35]

Although we want to attune to a wider range of frequencies as we probe the place of totalitarianism in the interaction, we cannot simply accept whatever those using the category at the time said about it. We need some notion of what could plausibly have counted as a totalitarian direction, but we can be more open as to what it might have entailed, especially more open as to what vision, what originating aspirations, were fueling it. At the same time, we have to ask what those using the category at the time knew of its meaning for others, its rationale, and its implications for practice—including its possible dangers. We must also assess the extent to which mere myth, slogan, or wishful thinking surrounded embrace of the category. So we need a baseline, but it can be loose, flexible—and, above all, congruent with the active and explicit adoption of "totalitarianism" in Fascist Italy.

Disagreement over "Totalitarianism" in the Italian-German Interaction

Although the Italian-German rivalry, and its effect on the self-understanding of each regime, has become reasonably well known, it is less widely recognized that it included explicit disagreement over totalitarianism, disagreement that implicated ancillary categories like statism, Hegelianism, and dynamism as well.[36] After some eagerness to embrace totalitarianism at the outset of the Nazi regime, the Nazis generally came to reject it. In doing so, they fastened especially upon the Fascist philosopher Gentile, whom they associated, plausibly up to a point but ultimately quite mis-leadingly, with Hegelian statism. For the most part the Nazis vehemently rejected any such accent on the state while trumpeting their own populist *movement*, linked to "blood." They tended to accept the Italian claim that Fascist Italy was moving toward totalitarianism, but for them that meant the advent of a total, legalistic state absorbing even the radical, dynamic party. On that basis the Nazis found the Italian Fascist direction, even as totalitarian, too static.

However, these Germans were not doing justice to the dynamic, post-Hegelian thrust of Italian totalitarian thinking. Although the Italians and the Nazis differed over the place of the state, they rejected *Hegelian* statism on much the same grounds—as static, precluding the open-ended dyna-mism that had come to seem necessary in a more radically historical and open-ended world. Though Gentile focused on the state as opposed to the movement-party, his was not Hegel's state, understood as the embodiment of reason and thus calculable in operation. Precisely because the statist liberalism of the Hegelian tradition was too static, it had to be transcended in a more deeply historical world. The Gentilian totalitarian state was the living and perpetually changing form or embodiment of the unified polit-ical people.

Still, the differences between the two sides were real and significant, even if the Germans did not fully grasp the basis for them. At issue was how to forge the instrument for the ongoing collective response both sides found essential. That concern led to questions about the uses of legal codifica-tion as sovereignty expands to infinity. The Germans were more resistant to codified law and fixed procedures as incongruent with the new action necessary. Action required flexibility, including the scope for improvised response. Still, the questions at issue occasioned tension and debate even within each regime. To what extent did an emphasis on the state—even a new totalitarian state—inherently mean a premium on codification and fixed procedures, and to what extent was any such premium incongruent with the new action necessary?

Whereas the Germans tended to take Italian Fascist totalitarianism as homogeneous, there was much disagreement in Italian Fascist legal discus-sion over party and state, codification and open-ended dynamism. Thus, for example, whereas Camillo Pellizzi, stressing provisionality and openness, portrayed laws as hieroglyphs in the sand, Alfredo Rocco accented cod-ification and the predictability of law even as the state's reach expanded indefinitely.[37] Rocco's legal rationalism, especially, stood diametrically opposed to the Nazi conception of law, based on race, blood, and the will of the Führer.[38] But there was contest in Germany as well, as Hans Frank and Wilhelm Frick, in their different ways, sought unsuccessfully to promote a greater measure of codification and regularized judicial procedure from within the Nazi framework.

As it turned out, Nazism certainly moved more radically beyond traditional state ideas, but that is no warrant for concluding, in simple dualistic terms, that Nazi Germany was totalitarian while Fascist Italy was merely traditionalist or authoritarian. To codify the law was indeed less "dynamic" in the sense the Nazis had in mind, but to expand to totality the scope for codified law was no less totalitarian. The criterion of totalitarianism was not the particular mode of dynamism embraced by the Nazis but the more general determination to act collectively in a newly total way.

Yet partly as a result of the early interaction between the Germans and the Italians, we have long been prone to some such dichotomy pitting the state, taken as conservative and authoritarian, against the movement-party, taken as dynamic and revolutionary. The combination of competition and confusion at the time has fed modes of analysis that have impeded understanding ever since.[39] This is a prime indication that we need reflexively to integrate understandings and conflicts at the time into our present categories. We will consider more deeply how we might do so when we come to the present uses of "totalitarianism" in the next chapter.

Encompassing Totalitarianism in Treating the Interaction

For now our concern is how we might better encompass totalitarianism in considering the interaction at the time. Doing so can be highly illuminating, but not if it is done on the basis of a delimited, a priori notion of what totalitarianism portended and an inadequate grasp of how it was understood. Despite the more general inadequacies we noted in Federico Finchelstein's treatment of Argentina and Italy, totalitarianism plays usefully in his account as he shows how disagreement among the Argentinian *nacionalistas* over the meaning and relevance of the category complicated the interaction—and ultimately furthered the disconnect—between the Argentinians and the Italians over the relationship between fascism and religion.[40] The *nacionalistas* generally sought to play up the Catholicism of Italian Fascism; the question was whether "totalitarianism" was compatible with any such emphasis.

To some extent, Finchelstein notes, the *nacionalistas* disagreed even among themselves over the compatibility of totalitarianism with the combination of Catholicism and fascism they claimed to embrace.[41] Although, in looking to Italy, individual *nacionalistas* often managed to find what they wanted, they generally viewed totalitarianism as a negative. And most tended to associate it with Nazi Germany and to deny that Italian Fascism was totalitarian—a good example of the disconnects and uncertainties at the time. But this reading among the *nacionalistas* was part of their effort to minimize the import of the statist and secular or even pagan tendencies of Italian Fascism in order to play up Fascist Catholicism.[42] And this even as they insisted that their own version was purer, precisely as less subject to that statist, secular, or pagan direction. But a visit to Argentina by the noted French Catholic intellectual Jacques Maritain in 1936 provoked much soul-searching and debate over the issue, for Maritain insisted that fascism in general was totalitarian and could not be the instrument of God.[43]

In conveying the muddle at the time, Finchelstein provides precisely the sort of attention to the interaction that deepens our understanding. Not only does he show that totalitarianism was importantly at issue, but he makes especially clear that it could be even more of a lightning rod than "fascism" itself. Yet his account also makes it clear that totalitarianism came up as a highly fluid and unstable notion.

In the last analysis, however, Finchelstein does not sort out the issues effectively because his conception of totalitarianism, like his understanding of fascism, is at once abstract and teleological. In insisting on violence, terror, and torture as the ultimate attributes of totalitarianism, he necessarily sows confusion over the stakes of the Italo-Argentine interaction.[44] If only because of the contest within Italian Fascism over the interface between totalitarianism and Catholicism, that interaction was inherently more fluid than Finchelstein's account suggests.

Treating the place of totalitarianism in the thinking of the Romanian Legion of the Archangel Michael, Constantin Iordachi is far more flexible and open. He makes it clear, most basically, that the category was actively embraced by some key figures—more so, it would seem, than in Argentina. There was talk of "building the totalitarian state," in a way combining nationalism with Orthodoxy, as one key to fascist revolution.[45] But even as Iordachi convincingly portrays the totalitarian aspiration as modern and fascist, he leaves much looseness concerning the Romanian understanding. Certainly his reference to the totalitarian state in Ilie Imbrescu's thinking, as combining nationalism with Orthodoxy, remains too vague to help pin it down.[46]

In concluding his essay, Iordachi seeks to provide more substance on the totalitarian state, but even there the discussion raises more questions than it answers. It refers to (a) replacing the multiparty system with a single-party dictatorship; (b) remodeling the state along corporatist lines; (c) conceiving citizenship in ethnic terms; and (d) understanding societal and gender relations in a newly patriarchal way.[47] But even in combination these directions do not add up to constructing a totalitarian state. They might have been steps in that direction, but we would need to understand the rationale for and the implications of each of those steps. If we are to speak of totalitarianism, we would need to know, above all, what the new state was actually to do, in light of what would necessarily have been a radical expansion of state sovereignty and responsibility. How did proponents of a totalitarian direction envision acting in the new ways through the state, including actually engineering societal and gender relations along newly patriarchal lines? As it is, we wonder what was new about the patriarchal understanding of societal and gender relations. The novelty would have to have been in discerning the scope for a new mode of action actually to re-engineer those relations through a radically expanded state.

Elsewhere Iordachi refers in passing to "Catholic totalitarianism" in Poland, as if we already knew what totalitarianism might mean—even in this problematic juxtaposition with Catholicism.[48] In probing the interaction, we simply need further research into what those embracing—or eschewing—the totalitarianism category in Romania, Poland, and elsewhere knew of it and intended by it. This entails asking the questions we noted above about depth of understanding, recognizing the possibility of mere myth or slogan. But we can fruitfully frame those questions only if we eschew the teleological thinking that compromises Finchelstein's account and attend to a wider range of frequencies. Again, however, insofar as we are seeking a deeper understanding of usages at the time, we need not seek to determine whether any particular direction was *really* totalitarian or not. What matters is the place of the category at the time, as bound up with the web of interaction.

Conclusion: Returning to the Left-Right Axis

Having discussed interaction with the Soviet Union and the place of the totalitarianism category at the time, we can usefully return to the more general question of the Left-Right axis that we considered in the first section. Focusing on the several modes of interaction across that axis enhances our sense of the slipperiness and uncertainty at the time. To be sure, anti-communism was essential to the fascist self-understanding, and that animosity helped assign fascism to the Right from the communist perspective. Moreover, the fact that the fascists and communists remained mortal enemies helped make the Left-Right axis seem central to the time, and has helped make it seem an essential feature of the political landscape ever since.

But we suggested near the outset of chapter 1 that insistence upon the Left-Right axis might keep us from grasping the energizing sense of openness at the time, even with respect to what was modern and progressive. And thus it might compromise our understanding of the aggregate and the texture of the era. That axis was itself historically specific, of course—a product of the French Revolution. Though characterological underpinnings can plausibly be suggested, the criteria of Left and Right were never altogether neat. J.L. Talmon's classic distinction, based on perceptions of human nature, surely retains some force; thus, for example, both Renzo De Felice and Meir Michaelis, major authorities on Italian Fascism, were quick to embrace it. Yet it was symptomatic that they differed over where Italian Fascism fit.[49] Moreover, even Talmon's criterion could blur with further historical experience.

The Left-Right axis could seem open to revision as, with the implications of mainstream liberal democracy becoming clearer, new questions about the requirements for a systematic alternative emerged at the same time. Such thinkers as Gentile, Sorel, and Vilfredo Pareto, seeking fresh approaches around the turn of the century, are notoriously difficult to place on any Left-Right axis. Whereas some fascists, like Alfredo Rocco in Italy, can surely be assigned to the Right, we noted that Giuseppe Bottai claimed that Italian Fascism was not denying but bringing to fruition the ideas of 1789. Much obviously depends on criteria, but the criteria themselves were being contested at the time, and thus, in part, the slipperiness and uncertainty.

Michael Mann's treatment of the fascist claim to transcend class differences affords a good example. As part of his effort to take the fascists seriously, he suggests that rather than privilege class, as was done for so long, we should start with the rationale for the fascist claim to be transcending class—as a key both to individual identity and to the understanding of society.[50] From a communist perspective, that claim would itself suffice to place fascism on the Right. What needs to be assessed, however, is the claim's plausibility. From a non-Marxist perspective, the scope for transcending class cannot be ruled out a priori. But whether fascism was actually doing so is of course another matter—and that was being hammered out at the time as the trajectory continued.

Even if we do not simply insist that fascism offered mere palliatives, papering over class differences, we may conclude, in retrospect, that the effort to transcend class did not get very far. But we still must take seriously the effort to transcend class distinctions and, more generally, the Left-Right distinction as it was then understood. If we simply assume that the Left-Right distinction structures the political universe, we cannot understand the stakes of the interaction at the time.

Notes

1. Gerhard Botz, "The Coming of the Dollfuss-Schuschnigg Regime and the Stages of Its Development," in *Rethinking Fascism and Dictatorship in Interwar Europe,* ed. António Costa Pinto and Aristotle Kallis (Basingstoke: Palgrave Macmillan, 2014), 131–32.

2. Dennis Deletant, *Hitler's Forgotten Ally: Ion Antonescu and His Regime, Romania 1940–44* (Basingstoke: Palgrave Macmillan, 2006), 72.

3. Abbott Gleason, *Totalitarianism: The Inner History of the Cold War* (New York: Oxford University Press, 1995), 29.

4. Erwin von Beckerath, *Wesen und Werden des fascistischen Staates* (Berlin: Julius Springer, 1927), 147–50.

5. William D. Irvine, "Beyond Left and Right: Rethinking Political Boundaries in Interwar France," in *The French Right between the Wars,* ed. Samuel Kalman and Sean Kennedy (New York and Oxford: Berghahn, 2014), 227–39.

6. Translated by David Maisel as *Neither Right nor Left: Fascist Ideology in France* (Berkeley: University of California Press, 1986).

7. Zeev Sternhell, *The Anti-Enlightenment Tradition,* trans. David Maisel (New Haven, CT: Yale University Press, 2010).

8. Mark Antliff, *Avant-Garde Fascism: The Mobilization of Myth, Art, and Culture in France, 1909–1939* (Durham, NC: Duke University Press, 2007), 160, 162–64, 167, 185–201.

9. Ibid., 163–64.

10. Giuseppe Bottai, *Esperienza corporativa (1929–1934)* (Florence: Vallecchi, 1934), 569–77, 583–85.

11. Ruth Ben-Ghiat, *Fascist Modernities: Italy, 1922–1945* (Berkeley: University of California Press, 2001), 119.

12. See, e.g., Bottai's interview with *Deutsche Allgemeine Zeitung* (1929), in Bottai, *Esperienza corporativa,* 669–70.

13. Bottai, *Esperienza corporativa,* 677–711. See esp. 681–87 (1929) for Bottai's praise of a recent speech by the veteran syndicalist A.O. Olivetti.

14. Michael Geyer, with assistance from Sheila Fitzpatrick, "Introduction: After Totalitarianism—Stalinism and Nazism Compared," in *Beyond Totalitarianism: Stalinism and Nazism Compared,* ed. Michael Geyer and Sheila Fitzpatrick (Cambridge: Cambridge University Press, 2009), 23.

15. Mark Edele and Michael Geyer, "States of Exception: The Nazi-Soviet War as a System of Violence, 1939–1945," in *Beyond Totalitarianism,* ed. Geyer and Fitzpatrick, 349, 373–74. See also Timothy Snyder, *Bloodlands: Europe between Hitler and Stalin* (New York: Basic Books, 2010), on how the two sides fed each other.

16. Christian Gerlach and Nicholas Werth, "State Violence—Violent Societies," in *Beyond Totalitarianism,* ed. Geyer and Fitzpatrick, 172.

17. Ibid., 140–41.

18. Katerina Clark and Karl Schlögel, "Mutual Perceptions and Projections: Stalin's Russia in Nazi Germany—Nazi Germany in the Soviet Union," in *Beyond Totalitarianism,* ed. Geyer and Fitzpatrick, 412, 420–21.

19. Roger D. Markwick, "Communism: Fascism's 'Other'?," in *The Oxford Handbook of Fascism,* ed. R.J.B. Bosworth (Oxford: Oxford University Press, 2009), 339–61. The quoted passage is from 340.

20. Ibid., 340, 341.

21. Benito Mussolini, speech to the Chamber of Deputies, 21 June 1921, in Benito Mussolini, *Scritti e discorsi di Benito Mussolini,* vol. 2, *La rivoluzione fascista (23 marzo 1919–28 ottobre 1922)* (Milan: Ulrico Hoepli, 1934), 179–80.

22. Bottai, *Esperienza corporativa,* 546. Though typically provocative and a bit extreme, A. James Gregor usefully addresses the fascist understanding of the Soviet trajectory in *The Faces of Janus: Marxism and Fascism in the Twentieth Century* (New Haven, CT: Yale University Press, 2000); see esp. 128–48.

23. Renzo Bertoni, *Il trionfo del fascismo nell'U.R.S.S.* (Rome: Angelo Signorelli, 1934), esp. 144, 148–58.

24. See especially Pier Luigi Bassignana, *Fascisti nel paese dei Soviet* (Turin: Bollati Boringhieri, 2000), which provides a good overview of the activities of those Fascists in the Soviet Union together with a selection of the writings that resulted.

25. Jeffrey T. Schnapp, *Building Fascism, Communism, Liberal Democracy: Gaetano Ciocca—Architect, Inventor, Farmer, Writer, Engineer* (Stanford, CA: Stanford University Press, 2004), 21–32.

26. Gaetano Ciocca, *Giudizio sul bolscevismo: Com'è finito il piano quinquennale* (Milan: Valentino Bompiani, 1934), with a preface by *Il popolo d'Italia.* See also Schnapp, *Building Fascism,* 35–56, on Ciocca's writing in the wake of his Soviet sojourn.

27. Gleason, *Totalitarianism,* 14–20.

28. Ibid., 15–20, does not adequately distinguish Gentile from Nationalists like Alfredo Rocco. Moreover, Gleason implies a contrast between Gentile's statism and an emphasis on will and spirit, whereas Gentile plausibly claimed to encompass both.

29. See David D. Roberts, *The Totalitarian Experiment in Twentieth-Century Europe: Understanding the Poverty of Great Politics* (London and New York: Routledge, 2006), 271–335 (chapter 6, entitled "Conflicted Totalitarianism in Fascist Italy") for fuller a discussion and further references.

30. Gleason, *Totalitarianism,* 31–50. See also Peter Lassman, "Responses to Fascism in Britain, 1930–1945: The Emergence of the Concept of Totalitarianism," in *Sociology Responds to Fascism,* ed. Stephen P. Turner and Dirk Käsler (London: Routledge, 1992), 214–40.

31. Bernard Bruneteau, *Le totalitarisme: Origines d'un concept, genèse d'un débat, 1930–1942* (Paris: Les Editions du Cerf, 2010). After a substantial seventy-seven-page introduction, Bruneteau presents a rich selection of texts, primarily from the 1930s, with useful biographies of the authors represented.

32. Gleason, *Totalitarianism,* 29–30.

33. Miguel Jerez Mir and Javier Luque, "State and Regime in Early Francoism, 1936–45: Power Structures, Main Actors and Repression Policy," in *Rethinking Fascism and Dictatorship,* ed. Pinto and Kallis, 191.

34. Aristotle Kallis, "Neither Fascist nor Authoritarian: The 4th of August Regime in Greece (1936–1941) and the Dynamics of Fascistisation in 1930s Europe," *East Central Europe* 37 (2010): 307, 313.

35. Ibid., 319.

36. Gleason, *Totalitarianism,* 27–28, 29, provides a good sense of the basis for the German rejection of the term, after the initial interest in 1933. See Roberts, *The Totalitarian Experiment,* 433–37, for a fuller discussion.

37. Camillo Pellizzi, *Problemi e realtà del fascismo* (Florence: Vallecchi, 1924), 161, 163–65.

38. Paolo Ungari, *Alfredo Rocco e l'ideologia giuridica del fascismo* (Brescia: Morcelliana, 1963) is the classic account of the difference.

39. Even Abbott Gleason seems implicitly to endorse the German notion that to take the state as the focus of totalitarianism inherently meant conservative authority as opposed to radical dynamism. See, e.g., Gleason, *Totalitarianism,* 35, 164.

40. Federico Finchelstein, *Transatlantic Fascism: Ideology, Violence, and the Sacred in Argentina and Italy, 1919–1945* (Durham, NC: Duke University Press, 2010), 132.

41. Ibid., 131.

42. Ibid., 136, 143.

43. Ibid., 140.

44. Ibid., 75.

45. Constantin Iordachi, "God's Chosen Warriors: Romantic Palingenesis, Militarism and Fascism in Modern Romania," in *Comparative Fascist Studies: New Perspectives,* ed. Constantin Iordachi (London and New York: Routledge, 2010), 342–43, 349.

46. Ibid., 349.

47. Ibid., 352.

48. Constantin Iordachi, "Fascism in Interwar East Central and Southeastern Europe: Toward a New Transnational Research Agenda," *East Central Europe* 37 (2010): 176.

49. J.L. Talmon, *The Origins of Totalitarian Democracy* (New York: W.W. Norton, 1970; first published 1952), 6–8. De Felice endorsed Talmon's criteria even as he assigned fascism, the original movement with totalitarian potential, to the Left. Disputing De Felice, Michaelis insisted that fascism belongs on the Right, but he well articulated the need to encompass *both* the Left-Right distinction and totalitarianism in any effort to place Italian Fascism. See Meir Michaelis, "Anmerkungen zum italienischen Totalitarismusbegriff: Zur Kritik der Thesen Hannah Arendts und Renzo De Felices," *Quellen und Forschungen aus italienischen Archiven und Bibliotheken* 62 (1982): 287–89, 300–2.

50. Michael Mann, *Fascists* (Cambridge: Cambridge University Press, 2004), 97, 100, 112.

PART III

SOME TENTATIVE
PRESCRIPTIONS

Chapter 8

CATEGORIES FOR US
Blurring and Rigor

Transition: The Ending of the Braided Dynamic

Probing four modes of interaction in the preceding chapters has shown how open-ended domestic trajectories intertwined with multinational encounters in a braided dynamic, though obviously modes of interaction differed, as did the modes of braiding. The variation depended to a considerable extent on geographical positions and territorial situations resulting from World War I. Those factors, especially, made Austria, Hungary, and Romania extreme examples, but they are worth recalling here because the interweaving of domestic and multinational factors in each case especially exemplifies the braided dynamic.

With the newly truncated Austria wedged between the two major fascist powers, each of which had major reasons—though, for a time, seriously conflicting reasons—for concern with Austrian affairs, and with two conflicting indigenous fascist movements, each linked to one of those conflicting outside powers, the evolution of fascism in Austria was inevitably caught up in wider multinational interaction. We noted Gerhard Botz's insistence that the decline of influence of the Heimwehr from 1934 until its dissolution in 1936 was determined more by the changing relationship between Italy and Germany than by internal developments. More generally, Botz insists that in light of the fluctuating influence of the two fascist powers, a diachronic, developmental approach to the Austrian corporatist regime is especially necessary.[1] In other words, there was no "Austrian fascism" to be disembedded from the uncertain trajectory.

The Hungarian case is significant not primarily because Hungary had, in the Arrow Cross, by some measures the largest and most successful "authentically fascist" movement outside Italy and Germany. It is significant, rather, because of the complex, contingent interweaving of positive interaction, negative interaction, and asymmetry that produced a certain relentless momentum and a fascistizing direction. That was not the sort of fascistizing direction Gyula Gömbös had sought from 1932 to 1936, yet his efforts helped make it possible, a good example of layering within the diachronic dynamic. The outcome in Hungary was especially horrific, even as the Arrow Cross had been losing support and seemed to have been marginalized. Each step changed the situation, with international interaction feeding back on the domestic situation and vice versa. Although the braided dynamic cannot be conceived without the fascist Arrow Cross, it is the whole braided dynamic, and not the Arrow Cross itself, that must be our focus if we are to conceive the new universe on the Right and the place of fascism within it.

In Romania, too, we noted a complex, contingent interplay as two different putatively conservative authoritarians, King Carol II and Ion Antonescu, actively suppressed the "authentically fascist" Iron Guard in the process of moving in a fascistizing direction. And that process was bound up with Romania's interaction with Nazi Germany, reflecting the idiosyncratic vulnerabilities of Romania's territorial situation in the wake of World War I.

Finally, we might also recall a less dramatic but still highly symptomatic instance of the braided dynamic from a different region. Following Manuela Williams's account, we noted how Italy's turn to a more aggressive imperialism entailed complex interaction with the Arabs, on the one hand, and the British, on the other. This resulted in changing perceptions, illusions, and eventually self-deception and mythmaking that affected Italy's relations with Nazi Germany as well as the internal trajectory of the Italian regime.

Of course each case had its own unique, distinctive places in the new Right universe, and each is still to be researched on its own. But the braided dynamic encompassing the web of interaction constitutes an aggregate, the new universe on the Right, which was not a collection of individual cases that can be taken in isolation.

Probing the interaction not only brings the braided dynamic into focus but indicates the slipperiness and uncertainty in the meaning of categories at the time. And such slipperiness and uncertainty reinforced the openness of the interweaving trajectories. The future is always opaque, of course, but in this situation of novel experiment and multiple interaction, it was especially hard to know what was what, what might lead where.

Even as the double asymmetry became overwhelming, the uncertain braided dynamic, having become bound up with World War II, continued to the end, yielding new and unforeseen combinations, revealing more about what had become possible with the break into the new universe. During 1943–45, in what proved the last phase of the overall experiment, we find such new combinations perhaps most dramatically in Italy, Hungary, Romania, and France. Who, even in 1942, could have foreseen what would transpire in Italy and Hungary by 1944?

Despite the openness and unforeseeability, however, the scope for experiment was being radically skewed and in some ways narrowed by the time of World War II—a fact that proves central to the overall trajectory of the era. Because the narrowing of possibilities stemmed partly from the double asymmetry coming ever more to bear on the interaction, the trajectories of Italy and Germany again prove crucial. But what was happening in each country reveals an essential aspect of the fascist dynamic itself.

In both Italy and Germany, as on the aggregate level, a modicum of openness remained until the end. Questioning and further experiment seemed to remain possible, a fact that continued to sustain even some of the discontented. In chapters 4 and 5 we noted that even as corporatism seemed to lose whatever radical potential it may have had, committed corporatists kept pushing. Even Italy's intervention in the war in 1940 led to stepped-up calls: winning the war required deepening the corporatist revolution.[2] Only in retrospect, with the trajectory ended, do we see how futile the ongoing hopes and efforts were.

Whereas images of a "new man" and a new world remained in both Italy and Germany, they became ever more mythical as "fascism" reduced to capricious dictatorship, with ever greater reliance on an erratic, unchecked leader. To stress a narrowing reduction to Hitler and Mussolini by the end does not remotely let everyone else off the hook. Avoiding teleological thinking, we remember that though an emphasis on strong leadership was important to the emergence of fascism in Italy and Germany, as elsewhere, fascism was not merely about the cult of the leader all along. But the ever more central role of the leader helps explain why the fascist regimes proved merely improvised, ramshackle, riddled with cognitive dissonance. And this way of ending up—hollow and ephemeral—was central to the winding down, and ending, of the braided dynamic.

Even as we open with Constantin Iordachi to a wider range of experiment, responding to whatever aspects of modern experience—parliamentary government, trade unions, the Depression—such experiment had been increasingly pursued in light of the seeming success of fascism in Italy and Germany. But to the extent the aggregate of the new Right was based on such perceptions and expectations, it was built on a house of cards and could simply implode. The era itself proved hollow and ephemeral, despite its disastrous outcomes.

Meanwhile, Spain and Portugal, relatively isolated geographically and neutral in World War II, could stand apart to some extent. Yet even they remained caught in the multinational interaction in ways that help fix their place in the new Right universe. Their complex, sometimes vacillating responses to the Holocaust reflected conflicting pressures from both Germany and the democracies. Spain and Portugal were seeking primarily to preserve their neutrality and independence; on that basis their unforeseeable responses to the Holocaust entailed at least some measure of openness to Jews seeking to escape from the Nazis. The overall experiment remained sufficiently open-ended that it was unclear what the interaction would draw forth from the two Iberian regimes as long as the braided dynamic continued.

Specialists on the Franco regime disagree about nomenclature, but there is general agreement that whether it was "quasi-fascist" or merely "pseudo-fascist," the regime went through a somewhat fascist phase from 1937 into World War II. But they also agree that that phase ended, whether in 1941 or 1945, as the wider framework was being radically transformed.[3] Having maintained the neutrality of their respective countries, both the Franco and the Salazar regimes survived the war, but it was clear when the war ended in 1945 that an epoch was ending with it. And with Italy ever more subservient to Germany, it was the trajectory of the German regime that ended the epoch. After a particular process of ending, the end did come.

Still, sorting out what did and did not end with the end of World War II in 1945 is a big part of the overall problem. On the one hand, the framework was entirely different once the seemingly successful, if possibly menacing and imperialistic, fascist model had been so thoroughly discredited as a potential political alternative. In that sense 1919–45 was a distinct period. But whether fascism remained an ongoing possibility is an altogether different question, one that we will tackle in the next two chapters. Moreover, as the overall modern political experiment continued, significant new Right experiments continued or emerged in places like Brazil and Argentina, still playing to some extent off the enduring Salazar and Franco regimes in Portugal and Spain. Indeed, corporatist development in Latin America even after World War II was generally more substantive than it had been in Europe, a further indication that the new Right must be conceived globally.[4]

Aristotle Kallis and António Costa Pinto convincingly maintain that many of the institutions shaped in the political laboratory of "the era of fascism" in Europe expanded to dictatorships across the globe after 1945.[5] But to emphasize what continued to this extent deflects from what ended, and thus from the nature of that "era of fascism," which was not only, or even primarily, such a laboratory. It entailed not just the circulation and recontextualization of new Right ideas and innovations, but a particular dynamic, a braided dynamic. In their insistence on the ongoing relevance of certain of the institutional innovations, Kallis and Pinto do not do justice to the elements of hollowness, illusion, and wishful thinking that helped give the era its particular consistency—and that meant it could and did end.

Then and Now: Reflexivity in Our Present Categories

So the overall braided dynamic came to a particular sort of end. In light of openness and ongoing uncertainty, and despite the narrowing of possibilities, the meaning of categories was in play until that end was reached. And only after reaching the end can we consider the implications of the uncertainty and open-endedness at the time for our own categories as we seek understanding after the fact. In treating the recent restiveness, we noted renewed or even deeper questions about some of the categories centrally at issue, such as generic fascism and palingenesis, and about some of the key distinctions or contrasts, such as fascism/para-fascism and totalitarianism/authoritarianism. Focus on the web of interaction seems to place in still sharper relief the problematic side of the standard categories and distinctions. We again recall Michel Dobry's important point about the contestedness of the term "fascist" itself at the time.[6]

Better integrating the uncertainty at the time into our present categories is congruent with the imperative of a deeper reflexivity that we find in the calls for a new agenda by Dobry and Stein Ugelvik Larsen, but also, in a more general way, in the proposal for *histoire croisée* by Michael Werner and Bénédicte Zimmermann. And it inherently entails the blurring and fuzziness that Dobry and Larsen, especially, suggest we must better come to countenance.

We recall that whereas fascism was novel and central, there was a larger universe on the new Right to be encompassed, with fascism a subset within that larger universe. Preoccupation with fascism, with whether or not this or that counts as fascist, might even compromise our understanding of fascism itself. Thus, for example, Mary Vincent, in contending that the radicalizing interaction with wider European fascism on the part of the Spanish anti-Republican Right blurred the distinction between fascism and authoritarianism at the time, implies that we ourselves need to loosen up on that long-standing distinction in approaching the Franco regime—and, by implication, the whole universe of the new Right.

But obviously we can see in retrospect what was happening as the actors at the time could not, and we can determine which categories are the most illuminating, whatever the usages at the time. Moreover, we surely continue to demand some measure of rigor, which requires, first, comparison, distinction, and differentiation. We still need some basis for distinguishing novel from earlier political forms, and especially for distinguishing among the innovations on the Right during the period. So even as we need to countenance greater blurring over what counts as what, we still need to differentiate fascist from non-fascist phenomena.

Recalling Vincent's implication that even Stanley Payne's way of distinguishing "fascism" from José Maria Gil Robles's conservative nationalism is iffier than Payne seemed to recognize, the key proves to be that we must find room for both positions. Vincent shows that interaction changed the equation, blurring the distinction, making neat comparison less appropriate or relevant. But Payne was right in suggesting that José António Primo de Rivera and the Falange differed from Gil Robles on a basis that must be pinned down. Indeed, what differentiates fascism within the wider universe is the obvious first question. And whether this or that novel phenomenon on the new Right was "fascist" or not remains at issue even as we adjust to blurrier lines. But we must ask what criteria of differentiation are appropriate and how blurring and rigor are to come together.

At the same time, we must recognize that to conceive the new universe on the Right, we may need more bases or axes of differentiation than fascism versus whatever else. Insofar as we are concerned to transcend nominalism, moreover, rigor requires a further step, a way of conceiving the relationships among the bits and pieces in play, a way that will suggest itself as we proceed in this chapter and that the concluding chapter will seek to specify.

Adjusting to Greater Looseness

But first we must consider what is entailed in adjusting to greater looseness. In treating the web of interaction, we brushed up against some indications of ongoing uncertainty and controversy about where lines are to be drawn, about whether this or that counts as "fascist" (or "totalitarian") or not. And indeed we find explicit and symptomatic scholarly disagreement over the issue, ranging from the nature of the Metaxas or Antonescu regimes to the place of Nazi Germany, which some take as a case apart. The question of the singularity of Nazi Germany is best held for the concluding chapter, but let us consider a few of the other examples here.

We noted that Gerhard Botz has found the corporatist regime in Austria merely a traditional dictatorship, relying on the police and the bureaucracy, and demobilizing the crisis-driven middle classes.[7] Such dictatorships, as he sees it, were common in much of Europe at the time. Plausible though it is up to a point, this familiar line of argument seems too caught up in the old either-or framework, without sufficient attention to the novelty of the Austrian regime. In his more recent work, Botz seems to back off a bit in portraying the regime as a ramshackle, ever-shifting mixture; improvised, it was a mere Potemkin Village that never achieved institutionalization. And for Botz, this makes it anything but a genuinely fascist regime.[8] These are effective characterizations, but was the Austrian regime on that basis qualitatively different from the "real" fascist regimes? Even Botz's more recent perspective seems to entail inappropriate either/or assumptions; we can settle for blurrier lines instead.

Tim Kirk similarly finds the Austrian regime superficial in key respects. But he seems implicitly to dissent from Botz, at least in part, in noting that much recent writing suggests that Austro-fascism, as an alliance of the avowedly fascist Heimwehr and *fascisant* authoritarian conservatives, was in many ways more successful than a number of similar movements. However, it was uniquely vulnerable in having grown from one of two competing indigenous fascisms, and it ended up undercut by the popular success of the rival Nazis.[9] This would suggest that the outcome in Austria reflects the contingency of the trajectory more than some overall superficiality.

Kirk also contends that "fascism" may be not so much inaccurate as unhelpful in advancing our understanding of the Austrian regime because it deflects from the political realities and socioeconomic consequences.[10] This is useful in addressing the key point: in light of the undoubted ambiguity and long-standing uncertainty, why does it matter if the regime is deemed "fascist" or not? Still, Kirk's sense of what matters instead seems to invite nominalism, deflecting from attention to the place of the novel Austrian regime in the new universe. That place was especially significant, thanks in large part to both positive and negative interaction in which the regime was caught up.

In the Romanian case, the nature even of the Iron Guard itself has been at issue. Although generally considered "fascist"—certainly so by Iordachi and Philip Morgan, for example—Dennis Deletant questions the attribution in light of the Guard's religious orientation, including its attachment to the Book of Revelation, in contrast with what seemed the secular orientations of Hitler and Mussolini. Deletant concludes that the Iron Guard was closer to the nineteenth-century Russian Narodniks than to any Western model.[11] He seems to waffle, however, when at another point he finds the Iron Guard unique in the *fascist* universe. It alone came to power without the help of Italy or Germany, and it alone was toppled from within German-dominated Europe.[12]

But in the Romanian case, it is especially the nature of the Antonescu regime that has been controversial, with uncertainties over the criteria of fascism that especially reflect the uncertainties at the time. We have seen that Vladimir Solonari and Radu Ioanid are comparably critical of efforts, especially after the fall of the Romanian communist regime, to rehabilitate Antonescu and to minimize Romania's role in the Holocaust. But even as Solonari comes to feature Antonescu's effort not merely to accommodate to, but even to become the most favored partner in, the new Nazi-dominated Europe, he, like most specialists, denies that Antonescu and his regime were "fascist." Suppressing the mass, fascist-style party in Romania, Antonescu ruled through trusted generals. Conversely, Solonari goes on, the genuine fascists in Romania played no role in implementing what might seem the regime's most "fascist" measure, the program of radical population engineering we encountered in chapters 4 and 5.[13]

In contrast, Ioanid portrays Antonescu as a fascist dictator, and his regime as totalitarian.[14] The dictator suppressed the Iron Guard not because of but despite his fascist convictions and behavior. With his military background, he could not abide the Guard's greed and incompetence, which, as we noted, led to administrative and economic disorder when the Guard was entrusted with power for a few months in 1940.[15]

Deletant gives a good sense of both sides of the question before coming down clearly on the non-fascist and "merely" authoritarian side. While recognizing that Antonescu's rule was overtly anti-Semitic and entailed a monopoly of power, he makes the standard distinction, noting that unlike the Italian and German cases, the Romanian dictatorship was not based on a new mass party or ideology. Antonescu's program was simple, based on internal order, entrusted to the police, and on secure borders, entrusted to the army. Moreover, Antonescu tolerated the two opposition parties, thereby causing friction with his German allies, as we noted in chapter 5.[16]

But Deletant's way of posing the questions—was Antonescu a fascist? was he totalitarian or authoritarian?—betray the assumption that must be called into question, the assumption that clean, either/or distinctions are what we need.[17] Deletant and Solonari have good reasons for denying that Antonescu's regime was fascist, but if not fascist, what instead? Especially in pursuing its program of population engineering and ethnic cleansing, it was surely not merely authoritarian, traditionalist, or conservative. Nor was it merely para-fascist in the original sense, using the trappings of fascism for defensive purposes. And whereas it is true and important that accommodation with Nazi-dominated Europe did not make one "fascist," interaction on that level especially muddied the lines, as we saw not only in the Romanian case.

Solonari, especially, but to a lesser extent Deletant as well, come too close to begging the question in invoking, as evidence that the Antonescu regime was not fascist, the suppression of the Iron Guard and the lack of

Guard involvement in the radical population program. They take it for granted that those whom Antonescu marginalized were the "genuine" fascists. This is the sort of bifurcating that we must get beyond. The important differences between Antonescu and the Iron Guard remain, but Antonescu, too, was using novel, extreme means to address a novel challenge and opportunity, and thus his place in the universe of the new Right.

Keeping such questions about the Antonescu regime in mind, let us recall again that even in the Italian case, who qualified as a genuine Fascist was disputed—and remains so. The degree to which Mussolini ruled through the Fascist Party, as opposed to his own loyal subordinates, similarly remains in dispute. Mussolini, too, marginalized some of the more radical Fascists on occasion—if never so dramatically as in Romania. Insofar as we better incorporate the fuzziness at the time, fuzziness that the interaction helped bring about, we recognize that the line between the Mussolini and Antonescu regimes is simply not as clear as we have tended to make it.

Let us compare Italy in a different direction. Questioning our tendency toward rigid distinction, Mary Vincent notes that "like Mussolini's regime before it, Franco's New State represented an alliance between the radical and conservative right."[18] And, from another angle, let us recall Ian Kershaw's point that pseudo-religious notions of national salvation, of the sort that some, at least, take to have been essential to fascism, were stronger in Franco's Spain than in Mussolini's Italy.[19] It can also be argued that Franco's regime was more violent than Mussolini's in important respects. Miguel Jerez Mir and Javier Luque note how extraordinary was the violence and repression in Spain even well after the Civil War.[20] More generally, Roger Griffin, in reconsidering the para-fascism category, stresses that violence against internal enemies breaks down as a criterion for distinguishing fascist regimes from those like Franco's that he continues to label parafascist.[21] Among other things, this reminds us that the widespread tendency to associate fascism with violence, as a defining category, is arbitrary.

In any case, the importance of all these criteria can be disputed, but they are all plausible, and they suggest that the line between Mussolini's Italy and Franco's Spain, too, is fuzzier than we tend to make it. Moreover, drawing out certain implications of Vincent's emphasis on the blurring that resulted from the interaction, we note that "authoritarianism," as an alternative within the illiberal universe, was not merely static and "given," as nothing but traditionalist conservatism. Once totalitarianism was on the table, what had been authoritarianism could no longer be the same, even if it remained primarily defensive. And this, too, blurs the distinction between Spain and Italy.

In considering Italian examples, we encountered Alfredo Rocco and Alberto Beneduce, each of whom, we concluded, ended up as "fascist" as anyone else in Italy, even though neither started as a Fascist. This was to allow for synergy. But insofar as we allow for blurring as well, we need not get worked up over any such matters of classification.

Discussing Dobry in chapter 2, we noted the long-standing controversy over the "immunity thesis" in France. In the face of the seemingly self-serving claim that France had been immune to genuine fascism, for decades a number of scholars have been determined to identify a "French fascism." And Colonel François de La Rocque's Croix de Feu, launched as a movement in 1928 and converted into the Parti social français in 1936, has been widely seen as the most likely candidate. But whereas such authorities as Robert Soucy and Kevin Passmore take the Croix de Feu as the quintessential French expression of fascism, Albert Kéchichian claims that it lacked the totalitarian component essential to genuine fascism, that it was comparable to Franco's Spain and Salazar's Portugal in seeking to stabilize institutions and depoliticize society.[22] We will return to this point when we consider the uses of "totalitarianism" as a criterion of differentiation. For now we can note simply that, as Dobry implies, the Croix de Feu need not be understood in such either/or terms, precisely because it, too, was caught up in the web of interaction.

We could continue to go back and forth discussing whether this or that movement or regime was "fascist" or not, or the degree to which it was "fascist," but what matters is how each played into the wider contingent interaction and thus into a particular aggregate trajectory leading to a particular outcome. Each trajectory fed into the wider interaction that helped constitute the new universe on the Right. Even insofar as we focus on "fascism" itself, up to a point we find it necessary to turn from any notion that there was some authentic or genuine fascism that provides the touchstone, that our priority is to determine, on that basis, the extent to which this or that instance deviates.

In chapter 5 we noted that either/or thinking with respect to fascism seems especially to have compromised efforts to place the Japanese case within the new Right of the period. Perhaps we need some new categories. We will return to Gregory Kasza's "*kakushin* right" below, but let us also note Paul Brooker's comparative sociological study of the effort to forge solidarity in Japan, Italy, and Germany. Although he does not treat interaction among them, he concludes that whereas the three had something distinctive in common, it might be better understood as "fraternalism" than "fascism." Even as he finds limits in all three cases, he judges Japan the most successful in manufacturing solidarity in light of the responses of the Japanese people throughout the course of World War II. This greater success stemmed primarily from differences in background factors of the sort we encountered in chapter 5.[23] Whatever the merits of his particular category "fraternalism" (which is surely too gender specific), Brooker usefully implies that various axes were salient on the new Right during the period and that we would do well to look more widely, less preoccupied with the question of "fascism."

"Hybrid" and "Fascistization"

But even as we pull back from clean lines, the question of what differentiates "fascism" as a subset within the new universe will not go away. The blurring and uncertainty we noted suggests that "fascism" itself does not work as a differentiating category, but other categories might work better. At this point we might distinguish between macro-variables like totalitarianism, palingenesis, political religion, or fascism itself and micro-variables like elite-recruitment, party-state relations, and modes of leadership. At the same time, we must keep in mind that to conceive the aggregate universe, we may need more bases of differentiation than fascism versus whatever else.

Even those like Mary Vincent and Aristotle Kallis, prominent in calls for less rigidity, propose categories that they believe will enable us to better encompass cases like Spain and Greece. It is striking that both start by specifying that the regime at issue was *neither* fascist nor authoritarian.[24] And as for an alternative, each suggests that we might pin things down through the related but distinguishable categories "hybrid" and "fascistization." Hybrid, especially, is at least implicit in the earlier analyses of Martin Blinkhorn and others, and it seems increasingly prominent.[25] "Hybridization" is central to the reorientation that Pinto and Kallis advocate, as we noted in chapter 2. It is worth considering the uses and limitations of both hybrid and fascistization. Insofar as we find limitations, probing them should help us specify a more promising alternative.

Whereas Hagen Fleischer is fairly typical in deeming the Metaxas regime "fascist more in appearance than substance," though without much attention to criteria, Kallis uses both "hybrid" and "fascistizing" in seeking to bring the Greek case into the mainstream of fascist studies.[26] And Kallis casts his net widely: the Metaxas regime "was a distinctly Greek facet of the 'fascistisation' of large sections of the interwar European right—and a 'hybrid' political phenomenon alongside others in Portugal, Romania, Bulgaria, Hungary or even Austria that theories of 'generic fascism' can no longer afford to shun as irrelevant or 'failed.'"[27]

Kallis takes particular care with the "hybrid" category, which he finds too limited as conventionally applied. As he sees it, hybridization was at work throughout the new Right universe, including Italy and Germany, because there was always some degree of fascist-conservative interaction, which, as we discussed in chapter 4, is widely held to have entailed conservative efforts from above to tame, channel, or exploit a fascist movement emerging from below.[28] As Kallis sees it, that conventional conception of hybridization presupposes too rigid a distinction between "genuine" fascism and other new Right departures. The Metaxas regime in Greece did not emerge to head off fascism from below; Greece lacked any such thing. But that regime was quite clearly novel, owing something to fascism elsewhere, and not merely an instance of old-fashioned conservatism. Metaxas moved Greece in a fascist direction from above, though, as we saw, doing so necessarily entailed interaction with other conservative elites, most obviously those around the monarchy.

In characterizing the Franco regime as a hybrid, Vincent, too, clearly intends the category as a useful step beyond the notion of taming or channeling so long applied to the Spanish case. She was writing in the context of long-standing debates about the nature of Franco's regime, debates revolving precisely around comparison with fascism and/or totalitarianism. Central to that discussion has been the noted social scientist Juan Linz, whose insistence that the Franco regime was authoritarian, as opposed to fascist or totalitarian, has led some to accuse him of exculpation.[29] Linz warned against thinking in terms of continua, which would be to underplay the uniqueness and sui generis quality of each regime, but he still adduced criteria, such as the Franco regime's modicum of pluralism and legal predictability, to deny that it was fascist or totalitarian.

Franco's regime of course lasted until his death in 1975, three decades after the end of World War II. In making her argument, Vincent was concerned especially with that regime's origins and early trajectory—and thus, by implication, its place in the universe at issue for us. She was not as concerned as Linz to characterize or classify the regime overall. But in concluding that, as the result of the Spanish Right's radicalizing interaction with European fascism, the emerging Franco regime was neither fascist nor merely authoritarian but rather—having undergone a "process of fascistization"— a hybrid, a "fascistized" state, she was certainly seeking to transcend the terms of the debate long surrounding Linz's work.[30] As we have noted, she was also denying that the Franco regime was merely "para-fascist" in the sense of manipulating novel forms for familiar, traditional purposes.

Although, as Vincent makes clear, interaction with wider European fascism was crucial, we must remember that indigenous fascism, with some distinctive features of its own, was also essential to the mix in Spain. José Antonio Primo de Rivera insisted plausibly that his Falange was an innovative Spanish response, with indigenous sources, not remotely a mere imitation. And as Vincent makes clear, novel modes of Catholic political involvement came to characterize the Spanish Right during the 1930s: "The circumstances of the Civil War, in particular the anticlerical massacres in the Republican zone, had given Catholicism a purchase it had not had before, not even in Spain. Indeed, this transfer between Catholicism and fascism, religion and politics, was part of the process of fascistization."[31]

Just as both Vincent and Kallis imply, "hybrid" usefully points beyond either/or, and in adopting the term, each of the two scholars seems to intend a kind of synergy. But even as an *ex post* category, hybrid is problematic, suggesting a static synthesis, an amalgam of stable elements, whereas in the Spanish case a more dynamic trajectory is clearly at issue. In light of Vincent's own argument, hybrid does not do justice to the novelty, singularity, and uncertainty of the combination that coalesced, contingently. In treating a number of examples in chapter 4 we noted how the interaction of elements often transformed them, engendering an uncertain, open-ended dynamic in the process. The course in both Hungary and Romania, well before the turn of the tide during the war, especially defies the hybrid notion in light of the complex, uncertain dynamic resulting from the interaction on both the domestic and the international levels. In short, in these cases at least, hybrid does not seem sufficiently reflexive to be open to the array of possibilities at the time.

"Fascistization" is a more dynamic and thus more promising category, and I have adopted it to characterize the trajectories in both Hungary and Romania. In their joint work, Pinto and Kallis seem to use fascistization and hybridization as essentially synonymous. But *as* dynamic, can fascistization be combined with hybrid, as Vincent, Kallis, and Pinto do, as if each category implied the other? Did hybrid yield or produce fascistization or result from it? How did the process work? Especially in pondering the Greek case, with its brief trajectory, we wonder if fascistization means that the fascist side was ascendant, or at least expanding, on the domestic level or simply that conservative sectors were being influenced by fascism elsewhere, resulting in a hybrid. There is an element of dynamism either way, but we still need to better understand the relationship between fascistization and hybrid.

However, Vincent's use of "fascistization" raises a still trickier question about the axes of interaction and the field of possibilities. Plausibly determined to bring the Spanish case closer to the mainstream of the discussion, she is quick to impute the novelty on the Right precisely to fascistization. Although the fascist example surely stimulated fresh thinking, the new politicizing of religion in Spain did not require a fascist model, nor was the mode of politicizing at work comparable to what we find in either Fascist Italy or Nazi Germany. The particular new Right that emerged in Spain, in light of the particulars of the crisis of the Republic and the Civil War, involved the Catholic Church and politicized religion in new ways, but the process seemed to owe relatively little to fascism. We must at least consider the possibility that, especially in light of the militant anti-clericalism of the Left, it would have happened even without foreign models. So what emerged in Spain may have been a novel and distinctive phenomenon, not only transcending mere hybrid, but also not resulting from anything usefully called fascistization. It would still have a place in the new universe on the Right, but it would be a more autonomous place, relating differently to the other phenomena in that universe.

To be sure, the Spanish case, in light of Spain's idiosyncratic circumstances, may be the exception that proves the rule, but it brings home a possibility to be kept in mind. Even as "fascistization" surely has its uses, it still reflects the sense that the place of this or that innovation vis-à-vis fascism determines its place in the new Right universe. And even as we may want to conceive the place of fascism itself during the era more broadly, we must be open to the possibility of innovation and experiment on the new Right that transcends either/or in other ways.

In the context of hybrid and fascistization, and recalling the possibility of alternative categories like Brooker's "fraternalism" to encompass the difficult Japanese case, we can usefully return to Gregory Kasza's "*kakushin* right." As we noted in chapter 5, Kasza suggests that we adopt this untranslatable Japanese term to characterize the selectively revolutionary initiatives that were prominent at various points during the period, not only in Japan but in much of Europe, including Romania, Greece, and Poland among others. This, for Kasza, is the key to transcending the either/or thinking that has especially bedeviled efforts to place the Japanese case. But in providing a category for innovations falling halfway between the conservative and the fascist Right, Kasza was also seeking to supplement a typology proposed by Stanley Payne.[32] The *kakushin* category surely serves comparison as well as characterization, just as Kasza contends. But how does it relate to hybridization and fascistization, categories that might seem more dynamic?

As with Griffin's recasting of para-fascism to constitute a "fourth way," noted in chapter 2, positing the *kakushin* Right provides one way of recognizing that there were more than two possibilities on the new Right, so that we get beyond worrying about the fascist-conservative dichotomy. As an aspect of jettisoning that either/or straightjacket, Kasza usefully notes, congruent with the new agenda, that positing the *kakushin* Right invites analysis and comparison without taking Fascist Italy or especially Nazi Germany as the standard. Placed alongside them, everything else looks merely conservative.[33] And adding a category transcending either/or, fascist/conservative, helps Kasza make some effective comparisons between the Japanese and several European cases.

In treating Japan, Kasza certainly shows that those borrowing from European fascism were crucial, direct conduits of fascist influence on a substantial segment of the governing elite. But especially in seeking to specify the wider applicability of the "*kakushin* right" to Europe, Kasza seems mostly concerned simply to establish the category, as if doing so, thereby overcoming the inadequacies of either/or, were sufficient. But, congruent with the new agenda, we note that concern with classification deflects from attention to the contingent interaction between conservatives and fascism and especially the possibility of dynamic synergy. Surely "fascistization" or even "hybridization" works better.

The Uses of Comparison

But let us look further at the uses of comparison. Certainly differentiation implies comparison, which leads us to think in terms of continua, but we noted Linz's concern that doing so tends to smooth out the jagged singularity of the disparate responses at issue. In looking for factors that can be assessed in common, we may indeed miss or unduly play down idiosyncrasies, sui generis factors. Yet a preoccupation with singularity threatens to leave us with mere nominalism. The challenge is to maintain the jagged edges, even as we think in terms of continua.

Both in his own work and in editing several collaborative volumes, António Costa Pinto has offered a number of helpful comparative assessments, differentiating especially the German, Italian, Spanish, and Portuguese cases in terms of such micro-variables as elite recruitment, decision-making procedures, modes of charismatic leadership, the role of the single party, and the extent of tensions between party and state.[34] Such factors, he emphasizes, were central to actual functioning, as ideology and program often were not. So it is by focusing on such factors that we get at the operational elements distinguishing fascist regimes from other twentieth-century European Right-wing dictatorships.[35] The type of comparison at issue can illuminate degrees of fascism, but it can also differentiate fascism.

It goes without saying that such variables are important and that inquiries pinpointing them have a significant ongoing place. But such inquiries can throw us off insofar as they tend to make the variables too static, and insofar as they too rigidly distinguish "operational" elements from aspiration, ideology, program, or theory.

Comparison can be diachronic, to be sure, but even with diachronic comparison the tendency is to compare static slices abstracted from the trajectory or dynamic, as if these were stable entities, capable of isolation. Essentialism and reification lurk in such approaches. Insofar as we are better attuned to the openness and fluidity at the time, including the dia-chronic dimension of the interaction, we consider more deeply at what point in the trajectory the entity for comparison is to be found. We ask what decisions were about and why such decisions seemed apposite at that point. Comparison is thus not static but serves our understanding of the dynamic.

In treating the Italian case, Pinto features both increasing party influ-ence and the increasing role of charisma, as manifested in the cult of the Duce.[36] And in noting the tensions with the state apparatus produced by the party's expanding role, he plausibly claimed to find one of the key fac-tors distinguishing the practice of genuinely fascist regimes.

But whereas Pinto's comparisons have revealed significant differences, to focus on these variables apart from the wider internal dynamic, stem-ming from and continuing to reflect all that Pinto bracketed as "program," can mislead. Without deeper attention to what seemed the stakes of the party-state infighting in the Italian case, possible only if we encompass the array of aspirations for Fascism, we cannot know what it meant that, in one sense, the party's influence was growing during the 1930s. Nor can we know what it meant that charismatic leadership was becoming more central at the same time. Insofar as the expanding party reach and inflating cult of the Duce meant empty rituals and mere spectatorship, the regime might have fallen into a demobilizing mode of mobilization, blunting and frustrating originating aspirations still at work. But that would not justify bracketing those aspirations, which continued to intertwine with provi-sional outcomes to help generate the regime's particular trajectory.

So whereas these sorts of micro-variables certainly serve the compar-ison and differentiation we seek, we may sometimes put too much stock in comparison at the expense of attention to wider dynamic trajectories. At the same time, we note that the array of variables that might attract our focus is enormous. In addition to those Pinto fastens upon, we might note differences over the role of violence, for example, or over the import of religious tradition and relations with existing churches, or over degrees of top-down and bottom-up agency, and over modes of mass mobilization. We are bound to assess the relative importance of the numerous variables, and Pinto makes a good case for the combination he has chosen. But en-compassing a greater measure of blurring entails recognizing the inevitabil-ity of a measure of arbitrariness as we chose this or that combination. No one combination is essential or definitional for "fascism," based on what-ever set of criteria. So even as we can usefully isolate this or that, we need not insist too strongly on any particular combination.

Although they, too, resist clean lines and clear distinctions, the macro-categories palingenesis, political religion, and totalitarianism can be useful for comparison and differentiation, perhaps even for distinguishing fascism from non-fascism or establishing degrees of fascism. In this context, political religion can be understood as encompassing modes of relationship with traditional religion and existing religious institutions. But considering the applicability of both palingenesis and political religion to the Romanian and Italian cases indicates, first, that each category was more central in some instances than others and that neither is a defining feature of fascism. After considering those two categories, however, we will need to ask about the relevance of totalitarianism.

The Romanian Legion of the Archangel Michael seems to offer an extreme example of both palingenetic thinking and the sacralization of politics. As we noted in chapter 6, Iordachi shows that Corneliu Codreanu and other Legion intellectuals adapted a long tradition of palingenetic thinking in Romania to profess an ecumenical form of "heroic Christianity." Romania was to play a unique historical role, wound around expiation and suffering, to spearhead resurrection, the literal fulfillment of Christianity, bringing about the end of history.[37] We also noted that the Legion's extreme religiosity led Deletant to deny that the Legion was modern or "fascist" at all. And it is certainly true that any such vision may suggest a renewed millenarianism, if not mere blasphemy or *Ersatzreligion*. But Iordachi insists convincingly that something more modern was at work, that the Legion was part of the wider novel, revolutionary nationalist political universe.[38]

Certainly the Legion was not some Orthodox "sect"; it violated Orthodox dogma and even proclaimed itself superior to the Orthodox Church. Still, precisely because it professed Christianity, the Legion's relationship with the church could only have been ambivalent and uncertain, entailing intimacy and collaboration on the one hand, competition and conflict on the other.[39]

We have seen that the relationship between Fascism and Catholicism was similarly contested in Mussolini's Italy and remains an area of controversy today, in light of ongoing research and reconceptualization. But even granting the disagreement over priorities and proportions in Italy, the relationship between the fascist movement and the church in the two countries was bound to differ considerably.

In Italy many Fascists embraced aspects of Catholic liturgy and sought to mesh Catholicism, Fascism, and Italian tradition, and some, as Walter Adamson shows, went further, conceiving Fascism as a means to further a Catholic agenda. But extreme modes of religious palingenesis, of the sort envisioned by the Romanian Legion, were little in evidence among Italian Fascists. The thrust of fascism in Italy was much more secular, more obviously reflecting modern experience to that point, including the performance of parliamentary government, the advent of trade unionism, and the revision of Marxism. For major components, including Mussolini himself, Italian Fascism was not remotely about the literal realization of Christianity. Italian Fascism was wound around a sense of the human place in history that was not merely different from, but incompatible with, Codreanu's notion of resurrection as the end of history. Conversely, we noted that the Iron Guard worried about the seeming atheism of both Mussolini and Hitler.

In the last analysis, both palingenesis and political religion seem more relevant to Romania than to Italy. But to do justice to the place of both cases in the mix, we recognize that the differences over palingenetic religion do not suggest that Italy was genuinely fascist whereas the Legion was merely millenarian—let alone merely para-fascist as opposed to fascist. Conversely, the fact that the Romanian Legion offers an extreme example of both palingenetic thinking and the sacralization of politics does not make it the archetypal instance of fascism. In the fluid, uncertain field on the new Right, palingenesis, political religion, anti-communism, totalitarianism, charismatic leadership, an energizing sense of special mission, and much else were among the possibilities.

So the considerable differences in the new Right universe need to be pinpointed, and axes of differentiation need to be established, but doing so need not focus on palingenesis and political religion, let alone "fascism" or "fascistization." Indeed, no one category or axis of differentiation needs to be taken as the key. Still, fascism of course remains central to the mix, as a subset within the wider field, and sometimes we still need to ask about fascist or not, or about degrees of fascistization. Even as Romania and Italy differed over palingenesis and the role of Christianity, and even as those differences do not make either, as opposed to the other, "fascist," the two had other things in common, not least because each was caught up in the wider web of interaction at the time. For all its indigenous sources, the palingenetic religious impulse in Romania developed in interplay with other impulses that owed something to Nazi Germany and especially to Fascist Italy, including a would-be totalitarianism.

"Totalitarianism" as a Basis of Comparison and Differentiation

Totalitarianism has long served as a differentiating principle. For example, Peter Sugar concluded his important collaborative volume of 1971 on fascism in the Habsburg successor states by noting that the several essays agreed in taking totalitarianism, especially as derived from Hannah Arendt, as what differentiated fascists from those like Regent Horthy in Hungary and King Carol II in Romania.[40] The problem is that the notion of totalitarianism, uncertain and contested at the time and long controversial thereafter, might seem even more problematic in light of our considerations so far. Whatever its origins, the category might seem to have become espe-cially ahistorical, making the phenomena too familiar, obscuring what was at issue at the time, and thereby keeping us from grasping originality and experiment. The fact that its meaning and desirability were earlier at issue does not mean the category is appropriate for us, in light of its potential for misuse and the misleading connotations that have come to attach to it.

Moreover, it is well known that "totalitarianism" long entailed a "struc-tural" model of top-down, total control, one that has been exploded through research over the last forty years showing internal divisions, insti-tutional rivalries, and lack of control—even in Nazi Germany and in the Soviet Union under Stalin during the 1930s. For this reason, especially, "totalitarianism" has come to seem singularly inappropriate and misguided to some. Even as Richard Overy, for example, makes points that might seem to support a recast use of the category, he links totalitarianism to a "political-science fantasy" presupposing "domination through fear by psy-chopathic tyrants" who wield "total, unlimited power."[41]

Focusing on the web of interaction seems only further to bring home the inappropriateness of the category. Arnd Bauerkämper features the con-flicting impulses, institutional rivalries, and lack of coordination that com-promised the efforts of both Italy and Germany to influence revolutionary nationalist movements elsewhere.[42] While also magnifying the scope for selective borrowing, these weaknesses might seem still more evidence that the two key fascist regimes were anything but totalitarian.

Still, to some extent "totalitarianism" survived the discredit of the struc-tural model and even got something like a new lease on life in tandem with "political religion" as this latter category returned to prominence in the later 1990s.[43] However, the relationship between totalitarianism and po-litical religion is anything but straightforward and opens a new universe of questions. To be sure, linking the two entailed a substantial departure from the discredited structural model, attributing the totalitarian departures to a quest for total control. For Emilio Gentile, perhaps the most influential proponent of "political religion," the earlier tendency to attribute total-itarianism to some self-explanatory quest for total power was too simple and obscured more significant, historically specific sources. But neither, Gentile makes clear, can we understand totalitarianism as a mere corollary of political religion. Warning explicitly against the indiscriminate use of "political religion," he insisted that it is but "one element of totalitarian-ism, not the principal element and not even the most important in defining its essence." And the nature of totalitarianism itself, he added, "remains a wholly open question."[44]

But even apart from the vogue of political religion, "totalitarianism" has remained widely used, especially as a means of differentiating among new phenomena on the Right. Iordachi uses it for this purpose, seemingly taking its utility for granted, in discussing east central and southeastern Europe.[45] The totalitarian-authoritarian binomial itself is still routinely assumed, whatever the concerns of Iberianists like Vincent and Pinto. Morgan explicitly invokes the contrast, seemingly taking it as unproblematic.[46] Robert Paxton similarly employs the term "authoritarian" unapologetically, for the conventional reasons, with extended use of the Franco example.[47]

Although "totalitarianism" remains widely used to characterize some subset of the phenomena at issue, it tends to be invoked without much depth or sense of what was intended by it at the time. And used as a present analytical category, it still often carries the assumption, even when the issue is not confronted explicitly, that totalitarianism was embraced at the time primarily for instrumental purposes, as a means of cementing power and domination.[48]

Although we need "totalitarianism" first to understand certain novelties of aspiration and direction at the time, the category can serve us as a criterion of differentiation if we use it in a more genuinely historical way, better informed by usages and conflicts then. This entails reflexively integrating what *they* meant by it, what they knew of it elsewhere, recognizing that "totalitarianism" might have been a mere myth or slogan.

Because uses at the time were uncertain, contested, and evolving, such a reflexive use of the category cannot be expected to reveal clear distinctions or static dichotomies. Yet even a somewhat ragged notion of totalitarianism affords greater rigor than palingenesis, political religion, or fascism itself as a differentiating factor. And though we need to be open to an array of impulses fueling a totalitarian direction, we can grasp the family resemblance, precisely as "totalitarian," in the radical departures at issue.

However, insofar as we find "totalitarianism" useful for differentiation on the Right, we are bound to ask at some point what differentiates "fascism" from communism, or at least the Stalinist regime, if, as I am among those to insist, a totalitarian direction is common to both.[49] We will confront that long-standing question in the concluding chapter.

Recasting "Totalitarianism" as an Analytical Category

Although even our own use of "totalitarianism" must be somewhat flexible, encompassing variations and degrees, it helps to have a kind of baseline, based on the positive embrace of the notion in Fascist Italy. Let us establish that baseline in this section, then note the need and scope for blurring as we actually try using totalitarianism as a differentiating category in the next section.

Totalitarianism is best conceived as a novel aspiration, a direction for practice, and a characteristic dynamic. It is not to be understood as a mode of governance or system of rule—let alone as a quest for something like "total control." Rather than a blueprint, it was merely a direction for collective action. The novel totalitarian departure stemmed from a sense of challenge, opportunity, and even responsibility that emerged at a historically specific moment, in light of a modern configuration that seemed to demand that new mode of collective action. It was essential to transcend liberal democracy by expanding state sovereignty, in principle without limit, but also by involving people—everyone—more constantly and directly, again in principle without limit. The distinction between public and private would dissolve; individuals would experience virtually anything they did, from labor to child-rearing, in public or political terms. Thus the proclamation of Nazi Germany's labor front chief Robert Ley that "the private citizen has ceased to exist."[50]

As a mode of *doing*, as opposed to mere being, totalitarianism envisioned not simply a sacralization of politics, nor, contrary to many, was its aim some "utopia" or final equilibrium. It was an instrument for *ongoing* collective action in the face of a history now experienced as more radically open-ended, with more that could be, and had to be, done collectively. It is partly thus that it is not to be conflated with political religion, which, as we noted, was more central in some instances than others and is not a defining feature of either fascism or totalitarianism. Indeed, precisely because it entailed a mode of doing and not merely being, "totalitarianism" proves more helpful than "political religion" to characterize certain of the genuinely fascist phenomena at issue.[51]

The totalitarian impulse had its own historically specific sources that we need better to understand. Because of limits to the range of frequencies we have been prepared to hear, invoking political religion too often has seemed to obviate any need to consider the sources and implications of totalitarianism on its own terms. Impulses that look like political religion are often better understood as corollaries of totalitarianism itself.

Although the totalitarian impulse was novel and a significant part of the new universe, it was sometimes rudimentary, and even in practice totalitarianism was only a direction. Obviously we must allow room for differentiation among totalitarian impulses—including the sense of the requirements for the greater dynamism that seemed essential. We have already noted the differences between the Nazis and the Italian Fascists over the uses of codified law. But, as we also noted, neither can be considered more totalitarian than the other on that basis. Moreover, what those at the time wanted to do, and in some cases actually set out to do, by means of the totalitarian mode of action varied considerably. Still, the distinctive direction was and remains clear—and so, once we open and listen, is the rationale for that direction in light of the sense of challenge and opportunity that the historical moment seemed to entail.

For those in power, however, the longer the occasion to move in a totalitarian direction, the more the ensuing dynamic proved to entail all sorts of unintended consequences, including, most basically, a tendency to spin out of control. Indeed, a certain "chaos" was one characteristic outcome of the totalitarian effort, which proved to entail hubris and overreach. This tendency toward chaos and lack of control obviously was not part of the original vision, and it could not have been fully grasped in the interaction at the time, even by those critical or skeptical. But in light of that tendency, it is not at all surprising that the structural model has been so readily exploded in recent decades. Still, appropriately recast as a novel aspiration and direction, totalitarianism is not only relevant but essential to distinguish and characterize a subset of the novel phenomena in the new Right universe.

In light of the uncertainties at the time, we must of course be alert to both explicit embrace and explicit rejection of the totalitarianism category as we assess aspirations and departures. But we may find an ideal or a potential direction that can usefully be understood as "totalitarian" even if proponents did not use the term—or even if they actively rejected it. The key example is obviously Nazi Germany itself.

In his recent *Modernism and Totalitarianism*, Richard Shorten proposes an alternative to the structural model, one that seems promising in taking ideas seriously and in seeking to encompass the quest for an alternative modernity. And he usefully disputes political religion, insisting on historical specificity and secularization instead. But he proves teleological in insisting on what he calls the "genocidal model" as an alternative—and then in featuring utopianism, scientism, and regenerative violence, all linked to that genocidal model, as the key dimensions of totalitarianism. Shorten's alternative stems from an explicitly moralistic notion: because the violent outcomes of the Nazi and Soviet experiments are what most trouble us, it is those outcomes that make the term "totalitarianism" essential to our vocabulary.[52]

Partly on that basis, Shorten privileges the Nazi and Soviet cases and explicitly precludes Fascist Italy.[53] Indeed, even as he endorses Michael Geyer and Sheila Fitzpatrick on the need for new research, his thrust is precisely the opposite of theirs, which is putatively "beyond totalitarianism," for he takes totalitarianism precisely as the way to get at what the Nazi and Soviet regimes had in common and insists that the common totalitarianism was what was most important about them.[54] This is not in itself to fault Shorten, of course, and we will soon consider the serious limits in the overall conceptualization that informs the Geyer-Fitzpatrick volume. But several of this latter book's essays indicate, if only indirectly, the problems with a teleological approach to totalitarianism like Shorten's.

Although Christian Gerlach and Nicholas Werth do not make the point explicitly, their evidence shows that even when violence in Nazi Germany and the Soviet Union became literal extermination, the outcome cannot be understood simply as "genocide" because it resulted from a broader process, an interactive escalation.[55] So to understand the outcome we must not start with the Nazi and Stalinist exterminations, as a sort of telos, and back up from there, though doing so is what Shorten explicitly advocates in claiming to recast totalitarianism. Even to understand the Holocaust, we must start with the wider departure and the resulting dynamic, including the several modes of binational interaction. It is clear from Gerlach and Werth that Nazi violence was stimulated in part by the big increase in the violent persecution of those marginalized in the Soviet Union, which responded to the unforeseen disruptions and frustrations that the Stalinist revolution encountered.[56] In the Nazi case, too, the increasing violence, leading to mass extermination, stemmed partly from the magnitude of the task undertaken and the inability to carry out the requisite territorial and ethnic engineering effectively, as even maintaining control and organizing deportation proved difficult.[57]

Shorten's genocidal model, based on certain outcomes in practice, restricts the terrain a priori, whereas we need to expand the range of inquiry and consider a wider array of possibilities. "Totalitarianism" can and should be understood more broadly and loosely in light of the array of impulses at work. But Shorten, in light of his teleological approach, seems little interested in how the category was used and understood at the time, as one of the novel possibilities on the table, capable of attracting, repelling, or confusing others from within the web of interaction. To take totalitarianism in a more deeply historical way, without teleology, is to give up any claim to know a priori what its implications were, where it would lead.

Shorten's reasons for precluding the Italian case are especially problematic—and symptomatic. First, he uncritically accepts the Nazi case against the putative statism of the Italians to deny that Fascist Italy was totalitarian.[58] In one sense, this is curious on the face of it because, as we saw, the Nazis were quite willing to attribute a totalitarian direction to Fascist Italy even as, pointing to that putative statism, they denied that they themselves were totalitarian. Although we of course are not bound to parrot usages at the time, the disconnect in this instance especially gives pause. As I have emphasized, the differences between the Germans and the Italians were very real, but they do not warrant Shorten's way of determining who and what counts as totalitarian.

Shorten goes on to portray the German-Italian difference over statism as underlying the difference in genocidal outcome. But it was not mass murder, nor was it primarily coercion and violence, that made the new term "totalitarianism" apposite at the time. So it is not these dimensions that make the notion essential to any inquiry into the new political universe at issue. And the centrality of the category to the Italian Fascist self-understanding, and to Italy's place in the wider discussion, surely suggests that any inquiry encompassing "totalitarianism" must include the Italian case.

Moreover, treating totalitarianism in a more deeply historical way makes it clear that its aim was not some "utopia" or final equilibrium, as Shorten assumes. At issue, we noted above, was forging the instrument for *ongoing* struggle in action instead. Shorten's account is a prime indication of the need for greater flexibility in our understanding.

Fortunately, however, other recent research and reconceptualization, even if not always using totalitarianism explicitly, helps us see how we might apply the category more flexibly to characterize novel aspirations and directions in a way more congruent with uses at the time—yet still illuminating for us. In the case of Nazi Germany, studies by Robert Gellately, Peter Fritzsche, and Thomas Kühne have made it clearer how ordinary people came to identify with and participate in the regime's grandiose projects, even to take initiatives from below once they had internalized something like the Nazi frame of mind.[59] We also recall Michael Burleigh's pioneering work showing how even the "euthanasia" program elicited the cooperation of ordinary people.[60] Yet Burleigh came to rely on "political religion," whereas a distinguishable, historically specific totalitarian syndrome seems to have been at work.

In the case of Italy, Emilio Gentile, especially, has pointed us beyond Hannah Arendt and even Renzo De Felice to take the totalitarian thrust of Italian Fascism more seriously, as a direction central to the Fascist self-understanding, even if it was obviously seriously blunted in practice.[61] Doing so, however, has opened a deeper array of questions about the basis and implications of totalitarianism in the Italian case. Just as there remains controversy over how totalitarianism relates to political religion, we find disagreement about its implications for the role of the Fascist Party and especially for the party's relationship with the Italian state, including the would-be corporate state.

Despite their claim to point "beyond totalitarianism," even Geyer and Fitzpatrick, almost in spite of themselves, similarly point the way to a recasting of the category. In claiming to go beyond, they are simply hung up on the old model of total control and the concomitant tendency to accent

German-Soviet commonalities on that basis. So determined are they and their collaborators to undercut that model that they tend even to slant their evidence the other way, playing up differences at the expense of commonalities. They thereby miss how totalitarianism, appropriately recast, becomes precisely the category we need to make sense of the rather different, but still quite striking and symptomatic commonalities that their invaluable researches reveal.[62]

In the preceding chapter we noted that those researches also show the import of Nazi–Soviet interaction in feeding the extremism of each side, thereby constituting what we suggested might be considered the archetypal instance of *histoire croisée*. The reciprocity explored, for example, in Mark Edele and Michael Geyer's essay on the Nazi-Soviet war is a central aspect of the way totalitarianism is to be understood—not as a static, reified system, but as "epochal," with a particular mode of interplay crucial to the dynamic as each claimed the post-liberal space.[63] The sense that they were involved in the same kind of departure, doing the same grandiose, history-making kind of thing, was comparably energizing and comparably fed the tendency toward out-of-control excess on both sides.

But if we are to turn the tables on the Geyer-Fitzpatrick team and insist that what they show is not "beyond totalitarianism" but rather the need and scope for a recast "totalitarianism," it becomes even more imperative to address the differences between fascism and Soviet communism in the concluding chapter.

Using "Totalitarianism" to Differentiate Fascism

But the point for now is that if we overcome the confusions that Shorten and Geyer-Fitzpatrick, in their different, even conflicting ways, add to those already dogging the category, an appropriately recast notion of totalitarianism provides our best means of differentiating among the new phenomena on the Right—and even of deepening our understanding of the differences. A sense of the imminent possibility of, or an actual attempt at, a totalitarian mode of action is what such disparate cases as Italian Fascism and the Romanian Iron Guard most significantly had in common. Despite their differences, they were both sufficiently totalitarian in aspiration and direction to count as fascist. Thus, for example, the Guard envisioned the new mode of action to at last implement the essential eugenics program. As a corollary of the totalitarian impulse, the sense of leapfrogging the mature democracies that we considered in chapter 6 adds to the value of "totalitarianism," because it was especially the totalitarian mode of action that seemed to warrant the sense of leapfrogging.

But let us get yet another possible objection on the table up front. Insofar as I claim that totalitarianism affords a better criterion of differentiation than the other obvious candidates, am I saying that it is uniquely definitional? Am I not letting essentialism in through the back door? We must recognize this objection here, but we can best address it after, first, following the ins and outs of totalitarianism as differentiating, but then especially after considering how we can best conceive the whole braided dynamic. At this point let us simply say that insofar as we do justice to the fluidity, uncertainty, and open-endedness surrounding totalitarianism at the time, to say that some were more totalitarian than others is relatively weak and does not specify determinate directions or outcomes.

But even as totalitarianism proves best for distinguishing fascism, other categories, especially palingenesis and political religion, insofar as they are comparably reflexive, remain relevant as well, differentiating along other axes. Totalitarianism, like fascism itself, proves embedded in the aggregate along with the other macro-categories. Crisscrossing axes delineate the field. Even as all these categories serve the essential differentiation, they do so loosely; we still need to countenance blurring, even after the fact. We noted that once totalitarianism was on the table, what had been authoritarianism could no longer be the same—an indication that even as totalitarianism is a criterion of rigor, the totalitarianism-authoritarianism distinction blurs to some extent.

Still, totalitarianism works as a criterion of differentiation up to a point. In comparing aspects of the Italian and Spanish cases above, we recognized that the difference between them can be overemphasized. Yet the grounds for differentiation are clear. Indeed, even Pinto and Vincent, while plausibly questioning long-standing ways of applying the totalitarian-authoritarian and comparable binomials to the Iberian regimes, implicitly recognize that those regimes, novel and significant though they were, were *less* totalitarian than the Italian and German regimes.

In chapter 4 we saw that Blinkhorn subscribes to the fairly widespread notion that the single party in the new anti-democratic regimes tended to be a fusion of radical fascists and conservatives, with conservatives gaining the upper hand, leaving radicals marginalized and somewhat discontented.[64] And he especially featured the putative parallels between the Spanish and Italian cases on that basis. Invoking especially the example of Alfredo Rocco, we argued that Blinkhorn's notion misses the scope for the synergy that, in the Italian case, carried beyond mere fusion. But we also encountered a wider question, better considered here, about the uses and limitations of lumping Spain and Italy on the basis of Blinkhorn's notion.

Blinkhorn's way of bringing Spain and Italy together around the fusion notion is too static, too pat, and thereby invites *unwarranted* blurring at the expense of the scope for rigor and distinction. In contending that Fascist radicalism in Italy was channeled into Germanophilia and racism, he not only betrays a restricted notion even of late Fascist radicalism, but he glosses over the role of the totalitarian aspiration and direction in the dynamic of Fascist Italy.[65] The greater totalitarian aspiration in Italy, and the concomitant sense of leapfrogging through great tasks, prove the key basis for differentiating the Italian from the Spanish regime.

For comparative purposes, Kéchichian brings Franco's Spain and Salazar's Portugal into his study of François de La Rocque's Croix de Feu. But thus Kéchichian's treatment affords both an excellent example of the illuminating use of totalitarianism as a differentiating variable and an indication that such use entails a measure of risk. In the face of long-standing debates over whether the Croix de Feu was fascist, we noted, following Dobry, that we need not force the organization in either direction. But still there are distinctions to be made, and Kéchichian uses totalitarianism convincingly for that purpose, arguing precisely that the Croix de Feu lacked the totalitarian component essential to genuine fascism. But in claiming that it was thereby comparable to Franco's Spain and Salazar's Portugal in seeking to stabilize institutions and depoliticize society, he seems too quick to preclude blurring and to accept, and thereby to reinforce, the rigid conventional dualism. Still, the bottom line remains that even as we do not expect clear distinctions, the Croix de Feu was *less* fascist than those like Robert Soucy and Kevin Passmore have claimed, precisely in the sense that it was less totalitarian.[66]

We have noted the particular difficulties of placing the Japanese case. So does totalitarianism work to differentiate Japan, indicating how fascist it ended up by the early 1940s? As we noted in chapter 5, the applicability of the category to Japan is tricky because distinctive Japanese cultural characteristics, entailing something like obedience, solidarity, and self-sacrifice, seem to cut both ways. That cultural backdrop arguably made Japan at least proto-fascist and proto-totalitarian in one—let us say "passive"—sense. But because it had that cultural backdrop, the Japanese New Order needed to be less radical, less totalitarian in the "active" sense, to produce the desired third way. On those grounds it might be judged less fascist.

Those like Bruce Reynolds and Rikki Kersten, seeking to show why Japan must be included, have essentially the "passive" understanding of totalitarianism in mind. But the need actively to create a fascist society, constantly renewing it, makes a greater difference than their characterizations suggest. They miss the dynamism, the need to mobilize, the sense of constant active involvement, that characterized fascism in Italy and Germany.

But we need not insist on that as the definitive criterion of totalitarianism or fascism; we need not posit a qualitative difference on that basis.

Reynolds and Kersten appropriately take totalitarianism as a key criterion of fascism, and though they miss some of what totalitarianism might encompass, they certainly get part of it. The category entails ambiguities that the Japanese case especially brings to light. The distinction between "passive" and "active" is itself permeable. We might specify differences of degree, but because, depending on the criteria, Japan could be taken as either more or less totalitarian than Italy or Germany, any such differences would rest on the choice of criteria, which would necessarily be somewhat arbitrary. In the last analysis, the Japanese case especially indicates that even "totalitarianism" can only take us so far in differentiating fascism.

In one sense the Romanian Codreanu's notion of the literal end of history is obviously incompatible with the new sense of the open-endedness of history that I am associating with totalitarianism; indeed, Codreanu's notion would seem to suggest something approximating the "utopia" or final equilibrium that I ruled out. Yet though they had little opportunity to move in a totalitarian direction in practice, the Romanian Legion claimed that totalitarian means were necessary to bring about the desired end— and claimed to be devising those means. But for them, too, history itself had come to seem dramatically more open-ended at that historical moment, though history also seemed subject to human organization and will. The sense that the totalitarian mode of action was possible and could be adapted to their particular radical ends surely energized the Legion, galvanizing action in certain extreme directions. And the overall direction surely must be accounted totalitarian, even as seizing the present opportunity through history-making collective action could actually, as they saw it, bring about the literal fulfillment of Christianity and the end of history.

Solonari's treatment of the Antonescu regime in Romania especially raises the question of whether totalitarianism proves more useful than "fascism" itself as a differentiating factor. We saw that Solonari denies that Antonescu and his regime were fascist, even in light of the interaction with Nazi Germany, but what if we ask about totalitarianism, again keeping in mind the place of the regime within the wider web of interaction? Let us return to the regime's program of radical population engineering, which, as we noted, entailed eugenic measures, the repatriation of Romanians living abroad, and "ethnic cleansing" to rid the country of minorities. Was such a program itself totalitarian, or must totalitarianism encompass something more?

To some extent, at least, Romanian population engineering was surely intended to fabricate a more effective nation, better able to act collectively. However, the question is what type of long-term collective action the Romanian regime envisioned. As best understood, totalitarianism entails not a single effort that might be accomplished once and for all—

mobilizing to fight a war, for example—but a more comprehensive program of *enduring* collective action in light of a sense of having entered a new era of challenge and possibility.

In embarking on their radical population program, the Romanians were surely moving in a totalitarian direction away from traditionalist authoritarianism. And this is true whatever the role of "fascists" in implementing the policy. But as we saw in chapter 5, the impetus was somewhat defensive in response to the idiosyncratic situation facing Romania in the wake of the settlement after World War I. Vulnerabilities would remain, to be sure, but from Antonescu's perspective, Romania might settle down once the immediate crisis had been surmounted. Thus the force of Deletant's argument, noted above, that Antonescu's program was simple, based on internal order and secure borders. Moreover, Antonescu tolerated the two opposition parties. However, Deletant makes these points in arguing not only that Antonescu's regime was not "fascist," but that it was authoritarian as opposed to totalitarian.[67] Just as we need not expect clean lines around fascism, we can blur the authoritarian-totalitarian dichotomy a bit as well. Still, the *wider* totalitarian aspiration was clearer and the direction more consistently pursued in Fascist Italy, based on precisely that sense of having broken into a new era of challenge and possibility requiring enduring collective action. So totalitarianism proves useful as a differentiating factor, even though we need not posit some clear either/or distinction.

In treating the Metaxas regime in Greece, Kallis finds it appropriate to follow Metaxas himself in adopting totalitarianism to characterize aspects of the regime, or at least its direction. A central role for a mass-mobilizing single party is often taken as a key criterion of both fascism and totalitarianism. And where, as in Greece, the push for innovation on the Right was not coming from below, such a party might be constructed from the top down. Yet whereas Engelbert Dollfuss and Gyula Gömbös, pursuing their top-down experiments in Austria and Hungary, respectively, took significant steps in that direction, Metaxas did not even try. Instead he focused on the National Youth Organization, established in October 1936, just two months after launching his new regime, as the regime's centerpiece.

As Kallis tells it, the Greek polity seemed too polarized to be mobilized through a single party, but through the totalitarian indoctrination of youth, unaffected by the divisive legacy of previous decades, it might be possible to produce the enduring fascistization of Greek society. Metaxas himself conceived the youth organization as a totalitarian device for social engineering, and though it was not the expected single party, Kallis finds it genuinely totalitarian in both objective and operation.[68] Membership was obligatory. Ethnic and religious minorities were excluded, though Mogens Pelt, stressing that Metaxas was not anti-Semitic, notes that the regime envisioned assimilating Jews, Muslims, and other minorities.[69] In other words, there was to be no separate identity; this was totalitarianism. But any one could and presumably should assimilate and adhere to the organization. However, Kallis points out that because it was being nurtured from above, the process of totalitarian penetration had to be gradual, supported by, among other things, a carefully choreographed liturgy supporting a new leadership cult. And the organization did gradually expand its functions.

None of this makes the Metaxas regime itself fascist or totalitarian, nor does Kallis claim it does. But for understanding the universe at issue, intentions and departures matter. The effort to move, through the totalitarian mode of action, toward the enduring fascistization of Greek society distinguishes the regime from others during the period. If anything, the National Youth Organization in Greece was *more* totalitarian in direction than the Fatherland Front, the single-party organization in Austria.

We find a different indication of the uses of totalitarianism for differentiation in James Frusetta's recent article on the Bulgarian case and in Iordachi's gloss on the article. But this is because totalitarianism is missing from their discussions, which feature palingenesis instead. Asking why fascism proved considerably less successful in Bulgaria than Romania, Hungary, or Yugoslavia, Frusetta argues that Bulgarian fascists and proto-fascists were largely unsuccessful in distinguishing their political profile and ideological vision from the conservative Right that ruled the country from 1934 to 1944.[70]

Frusetta himself was quick to take palingenesis as the essence of fascism, but Iordachi's commentary is of greater symptomatic importance. As Iordachi sees it, Frusetta's argument "denies the palingenetic nature of Bulgarian fascism, crediting instead the conservative right with effectively monopolizing the drive for the regeneration of the nation."[71] Recognizing that some mode of differentiation is needed, Iordachi is careful not to conflate "nationalist palingenetic projects" with "fascism." Thus the conservative Right, as opposed to the would-be Bulgarian fascists, could grasp the political space bound up with "regeneration of the nation." But mere "regeneration of the nation" is too vague to get at what was at issue, and for the differentiation that Iordachi himself wants, palingenesis quite obviously breaks down. Indeed, his argument is almost circular because he lacks the other category, necessary for the differentiation he posits but pulls back from actually explaining. And totalitarianism seems the missing differentiating factor. What would-be fascism lacked in Bulgaria, necessary to differentiate itself from others seeking national renewal, was totalitarian will.

The relative merits of totalitarianism and palingenesis as differentiating categories are also implicitly at issue in Roger Griffin's notion that whereas fascism, revolving around a palingenetic vision, has continued to well up after World War II, its historically specific totalitarian form ended in 1945. As he sees it, classic fascism became totalitarian only because of the contingencies of "an age shaped by World War I, the collapse of absolutist empires and the Russian Revolution of 1917."[72] That might seem to suggest that totalitarianism affords greater rigor than palingenesis for distinguishing among new phenomena on the Right during the era of the two world wars, yet clearly for Griffin palingenesis remains the deeper variable. To understand the period, he implies, we need both, but we should not assume that totalitarianism is a defining feature of fascism. This suggests, however, that the relative merits of totalitarianism and palingenesis as differentiating categories are bound up with the question of whether "fascism" ended in 1945 or continued in whatever form thereafter—a question to be considered in the next chapter. Doing so carries us beyond blurring and rigor and the uses of this or that ancillary category and back to fascism itself, especially to the implications of all we have noted about its embeddedness in a braided dynamic that ended in 1945.

Notes

1. Tim Kirk, "Fascism and Austrofascism," in *The Dollfuss/Schuschnigg Era in Austria: A Reassessment*, ed. Günter Bischof, Anton Pelinka, and Alexander Lassner (New Brunswick, NJ: Transaction, 2003), 25.

2. For example, see Vito Panunzio, *Fedeltà al sindacato e alla corporazione* (Rome: L'economia italiana, 1942). Vito was the son of Sergio Panunzio, a veteran syndicalist who became one of the Fascist regime's leading ideologues. See also Vito Panunzio's retrospective account, *Il "secondo fascismo," 1936–1943: La reazione della nuova generazione alla crisi del movimento e del regime* (Milan: Mursia, 1988).

3. Miguel Jerez Mir and Javier Luque, "State and Regime in Early Francoism, 1936–45: Power Structures, Main Actors and Repression Policy," in *Rethinking Fascism and Dictatorship in Interwar Europe*, ed. António Costa Pinto and Aristotle Kallis (Basingstoke: Palgrave Macmillan, 2014), 192.

4. Didier Musiedlak, ed., *Les Expériences Corporatives dan l'aire Latine* (Berne: Peter Lang, 2010), editor's conclusion, 474–76.

5. Aristotle Kallis and António Costa Pinto, "Conclusion: Embracing Complexity and Transnational Dynamics: The Diffusion of Fascism and the Hybridization of Dictatorships in Inter-War Europe," in *Rethinking Fascism and Dictatorship*, ed. Pinto and Kallis, 272.

6. Michel Dobry, "Desperately Seeking 'Generic Fascism': Some Discordant Thoughts on the Academic Recycling of Indigenous Categories," in *Rethinking the Nature of Fascism: Comparative Perspectives*, ed. António Costa Pinto (Basingstoke: Palgrave Macmillan, 2011), 60, 71–72, 76–77.

7. Gerhard Botz, "The Short- and Long-Term Effects of the Authoritarian Regime and of Nazism in Austria: The Burden of a 'Second Dictatorship,'" in *Totalitarian and Authoritarian Regimes in Europe: Legacies and Lessons from the Twentieth Century*, ed. Jerzy W. Borejsza and Klaus Ziemer (New York and Oxford: Berghahn, 2006), 189.

8. Gerhard Botz, "The Coming of the Dollfuss-Schuschnigg Regime and the Stages of Its Development," in *Rethinking Fascism and Dictatorship*, ed. Pinto and Kallis, 122, 137, 140–41.

9. Kirk, "Fascism and Austrofascism," 26.

10. Ibid. See also 22–23 on the controversies over the nature of the corporatist regime, including how "fascist" it was.

11. Dennis Deletant, *Hitler's Forgotten Ally: Ion Antonescu and His Regime, Romania 1940–44* (Basingstoke: Palgrave Macmillan, 2006), 30–31.

12. Ibid., 66–67.

13. Vladimir Solonari, *Purifying the Nation: Population Exchange and Ethnic Cleansing in Nazi-Allied Romania* (Washington, DC: Woodrow Wilson Center Press; Baltimore: Johns Hopkins University Press, 2010).

14. Radu Ioanid, *The Holocaust in Romania: The Destruction of Jews and Gypsies under the Antonescu Regime, 1940–1944*, trans. Marc J. Masurovsky (Chicago: Ivan R. Dee, 2000), 293.

15. Radu Ioanid, "Romania," in *The Oxford Handbook of Fascism*, ed. R.J.B. Bosworth (Oxford: Oxford University Press, 2009), 411.

16. Deletant, *Hitler's Forgotten Ally*, 71–74.

17. Ibid., 70–71.

18. Mary Vincent, "Spain," in *Oxford Handbook*, ed. Bosworth, 375.

19. Ian Kershaw, "Hitler and the Uniqueness of Nazism," *Journal of Contemporary History* 39, no. 2 (April 2004): 247.

20. Jerez Mir and Luque, "State and Regime in Early Francoism," 188–191.

21. Roger Griffin, "Foreword: Il ventennio parafascista? The Past and Future of a Neologism in Comparative Fascist Studies," in *Rethinking Fascism and Dictatorship*, ed. Pinto and Kallis, xvi–xvii.

22. Albert Kéchichian, *Les Croix de Feu à L'Âge des Fascismes: Travail, Famille, Patrie* (Paris: Champ Vallon, 2006). For the alternative view, see esp. Kevin Passmore, *From Liberalism to Fascism: The Right in a French Province, 1928–1939* (Cambridge: Cambridge University Press, 1997).

23. Paul Brooker, *The Faces of Fraternalism: Nazi Germany, Fascist Italy, and Imperial Japan* (Oxford: Clarendon, 1991).

24. For Aristotle Kallis, note first the title of his article "Neither Fascist nor Authoritarian: The 4th of August Regime in Greece (1936–1941) and the Dynamics of Fascistisation in 1930s Europe," *East Central Europe* 37 (2010): 303–330. For Vincent, see her "Spain," 365, 375, 378–79.

25. For example, Botz, "The Coming of the Dollfuss-Schuschnigg Regime," 122.

26. Fleischer takes so much for granted at least partly, no doubt, because his major concern is with the resonance of the Metaxas regime in subsequent Greek political culture. On that level his account is particularly illuminating. See Hagen Fleischer, "Authoritarian Rule in Greece and Its Heritage (1936–1974)," in *Totalitarian and Authoritarian Regimes in Europe*, ed. Borejsza and Ziemer, 238–39.

27. Kallis, "Neither Fascist nor Authoritarian," 327.

28. Ibid., 309–10.

29. Juan J. Linz, *Totalitarian and Authoritarian Regimes* (Boulder, CO: Lynne Rienner, 2000). This is for the most part a republication of Linz's classic work, first published in 1975, offering a highly influential basis for differentiating the two types of regime. This newer edition includes a substantial new introduction considering recent scholarship. On the debates surrounding Linz's work, see Thomas Jeffrey Miley, "Franquism as Authoritarianism: Juan Linz and His Critics," *Politics, Religion & Ideology* 12, no. 1 (2011): 27–50, esp. 41–42.

30. Vincent, "Spain," 365, 375–76, 378–79.

31. Ibid., 376. See also 367.

32. Gregory J. Kasza, "Fascism from Above? Japan's *Kakushin* Right in Comparative Perspective," in *Fascism outside Europe: The European Impulse Against Domestic Conditions in the*

Diffusion of Global Fascism, ed. Stein Ugelvik Larsen (Boulder, CO: Social Science Monographs, 2001), 186–87, 199, 225–27.

33. Ibid., 226–28.

34. See especially António Costa Pinto, "Single Party, Cabinet and Political Decision-Making in Fascist Era Dictatorships: Comparative Perspectives," in *Ruling Elites and Decision-Making,* ed. António Costa Pinto (Boulder, CO: Social Science Monographs, 2009), 215–51; and António Costa Pinto, "Elites, Single Parties and Political Decision-Making in Fascist Era Dictatorships," *Contemporary European History* 11, no. 3 (2002): 429–54. As indicated in chapter 2, note 40, I was invited to comment on the latter, and Pinto provided a counter-response.

35. António Costa Pinto, "Reply: State, Dictators and Single Parties—Where Are the Fascist Regimes?," *Contemporary European History* 11, no. 3 (2002): 462, 465.

36. Pinto, "Elites, Single Parties," 445–46.

37. Constantin Iordachi, "God's Chosen Warriors: Romantic Palingenesis, Militarism and Fascism in Modern Romania," in *Comparative Fascist Studies: New Perspectives,* ed. Constantin Iordachi (London and New York: Routledge, 2010), 340.

38. Ibid., 350, 354.

39. Ibid., 350, 353.

40. Peter F. Sugar, "Conclusion," in *Native Fascism in the Successor States, 1918–1945,* ed. Peter F. Sugar (Santa Barbara, CA: ABC-Clio, 1971), 148.

41. Richard Overy, *The Dictators: Hitler's Germany and Stalin's Russia* (New York: W.W. Norton, 2004), xxvii, 73. See also the characterizations on 73–75, 636–37, which especially suggest the scope for a fruitful recasting of the category.

42. Arnd Bauerkämper, "Transnational Fascism: Cross-Border Relations between Regimes and Movements in Europe, 1922–1939," *East Central Europe* 37 (2010): 228.

43. Constantin Iordachi, "Fascism in Interwar East Central and Southeastern Europe: Toward a New Transnational Research Agenda," *East Central Europe* 37 (2010): 166. Philip Morgan makes this point specifically with reference to the Romanian Iron Guard; see his "Studying Fascism from the Particular to the General," *East Central Europe* 37 (2010): 336.

44. Emilio Gentile, "Fascism, Totalitarianism and Political Religion: Definitions and Critical Reflections on Criticisms of an Interpretation," in *Fascism, Totalitarianism and Political Religion,* ed. Roger Griffin (London and New York: Routledge, 2005), 65–66.

45. Iordachi, "Fascism in Interwar East Central and Southeastern Europe," 164, 189.

46. Morgan, "Studying Fascism," 335.

47. Robert O. Paxton, *The Anatomy of Fascism* (New York: Random House [Vintage], 2005), 216–18. And whereas at this point in his argument, the contrast is with "fascism," not "totalitarianism," the later notion is implicit in his reference to "fascism's urge to reduce the private sphere to nothing" (217).

48. Jerez Mir and Luque, writing on the Franco regime, afford a symptomatic recent example of looseness and seeming uncertainty in our present uses of "totalitarianism." Lumping repression, the unification decree, and the labor charter, they conclude that the regime was quasi-totalitarian from 1937 to 1945. But they also find that, though with some significant nuances, it had every trait in the classic model of Carl J. Friedrich and Zbigniew Brzezinski. Then why only *quasi*-totalitarian? And are we still relying on the criteria Friedrich and Brzezinski outlined over sixty years ago, at the height of the Cold War? See Jerez Mir and Luque, "State and Regime in Early Francoism," 191–92.

49. David D. Roberts, *The Totalitarian Experiment in Twentieth-Century Europe: Understanding the Poverty of Great Politics* (London and New York: Routledge, 2006).

50. As cited in Karl Dietrich Bracher, *The Nazi Dictatorship: The Origins, Structure, and Effects of National Socialism,* trans. Jean Steinberg (New York: Praeger, 1970), 340.

51. David D. Roberts, "'Political Religion' and the Totalitarian Departures of Interwar Europe: On the Uses and Disadvantages of an Analytical Category," *Contemporary European History* 19, no. 4 (November 2009): 379–412.

52. Richard Shorten, *Modernism and Totalitarianism: Rethinking the Intellectual Sources of Nazism and Stalinism, 1945 to the Present* (Basingstoke: Palgrave Macmillan, 2012), 25, 50.

53. Ibid., 60, 230.

54. Ibid., 6.

55. Christian Gerlach and Nicholas Werth, "State Violence—Violent Societies," in *Beyond Totalitarianism: Stalinism and Nazism Compared*, ed. Michael Geyer and Sheila Fitzpatrick (Cambridge: Cambridge University Press 2009), 138.

56. Ibid., 140–41.

57. Ibid., 151–57.

58. Shorten, *Modernism and Totalitarianism*, 40–43, 239–40.

59. I again refer to works by Peter Fritzsche, Robert Gellately, and Thomas Kühne cited in a different context in chapter 4 (note 92).

60. Michael Burleigh, *Death and Deliverance: "Euthanasia" in Germany, c. 1900–1945* (Cambridge: Cambridge University Press, 1994); note his question on 4.

61. Emilio Gentile, *La via italiana al totalitarismo: Il partito e lo Stato nel regime fascista* (Rome: La Nuova Italia Scientifica, 1995). But note also Meir Michaelis's seminal "Anmerkungen zum italienischen Totalitarismusbegriff. Zur Kritik der Thesen Hannah Arendts und Renzo De Felices," *Quellen und Forschungen aus italienischen Archiven und Bibliotheken*, 62 (1982): 270–302.

62. Michael Geyer, with assistance from Sheila Fitzpatrick, "Introduction: After Totalitarianism—Stalinism and Nazism Compared," in *Beyond Totalitarianism*, ed. Geyer and Fitzpatrick, 1–37. The Geyer-Fitzpatrick volume is usefully compared with Leonid Luks's almost contemporaneous *Zwei Gesichter des Totalitarismus: Bolschewismus und Nationalsozialismus im Vergleich* (Cologne: Böhlau, 2007), which makes clear that the category can still illuminate the comparison between Nazi Germany and the Soviet Union.

63. Mark Edele and Michael Geyer, "States of Exception: The Nazi-Soviet War as a System of Violence, 1939–1945," in *Beyond Totalitarianism*, ed. Geyer and Fitzpatrick, 345–95.

64. Martin Blinkhorn, "Introduction: Allies, Rivals, or Antagonists? Fascists and Conservatives in Modern Europe," in *Fascists and Conservatives: The Radical Right and the Establishment in Twentieth-Century Europe*, ed. Martin Blinkhorn (London: Unwin Hyman, 1990), 10.

65. Ibid.

66. Kéchichian, *Les Croix de Feu*, 8–10, 378–80.

67. Deletant, *Hitler's Forgotten Ally*, 71–74.

68. Kallis, "Neither Fascist nor Authoritarian," 311, 317, 319–20.

69. Mogens Pelt, "Stages in the Development of the 'Fourth of August' Regime in Greece," in *Rethinking Fascism and Dictatorship*, ed. Pinto and Kallis, 211.

70. James Frusetta, "Fascism to Complete the National Project? Bulgarian Fascists' Uncertain Views on the Palingenesis of the Nation," *East Central Europe* 37 (2010): 280–302.

71. Iordachi, "Fascism in Interwar East Central and Southeastern Europe," 197.

72. Roger Griffin, "Uniqueness and Family Resemblances in Generic Fascism," *East Central Europe* 37 (2010): 339.

Chapter 9

FASCISM AS "EPOCHAL" OR CONTINUING POSSIBILITY?

The Question of Neo-Fascism

Even if classic fascism, as caught up in a braided dynamic, ended in 1945, could new instances erupt thereafter, perhaps taking different form? The question of whether fascism is better understood as a continuing possibility or as an "epochal" phenomenon, characteristic of and confined to the era of the two world wars, is obviously central to our overarching question concerning the place of fascism in the aggregate of responses constituting the new Right during that period. Ultimately, neither the epochal question nor the question of the aggregate can be answered independently of the other, but we must ponder the possible temporal limits first. After we have done so in the present chapter, I will seek to formulate some concluding points about the aggregate and the epoch in the final chapter.

The question of the temporal limits of fascism has long sparked disagreement. Which way we turn obviously has implications for our approach to various novel, often troubling political phenomena that have emerged on the Right since 1945. But our answer is also bound up with our conception of fascism during the "classic" period—and with our conception of the classic period itself. To what extent did the framework from which fascism emerged end in 1945, perhaps consumed by fascism itself? Especially insofar as we accept that the framework was radically altered, we must ask whether fascism could emerge again in different form. There are no easy answers, and no doubt, here again, we must be prepared for some blurring. But to treat the question of the aggregate, we need to be clearer about what might have ended in 1945—and about the implications of the ending of whatever it was. To grasp the stakes and to get a preliminary sense of what we need, let us consider some prominent arguments along a kind of continuum, from those finding a reasonably clean break in 1945 to those insisting that fascism is an ongoing possibility, not confined to the era.

A Range of Possibilities: From Ernst Nolte and Michael Mann to Roger Griffin and Geoff Eley

Over half a century ago, in a book translated as *Three Faces of Fascism*, Ernst Nolte famously wrote of "fascism in its epoch," making a classic case for viewing fascism as characteristic of and limited to precisely the period at issue for us, the era of the two world wars. As the long-term modern "emancipatory process" was about to overwhelm certain key structures of traditional society, it provoked a paroxysm of resistance—ultimately resistance to transcendence itself. Fascism was that paroxysm; it was the death throes or life-and-death struggle of the martial, sovereign, inwardly antagonistic group.[1] So Nolte linked what changed beginning in 1945 to what fascism had been a last desperate effort to preserve.

In the book's concluding paragraph, Nolte introduced some slight ambiguity about whether the conditions for fascism had indeed ended.[2] The ambiguity stems from positing a single emancipatory process, overloaded and thus vague. In light of changes since 1945, it seemed no longer possible for Western societies to be martial, sovereign, and inwardly antagonistic as they had been, but they were not fully emancipated either. Yet Nolte's overall emphasis on fascism as an epochal phenomenon, bound up with death throes, suggested that the conditions for fascism had ended along with fascism itself. Positing fascism as an epochal phenomenon means that it was at once characteristic of the era and over as of 1945.

When first published in English in 1966, Nolte's book had a major impact; indeed, it was widely considered the most important book on fascism ever written. To be sure, it was notoriously difficult as well, but a noted review essay by Klaus Epstein helped many grasp the argument.[3] However, even as Nolte expanded his argument in subsequent works, specialists tended to pull back, though for somewhat disparate reasons.

Gilbert Allardyce's debunking stance in his 1979 article was one manifestation. Whereas Nolte could speak confidently about "the emancipatory process," and on that basis posit fascism as a single big phenomenon defining the epoch, Allardyce took much the opposite tack, seeking to deflate generic fascism, stressing hollowness and ephemerality, and disparaging the notion that there had been an "era of fascism."[4] Still, even if for Allardyce fascism had not had sufficient consistency to define or structure the era, on his account, too, it was over after 1945, having burned itself out. Fascism was a unique happening that ended.

Surely Nolte's way of tracing fascism to resistance to a single grand macro-process no longer convinces, if it ever did. Rather than determined by or built into longer-term trends, fascism has come to seem more contingent, ad hoc, along Allardyce's lines. To be sure, Nolte's schema entailed a way of accounting for the hollow and ephemeral side of fascism, but it was too bound up with fascism's putative resistance to a dominant master process to be convincing. And Nolte was too close to positing fascism as mere resistance to mainstream modernity, whereas, as I have emphasized, it has come to be understood in many quarters as a quest for an alternative modernity.

Moreover, whereas for Nolte fascism was fundamentally "anti-Marxism," emerging in resistance to what Nolte took for granted as *the* modern revolution, fascism now seems better understood as "revolutionary in its own right," its undoubted anti-Marxism an indication of *competition* with Marxism and communism for the space beyond mainstream liberal modernity. To be sure, Nolte made much of the fact that fascism, precisely as anti-Marxism, had to fight by means of "a radically opposed and yet related ideology and by the use of almost identical and yet typically modified methods."[5] But fascism, on his reading, was fundamentally reactive, just as Nietzsche, foreshadowing fascism, was fundamentally reacting against Marx, with his vision of literally changing the world.[6]

But though aspects of Allardyce's debunking, including his deflation of reified concepts and his insistence on an element of hollowness and ephemerality, still convince up to a point, his argument, as we noted in chapter 1, entailed its own sort of one-sidedness. He was so determined to emphasize hollowness and ephemerality that he could not do justice to the deeper issues Nolte's account raised in positing fascism as an epochal phenomenon.

First, even if fascism is not to be understood as the moment of crisis in a macro-process, it might still have been characteristic of the era, and might still need to be located on that level, in ways Allardyce precluded. He was ultimately *too* disparaging, not doing justice to the force and import of fascism at the time. Moreover, in deflating the reified generic concept, he was too prone to settle for mere nominalism, leaving fascism as a set of individual strands, which itself tends to preclude any understanding of its epochal import. Insofar as we better encompass the aggregate as a field of relationships, we open to a different sense of the epoch. And whereas Allardyce was on the right track in denying that there is any such *thing* as fascism, we need to make deeper sense of what that means, which might be precisely that fascism was epochal—that it was *so* embedded in its epoch that little if anything of it could have survived. We will address that possibility in the next chapter.

Second, Allardyce's way of showing how fascism, even as it did not define the epoch, could and did end in 1945 is too sketchy because it is relies on hollowness and ephemerality without sufficient attention to the elements of substance and their implications. Even as more contingent and ad hoc than generic concepts tend to suggest, fascism entailed corpuscles of innovation, though they wove in and out and were often diluted or absorbed. But neglecting those elements, Allardyce missed the interplay and the resulting trajectory. His way of positing the ending in 1945 comes close to begging the question; because it ended in 1945, fascism must have been hollow and ephemeral. But the nature of the forces in play was certainly not obvious during the period itself. Even Antonio Gramsci, who, as we will see, grasped better than most the bases of the superficiality and fissuring of Fascism in Italy, did not foresee how hollow and ephemeral the Italian regime would prove to be. We need the whole trajectory to grasp the sense in which what ended in 1945 may have been not only classic fascism itself but the very conditions for anything we could usefully term fascism.

Meanwhile, Nolte's thinking came to seem idiosyncratic and even wayward in subsequent works that helped fuel the famed German *Historikerstreit*, or historians' quarrel, of the later 1980s. He suggested that Nazi Jewish policy, even including its genocidal outcome, might be understood as a sort of pre-emptive strike against the menace of Soviet communism.[7] This way of glossing his earlier notion of fascism as anti-Marxism was bound to reflect back on the earlier work and made his whole approach seem suspect. By 2004 Nolte was prominent in an illuminating multinational exchange in *Erwägen, Wissen, Ethik* (EWE) centering around a lead article by Roger Griffin.[8] But the tendency of Anglophone scholars to steer clear of Nolte was manifest. In his contribution to this exchange, Philip Morgan seemed to take pride in insisting he had always found Nolte's *Three Faces of Fascism* incomprehensible, though he seemed to understand it well enough to contend that it was ultimately concerned with Nazism, not really with generic fascism at all.[9]

Although most of the recent generic accounts engaged Nolte's work to some extent, his argument and questioning on the abstract level he proposed were decidedly out of fashion. But aspects of his challenge, raising the epochal question in both senses—fascism as at once characteristic of and confined to the era—still had not been fully addressed. If Nolte did not adequately pinpoint what might be said on the aggregate level to transcend singularity and nominalism, what instead? And if his particular way of positing historical specificity does not convince, he forcefully posed the question.[10] What are the implications of the undoubted changes in the framework after 1945 for the possibility of fascism? Conversely, if, contrary to Nolte, fascism has remained an ongoing possibility, what does that say about its place in the era of the two world wars? More generally, what, if anything, can be said on the supranational, historically specific level? If the answer is "nothing," why is that, and what does it say about "fascism"?

Though without reference to Nolte, Michael Mann treats the matter extensively in concluding his book *Fascists,* and he is especially good in addressing what might be considered fascist and non-fascist within the major postwar candidates.[11] While recognizing certain parallels with classic fascism, his accent is overwhelmingly on why postwar phenomena are different—are not fascist—and on why "European fascism is defeated, dead and buried."[12] He insists that there can be degrees, that movements can be more or less fascist, so it is hardly surprising that on the postwar Right we find *some* of the five elements he had identified as the keys to fascism as it emerged during the classic period.[13] But we do not find the combination of all five, nor are we apt to. Even as we can continue to expect crises, "it is ever less likely that a combination of transcendent, cleansing, paramilitary nation-statism will be seen as providing the best solution."[14]

As for what has changed, Mann points especially to the institutionalization of liberal democracy, the absorption of class conflict—which thus no longer needs to be "transcended"—and the ending of organized paramilitary violence and, for the most part, even of militarism itself. All this is to say something about what characterized the era of the two world wars and about what ended with World War II. But taking fascism as more definitive or characteristic of the era than the debunking Allardyce did, Mann addresses the epochal issue more explicitly:

> Fascism was generated by a world-historical moment when mass citizen warfare surfaced alongside mass transitions toward democracy amid a global capitalist crisis. Fascism made a not implausible claim to solve these worldly problems in a brave new world in which the nation, the state and even war might be seen as the bearers of progress. That moment has passed.[15]

So even if what followed World War II was not precisely Nolte's change in framework, for Mann there was surely a change that made the re-emergence of fascism far less likely, if not impossible. And for him, too, that was because core aspects of what had changed had been essential to fascism. But though Mann's is especially significant testimony, his sense of fascism's place in its time, and thus of what ended in 1945, necessarily reflects his sense of what had fueled and constituted fascism in the first place. And that not only entailed the five attributes he pinpointed but reflected, at bottom, a master narrative of normal, healthy development. That master narrative entailed anything but the openness to experiment and to the import of interaction that Constantin Iordachi, for example, calls for. So Mann leaves room for further questioning.

Contributing to a debate moderated by Iordachi, Morgan recently addressed the issue explicitly, taking us a step closer to fascism as an ongoing possibility. He may seem to waffle a bit, but this is mostly because he was making two different points in response to two somewhat distinguishable questions posed by Iordachi as moderator. Addressing the question "Was Fascism a Synchronic-Epochal or a Generic-Diachronic Phenomenon?" Morgan warns that we should start with specifics, analyzing postwar phenomena in their own right. Taking fascism out of context and applying it broadly can lead us to miss the novelty of those phenomena. The test is pragmatic: does viewing some novel political formation in terms of "fascism" help us to understand it? For the most part Morgan doubts that "fascism" can fruitfully be applied to post-1945 phenomena—or even to non-European areas during the "classic" period.[16] Constantly invoking "fascism" may actually impede analysis of the novel and perhaps dangerous phenomena at issue.

But in addressing the question "Can One Speak of a Recrudescence of Fascism in Contemporary Europe, or [*sic*] We Deal here with an Essentially New Political Phenomenon?" Morgan, taking a step beyond Mann, believes we can indeed recognize fascism in some post-1945 phenomena: "I think we are justified in seeing these movements as fascist, if only because many of their supporters acknowledge, more or less openly, their ideological debts to interwar and wartime fascism and to extreme and idiosyncratic fascist thinkers." Morgan went on to note that the anti-Semitism and xenophobia that had been contained or channeled by the communist regimes in eastern Europe could flourish in the post-communist context, especially, of course, where the post-communist transition proved difficult and even disillusioning.[17]

But it may be doubted whether the sort of nostalgia or influence Morgan mentions makes a political phenomenon fascist. The second time around, knowing the trajectories and outcomes after original fascism was over, can only be qualitatively different. What fueled original fascism was a sense of *imminent* possibility. Moreover, the anti-Semitism and xenophobia that Morgan ends up invoking surely do not make for fascism in themselves. Mann was on much firmer ground in looking for some wider combination of elements.

In earlier warning against focusing on trappings and overt imitation, both Walter Laqueur and Robert Paxton point beyond Morgan's skepticism. Each sees a definite ongoing or, especially in the case of Laqueur, an actual renewed threat of what must indeed be considered fascism, but each also stresses that any genuine fascism would likely take different form after the end of the classic regimes.[18] To head off the danger, we must grasp elements of originality and novelty that we might not immediately recognize. Understanding the trajectory of classic fascism can surely help, but obsession with merely superficial resemblances, bound up with trappings and overt imitation, will not.

Although the arguments of Laqueur and Paxton run parallel up to a point, a difference between them is worth considering. Laqueur, writing in 1996, was especially concerned with seeming instances of fascism in the former communist countries. Paxton, writing in 2004, was more concerned with hypothetical possibilities, to be considered in light of what we putatively know of "the fascist cycle," from studying the classic period:

> The well-known warning signals—extreme nationalist propaganda and hate crimes—are important but insufficient. Knowing what we do about the fascist cycle, we can find more ominous warning signals in situations of political deadlock in the face of crisis, threatened conservatives looking for tougher allies, ready to give up due process and the rule of law, seeking mass support by nationalist and racialist demagoguery. Fascists are close to power when conservatives begin to borrow their techniques, appeal to their "mobilizing passions," and try to co-opt the fascist following.[19]

But is this really what we know of "the fascist cycle"? It certainly reflects something about how fascism came to power in Italy and Germany, but what of the two trajectories from there? The question is what would make some subsequent phenomenon "fascist." For Paxton, as for Mann, it seems a combination, but why this particular combination, including "mass support by nationalist and racialist demagoguery"? Is such demagoguery really what open-minded attention to the actual history, which is what Paxton claims to start with, shows to be the key to mass support? Are all appeals to nationalism demagogic? Paxton's combination seems facile, based on a combination of essentialism and hindsight.

In chapter 1 we noted briefly the scope for objection to Paxton's account. It is also striking that Michel Dobry objected specifically to it, in the context of arguing, first, for a deeper sense of the contingency of the actual fascist trajectory and, second, as a corollary, for a recognition that what we might still justifiably call fascism could have produced a different trajectory and different outcomes.[20] We will address that latter contention below; it may not convince us. But it usefully challenges Paxton's suggestion that we can characterize what might count as fascist in his conventional negative terms.

Roger Griffin shares the sense we find in Laqueur and Paxton that any renewed fascism would take different form after 1945, and he explicitly criticizes those who look for the earlier trappings. But having been particularly concerned with the scope for neo-fascism, he goes well beyond

Laqueur and Paxton to specify a wide range of postwar phenomena that he believes must be considered fascist, even if the framework has been radically different, and even if none has produced a new regime.[21]

As we have seen, Griffin's continued insistence on an abiding core myth of fascism, positing palingenesis, or ethnic/national rebirth, has provoked periodic charges of essentialism, which he has taken pains to deny. And despite some loose language, suggesting that, for example, there is such a thing as "fascism" that can perform such acts as "adapt" and "mutate," Griffin's position, at bottom, is not really essentialist.[22] He means to argue that the core myth of fascism reflects a historically specific but still continuing phase in our confrontation with modernity and its attendant "canopy loss," and that this myth has continued to manifest itself, albeit in new forms, as our confrontation with modernity has continued after 1945. Put differently, we can isolate a residuum from classic fascism, a residuum that is *relatively* suprahistorical, in the sense of transcending the earlier epoch and surviving its ending, though this is not to argue that the conditions for fascism are built into the human condition and could never be transcended altogether. Although it sometimes appears otherwise, Griffin is not tracing fascism to some common *ahistorical* psychological propensity—to some "ur-fascism," as Umberto Eco called it.[23]

As we have seen, Griffin argues that the fascist response to the ongoing pressures of modernity took a particular totalitarian form during the era of the two world wars for contingent, historically specific reasons that he seems to find relatively easy to grasp. Triggered especially by the contingent concatenation surrounding World War I, classic fascism was an innovative, if disastrous, experiment, departure, or eruption at a particular moment within the wider ongoing modern experiment.[24] So although, from Griffin's perspective, that experiment and the process of adjusting to modernity have obviously continued, it is indeed possible to draw lines around classic, totalitarian fascism, which ended in 1945. In this sense, for Griffin, too, fascism was characteristic of the epoch, but it was only fascism in its totalitarian form. Extending the argument a bit, we might even say that the epoch ended because of the chaotic, overreach tendencies of totalitarianism, not because the conditions for *fascism* were transcended or because *fascism* destroyed itself.

But for Griffin, the deeper conditions of possibility for fascism remain. It is obviously true that our modern political experiment and our wider confrontation with modernity have continued after 1945, and we have seen, and will surely continue to see, a variety of new, sometimes extreme phenomena on what we persist in calling the Right. Just as Morgan insisted, we must first ask whether the use of "fascism" as a label for such later phenomena furthers or impedes understanding. As Griffin sees it, not only do we still have the conditions of possibility for fascism, but we have encountered a variety of actual instances, reflecting the same longing for palingenesis, in response to the pressures of modernity, that fueled classic fascism. To our peril, he implies, we fail to understand these phenomena as instances of fascism insofar as we assume that *any* fascism must take totalitarian form. Indeed, he is highly critical of Nolte and Mann, as well as Stanley Payne and A. James Gregor, for taking aspects of fascism during the earlier period as true fascism, as definitional, thus rendering what he takes to be postwar fascism a mere coda.[25]

In opposition to those who look for earlier trappings and overt echoes, Griffin stresses "the need to track fascism's evolution as a genus, its adaptation to different local historical conditions and its ability to mutate into new forms (e.g. cyberfascism or the New Right) outwardly different from Nazism or Fascism while retaining its core myth of national/ethnic rebirth."[26] Those who take classic fascism as definitional "fail to recognize the profound and empirically demonstrable continuity and kinship of interwar variants of fascism with such phenomena as White Noise music, International Third Position, and acts of lone-wolf terrorism carried out against multi-culturalism or the 'One World' society with no trace of leader-cult or coloured shirts."[27]

For Griffin these phenomena were all based on the same fascist minimum he had posited earlier, though to encompass such a diverse array he has had to water down that minimum a bit. Above all, he pulls back, as he has done to a lesser extent before, from what seemed a key aspect of his influential earlier definition: the expectation of *imminent* palingenetic renewal.[28] Thus he now argues, for example, that the early postwar visions of Armin Mohler and Julius Evola count as "fascist," even if each thinker saw the present as an interregnum, with the expected breakthrough to a new era indefinitely postponed.[29]

But because it requires watering down so much, Griffin's way of denying that fascism itself was confined to its epoch does not convince. In chapter 1 we noted objections to his use of "palingenesis" for classic fascism, especially to his tendency to reduce the palingenetic impulse to common psychological maladjustment in the face of "canopy loss." In treating postwar phenomena, Griffin stretches "palingenesis" even further, making it elastic and protean. Indeed, it becomes so all-encompassing as to be applicable virtually by definition to all forms of radical alienation calling for a new dispensation. So use of the term tells us very little, other than that those who seek a radical alternative to the status quo are alienated.

Like Griffin, Geoff Eley usefully links original fascism to the immediate conjuncture growing from World War I. Indeed, his way of doing so might particularly seem to suggest that fascism was confined its epoch. Yet he still finds the category at least potentially relevant even for characterizing contemporary phenomena. However, he is less concerned than Griffin to pinpoint actual instances of neo-fascism, and thus he does not focus, like Griffin, on phenomena taken as manifesting abiding psychological vulnerabilities. Instead, Eley links his claim of relevance to "times of emergency." Although the particular concatenation that led to classic fascism ended decades ago, the possibility of something like a fascism-producing crisis has continued, and is perhaps even intensifying at present, in light of the all-too-familiar litany of problems Eley mentions in concluding.[30]

If anything, Eley is even more determined than Griffin to specify why changes in the framework would mean differences in the resulting political phenomena. He is most struck by the difference between the deliriously futural orientation of fascism between the wars and the paranoia and apocalyptic fear now evident, though he enumerates a number of ways in which a contemporary crisis would differ from the crisis that yielded the first fascism. But, he goes on, "if we theorize fascism as an exceptional set of relations to politics made feasible and compelling by the intensifying of a particular type of crisis, then we can surely deploy the same term."[31] He had already argued that "fascism is *first and foremost a type of politics, or a set of relations to politics*. That is what allows us to decontextualize, ... freeing the term from its immediate crucible of time and place."[32] But he has in mind a more definite content, abstracted from what he takes to have been the essentials of original fascism: "If we limit fascism to a type of politics—the coercively nationalist recourse to political violence and exclusionary authoritarianism under worsening conditions of governmental paralysis and democratic impasse—then we can explore the differing and particular ways in which this distinctive fascist relation to politics might be inscribed in our contemporary circumstances, too."[33]

It may well be that our present problems entail the potential for crisis, and the configuration Eley pinpoints could perhaps be replicated in response. But is that to be identified with fascism? Eley says "if we limit fascism to" the type of politics he outlines, then we see the potential uses. But why should we limit it in this way? He seems to want to draw out a conception of fascism that would conform to the likely scenario of a contemporary crisis. That doing so is incompatible with the new agenda would not rule Eley out of court, but it does suggest reasons for doubt. Quite apart from the formulation quoted above, Eley's conception of fascism, based on defining attributes from violence to expansionism, is based especially on the Nazi German version.[34] At the very least, Eley implicitly privileges Germany and to a lesser extent Italy in precisely the ways Iordachi, Dobry, and Stein Ugelvik Larsen find too limiting. And thus his lack of openness to the uncertain trajectory of classic fascism overall.

As one example, let us note that in considering the differential space for conservative intellectuals to remain active in Nazi Germany and Fascist Italy, Eley offers a highly misleading contrast between Giovanni Gentile, allowed to continue in Italy, with those marginalized or kept at a distance in Germany, such as Oswald Spengler, Stefan George, and Ernst Jünger.[35] So Gentile was not a fascist but a conservative tolerated by the less rigorous Italian regime? Gentile's central but varying and much-contested role is but one indication that in Italy as elsewhere what fascism was, or could be made to become, was fluid, uncertain, and would only be hammered out through interaction over the course of the trajectory. Any effort to specify a litany of defining characteristics keeps us from grasping the uncertainty and contingency of that trajectory.

Eley's notion that fascism should be theorized in terms of the crisis that produces it, and that the character of the immediately fascism-producing crisis is the best place to begin, is in itself prejudicial and limiting. Let us ponder the difference between seeing fascism as a response to crisis and seeing fascism as a response to a new sense of challenge and opportunity, developing in uncertain, contingent trajectory in interaction with other components. We again recall Iordachi's emphasis on the scope for experiment and multipolar creativity, which might lead in varied directions.

New crises or emergencies might yield dangerously radical departures, to be sure, and we might learn from comparing them with fascism. As we saw, Mann notes *some* convergence with fascism in varied post-1945 phenomena while still denying that they count as fascist overall. But Eley goes much further in insisting that these new phenomena would be instances of fascism every bit as much as those of the earlier period. Whether or not it alerts us to the potential for crisis, this threatens to misconstrue the place of fascism in the earlier period.

Deeper into the Implications of the Ending of What Ended

Turning again to actual as opposed to potential phenomena, Roger Eatwell and Cas Mudde are more convincing than Griffin in assessing some of the recent instances at issue. They discern a serious challenge from the recent European new Right, which, as they see it, has raised genuine issues in light of tensions surrounding globalization, immigration, and Islamic fundamentalism. And they find serious questions about the capacity of mainstream democratic politics to address those issues. But the two authors also note that the parties and movements in question do not appeal to the fascist past or adopt specifically fascist themes and motifs. Judging the overtly neo-fascist parties to have been largely marginalized, they conclude that this newer challenge should be sharply differentiated from "fascism."[36] Like Morgan, Eatwell and Mudde imply that stretching the category to encompass subsequent phenomena, no matter how distasteful we may find them, does not serve but rather impedes our quest for understanding. What is most important about them is not what was most important about classic fascism, and insofar as we insist on the conflation, we cannot grasp their novelty and assess whatever danger they pose.

But more important to the present study is essentially the converse: stretching the category, as Griffin does, or shaping it to fit a new potential crisis, as Eley does, compromises our focus on fascism during the classic period, in its historical specificity, and thus may dilute our understanding. But to counter those like Griffin and Eley, we need to show that it *does* dilute our understanding—and *how* it does so. And that necessitates going beyond earlier authorities from Nolte to Mann. Their overall "epochal" contention convinces, but we need an alternative way of linking fascism to the epoch, of understanding how it was embedded, what the embeddedness entailed—and the implications of *that* having ended.

The point is not simply that the change in framework seemed to make any re-emergence of "fascism" far less likely, if not impossible. To understand how fascism might have been confined to an epoch that ended in 1945, our concern is the other side of the coin. The change of framework suggests that the period from 1919 to 1945 was a very particular and delimited era, making for interaction and thus embeddedness of a particular sort. And the alternative to Nolte and Mann requires most basically drawing out the implications of that embeddedness. Moreover, we need to do greater justice to the peculiar fascist combination of innovative substance, contingency, hollowness, and ephemerality. We also need better to incorporate the sense in which the heterogeneity and fissuring were themselves characteristic of the epoch. Deepening along these lines will enable us better to address the overarching questions concerning the aggregate, including what can be said about fascism in general.

However, drawing out the implications of the epochal embeddedness of fascism, and on that basis better assessing what ended, may still reveal a sort of fascist residuum transcending the epoch. Insofar as it does, we would need to revisit the question of neo-fascism.

Notes

1. Ernst Nolte, *Three Faces of Fascism: Action Française, Italian Fascism, and National Socialism*, trans. Leila Vennewitz (New York: Holt, Rinehart and Winston, 1966), 421–22, 429, 446. The book was first published in German as *Der Faschismus in seiner Epoche* (Fascism in Its Epoch), in 1963.

2. Nolte, *Three Faces of Fascism*, 454.

3. Klaus Epstein, "A New Study of Fascism," first published in 1964, now in *Reappraisals of Fascism*, ed. Henry Ashby Turner (New York: Franklin Watts [New Viewpoints], 1975), 2–25.

4. Gilbert Allardyce, "What Fascism Is Not: Thoughts on the Deflation of a Concept," *American Historical Review* 84, no. 2 (April 1979): 376.

5. Nolte, *Three Faces of Fascism*, 20–21.

6. Ibid., 443–46.

7. Ernst Nolte, "Between Myth and Revisionism? The Third Reich in the Perspective of the 1980s," in *Aspects of the Third Reich*, ed. H.W. Koch (New York: St. Martin's, 1985), 17–38.

8. Subsequently published in book form as *Fascism Past and Present, West and East: An International debate on Concepts and Cases in the Comparative Study of the Extreme Right*, ed. Roger Griffin, Werner Loh, and Andreas Umland (Stuttgart: Ibidem, 2006).

9. Philip Morgan, "Recognizing the Enemy," in ibid., 156.

10. I addressed this issue in my second contribution to the *EWE* discussion: David D. Roberts, "Roger Griffin, Ernst Nolte, and the Historical Place of Fascism," now in *Fascism Past and Present*, ed. Griffin, Loh, and Umland, 376–80.

11. Michael Mann, *Fascists* (Cambridge: Cambridge University Press, 2004), 365–75.

12. Ibid., 370.

13. Ibid., 365.

14. Ibid., 374.

15. Ibid.

16. Philip Morgan, "Studying Fascism from the Particular to the General," *East Central Europe* 37 (2010): 334–35.

17. Ibid., 337.

18. Walter Laqueur, *Fascism: Past, Present, Future* (Oxford: Oxford University Press, 1996), 235; Robert O. Paxton, *The Anatomy of Fascism* (New York: Random House [Vintage]: 2005), 205.

19. Paxton, *The Anatomy of Fascism*, 205.

20. Michel Dobry, "Desperately Seeking 'Generic Fascism': Some Discordant Thoughts on the Academic Recycling of Indigenous Categories," in *Rethinking the Nature of Fascism: Comparative Perspectives*, ed. António Costa Pinto (Basingstoke: Palgrave Macmillan, 2011), 58, 68–69.

21. See first Roger Griffin, "Fascism's New Faces (and New Facelessness) in the 'Post-Fascist' Epoch," in *Fascism Past and Present*, ed. Griffin, Loh, and Umland, 29–67.

22. Roger Griffin, "Uniqueness and Family Resemblances in Generic Fascism," *East Central Europe* 37 (2010): 338–39.

23. Umberto Eco, "Ur-fascism," *New York Review of Books*, June 22, 1995, 12–15. A slightly altered version is included in Umberto Eco, *Five Moral Pieces*, trans. Alastair McEwen (New York: Harcourt, 2001), 65–88.

24. Griffin, "Uniqueness and Family Resemblances," 339. For the wider argument, see Roger Griffin, *Modernism and Fascism: The Sense of a Beginning under Mussolini and Hitler* (Basingstoke: Palgrave Macmillan, 2007).

25. Griffin, "Uniqueness and Family Resemblances," 338–39.

26. Ibid., 338–39.

27. Ibid., 339.

28. I note his way of doing so earlier in David D. Roberts, "Understanding Fascism as Historically Specific," in *Fascism Past and Present*, ed. Griffin, Loh, and Umland, 202–4.

29. Griffin, "Uniqueness and Family Resemblances," 338.

30. Geoff Eley, *Nazism as Fascism: Violence, Ideology, and the Ground of Consent in Germany, 1930–1945* (London and New York: Routledge, 2013), 214–18.

31. Ibid., 218.

32. Ibid., 214. Emphasis in the original.

33. Ibid., 215.

34. Ibid., 207–14.

35. Ibid., 211.

36. Roger Eatwell and Cas Mudde, eds, *Western Democracies and the New Extreme Right Challenge* (London and New York: Routledge, 2004).

Chapter 10

THE EPOCHAL AGGREGATE

Deeper into the Relationship between Fascism and the Era

All historical phenomena are of course embedded—bound up with others. The question is the scope for disembedding fascism in particular, in light of its particular modes of embeddedness in the era of the two world wars. Let us consider two modes of embeddedness and, from there, what disembedding fascism, insofar as it proves possible, would seem to give us. First, in this section, we will consider the implications of its embeddedness in the framework of this historically specific period. Doing so entails rethinking the historical negativity of fascism, all that yielded a certain hollowness and ephemerality, even in light of elements of genuine substance in response to modern problems. In the next section, we will consider the implications of the embeddedness of fascism in the braided dynamic, which means, as we will see, a field of partly overlapping pieces. Obviously the more deeply fascism seems embedded in both senses, and the less the scope for disembedding it, the more fascism seems confined to its epoch. Yet even doing full justice to its embeddedness, we still might find it possible to isolate some specifically fascist residuum transcending the epoch.

What the departures on the Right had most deeply in common, and what bound them together, was the novel conjuncture that resulted especially from World War I. Whereas historical agents can never be sure what will result from their actions, that framework was unusual in the novel sense of challenge and possibility it entailed. It was more uncertain and open-ended than the frameworks posited by Nolte and Mann.

Fascism and the new Right developed in interplay with the particulars of that framework, which included, most obviously, new territorial concerns and the threat from the extreme Left, then on to the challenges of the Depression. But the broader sense of challenge and opportunity seemed to many to require an alternative to parliamentary government. Still, whereas a new mode of collective action, an alternative to both liberalism and communism, seemed necessary, there was much disagreement about what was required.

Treating this framework demands particular care to minimize teleological thinking and, partly as the other side of the coin, to do justice to contingency. This imperative is of course congruent with aspects of the new agenda. Just as all historical phenomena are embedded, they also all entail a measure of contingency, but precisely because the new mode of action was particularly uncertain and open-ended, the contingency was particularly salient in the case of fascism and the new Right. The framework entailed deeper contingency than the frameworks posited by Nolte and Mann encompass.

We first recall the contingency of fascism's Italian birth and subsequent development, accented in chapter 3. It was only because of contingent concatenations that what we now know as "fascism" came to be at all—and that it could have played out, interacting, ramifying internationally as it did.

Such concatenations actualized what had been only possibilities, with implications not readily visible. John Pollard notes, for example, that anti-Semitism was an almost universal feature of Christian Europe, from Scandinavia to Romania.[1] But in terms of our framework, the key is that whereas Europe had long known not only anti-Semitism but also, periodically, violent pogroms, what was new in our period, requiring further explanation, was the determination to act in a new, more systematic way to deal with the perceived "Jewish problem." That determination was epochal, reflecting the sense of new challenges and possibilities demanding new modes of collective action.

Fascism was central, but it did not exhaust the space for experiment on the new Right, as the Salazar and Franco examples make clear. Yet the epochal question is generally taken as dealing strictly with fascism. To be sure, this is plausible in light of the endurance of the Franco and Salazar regimes well after 1945. Yet we have seen that during the era of the two world wars fascism developed in interaction with the wider new Right, producing blurring on occasion, whereas Nolte and Mann are typical in assuming cleaner lines. Conceiving the epochal place of fascism requires doing greater justice to its interaction with or embeddedness in the wider new Right. Doing so then makes it possible to consider more deeply the epochal nature of fascism specifically.

The interaction, blurring, and overlap we have encountered buttress the implication of restives like Mary Vincent that we need to go beyond the question of fascism-or-not to address the wider aggregate, all that was taking place on the new Right. Insofar as we first seek to pinpoint, and then privilege, what we take to be specifically fascist movements at the expense of the interaction that helped constitute the braided dynamic, we miss the scope for fascistizing directions that might, as in Hungary, involve a specifically fascist movement but from which fascism cannot be readily disembedded.

As we have seen, the Austrian, Hungarian, and Romanian cases especially show how interaction on the domestic and international levels intersected to spawn new Right departures—departures that then developed in highly contingent ways through various stages to yield directions that can be called fascistizing, if not fascist. Because fascism cannot be readily disembedded from them, those trajectories must be part, even the first part, of the focus when we ask the epochal question. To recall just one example, the several components in the Hungarian mix, including the Arrow Cross, were what they were, or became what they became, only through the contingencies of that interaction.

In focusing on interaction, we have found fascism developing, becoming a certain way, in relationship with others, especially establishment conservatives, who were not necessarily part of the *new* Right—though interaction with fascism might pull them into it. In any case, emphasis on interaction itself delimits the scope for disembedding. Drawing out the implications of Walter Adamson's discussion of the interaction between Italian Fascism and the Catholic Church, we found not only that what counted as fascism was contested and malleable but also that what fascism became depended in large part on the contingencies of the interaction. And those contingencies included the interplay of factors in one sense exogenous, especially the change in the international situation with the advent of Hitler to power in Germany. In cases more clearly entailing synergy, as with Italian Fascism and economic elites or German Protestants and the Nazi regime, it is even more difficult to specify where fascism starts or stops, so the scope for disembedding it from the contingent network of relationships shrinks further.

Yet even as embedded in the wider new political universe, and even as lines blur, fascism was central to the mix. And if we seek an alternative to Nolte and Mann, we still face the question of what was epochal about fascism specifically. Some of the particulars of that alternative are better held for below, when we ask whether some fascist residue can be isolated. But here we can take the first steps in light of what can be said about the contextual framework.

Especially after Nazism came to power in Germany, fascism increasingly came to dominate the new Right framework. Nazi Germany and Fascist Italy were restless, innovative, revisionist powers willing to act. Other countries became caught up with them differently, depending especially on geography, but also on economic, historical, and ideological factors. The different modes of interaction with the fascist powers affected domestic developments in those other countries. In chapter 1 we noted Tim Kirk's insistence that "fascism determined the political agenda in Europe for a quarter of a century, from its origins in the right-wing political violence that followed the First World War to the defeat of Nazi Germany in 1945."[2] Even if Kirk may slightly overstate the point for effect, it was indeed an epoch of fascism, the debunking of Gilbert Allardyce and others notwithstanding.

Yet, as I have continued to insist, there was still something hollow and ephemeral about fascism; Allardyce was "half" right. To be sure, fascism yielded unprecedented devastation, thanks partly to its terroristic apparatus, its military power, and its willingness to act in unprecedented ways. There was nothing hollow and ephemeral about that devastation, as we have also noted more than once. But there was something about the framework, and the fascist mode of responding to that framework, that made fascism hollow and ephemeral in ways that the accounts of Nolte and Mann do not adequately encompass. And encompassing this peculiar combination of centrality and hollowness is essential to a better understanding of the embeddedness of fascism in its particular epoch.

Fascism seemed a promising alternative to liberalism and communism, but because it was not clear what such an alternative needed to entail, new fascist movements took on a catchall quality, making for particular fissiparousness. Some degree of division is inherent in any polity, of course, but it was especially debilitating for fascism overall as an attempt at innovation from within this especially uncertain framework.

The debilitating heterogeneity of fascism or the new Right in France affords a prime example. Specialists are still seeking better to understand the sources of that fissiparousness.[3] Let us also recall the Austrian Heimwehr, which at least crystalized as a single movement but which, Lothar Höbelt maintains, was as heterogeneous ideologically as it was possible to be. It was anti-communist but otherwise open to all, including Jews.[4] However, it was unable to come together around a common ideology or unified program. Even the most concerted effort to deepen and unify the Heimwehr around a clearly fascist direction, the Korneuburger Oath of 1930, proved divisive.[5]

Still, some generalization about fascism is possible, and we have found totalitarianism the most useful differentiating principle. What distinguished fascism from within the new universe was not so much the totalitarian direction itself but a particular variation on the wider sense of the historical moment, a variation that itself underpinned the choice for a novel totalitarian direction. For fascism the new historical sense entailed a perception of immediate challenge and opportunity of a certain sort, seemingly mandating immediate action of a certain sort. It was necessary not merely to act but to hurry, even to improvise, in light of what seemed to be required to master the historical moment. The orientation entailed hubris, including the sense of the scope for leapfrogging we have discussed, but also shrillness, reflecting a feeling of risk and vulnerability. That whole syndrome was central to the novel fascist self-understanding or frame of mind.

Fascism was unusual, if not unique, in becoming what it was only in action—action of this particularly uncertain, open-ended sort. But the need to hurry and to improvise did not preclude elements of innovative "substance," which stands as the contrary of both myth and style, though myth and style were also in play as part of the field. Mann is more open than Nolte, but as we noted, even his conception is still based to a considerable extent on a master narrative of normal development. And thus we have emphasized the need for greater openness, along the lines Constantin Iordachi has advocated, to the scope for innovation, varied experiment, and multipolar creativity, to the scope for departures that were revolutionary in their quest for an alternative modernity. But though we must take seriously and reconnect with such elements if we are to understand the trajectory of each case, to do justice to embeddedness we must consider why such substantive elements so readily got absorbed, diluted, submerged, deflected, or hollowed out from within this particularly uncertain, open-ended situation.

The hollowness and ephemerality do not indicate mere opportunism, or a lack of seriousness, or even a lack of ideology; nor can fascism be reduced to a mere "happening" to the extent Allardyce argued. But despite some distinctive achievements by fascist movements in power, we noted in treating the ending of the braided dynamic that the possibilities narrowed, the substance tended either to thin or to be channeled in extreme and ultimately out-of-control, self-destructive directions. There were grandiose, megalomaniacal visions, like Hitler's for the rebuilding of Berlin, but they were ever more mythical, blinding the fascists to their real prospects. In light of the particular mode of action that it entailed, fascism proved ramshackle, contradictory, capable of disintegrating and collapsing in unanticipated ways. Even the substance Allardyce missed, if it did not get diluted or absorbed, was of such consistency that it could and did get consumed by the action itself.

We saw how central corporatism was to aspiration and interaction at the time, yet the impulse got blunted or channeled; it, too, ended up largely a myth. As we noted in chapter 5, Gianpasquale Santomassimo highlights the paradox that as the actual course of corporatist development was producing disillusionment in Italy, Italian Fascist corporatism was widely influential on the international level, its putative achievements in producing socioeconomic coordination and harmony widely credited.[6] Thus it was easier for committed corporatists in Italy to continue believing that they were indeed onto something, that continued pushing could eventually bear fruit. But it was especially this element of smoke and mirrors that bred mythmaking. The fate of corporatism was central to the wider hollowness and ephemerality of fascism in Italy and elsewhere.

That outcome resulted partly from the catchall, fissiparous quality of fascism, reflecting the era's uncertainty and openness to experiment. In light of that fissiparousness, strong, charismatic leaders could make a major—and it may seem decisive—difference. We think of José Antonio Primo de Rivera of the Spanish Falange and Corneliu Codreanu of the Romanian Iron Guard, each of whom was killed early in his career, seriously weakening the movement in each case. To be sure, each movement survived to play significant roles for a while, in the Franco and Antonescu regimes, respectively, but in each case the absence of the unifying charismatic leader affected the dialectic, diluting the fascist element.

Still, in the larger scheme of things, how much difference did the loss of those leaders make? Mussolini and Hitler were charismatic leaders who survived to lead the two major regimes. But especially in Italy, though to some extent even in Germany, the emphasis on leadership from the top only papered over the cracks. Moreover, insofar as the leader was the key to holding the regime together, there was always the possibility that fascism might narrow into nothing but personal dictatorship. As early as 1926, referring to the Italian case, Roberto Michels astutely pinpointed the likely reasons for such a direction, even as he was largely sympathetic to Fascism in light of his disillusionment with political parties and parliamentary government.[7]

The noted Marxist thinker Antonio Gramsci, after being imprisoned by Mussolini's regime in 1926, developed a highly original understanding of the fascist dynamic. While examining Italy especially, he was also casting fascism as a wider phenomenon. We can today perhaps appreciate the strengths of Gramsci's analysis better than ever, even as we also recognize that it proved symptomatically wrong in significant respects.[8] Assuming that a viable alternative to the liberal order in Italy's postwar crisis—a genuine new hegemony—could only have been spearheaded by the working class and the Communist Party, Gramsci radically underestimated fascism prior to his imprisonment, and he was utterly mistaken about how the Italian Fascist regime would eventually end—and, as a result, about what would replace it. In viewing the ascendancy of fascism as beginning the final battle between the two contending sides in the class struggle, his sense of the alternatives was simply too restricted.

Still, in his mature analysis Gramsci saw into the contradictions of the Italian Fascist regime, the curious, distinctive, and deeply symptomatic combination it entailed. He came to grant a modicum of seriousness—with corporatism, for example—in the Fascist response to the problems of liberal capitalism. Moreover, he came to acknowledge that the regime had achieved a modicum of success, genuinely penetrating Italian society to some extent. Yet he also pinpointed sources of the brittleness and hollowness, the ramshackle superficiality, that portended Fascism's eventual failure. He did not adequately connect the dots, to be sure, but this is not surprising, in light of his death in 1937.

As Gramsci saw it, the postwar crisis of Liberal Italy was such that no viable alternative could emerge from it. Thus the mishmash quality of Fascism, with all the resulting fissuring, which reflected the incapacity of any Italian political force to produce the essential new hegemony. Fascism was too much a catchall, trying, helter-skelter, to do too much at once. Such heterogeneity and fissuring were characteristic of the wider epoch, as Gramsci also saw. But he missed the implications of the ramshackle quality, why it could yield ephemerality, and thus he missed the possibility that Italian Fascism would deflate and fizzle out. In other words, even Gramsci, pinpointing better than most the sources of the brittleness, did not grasp just *how* brittle and thus ephemeral fascism would prove to be.

Such brittleness and hollowness also characterized Nazi Germany as, following many others, I have sought to show elsewhere.[9] Although the Nazi regime was effective in some respects, certainly more so, in the last analysis, than the Fascist regime in Italy, it achieved hegemony only in a very limited sense—and certainly not in Gramsci's sense. Like Fascist Italy, it was too brittle, shallow, ramshackle. Such brittleness and hollowness were central to what was at once distinctive and surprising about what "fascism" became—or turned out to be.

In a memoir published in 1949, Giuseppe Bottai, whom we have encountered at several points as a leading Italian Fascist hierarch and ideologue, sought to distinguish genuine Fascism in Italy from its Mussolinian degeneration.[10] Although his argument was clearly self-serving, Bottai was right to insist that the possibility of a different outcome had remained until the end. But by its last years Fascism was left as a shadow of what its advocates had earlier imagined. And even as Bottai himself had maintained a modicum of independence and critical distance, he had been too willing to gamble on the leader, to fold in behind Mussolini, in light of the forces in play in this highly conflicted regime. So he shared responsibility for the outcome, even though he was central to the no-confidence vote that led to Mussolini's ouster and the end of the first Fascist regime in July 1943. But the key for us is that even as conflicting bits and pieces remained in that regime until the end, there was no "genuine" Fascism distinguishable from the Mussolini-dominated agglomeration that Italian Fascism ended up. In that sense, Fascism was nothing but the trajectory that led to that outcome.

Fascism could have been central to the epoch yet turn out to have been hollow and ephemeral because it was not at all clear at the time how the unstable, overloaded, uncertain mix was settling out. As the possibilities narrowed from within the overall trajectory, the significance of World War II began coming into focus only in 1943. But insofar as fascism narrowed, with its substantive elements being deflected, absorbed, or hollowed, it could and did use itself up, burn itself out. In that sense, quite apart from any moral judgment, fascism was a historical negativity, leaving nothing transcending the epoch, nothing to be disembedded. There was nothing to it beyond the response to the novel challenges and possibilities the historical moment seemed to entail.

Fascism within a Field of Partly Overlapping Pieces

Turning to the second angle on embeddedness, we note that the open-ended braided dynamic entailed further new and unforeseen combinations, with the pieces overlapping in changing ways, as it continued to the end. And even as we recognize the centrality of fascism to the era and, in light of the double asymmetry, the centrality of Germany to the outcome, the blurring and intertwining were such that we cannot pinpoint some "center" or core as we seek to characterize the epoch and the aggregate. What we find instead is a field of partly overlapping, intersecting, or interlocking pieces, resulting from the fluid, contingently developing braided dynamic.

In chapter 8 we saw the need to eschew clean lines, but to posit such a field of partly overlapping pieces is to take a further step. It affords, first, a mode of *ex post* classification avoiding excessively dichotomous either/or thinking. But above all it affords another way of understanding the embeddedness at the time, and this is central to conceiving the epochal nature of fascism differently than do Nolte or Mann.

As a kind of intermediate layer, the field of pieces was embedded in the epoch, and fascism was embedded in the field of pieces. So as a way of suggesting how intertwined everything was at the time, the field of pieces further suggests the difficulty if not impossibility of disembedding fascism.

We have encountered such overlapping or interlocking in our examples throughout this study. Indeed, we note such a field of pieces if we slice into the braided dynamic at any point. Or, more precisely, at every moment we find *something like* such a field, which was never static and which could not be pinned down while the process continued. Such a fluid field differs from the sort of oscillation that, as we noted at the outset of chapter 8, Martin Blinkhorn posited in seeking to characterize the uncertainty at the time about what was what on the new Right. Although he was surely on track in noting that the differences among Rightist movements and regimes "tended to be subtly nuanced and constantly shifting," we need better to understand the dynamic being generated.[11] It is only after the fact that we can begin to arrange the pieces, specifying the overlaps and intersections, while recognizing that what we have is precisely such a field as opposed to either the blurring we find at the time or the clean lines we tend to assume we require.

The pieces overlapped, intersected, or interlocked from various, sometimes odd, angles and often across the fascist–non-fascist axis. The field extended beyond fascism not least because of the uncertainty, resulting partly from the interaction itself, about the categories at the time. Depending on the variable, a component we deem fascist could overlap more with one we deem non-fascist than with another we deem fascist. Stein Ugelvik Larsen seems to have had something of the sort in mind when he observed that "fascism thus becomes a phenomenon of many shades which are sometimes not easy to distinguish from other political phenomena; perhaps some movements and regimes were fascist at one point in time, but for specific reasons chose another direction."[12]

So the field entailed the embeddedness of fascism in multiple relationships, from within some of which fascism proved especially prone to absorption and dilution, as we noted. To think in terms of such an uncertain field is reflexive, encompassing not only the blurring and fluidity at the time but also, more specifically, the centrality of interaction at the time, which, of course, contributed mightily to the blurring and fluidity. Moreover, thinking in terms of such a field enables us to combine jagged edges with continuities as we compare pieces within it.

The pieces in the field overlapped insofar as they had things in common from within the wider new framework, but the fact they only *partly* overlapped reflects significant differences. As we saw, the totalitarian directions in Italy and Romania overlapped in some ways but not in others, in light of differences in their sense of history. But the complexities of the Hungarian case were especially symptomatic.

In Hungary the Arrow Cross shared in the National Christian ideology that helped define the wider new radical Right in the country. And thus its ideal of a specifically Christian moral order differed significantly from the fascist ideal in Italy or Germany, even factoring in the arguments of Adamson and Richard Steigmann-Gall, respectively. Yet obviously Hungary ended up overlapping significantly with Nazi Germany. Hungarian population engineering and eugenics owed something to the German model, in light of seeming German successes. But of course Nazi Germany had such an impact on Hungary partly because of Hungarian irredentism, which fed the Hungarian determination to cement close ties. So Hungarian population policy overlapped with the German in some ways but not in others.

The variety was especially rich with respect to the relationship of fascism with religion and the churches, as we noted especially in comparing Romania and Italy in chapter 8 and in treating Italy, Germany, Austria, and Hungary in chapter 4. The Catholic Church is widely held to have been a moderating force on the Austrian corporatist regime. Adamson's work on Italy suggests some overlap with the Austrian case, but also significant differences. In Romania, Orthodox priests were being shot in February 1941 as part of Antonescu's punitive revenge against the Iron Guard rebellion. Nothing of the sort would have been conceivable in Italy at around the same time, despite the growing Catholic misgivings about the Fascist government's alliance with Nazi Germany and decision for war. But there still were overlaps in the sometimes fraught, sometimes cordial relationships between regime and church in the two cases.

Pollard notes the ambivalence of the Spanish Falange leaders José Antonio Primo de Rivera and Onésimo Redondo toward Catholicism. It was central to Spanish tradition, but the Catholic Church could not be allowed to compromise state sovereignty or national integrity. Pollard goes on to note the quite different relationships that were envisioned, or that actually developed, between extreme Right groups and the Catholic Church elsewhere. The Slovakian People's Party, the Croatian Ustasha, and the Belgian Rexist movement were sufficiently Catholic to warrant the term "clerical-fascism."[13] Or let us return to our suggestion that attributing to "fascistization" the process through which a new political role for Catholicism resulted in Spain might restrict unduly, denying the Spanish case its own, more autonomous place in the new universe on the Right. Even if so, the Spanish case would still overlap and contrast, but in different ways, along different axes, than if the outcome had resulted from "fascistization."

The pieces did not merely overlap but intersected or even interlocked insofar as what any particular piece came to mean depended to some extent on the interaction. The fact that interaction with "totalitarianism" necessarily affected "authoritarianism" is a prime example. Even if they were at issue in the interaction only indirectly, the pieces were bound to affect each other; indeed, merely a sense of assuming a place alongside others in the new Right universe could be energizing. So the lines between overlapping and intersecting also blur.

The experiment engineered by the Metaxas regime in Greece proved in some ways purer than those in Hungary and Romania, partly because, in light of Greece's geographical situation and the outcomes of World War I, Metaxas for a time was able to play off the great powers as Hungary and Romania could not. But Greece ultimately proved more vulnerable, for contingent reasons involving Fascist Italy, so ended up being attacked by Nazi Germany early in 1941. By that point Hungary and Romania were both allied with Germany, though first because of territorial as opposed to ideological concerns. Still, in each case the long-standing relationship with Nazi Germany helped produce a fascistizing direction.

At the same time, Greece lacked an indigenous fascist movement comparable to the Arrow Cross in Hungary or the Iron Guard in Romania. As merely top-down, the Metaxas experiment overlapped in some ways with that of Gyula Gömbös in Hungary and King Carol II in Romania. But Carol had to deal with the Iron Guard, as did Antonescu a bit later, and just as Hungarian Regent Horthy had to deal with the Arrow Cross. In both Hungary and Romania, the interplay made for a very different dynamic than in Greece, a dynamic usefully considered fascistizing, though not as fully fascist as Metaxas's, delimited though Metaxas's experiment was in other respects.

As central to but still only part of the field of pieces, fascism comes to appear less isolable, and even the distinction we made earlier between interaction within fascism and wider interaction on the Right between fascists and more traditional authoritarian conservatives becomes less salient. Thus, again, we can worry less about whether this or that during the period was "fascist" or not. We need not insist on any particular defining categories, and certainly not "palingenesis" or "political religion," which, as we noted, some take as defining fascism. Nor need we insist on totalitarianism, even though it proves a more useful differentiating category than the others. Because it does so, however, totalitarianism raises further questions that we will consider shortly. But it is worth specifying here that all these categories, as themselves partly overlapping pieces, were in uncertain, dynamic interplay within the braided dynamic.

In light of the field of pieces, we can make better sense of the tricky distinction in chapter 8 suggesting that even insofar as we focus on fascism itself, we turn from any notion that there was some authentic or genuine fascism that provides the touchstone. We simply must distinguish a criterion for differentiating fascism from a criterion for differentiating *authentic* fascism. Whereas the latter implies some essence, the former is consistent with a measure of blurring and with partly overlapping pieces.

In light of this embeddedness in a field of pieces, we must at last address the question of the singularity of Nazi Germany. Such singularity is disputed implicitly by most students of generic fascism, who routinely encompass Nazi Germany, and explicitly by such prominent authorities as

Roger Griffin and Geoff Eley.[14] But proponents of singularity have important arguments, with significant implications for our effort to conceive the new Right universe. In fact, several modes of singularity are at issue, with different implications for us, but in each case positing a field of pieces helps us see how to encompass the German case, including its undoubted singularities.

Most basically at issue is the notion that German Nazism and Nazi Germany were not instances of generic fascism but stand apart as sui generis. As we noted, such students of generic fascism as A. James Gregor and Zeev Sternhell neglect Nazism on those grounds, but the most powerful testimony comes from specialists on Nazi Germany. The point is of course not merely that the German case was unique, as is every case, nor even that it was the most extreme or "successful," for there was bound to be some such variation, with *some* instance at the extreme end. Rather, the point is that the German case was qualitatively different, not even to be measured on the same scale as the others.

Concluding their influential study of Nazi population policy, published in 1991, Michael Burleigh and Wolfgang Wippermann stressed "the specific and singular character of the Third Reich. ... Its objects were novel and *sui generis*." And they warned that "existing theories, whether based upon modernisation, totalitarianism, or global theories of Fascism, [are] poor heuristic devices for a greater understanding of what was a singular regime without precedent or parallel."[15] It was primarily the radical and systematic nature of Nazi population engineering that prompted Burleigh and Wippermann to set Nazi Germany apart, and surely that was a major part of what led Gregor and Sternhell to distinguish Nazism from fascism. But though it was indeed the most radical and systematic, Nazi population engineering was not qualitatively different. Indeed, interaction with Nazi Germany helped enable indigenous population initiatives elsewhere, as we have seen. Moreover, even though their energizing great tasks differed to some extent, Germany and Italy can be associated because of the common totalitarian mode of action. Again, rather than clean lines we find partly overlapping pieces.

More recently, Ian Kershaw has been a particularly forceful proponent of the singularity argument, as we have noted.[16] We addressed aspects of his case in contending that he misses leapfrogging when indicating that Fascist Italy had less sense of defensive mission even than Franco's Spain. In fastening upon such a sense of mission, Kershaw was indeed pinpointing a difference between Germany and Italy, but in missing the functional equivalent, he exaggerated the distinction. Again, partly overlapping pieces works better than singularity to account for the evidence.

It is generally agreed that even though, in the German case, too, interaction between fascists and conservatives entailed some measure of blunting and absorption, Nazi Germany was the most radical and successful in subordinating, penetrating, or fascistizing existing elites and institutions. Blinkhorn insists on the singularity of Nazi Germany precisely on this basis. Whereas Nazism as a departure was part of the wider new Right, he insists that the Third Reich, as *regime,* stands on its own. Although the process necessarily remained incomplete in the regime's twelve-year duration, "the German state, and elite corps such as the army and the bureaucracy, were subject to 'Nazification' in a way not approached, or even seriously attempted, by fascists elsewhere."[17] "Only in Germany," Blinkhorn goes on to say, "did the conservative right come close to being devoured by the tiger it had chosen to ride."[18]

This is to offer another plausible angle on the singularity of Nazi Germany, but we must ask *why* that greater penetration and, on that basis, whether it in fact indicates a qualitative difference from other cases, starting, obviously, with Italy. Blinkhorn was quick with an answer, attributing the uniqueness of Nazism on this level to the fact that "Nazism possessed an ideological content and thrust which most if not all other fascisms lacked."[19] There surely ended up *something* more unified and single-minded about Nazi Germany than Fascist Italy, but to posit up front such a difference in "ideological content and thrust" may be going too far. We must remember, first, that the difference may well have stemmed to some undecidable extent from the oft-cited strength of institutions like the monarchy and the Catholic Church in Italy, providing conservatives alternative sources, lacking in Germany, of unifying identity.

But more challenging is Blinkhorn's implication that Nazi Germany was qualitatively different not in the relative weakness of established institutions but in its own ideological strength. Indeed, he seems not merely to posit a difference in ideological content but to suggest that only Nazism had ideological content of the sort that would generate the requisite ideological thrust or will. In eliminating or marginalizing those from the Strasser wing to Ernst Röhm, and intellectuals from Carl Schmitt to Martin Heidegger, Nazism managed a greater ideological homogeneity than Italian Fascism, which was more obviously a catchall. We need only mention such disparate major figures as Giovanni Gentile, Alfredo Rocco, Roberto Farinacci, and Giuseppe Bottai, but there was also F.T. Marinetti, *stracittà, strapaese*—and on and on. But the resulting difference in ideological thrust did not reflect a lack of ideological content or even ideological will in Italy. The difference was in the degree of fissiparousness diffusing the ideological thrust. So Blinkhorn goes unnecessarily far in suggesting singularity and qualitative difference. In light of the combination of congruence and difference, we are again better advised to think in terms of partly overlapping pieces.

Still, by the late phase of the overall trajectory, Nazi Germany was surely singular in a different sense. Although there had been nodules of experiment and innovation on the new Right across Europe, by the later phase the fate of the new Right came to rest largely on the doubly asymmetrical power relationships, meaning the ultimate preponderance of Nazi Germany, that we discussed especially in chapter 5. Almost all the prior experiment now folded into the interaction on that level. But in the last analysis even the trajectory of Nazism and Nazi Germany cannot be conceived apart from the interplay, the relationships, during this late phase. Nazism became so destructive partly in interaction with others who had their own place in the wider universe.

The Scope for Isolating a Fascist Residuum

But if, in light of the modes of embeddedness we have considered, disembedding the fascist trajectory is difficult or impossible, we still must consider the scope for isolating a fascist residuum, something like a test-tube virus, that might transcend the epoch. This would give us at least a relatively supra-historical fascism, perhaps on Griffin's level, even if not an ahistorical ur-fascism of the sort that Umberto Eco claimed to pinpoint. To be sure, emphasizing embeddedness as we have might seem to preclude any isolable residuum on the face of it, but the question remains insofar as we posit a distinguishable fascist strand, however much, as "weak," it reduces to its trajectory. More particularly, positing hollowness and ephemerality might seem in itself to preclude any sort of fascist residuum. But again the question will not go away. Perhaps one characteristic of any such fascist germ would be a likeliness to yield a trajectory ending up in hollowness and ephemerality. Or perhaps, as Griffin might argue, fascism ended up hollow and ephemeral only under the particular circumstances of the epoch.

To assess the scope for an isolable residuum, we must return to totalitarianism as a criterion of differentiation. In this context, we can finally address an objection we encountered in chapter 8 but put off until this point to consider. In claiming that totalitarianism affords a better criterion of differentiation than the other obvious candidates, we might seem to be saying that it is uniquely definitional—thereby reintroducing essentialism through the back door. But in light of the question of an isolable residuum, we must reframe and even augment the objection, for to claim totalitarianism as a differentiating principle would seem precisely to specify such a residuum, and doing so might seem even more to suggest at least some degree of essentialism and reification. More generally, it might seem contradictory to claim both hollowness and a totalitarian direction strong enough to differentiate among the novel phenomena on the Right.

We stressed that totalitarianism was not a blueprint or system of rule but the new mode of collective action that seemed necessary to confront the challenges and seize the opportunities of the historical moment. Fascism was bound up with the totalitarian dynamic that resulted from action on that basis. But even as the totalitarian direction afforded a unifying dimension in the face of fragmentation, saying that fascism was totalitarian does not specify where it would lead or how it would end—and end up. Moreover, whereas totalitarianism might first seem to have provided fascism with a kind of backbone, as it happened the totalitarian mode of action proved something like the opposite; it ended up contributing to fascism's ragged, improvised, seat-of-the-pants quality. Totalitarianism itself turned out to be a façade, a myth that the fascists themselves believed in excessively. It was especially *because of* its totalitarianism that fascism proved so hollow and ephemeral.

So whereas totalitarianism can be pinpointed as the fascist residuum during the epoch, that residuum was self-consuming like fascism more broadly. Adding in totalitarianism simply makes it clearer why the dimension of fascism that can be understood as relatively supra-historical, that might in principle be understood as continuing beyond the epoch, shrinks dramatically. But does it shrink to zero?

Fascism and Soviet Communism

We also noted earlier that if we are to take totalitarianism as differentiating among phenomena on the new Right, we are bound to ask what differentiates fascism from communism, especially Soviet Stalinism, which developed alongside fascism and which is also widely viewed as totalitarian in some sense. The stakes of the comparison deepen as we ask whether, even taking fascism as embedded, we can still isolate some fascist residuum. Any such residuum might seem precisely what distinguishes fascism from communism or Stalinism. Conversely, to posit a difference between fascist totalitarianism and Soviet communist totalitarianism might itself seem to imply a fascist residuum, or even an essence.

To be sure, the situation is asymmetrical because we have, on the one hand, the single Soviet case and, on the other, numerous fascist cases, insofar as contemporaneous fascism in general is at issue. This makes for awkwardness but does not dissolve the question of what, if anything, the Soviet comparison tells us about an isolable fascist residuum.

Certain differences between the Soviet communist experiment and whatever we might count as fascism are beyond dispute, but do they point us to an isolable fascist residuum? Differences in ideology, worldview, and originating aspirations perhaps come first to mind, but we also recall that the Soviets unquestionably made a more thoroughgoing revolution, entailing a far more radical replacement of the old regime, than did the Nazis or the Italian Fascists. But the significance of those aspects of the Soviet case, and thus of the attendant differences, diminish once we focus on the trajectory of the Soviet regime in practice.

Still, let us start with intellectual origins. Although significant aspects of Italian Fascism can be traced to the turn-of-the-century revision of Marxism that also fed Leninism, the Soviet regime had deeper roots in Marxism and, most obviously for that reason, very different roots than fascism overall. And certainly the Soviets claimed to be following Marxism as they began constructing their new regime. But, having seized power in Russia, they soon found themselves facing an unforeseen situation for which Marxism provided no real blueprint.

In a crucial sense, then, fascism and Soviet communism each emerged from within the same brave new world, seemingly affording radically new challenges but also new possibilities in the quest for an alternative to mainstream liberal modernity. The more thoroughgoing removal of the old regime in the Soviet Union opened more space for experiment, but on each side history itself came to seem more open-ended, though subject to human organization and will.[20] On that basis fascists and Soviet communists adopted partly overlapping modes of action, with the common element usefully characterized as totalitarianism, characteristically combining hubris and shrillness. Although the residual Marxism bolstered confidence among the Soviets, each side was caught up in an uncertain, open-ended trajectory. If anything, Marxist ideology functioned ever more as myth within the Soviet experiment.

Once we focus on the trajectories, but then also on the dynamic interaction between the Soviets and the fascists, the undeniable differences in originating aspirations and even in aspects of practice shrink—and blur, another instance of the blurring of the wider Left-Right dichotomy that we find periodically during the period. The fascism-Soviet comparison suggests further, partly overlapping pieces in the field constituting the novel universe at the time. In that sense, the premium on isolating some pure fascism even vis-à-vis Soviet communism diminishes.[21]

It is hardly radical or innovative to suggest that for certain questions, Hitler's Germany had more in common with Stalin's Soviet Union than with Franco's Spain—or even, many would argue, Mussolini's Italy. Those adopting the totalitarian mode of action surely envisioned somewhat different tasks to be tackled, but those tasks do not break neatly between fascism and communism. Even limiting ourselves to the "fascist" Right, Fascist Italy and Nazi Germany embarked for a time on rather different projects.

Moreover, other axes crossed the Left-Right divide. For example, in policies toward diverse national or ethnic groupings, we find a significant if long-neglected parallel between Stalin and Mussolini, differentiating them from Hitler and Nazi Germany. Whereas the Italian and Soviet directions entailed the often forced relocation of ethnic minorities, they cannot be conflated with Nazi modes of ethnic hierarchy and systematic, murderous elimination. In the Soviet and Italian cases, the aim was to align each national or ethnic grouping with its own specific territory.[22]

But again we find partly overlapping pieces. Although the Italians, too, could be brutal in carrying out the policy, implementation in the Soviet case brought the regime ever closer to Nazi German modes of practice. Jörg Baberowski and Anselm Doering-Manteuffel show that Soviet population engineering, even on the basis of what began as a "universal" principle, led to the increasingly repressive use of ethnic categories, even forced mass deportations. As minorities became conflated with disorder, and especially as they became linked to outside threats—and thus even with treason—much of the distinction with Nazism, based on putative Soviet universalism, was lost.[23]

But situating the fascism-communism comparison within the field of partly overlapping pieces does not shrink the differences to zero. Because the pieces constituting the field were only partly overlapping, we have room for both common totalitarianism and differences within totalitarianism. And if there was *any* difference, there would seem to be something about fascism in general that must be specified. But what would be the nature of that "something"?

We find differences in totalitarian dynamics between fascism and communism that did not stem merely from the differences in tasks undertaken. Even as they blurred in practice, the differences in worldview, originating aspirations, and ideological depth remained operative to some extent, helping to differentiate the totalitarian dynamic in the Soviet Union. I have accented the heterogeneity on the fascist side, which contrasts, as many have stressed, with the at least somewhat unifying ideology that underpinned the Soviet experiment.

Although tendencies toward mythmaking and narrowing, encompassing reduction to the will of an erratic leader, were to be found on both the fascist and the Soviet sides, they were more pronounced in fascism. Partly because of the Soviet experiment's deeper roots and richer, more consistently elaborated ideology, both the party and the bureaucracy in the

Soviet Union provided a greater modicum of coherence and more seriously checked the leader.

Comparing the Soviet Union with Nazi Germany in the Geyer-Fitzpatrick volume, Yoram Gorlizki and Hans Mommsen show that the higher degree of party-based institutionalization in the Soviet case enabled the leadership over the long term to keep the dynamics of political mobilization in check, whereas in Germany the greater reliance on an amorphous cult of the leader and on the free-floating retinue structures around him, added to the expansionist ideology, led the dynamics of political mobilization to spin out of control.[24] Even at the height of Stalinism, the authors insist, the Communist Party remained more independent of the leader than did the Nazi Party in Germany, and the higher degree of party-based institutionalization in the Soviet case provided the basis for self-correction lacking in Germany.

This contrast illuminates the difference in the longevity of the two regimes, just as Gorlizki and Mommsen contend. But in their determination to stress difference, these authors, like the others in the Geyer-Fitzpatrick volume, make the distinction at issue too neat, and they, too, end up glossing over a deeper element of commonality not encompassed by the old totalitarianism model. For surely, especially with the Stalinist revolution, the Soviet experiment also spun out of control at several points during the 1930s, arguably with results decisive for its overall outcome, longer lived though it proved to be. The Soviet great project differed from Nazi territorial expansion, but the Soviet effort in crash industrialization and forced collectivization, and even in ethnic re-engineering, proved comparably overreaching based on a comparably grandiose sense of the historical challenge and opportunity. So, yet again, we find partly overlapping pieces.

It remains the case, however, that fascism was messier, more improvisational and open-ended. Thus, most obviously, fascism lacked the staying power of the Soviet regime. And thus the Soviet regime was more likely to end as it eventually did, in stultification, than as Fascist Italy and Nazi Germany did, reduced to reliance on an erratic leader who led each to defeat and ruin.

Although what we find are to some extent simply different modes of totalitarianism or differences within totalitarianism, the differences do suggest something like the residuum we are seeking. The key, however, is that the residuum does not transcend the epoch. Even insofar as the communist comparison reveals an isolable fascism, the residuum is overwhelmingly the "negative"—the heterogeneity and fissuring, the narrowing, hollowness, and ephemerality. But thus we more deeply understand how completely anything we can usefully understand as fascism was confined to the era of the two world wars. Even if the palingenetic impulse has continued, and even for something like Griffin's reasons, the phenomena it has fueled were not instances of "fascism," because all that we can usefully encompass through that category was bound up with both the epochal interaction and with totalitarianism, whether as actual deployment or seemingly imminent possibility. The whole package ended in 1945.

The Unbearable Lightness and the Unbearable Weight of Historical Fascism

To conclude, let us look again at the question of how we might put fascism in better proportion, at once taking it seriously—even *more* seriously— and deflating it at the same time. Adapting Milan Kundera's famous title, we might think in terms of the unbearable lightness and the unbearable weight of fascism.[25] Not surprisingly, lightness and weight are in interplay, and indeed we could start with either. The interplay is bound up with the particular consistency of European fascism as history during the era of the two world wars.

Insofar as we feature its embeddedness, hollowness, capriciousness, messiness, contingency, and superficiality, fascism seems to lack the weight we sometimes attribute to it. But the resulting lightness is unnerving, unbearable; given its heavy historical footprint and horrific outcomes, fascism continues to weigh on us, and we worry that we have not understood it as deeply as we need to—that despite having come to take it more seriously, in some sense we still have not taken it seriously enough. Deflation does not make fascism any less troubling, nor does it make understanding fascism any less important. But in light of the unbearable lightness, our efforts to get a handle on it may lead us to inflate it or force it in various ways. And we tend to want a *comfortable* handle, which means not fully confronting our tendencies, well pinpointed by Mark Roseman and Stephen Holmes, to sidestep certain discomforting aspects, to sweep them under the rug.[26]

Most obviously, we abstract from the actual history to privilege theory of some sort. It sometimes seems that "a general theory of fascism" or "a retrodictive theory of fascism" is the self-evident aim of our inquiries.[27] Any such theory would of course rest on the history and would result from research into the individual cases, but from this perspective the history is essentially preliminary. Understanding seems to entail and require building an edifice from which a certain perspective from above, and thus, it would seem, a certain mastery, becomes possible.

In our deflating mode, we suspect that fascism was too fractured, messy, embedded, capricious, and contingent to yield a general or even a retrodictive theory. But still seeking a handle as we pull back from that level, we may force in other ways, abstracting from the actual course of events to privilege this or that, especially through the standard pitfalls of reductionism, teleology, and essentialism or reification. In this way, too, we fail to do justice to the disparate components in the new universe at issue, and thus, again, we cannot convincingly account for the trajectory resulting from their interaction. Even the attempt to find such handles deflects us from the reconceptualization necessary.

What a new agenda most basically requires is a more deeply historical approach, and it is that that I seek to specify, and justify, in the present study. No doubt at best it would remain but one strand among others, as alternative comparative frameworks, as well as models and theories, continue to find a place as well. But we could be clearer on what such a more deeply historical approach might entail and why it might merit more of our attention, even at the expense of those alternatives.

It is generally agreed that history deals in unique, unrepeatable events, yet some instances more than others must be understood as singular contingent concatenations; from them it is especially difficult not only to devise some general or retrodictive theory but even to extrapolate factors that would relate them to others. In such cases each factor, to an unusual extent, is what it is only in relationship with others *within that case*. So we find ourselves more limited than usual to simply understanding the overall event as it happened, as a contingent concatenation.

Fascism as an aggregate historical phenomenon was sufficiently unusual, even extreme, that it is best understood as a unique, contingent sequence constituting a single, if obviously multifaceted, event. It entailed the braided dynamic yielding the field, or sequence of fields, of partly overlapping pieces. And that event was finite, epochal, in that, as it happened, it came to an end. In retrospect, certain outcomes and even modes of ending seem to have been more likely all along, but only the history would tell.

In light of what fascism turned out to be, and to have been, not only is there limited scope for a general or retrodictive theory, but even the scope for abstracting factors from within the event of fascism is limited. Whatever the combination or subset chosen, such extrapolation or abstraction is bound to be *especially* arbitrary and ahistorical, given the "negative" consistency of fascism. So in approaching fascism, more than is usually the case in dealing with historical experience, we can aspire only to understand the finite history—the actual contingent historical linkages producing the trajectory through which fascism became what it was. Put simply, the question is not how fascism *comes* to be, but how fascism *came* to be. And only insofar as we grasp why the past tense is appropriate can we grasp *how* fascism came to be.

In this light we can usefully return to Larsen and Michel Dobry, recalling their modes of deflating fascism and considering the uses for fascist studies that seem to remain. Each is prominent in the calls for a new agenda, and at least some of the findings of the present study seem congruent with the directions they have proposed. Among our restive authorities, they most explicitly address the balance of theory and history, though neither is remotely proposing some general theory of fascism. Indeed, even as their emphases differ considerably, each wants to deflate fascism in ways that seem to point beyond not only definitions like Griffin's but also even the possibility of some general theory. But theory pairs with history in various ways, and it is worth considering the theory each *does* propose, especially the implications of each for understanding the actual naked history of the epoch.

For Dobry especially, but for Larsen as well, putting fascism in proper proportion is valuable especially in opening the way to comparison with phenomena, even non-fascist phenomena, beyond the era. Such comparison is surely self-recommending up to a point, yet there are trade-offs, as well as questions of priority and proportion. The modes of deflating that we find in Larsen and Dobry prove to point us away from the deeper focus on the singular event of embedded fascism that we need.

Larsen surely convinces in noting that there can be no single theory for fascism during the period 1918–45. His reminder that, for example, we cannot explain the Holocaust by means of electoral statistics remains useful. Yet he also persuasively stresses that there are connections, inner links, that must be discovered among the bits and pieces at issue.[28] At the same time, however, we saw that Larsen envisions a "new theoretical platform" based on an inventory of findings about fascism. This would be to get all the variables as close to fixed as possible, giving us a kind of map. In fact, however, we can discover and explain those links not through some static inventory, not even a static inventory of such inner links, but only by laying out the contingent linkages that yielded the actual dynamic or trajectory—the actual particular history. Again, what we seek to understand is the aggregate *event*. In light of the dynamic quality of the interwoven strands, no static inventory of the sort Larsen recommends can give us the aggregate picture.

Extending the point beyond Larsen, once we understand the consistency of fascism, we grasp the limits of what we can learn from a catalog of familiar characteristics like dictatorship, mass mobilization, nationalism, and racism. Each was what it was only from within the trajectory and the braided dynamic, only in relationship with the others, only in response to the contingent concatenation that had resulted so far.

In chapter 2 we noted the tendency to assume that a web of comparisons might enable us to understand the aggregate. But while comparison remains essential, seeking such a web is too readily taken as a default setting at the expense of other modes of historical understanding. And conceiving fascism as an embedded, epochal event is the appropriate alternative in this case. Comparison serves understanding of the event.

Dobry is even more determined than Larsen to deflate fascism. And despite his own theoretical bent, he comes close to suggesting explicitly that fascism was too embedded, contingent, capricious, fractured, and messy to afford the basis for some general theory. Up to a point, his particular mode of deflating is especially valuable, bound up as it is with his call to avoid teleological thinking. Avoiding teleology, we have seen again and again, is essential to grasp the open-endedness of the braided dynamic. As one corollary, Dobry insists that we recognize the possibility of different trajectories and outcomes. As another corollary, he warns that our tendency, especially in light of its outcomes, to take fascism as an exceptional case from the outset keeps us from grasping the open-endedness of its contingent trajectory. *Not* taking fascism as exceptional up front surely would not preclude exceptionalism on other grounds, so accepting Dobry's imperatives would seem compatible with taking fascism as exceptionally embedded, as I am proposing. In fact, especially when we also note his concomitant call for a relational perspective, those imperatives help us understand fascism precisely as embedded in its epoch.[29]

But we also note tensions in Dobry's program. Although in one sense the possibility of different outcomes is a corollary of any accent on contingency, dwelling on the possibility in the case of fascism nets us very little. How would we isolate from within the actual trajectory the subset of fascist-like components that might have yielded different outcomes? The bits and pieces became what they were in their relationships, each responding to the contingent concatenation that had resulted so far. There are no "fascist" components to be isolated apart from the braided dynamic and the field of partly overlapping pieces. To abstract whatever combination would be too merely arbitrary.

Dobry also suggests that a deflated, less singular fascism might fruitfully be engaged in a wider range of comparison with political phenomena outside the universe of the new Right during its epoch. The web of comparison might even encompass what initially seems incomparable.[30] Such transhistorical comparison would transcend Larsen's inventory, limited to the fascist universe, and would differ considerably from Larsen's premium on discovering connections and inner links *among* specifically fascist phenomena. For Dobry, the universe of relationships involving fascist phenomena would expand to infinity.

In principle, comparison across the wider range Dobry has in mind would not be inconsistent with our emphasis on the embeddedness of fascism during the particular era. But what he recommends elicits much the same objection that was offered just above concerning the possibility of different outcomes. In leading to a premium on comparison, too, Dobry's mode of deflation reduces fascism to bits and pieces that can be compared this way and that. In principle, such comparison could illuminate even the components yielding the actual historical trajectory at issue for us. But as Dobry frames the possibilities and desiderata, opening the way to trans-historical comparison both abstracts and deflects from the actual fascist trajectory that produced the unbearably heavy outcomes.

Up to a point, to be sure, Dobry's mode of deflation, with its emphasis on contingency, seems to make clear the primacy of that actual historical trajectory. But the corollary should be precisely that all the elements are abstract, merely potential, until they are caught up in it. Yet for Dobry, with fascism deflated, transhistorical comparison becomes the priority, as if it might yield a wider theoretical or transhistorical sense of the role of, to cite his own examples, charismatic domination or the situational con-straints facing new entrants into the political arena. But an array of pos-sibilities come to mind, from particular phenomena like liturgy and ritual to some broader theoretical edifice more obviously transcending fascism.

Even if it is only via comparison, leaping to such a more abstract or supra-historical level tends to homogenize the phenomena at issue, thereby diluting the inquiry into fascism and its epoch. More specifically, such a premium on transhistorical comparison deflects us from attention to the contingent historical relations during the epoch of fascism. Probing them more deeply might enable us better to understand what fueled what and how, what got absorbed or consumed and how—so that we might better understand how the contingencies yielded the particular event. On that basis we might learn more deeply from the overall experience of the epoch. Those actual connections are precisely what a "relational perspective" might be expected to clarify.

We said that deflating fascism does not make it any less troubling, nor does it make understanding fascism any less important. In a key sense, in fact, deflating makes it even more troubling. Especially in view of the destructive and horrific outcomes, any suggestion that in some sense "it just happened," historically, contingently, that fascism was too slippery to afford theoretical handles or supra-historical reasons, seems offensive. It is especially in that sense that the lightness that seems to result from defla-tion is unbearable.

And it is partly for that reason that Richard Shorten and many others, guided by a moral concern that is surely laudable up to a point, feel that the most horrific outcomes must have emerged teleologically, in light of some essence. But what we must grasp and learn to digest is the contrary, how even the most horrific outcomes emerged historically, through nothing but the actual contingent process, entailing the braided dynamic we have pinpointed. The whole experience remains so troubling not only because of the horrific outcomes, or even because of the violence, coercion, and dictatorship along the way, but precisely because of the lightness of the process whereby it all became part of our world, to remain as a layer forever.

Proclaiming ourselves against violence, terror, atrocity, and genocide is no substitute for learning more deeply from the historical experience at issue. Such learning requires, as we have emphasized, putting the aggregate in better proportion, which entails not only deflation but also taking fascism more seriously and attuning to a wider range of frequencies. There is scope for doing so without even a hint of apology or rehabilitation, suggesting that they might have been right after all, or that it was not so bad after all. We learn to make the essential distinction between a mode of understanding that encompasses deeper challenge and the moralistic triumphalism that seems to obviate the need to confront that challenge. Only insofar as we take fascism more deeply seriously can we better understand how it all happened historically. And only on that basis can we at once more seriously deflate fascism and learn more deeply from the burdensome historical experience that it became—and bequeathed to us.

Notes

1. J.F. Pollard, "Fascism and Catholicism," in *The Oxford Handbook of Fascism,* ed. R.J.B. Bosworth (Oxford: Oxford University Press, 2009), 178.

2. Tim Kirk, "Fascism and Austrofascism," in *The Dollfuss/Schuschnigg Era in Austria: A Reassessment,* ed. Günter Bischof, Anton Pelinka, and Alexander Lassner (New Brunswick, NJ: Transaction, 2003), 10.

3. For a good sense, see Samuel Kalman and Sean Kennedy, eds, *The French Right between the Wars* (New York and Oxford: Berghahn, 2014). The introduction by the editors, 1–21, esp. 10–11, provides a valuable overview.

4. Lothar Höbelt, "Nostalgic Agnostics: Austrian Aristocrats and Politics, 1918–1938," in *European Aristocracies and the Radical Right, 1919–1939,* ed. Karina Urbach (Oxford: Oxford University Press, 2007), 170–71, 173.

5. Corinna Peniston-Bird, "Austria," in *Oxford Handbook,* ed. Bosworth, 439–40.

6. Gianpasquale Santomassimo, *La terza via fascista: Il mito del corporativismo* (Rome: Carocci, 2006), 10–11.

7. Roberto Michels, *First Lectures in Political Sociology,* trans. Alfred de Grazia (New York: Harper & Row [Torchbooks], 1965), 119–33, esp. 125–26, 131–32.

8. See David D. Roberts, "Reconsidering Gramsci's Interpretation of Fascism," *Journal of Modern Italian Studies* 16, no. 2 (March 2011): 239–55, for a fuller analysis and the relevant references to Gramsci.

9. David D. Roberts, *The Totalitarian Experiment in Twentieth-Century Europe: Understanding the Poverty of Great Politics* (London and New York: Routledge, 2006), 336–411 (chapter 7, entitled "The Hollow Triumph of the Will in Nazi Germany").

10. Giuseppe Bottai, *Vent'anni e un giorno* (Milan: Garzanti, 1949).

11. Martin Blinkhorn, "Introduction: Allies, Rivals, or Antagonists? Fascists and Conservatives in Modern Europe," in *Fascists and Conservatives: The Radical Right and the Establishment in Twentieth-Century Europe*, ed. Martin Blinkhorn (London: Unwin Hyman, 1990), 9.

12. Stein Ugelvik Larsen, "Was There Fascism outside Europe? Diffusion from Europe and Domestic Impulses," in *Fascism outside Europe: The European Impulse against Domestic Conditions in the Diffusion of Global Fascism*, ed. Stein Ugelvik Larsen (Boulder, CO: Social Science Monographs, 2001), 818.

13. Pollard, "Fascism and Catholicism," 169.

14. Roger Griffin, "Hooked Crosses and Forking Paths: The Fascist Dynamics of the Third Reich," in *A Fascist Century: Essays by Roger Griffin*, ed. Matthew Feldman (Basingstoke: Palgrave Macmillan, 2008), 83–113; Geoff Eley, *Nazism as Fascism: Violence, Ideology, and the Ground of Consent in Germany, 1930–1945* (London and New York: Routledge, 2013).

15. Michael Burleigh and Wolfgang Wippermann, *The Racial State: Germany 1933–1945* (Cambridge: Cambridge University Press, 1991), 306–7.

16. Ian Kershaw, "Hitler and the Uniqueness of Nazism," *Journal of Contemporary History* 39, no. 2 (April 2004): 239–54.

17. Blinkhorn, "Introduction," 11.

18. Ibid., 13.

19. Ibid., 11.

20. Alfred G. Meyer, *Leninism* (New York: Frederick A. Praeger, 1962), 276–77, 279, 288, 290–92; Moshe Lewin, *The Making of the Soviet System: Essays in the Social History of Interwar Russia* (New York: Pantheon, 1985), 202, 258–59.

21. Seeking to challenge Marxist thinking about fascism, Roger Griffin, too, strongly questions the Left-Right distinction in bringing both Marxism and the Soviet experiment together with fascism around palingenesis. See Roger Griffin, "Exploding the Continuum of History: A Non-Marxist's Marxist Model of Fascism's Revolutionary Dynamics," in Griffin, *A Fascist Century*, 46–68. In response, I questioned Griffin's way of challenging the Marxists; see David D. Roberts, "Fascism, Marxism, and the Question of Modern Revolution," *European Journal of Political Theory*, 9, no. 2 (April 2010): 183–201. Griffin and I then invited a group of Marxist or left-leaning scholars to respond to our two essays. The result was "'The Fascist Revolution': Utopia or Façade? Reconciling Marxist and Non-Marxist Approaches," ed. Roger Griffin and David D. Roberts, special issue, *European Journal of Political Theory* 11, no. 4 (October 2012).

22. On Italy see Davide Rodogno, *Fascism's European Empire: Italian Occupation during the Second World War*, trans. Adrian Belton (Cambridge: Cambridge University Press, 2006), 264–65, 298. On the Soviet case, see Jörg Baberowski and Anselm Doering-Manteuffel, "The Quest for Order and the Pursuit of Terror: National Socialist Germany and the Stalinist Soviet Union as Multiethnic Empires," in *Beyond Totalitarianism: Stalinism and Nazism Compared*, ed. Michael Geyer and Sheila Fitzpatrick (Cambridge: Cambridge University Press, 2009), 180–227.

23. Baberowski and Doering-Manteuffel, "The Quest for Order," 209–10. See also Christian Gerlach and Nicholas Werth, "State Violence—Violent Societies," in *Beyond Totalitarianism*, ed. Geyer and Fitzpatrick, 157–61, on violence toward "asocials," prisoners-of-war, and victims of ethnic resettlement.

24. Yoram Gorlizki and Hans Mommsen, "The Political (Dis)Orders of Stalinism and National Socialism," in *Beyond Totalitarianism*, ed. Geyer and Fitzpatrick, 42, 84–85. Although Moshe Lewin placed a different, more negative spin on something like the same syndrome in the Soviet Union, he too recognized that the contingent development of a particular, unexpected relationship between the leadership and the bureaucracy made for

stabilization of a sort. See Lewin, *The Making of the Soviet System*, 260–61, 263, 299; and Moshe Lewin, "Bureaucracy and the Stalinist State," in *Stalinism and Nazism: Dictatorships in Comparison*, ed. Ian Kershaw and Moshe Lewin (Cambridge: Cambridge University Press, 1997), 74.

25. Milan Kundera, *The Unbearable Lightness of Being*, trans. Michael Henry Heim (HarperCollins [Perennial], 1987). This book has much to do with the "unbearable lightness" of history itself, especially as we came to experience it—and manipulate it—during the cataclysmic twentieth century.

26. Mark Roseman, "National Socialism and Modernization," in *Fascist Italy and Nazi Germany: Comparisons and Contrasts*, ed. Richard Bessel (Cambridge: Cambridge University Press, 1996), 226–27; Stephen Holmes, *The Anatomy of Antiliberalism* (Cambridge, MA: Harvard University Press, 1993), 154.

27. Among prominent examples, "Toward a General Theory of Fascism" is the lead essay in George L. Mosse's *The Fascist Revolution: Toward a General Theory of Fascism* (New York: Howard Fertig, 1999), 1–44; "Elements of a Retrodictive Theory of Fascism" is one of the concluding interpretive chapters in Stanley G. Payne's *A History of Fascism, 1914–1945* (Madison: University of Wisconsin Press, 1995), 487–95.

28. Stein U. Larsen, "Decomposition and Recomposition in Theories: How to Arrive at Useful Ideas Explaining Fascism," in *Rethinking the Nature of Fascism: Comparative Perspectives*, ed. António Costa Pinto (Basingstoke: Palgrave Macmillan, 2011), 43.

29. Michel Dobry, "Desperately Seeking 'Generic Fascism': Some Discordant Thoughts on the Academic Recycling of Indigenous Categories," in *Rethinking the Nature of Fascism*, ed. Pinto, 54, 60, 72–74, 77.

30. Ibid., 79–80.

WORKS CITED

Adamson, Walter L. "Fascism and Political Religion in Italy: A Reassessment." *Contemporary European History* 23, no. 1 (February 2014): 43–73.

Adanïr, Fikret. "Kemalist Authoritarianism and Fascist Trends in Turkey during the Interwar Period." In *Fascism outside Europe: The European Impulse Against Domestic Conditions in the Diffusion of Global Fascism*, ed. Stein Ugelvik Larsen. Boulder, CO: Social Science Monographs, 2001, 313–61.

Adinolfi, Goffredo. "Political Elite and Decision-Making in Mussolini's Italy." In *Ruling Elites and Decision-Making in Fascist-Era Dictatorships*, ed. António Costa Pinto. Boulder, CO: Social Science Monographs, 2009, 19–54.

Adler, Franklin Hugh. *Italian Industrialists from Liberalism to Fascism: The Political Development of the Industrial Bourgeoisie, 1906–1934.* Cambridge: Cambridge University Press, 1995.

Allardyce, Gilbert. "What Fascism Is Not: Thoughts on the Deflation of a Concept." *American Historical Review* 84, no. 2 (April 1979): 367–98 (with comments by Stanley G. Payne and Ernst Nolte and a reply by Allardyce).

Andersen, Wayne. *German Artists and Hitler's Mind: Avant-Garde Art in a Turbulent Era.* Boston and Geneva: Editions Fabriart, 2007.

Antliff, Mark. *Avant-Garde Fascism: The Mobilization of Myth, Art, and Culture in France, 1909–1939.* Durham, NC: Duke University Press, 2007.

Arthurs, Joshua. *Excavating Modernity: The Roman Past in Fascist Italy.* Ithaca, NY: Cornell University Press, 2012.

Aschheim, Steven E. *The Nietzsche Legacy in Germany, 1890–1990.* Berkeley: University of California Press, 1992.

Baberowski, Jörg, and Anselm Doering-Manteuffel. "The Quest for Order and the Pursuit of Terror: National Socialist Germany and the Stalinist Soviet Union as Multiethnic Empires." In *Beyond Totalitarianism: Stalinism and Nazism Compared*, ed. Michael Geyer and Sheila Fitzpatrick. Cambridge: Cambridge University Press, 2009, 180–227.

Balbo, Italo. *Diario, 1922*, Milan: A. Mondadori, 1932.

Baldoli, Claudia. *Exporting Fascism: Italian Fascists and Britain's Italians in the 1930s.* Oxford: Berg, 2003.

Baranowski, Shelley. *Strength through Joy: Consumerism and Mass Tourism in the Third Reich*. Cambridge: Cambridge University Press, 2004.

Bassignana, Pier Luigi. *Fascisti nel paese dei Soviet*. Turin: Bollati Boringhieri, 2000.

Bauerkämper, Arnd. *Der Faschismus in Europa, 1918–1945*. Stuttgart: Philipp Reclam jun., 2006.

———. "Transnational Fascism: Cross-Border Relations between Regimes and Movements in Europe, 1922–1939." *East Central Europe* 37 (2010): 214–46.

Beckerath, Erwin von. *Wesen und Werden des faschistischen Staates*. Berlin: Julius Springer, 1927.

Ben-Ghiat, Ruth. *Fascist Modernities: Italy, 1922–1945*. Berkeley: University of California Press, 2001.

Bergen, Doris L. *The Twisted Cross: The German Christian Movement in the Third Reich*. Chapel Hill: University of North Carolina Press, 1996.

Bertoni, Renzo. *Il trionfo del fascismo nell'U.R.S.S.* Rome: Angelo Signorelli, 1934.

Bessel, Richard, ed. *Fascist Italy and Nazi Germany: Comparisons and Contrasts*. Cambridge: Cambridge University Press, 1996.

Bischof, Günter, Anton Pelinka, and Alexander Lassner, eds. *The Dollfuss/Schuschnigg Era in Austria: A Reassessment*. New Brunswick, NJ: Transaction, 2003.

Blackbourn, David. *The Conquest of Nature: Water, Landscape, and the Making of Modern Germany*. New York: W.W. Norton, 2006.

Blinkhorn, Martin. *Fascism and the Right in Europe, 1919–1945*. Harlow: Longman, 2000.

———. "Introduction: Allies, Rivals, or Antagonists? Fascists and Conservatives in Modern Europe." In *Fascists and Conservatives: The Radical Right and the Establishment in Twentieth-Century Europe*, ed. Martin Blinkhorn. London: Unwin Hyman, 1990, 1–15.

———, ed. *Fascists and Conservatives: The Radical Right and the Establishment in Twentieth-Century Europe*. London: Unwin Hyman, 1990.

Borejsza, Jerzy W., and Klaus Ziemer, eds. *Totalitarian and Authoritarian Regimes in Europe: Legacies and Lessons from the Twentieth Century*. New York and Oxford: Berghahn, 2006.

Bosworth, R.J.B. *The Italian Dictatorship: Problems and Perspectives in the Interpretation of Mussolini and Fascism*. London: Arnold, 1998.

———. *Mussolini*. London: Arnold, 2002.

———. *Mussolini's Italy: Life under the Dictatorship, 1915–1945*. New York: Penguin, 2006.

———, ed. *The Oxford Handbook of Fascism*. Oxford: Oxford University Press, 2009.

Bottai, Giuseppe. *Esperienza corporativa (1929–1934)*. Florence: Vallecchi, 1934.

———. *Vent'anni e un giorno*. Milan: Garzanti, 1949.

Botz, Gerhard. "The Coming of the Dollfuss-Schuschnigg Regime and the Stages of Its Development." In *Rethinking Fascism and Dictatorship in Interwar Europe*, ed. António Costa Pinto and Aristotle Kallis. Basingstoke: Palgrave Macmillan, 2014, 121–53.

————. "The Short- and Long-Term Effects of the Authoritarian Regime and of Nazism in Austria: The Burden of a 'Second Dictatorship.'" In *Totalitarian and Authoritarian Regimes in Europe: Legacies and Lessons from the Twentieth Century*, ed. Jerzy W. Borejsza and Klaus Ziemer. New York and Oxford: Berghahn, 2006, 188–208.

Bracher, Karl Dietrich. *The Nazi Dictatorship: The Origins, Structure, and Effects of National Socialism*. Trans. Jean Steinberg. New York: Praeger, 1970.

Brooker, Paul. *The Faces of Fraternalism: Nazi Germany, Fascist Italy, and Imperial Japan*. Oxford: Clarendon, 1991.

Bruneteau, Bernard. *Le totalitarisme: Origines d'un concept, genèse d'un débat, 1930–1942*. Paris: Les Editions du Cerf, 2010.

Bucur, Maria. "Remapping the Historiography of Modernization and State-Building in Southeastern Europe through Health, Hygiene and Eugenics." In *Health, Hygiene, and Eugenics in Southeastern Europe to 1945*, ed. Christian Promitzer, Sevastri Trubeta, and Marius Turda. Budapest: Central European University Press, 2011, 427–45.

Burleigh, Michael. *Death and Deliverance: 'Euthanasia' in Germany, c. 1900–1945*. Cambridge: Cambridge University Press, 1994.

————. *Sacred Causes: The Clash of Religion and Politics from the Great War to the War on Terror*. New York: HarperCollins, 2007.

Burleigh, Michael, and Wolfgang Wippermann. *The Racial State: Germany 1933–1945*. Cambridge: Cambridge University Press, 1991.

Carpi, Daniel. *Between Mussolini and Hitler: The Jews and the Italian Authorities in France and Tunisia*. Hanover, NH: University Press of New England, for Brandeis University Press, 1994.

Ciocca, Gaetano. *Giudizio sul bolscevismo: Com'è finito il piano quinquennale*. With a preface by *Il popolo d'Italia*. Milan: Valentino Bompiani, 1934.

Clark, Katerina, and Karl Schlögel. "Mutual Perceptions and Projections: Stalin's Russia in Nazi Germany—Nazi Germany in the Soviet Union." In *Beyond Totalitarianism: Stalinism and Nazism Compared*, ed. Michael Geyer and Sheila Fitzpatrick. Cambridge: Cambridge University Press, 2009, 396–441.

Corner, Paul. "Italian Fascism: Whatever Happened to Dictatorship?" *Journal of Modern History* 74, no. 2 (June 2002): 325–51.

Costa Pinto, António. *See* Pinto, António Costa.

Cronin, Mike, ed. *The Failure of British Fascism: The Far Right and the Fight for Political Recognition*. Basingstoke: Macmillan, 1996.

De Caprariis, Luca. "Fascism for Export? The Rise and Eclipse of the Fasci Italiani all'Estero." *Journal of Contemporary History* 35, no. 2 (April 2000): 151–83.

De Cecco, Marcello. "The Economy from Liberalism to Fascism." In *Liberal and Fascist Italy, 1900–1945*, ed. Adrian Lyttelton. Oxford: Oxford University Press, 2002, 62–82.

De Felice, Renzo. *Fascism: An Informal Introduction to Its Theory and Practice (an Interview with Michael A. Ledeen)*. New Brunswick, NJ: Transaction, 1976.

————. *Mussolini il Duce*, I, *Gli anni del consenso, 1929–1936*. Turin: Giulio Einaudi, 1974.

————, ed. *La Carta del Carnaro nei testi di Alceste De Ambris e di Gabriele D'Annunzio.* Bologna: Il Mulino, 1973.

De Grazia, Victoria. *The Culture of Consent: Mass Organization of Leisure in Fascist Italy.* Cambridge: Cambridge University Press, 1981.

Deletant, Dennis. *Hitler's Forgotten Ally: Ion Antonescu and His Regime, Romania 1940–44.* Basingstoke: Palgrave Macmillan, 2006.

Diggins, John P. *Mussolini and Fascism: The View from America.* Princeton, NJ: Princeton University Press, 1972.

Dobry, Michel., "Desperately Seeking 'Generic Fascism': Some Discordant Thoughts on the Academic Recycling of Indigenous Categories." In *Rethinking the Nature of Fascism: Comparative Perspectives,* ed. António Costa Pinto. Basingstoke: Palgrave Macmillan, 2011, 53–84.

————. "February 1934 and the Discovery of French Society's Allergy to the 'Fascist Revolution.'" In *France in the Era of Fascism: Essays on the French Authoritarian Right,* ed. Brian Jenkins. New York and Oxford: Berghahn, 2005, 129–50.

————, ed. *Le mythe de l'allergie française au fascisme.* Paris: Albin Michel, 2003.

Eatwell, Roger. *Fascism: A History.* New York: Penguin, 1995.

————. "Universal Fascism? Approaches and Definitions." In *Fascism outside Europe: The European Impulse Against Domestic Conditions in the Diffusion of Global Fascism,* ed. Stein Ugelvik Larsen. Boulder, CO: Social Science Monographs, 2001, 15–45.

Eatwell, Roger, and Cas Mudde, eds. *Western Democracies and the New Extreme Right Challenge.* London and New York: Routledge, 2004.

Ebner, Michael R. *Ordinary Violence in Mussolini's Italy.* Cambridge: Cambridge University Press, 2011.

Eco, Umberto. "Ur-fascism." *New York Review of Books,* June 22, 1995, 12–15. A slightly altered version is included in Umberto Eco, *Five Moral Pieces.* Trans. Alastair McEwen. New York: Harcourt, 2001, 65–88.

Edele, Mark, and Michael Geyer. "States of Exception: The Nazi-Soviet War as a System of Violence, 1939–1945." In *Beyond Totalitarianism: Stalinism and Nazism Compared,* ed. Michael Geyer and Sheila Fitzpatrick. Cambridge: Cambridge University Press, 2009, 345–95.

Einzig, Paul. *The Economic Foundations of Fascism.* London: Macmillan, 1933.

Eley, Geoff. *Nazism as Fascism: Violence, Ideology, and the Ground of Consent in Germany, 1930–1945.* London and New York: Routledge, 2013.

Epstein, Klaus. "A New Study of Fascism" (1964). In *Reappraisals of Fascism,* ed. Henry Ashby Turner. New York: Franklin Watts (New Viewpoints), 1975, 2–25.

Field, G. Lowell. *The Syndical and Corporative Institutions of Italian Fascism.* New York: Columbia University Press, 1938.

Finchelstein, Federico. *Transatlantic Fascism: Ideology, Violence, and the Sacred in Argentina and Italy, 1919–1945.* Durham, NC: Duke University Press, 2010.

Fleischer, Hagen. "Authoritarian Rule in Greece and Its Heritage (1936–1974)." In *Totalitarian and Authoritarian Regimes in Europe: Legacies and Lessons from the Twentieth Century*, ed. Jerzy W. Borejsza and Klaus Ziemer. New York and Oxford: Berghahn, 2006, 237–75.

Fletcher, William Miles, III. *The Search for a New Order: Intellectuals and Fascism in Prewar Japan*. Chapel Hill: University of North Carolina Press, 1982.

Franzina, Emilio, and Matteo Sanfilippo, eds. *Il fascismo e gli emigrati: La parabola dei Fasci italiani all'estero (1920–1943)*. Rome and Bari: Laterza, 2003.

Fritzsche, Peter. *Life and Death in the Third Reich*. Cambridge, MA: Belknap Press of Harvard University Press, 2008.

Frusetta, James. "Fascism to Complete the National Project? Bulgarian Fascists' Uncertain Views on the Palingenesis of the Nation." *East Central Europe* 37 (2010): 280–302.

Fuller, Mia. *Moderns Abroad: Architecture, Cities, and Italian Imperialism*. London and New York: Routledge, 2007.

Gagliardi, Alessio. *Il corporativismo fascista*. Rome: Laterza, 2010.

Gellately, Robert. *Backing Hitler: Consent and Coercion in Nazi Germany*. Oxford: Oxford University Press, 2001.

Gellately, Robert, and Nathan Stoltzfus, eds. *Social Outcasts in Nazi Germany*. Princeton, NJ: Princeton University Press, 2001.

Gentile, Emilio. "Fascism, Totalitarianism and Political Religion: Definitions and Critical Reflections on Criticisms of an Interpretation." In *Fascism, Totalitarianism and Political Religion*, ed. Roger Griffin. London and New York: Routledge, 2005, 32–81.

———. *The Sacralization of Politics in Fascist Italy*. Trans. Keith Botsford. Cambridge, MA: Harvard University Press, 1996.

———. *La via italiana al totalitarismo: Il partito e lo Stato nel regime fascista*. Rome: La Nuova Italia Scientifica, 1995.

Gentile, Giovanni. "Nazione e Nazionalismo" (1917). In *Guerra e fede*. Florence: Le Lettere, 1989, 35–38.

———. *Politica e cultura*. 2 vols. Ed. Hervé A. Cavallera. Florence: Le Lettere, 1990–91.

Gerlach, Christian, and Nicholas Werth. "State Violence—Violent Societies." In *Beyond Totalitarianism: Stalinism and Nazism Compared*, ed. Michael Geyer and Sheila Fitzpatrick. Cambridge: Cambridge University Press, 2009, 133–79.

Geyer, Michael, with assistance from Sheila Fitzpatrick. "Introduction: After Totalitarianism—Stalinism and Nazism Compared." In *Beyond Totalitarianism: Stalinism and Nazism Compared*, ed. Michael Geyer and Sheila Fitzpatrick. Cambridge: Cambridge University Press, 2009, 1–37.

Geyer, Michael, and Sheila Fitzpatrick, eds. *Beyond Totalitarianism: Stalinism and Nazism Compared*. Cambridge: Cambridge University Press, 2009.

Gleason, Abbott. *Totalitarianism: The Inner History of the Cold War*. New York: Oxford University Press, 1995.

Gorlizki, Yoram, and Hans Mommsen. "The Political (Dis)Orders of Stalinism and National Socialism." In *Beyond Totalitarianism: Stalinism and Nazism Compared*, ed. Michael Geyer and Sheila Fitzpatrick. Cambridge: Cambridge University Press, 2009, 41–86.

Gottlieb, Julie V. *Feminine Fascism: Women in Britain's Fascist Movement, 1923–1945*. London: I.B. Tauris, 2000.

Grandi, Dino. *Giovani*. Bologna: Nicola Zanichelli, 1941.

Gregor, A. James. *The Faces of Janus: Marxism and Fascism in the Twentieth Century*. New Haven, CT: Yale University Press, 2000.

Griffin, Roger. "Exploding the Continuum of History: A Non-Marxist's Marxist Model of Fascism's Revolutionary Dynamics." In *A Fascist Century: Essays by Roger Griffin*, ed. Martin Feldman. Basingstoke: Palgrave Macmillan, 2008, 46–68.

———. "Fascism's New Faces (and New Facelessness) in the 'Post-Fascist' Epoch." In *Fascism Past and Present, West and East: An International Debate on Concepts and Cases in the Comparative Study of the Extreme Right*, ed. Roger Griffin, Werner Loh, and Andreas Umland. Stuttgart: Ibidem, 2006, 29–67.

———. *A Fascist Century: Essays by Roger Griffin*. Ed. Martin Feldman. Basingstoke: Palgrave Macmillan, 2008.

———. "Foreword: Il ventennio parafascista? The Past and Future of a Neologism in Comparative Fascist Studies." In *Rethinking Fascism and Dictatorship in Interwar Europe*, ed. António Costa Pinto and Aristotle Kallis. Basingstoke: Palgrave Macmillan, 2014, viii–xix.

———. "Hooked Crosses and Forking Paths: The Fascist Dynamics of the Third Reich." In *A Fascist Century: Essays by Roger Griffin*, ed. Matthew Feldman. Basingstoke: Palgrave Macmillan, 2008, 83–113.

———. "Introduction: God's Counterfeiters? Investigating the Triad of Fascism, Totalitarianism and (Political) Religion." In *Fascism, Totalitarianism and Political Religion*, ed. Roger Griffin. London and New York: Routledge, 2005, 1–31.

———. *Modernism and Fascism: The Sense of a Beginning under Mussolini and Hitler*. Basingstoke: Palgrave Macmillan, 2007.

———. *The Nature of Fascism*. London: Routledge, 1993.

———. "The Primacy of Culture: The Current Growth (or Manufacture) of Consensus within Fascist Studies." *Journal of Contemporary History* 37, no. 1 (January 2002): 21–43. (Invited commentaries by David D. Roberts, Alexander DeGrand, Mark Antliff, and Thomas Linehan appeared in the next issue, *Journal of Contemporary History* 37, no. 2 [April 2002]: 259–74.)

———. "Uniqueness and Family Resemblances in Generic Fascism." *East Central Europe* 37 (2010): 338–44.

———, ed. *Fascism, Totalitarianism and Political Religion*. London and New York: Routledge, 2005.

Griffin, Roger, Werner Loh, and Andreas Umland, eds. *Fascism Past and Present, West and East: An International Debate on Concepts and Cases in the Comparative Study of the Extreme Right*. Stuttgart: Ibidem, 2006.

Griffin, Roger, and David D. Roberts, eds. "'The Fascist Revolution': Utopia or Façade? Reconciling Marxist and Non-Marxist Approaches." Special issue, *European Journal of Political Theory* 11, no. 4 (October 2012).

Griffiths, Richard. *An Intelligent Person's Guide to Fascism*. London: Duckworth, 2000.

Hanebrink, Paul A. *In Defense of Christian Hungary: Religion, Nationalism, and Anti-Semitism, 1890–1944*. Ithaca, NY: Cornell University Press, 2006.

Hayes, Peter. Foreword to Stephan H. Lindner, *Inside IG Farben: Hoechst During the Third Reich*, trans. Helen Shoop. Cambridge: Cambridge University Press, 2008), xiii–xviii.

———. *Industry and Ideology: IG Farben in the Nazi Era*. Cambridge: Cambridge University Press, 1987; new edn, 2001.

Himka, John-Paul. "The Importance of the Situational Element in East Central European Fascism." *East Central Europe* 37 (2010): 353–58.

Hitler, Adolf. *Hitler's Second Book: The Unpublished Sequel to* Mein Kampf. Ed. Gerhard L. Weinberg. Trans. Krista Smith. New York: Enigma Books, 2003.

Höbelt, Lothar. "Nostalgic Agnostics: Austrian Aristocrats and Politics, 1918–1938." In *European Aristocracies and the Radical Right, 1919–1939*, ed. Karina Urbach. Oxford: Oxford University Press, 2007, 161–85.

Holmes, Stephen. *The Anatomy of Antiliberalism*. Cambridge, MA: Harvard University Press, 1993.

Ihrig, Stefan. *Atatürk in the Nazi Imagination*. Cambridge, MA: Harvard University Press, 2014.

Ioanid, Radu. *The Holocaust in Romania: The Destruction of Jews and Gypsies under the Antonescu Regime, 1940–1944*. Trans. Marc J. Masurovsky. Chicago: Ivan R. Dee, 2000.

———. "Romania." In *The Oxford Handbook of Fascism*, ed. R.J.B. Bosworth. Oxford: Oxford University Press, 2009, 398–413.

Iordachi, Constantin. "Fascism in Interwar East Central and Southeastern Europe: Toward a New Transnational Research Agenda." *East Central Europe* 37 (2010): 161–213.

———. "God's Chosen Warriors: Romantic Palingenesis, Militarism and Fascism in Modern Romania." In *Comparative Fascist Studies: New Perspectives*, ed. Constantin Iordachi. London and New York: Routledge, 2010, 316–57.

———, ed. *Comparative Fascist Studies: New Perspectives*. London and New York: Routledge, 2010.

Irvine, William D. "Beyond Left and Right: Rethinking Political Boundaries in Interwar France." In *The French Right between the Wars*, ed. Samuel Kalman and Sean Kennedy. New York and Oxford: Berghahn, 2014, 227–39.

Jenkins, Brian, ed. *France in the Era of Fascism: Essays on the French Authoritarian Right*. New York and Oxford: Berghahn, 2005.

Jerez Mir, Miguel, and Javier Luque. "State and Regime in Early Francoism, 1936–45: Power Structures, Main Actors and Repression Policy." In *Rethinking Fascism and Dictatorship in Interwar Europe*, ed. António Costa Pinto and Aristotle Kallis. Basingstoke: Palgrave Macmillan, 2014, 176–97.

Kallis, Aristotle. *Fascist Ideology*. London: Routledge, 2000.

———. *Genocide and Fascism: The Eliminationist Drive in Fascist Europe*. New York and London: Routledge, 2009.

———. "Neither Fascist nor Authoritarian: The 4th of August Regime in Greece (1936–1941) and the Dynamics of Fascistisation in 1930s Europe." *East Central Europe* 37 (2010): 303–30.

Kallis, Aristotle, and António Costa Pinto. "Conclusion: Embracing Complexity and Transnational Dynamics; The Diffusion of Fascism and the Hybridization of Dictatorships in Inter-War Europe." In *Rethinking Fascism and Dictatorship in Interwar Europe*, ed. António Costa Pinto and Aristotle Kallis. Basingstoke: Palgrave Macmillan, 2014, 272–82.

Kalman, Samuel, and Sean Kennedy, eds. *The French Right between the Wars*. New York and Oxford: Berghahn, 2014.

Kasza, Gregory J. "Fascism from Above? Japan's *Kakushin* Right in Comparative Perspective." In *Fascism outside Europe: The European Impulse Against Domestic Conditions in the Diffusion of Global Fascism*, ed. Stein Ugelvik Larsen. Boulder, CO: Social Science Monographs, 2001, 183–232.

Katznelson, Ira. *Fear Itself: The New Deal and the Origins of Our Time*. New York: Liveright, 2013.

Kéchichian, Albert. *Les Croix de Feu à L'Âge des Fascismes: Travail, Famille, Patrie*. Paris: Champ Vallon, 2006.

Kershaw, Ian. "Hitler and the Uniqueness of Nazism." *Journal of Contemporary History* 39, no. 2 (April 2004): 239–54.

Kershaw, Ian, and Moshe Lewin, eds. *Stalinism and Nazism: Dictatorships in Comparison*. Cambridge: Cambridge University Press, 1997.

Kersten, Rikki. "Japan." In *The Oxford Handbook of Fascism*, ed. R.J.B. Bosworth. Oxford: Oxford University Press, 2009, 526–44.

Keyder, Çağlar. *State and Class in Turkey: A Study in Capitalist Development*. London: Verso, 1987.

Kirk, Tim. "Fascism and Austrofascism." In *The Dollfuss/Schuschnigg Era in Austria: A Reassessment*, ed. Günter Bischof, Anton Pelinka, and Alexander Lassner. New Brunswick, NJ: Transaction, 2003, 10–31.

Koch, H.W., ed. *Aspects of the Third Reich*. New York: St. Martin's, 1985.

Kühl, Stefan. *The Nazi Connection: Eugenics, American Racism, and German National Socialism*. New York: Oxford University Press, 1994.

Kühne, Thomas. *Belonging and Genocide: Hitler's Community, 1918–1945*. New Haven, CT: Yale University Press, 2010.

Kundera, Milan. *The Unbearable Lightness of Being*. Trans. Michael Henry Heim. New York: HarperCollins (Perennial), 1987.

Laclau, Ernesto. *Politics and Ideology in Marxist Theory: Capitalism, Fascism, Populism*. London: NLB, 1977.

Laqueur, Walter. *Fascism: Past, Present, Future*. Oxford: Oxford University Press, 1996.

Larsen, Stein U[gelvik]. "Decomposition and Recomposition in Theories: How to Arrive at Useful Ideas Explaining Fascism." In *Rethinking the Nature of Fascism: Comparative Perspectives*, ed. António Costa Pinto. Basingstoke: Palgrave Macmillan, 2011, 13–52.

———. "Was There Fascism outside Europe? Diffusion from Europe and

Domestic Impulses." In *Fascism outside Europe: The European Impulse Against Domestic Conditions in the Diffusion of Global Fascism*, ed. Stein Ugelvik Larsen. Boulder, CO: Social Science Monographs, 2001, 705–818.

———, ed. *Fascism outside Europe: The European Impulse against Domestic Conditions in the Diffusion of Global Fascism*. Boulder, CO: Social Science Monographs, 2001.

Lassman, Peter. "Responses to Fascism in Britain, 1930–1945: The Emergence of the Concept of Totalitarianism." In *Sociology Responds to Fascism*, ed. Stephen P. Turner and Dirk Käsler. London: Routledge, 1992, 214–40.

Ledeen, Michael. *Universal Fascism: The Theory and Practice of the Fascist International, 1928–1936*. New York: Howard Fertig, 1972.

Lewin, Moshe. "Bureaucracy and the Stalinist State." In *Stalinism and Nazism: Dictatorships in Comparison*, ed. Ian Kershaw and Moshe Lewin. Cambridge: Cambridge University Press, 1997, 53–74.

———. *The Making of the Soviet System: Essays in the Social History of Interwar Russia*. New York: Pantheon, 1985.

Lindner, Stephan H. *Inside IG Farben: Hoechst During the Third Reich*. Trans. Helen Shoop. Cambridge: Cambridge University Press, 2008.

Linehan, Thomas. *British Fascism, 1918–1939: Parties, Ideology and Culture*. Manchester: Manchester University Press, 2000.

Linz, Juan J. *Totalitarian and Authoritarian Regimes*. Boulder, CO: Lynne Rienner, 2000.

Longerich, Peter. *Holocaust: The Nazi Persecution and Murder of the Jews*. Oxford: Oxford University Press, 2010.

Luks, Leonid. *Zwei Gesichter des Totalitarismus: Bolschewismus und Nationalsozialismus im Vergleich*. Cologne: Böhlau, 2007.

Lyttelton, Adrian. "Concluding Remarks." In *Rethinking the Nature of Fascism: Comparative Perspectives*, ed. António Costa Pinto. Basingstoke: Palgrave Macmillan, 2011, 271–78.

———, ed. *Italian Fascisms from Pareto to Gentile*. New York: Harper & Row (Torchbooks), 1975.

———, ed. *Liberal and Fascist Italy*. Oxford: Oxford University Press, 2002.

Maertz, Gregory. "The Invisible Museum: Unearthing the Lost Modernist Art of the Third Reich." *Modernism/modernity* 15, no. 1 (January 2008): 63–85.

Mann, Michael. *Fascists*. Cambridge: Cambridge University Press, 2004.

Manoilescu, Mihail. *Le Siècle du corporatisme: Doctrine du corporatisme intègral et pur*, new edn. Paris: Félix Alcan, 1936 (first pub. 1934).

Markwick, Roger D. "Communism: Fascism's 'Other'?" In *The Oxford Handbook of Fascism*, ed. R.J.B. Bosworth. Oxford: Oxford University Press, 2009, 339–61.

Marrus, Michael R., and Robert O. Paxton. *Vichy France and the Jews*. New York: Basic Books, 1981.

Maruyama, Masao. *Thought and Behaviour in Modern Japanese Politics*. Expanded edn. Ed. Ivan Morris. London: Oxford University Press, 1969.

Meyer, Alfred G. *Leninism*. New York: Frederick A. Praeger, 1962.

Michaelis, Meir. "Anmerkungen zum italienischen Totalitarismusbegriff: Zur Kritik der Thesen Hannah Arendts und Renzo De Felices." *Quellen und Forschungen aus italienischen Archiven und Bibliotheken,* 62 (1982): 270–302.

Michels, Roberto. *First Lectures in Political Sociology.* Trans. Alfred de Grazia. New York: Harper & Row (Torchbooks), 1965.

Miley, Thomas Jeffrey. "Franquism as Authoritarianism: Juan Linz and His Critics." *Politics, Religion & Ideology* 12, no. 1 (2011): 27–50.

Ministero delle Corporazioni. *Atti del secondo convegno di studi sindacali e corporativi: Ferrara, 5–8 maggio 1932.* 3 vols. Rome: Tipografia del Senato, 1932.

Morgan, Philip. "Corporatism and the Economic Order." In *The Oxford Handbook of Fascism,* ed. R.J.B. Bosworth. Oxford: Oxford University Press, 2009, 150–65.

———. *Fascism in Europe, 1919–1945.* London and New York: Routledge, 2003.

———. "Recognizing the Enemy." In *Fascism Past and Present, West and East: An International Debate on Concepts and Cases in the Comparative Study of the Extreme Right,* ed. Roger Griffin, Werner Loh, and Andreas Umland. Stuttgart: Ibidem, 2006, 156–60.

———. "Studying Fascism from the Particular to the General." *East Central Europe* 37 (2010): 334–37.

Mosca, Gaetano. *The Ruling Class.* Ed. and rev. Arthur Livingston. Trans. Hannah D. Kahn. New York: McGraw-Hill, 1939.

Mosse, George L. *The Fascist Revolution: Toward a General Theory of Fascism.* New York: Howard Fertig, 1999.

———. "Toward a General Theory of Fascism." In *The Fascist Revolution: Toward a General Theory of Fascism.* New York: Howard Fertig, 1999, 1–44.

Musiedlak, Didier. "Le corporatisme dans la structure de l'Etat fasciste." In *Les Expériences Corporatives dans l'aire Latine,* ed. Didier Musiedlak. Berne: Peter Lang, 2010, 127–52.

———, ed. *Les Expériences Corporatives dan l'aire Latine.* Berne: Peter Lang, 2010.

Mussolini, Benito. Speech to the Chamber of Deputies, 21 June 1921. In Benito Mussolini, *Scritti e discorsi di Benito Mussolini,* vol. 2, *La rivoluzione fascista (23 marzo 1919–28 ottobre 1922).* Milan: Ulrico Hoepli, 1934.

Nolte, Ernst. "Between Myth and Revisionism? The Third Reich in the Perspective of the 1980s." In *Aspects of the Third Reich,* ed. H.W. Koch. New York: St. Martin's, 1985, 17–38.

———. Comment on Gilbert Allardyce, "What Fascism Is Not: Thoughts on the Deflation of a Concept." *American Historical Review* 84, no. 2 (April 1979): 391–94.

———. *Three Faces of Fascism: Action Française, Italian Fascism, and National Socialism.* Trans. Leila Vennewitz. New York: Holt, Rinehart and Winston, 1966.

Orlow, Dietrich. *The Lure of Fascism in Western Europe: German Nazis, Dutch and French Fascists, 1933–1939.* New York: Palgrave Macmillan, 2009.

Ormos, Maria. *Hungary in the Age of the Two World Wars, 1914–1945.* Trans. Brian McLean. Boulder, CO: Social Science Monographs, 2007.

Overy, Richard. *The Dictators: Hitler's Germany and Stalin's Russia.* New York: W.W. Norton, 2004.

Painter, Borden W., Jr. *Mussolini's Rome: Rebuilding the Eternal City.* New York: Palgrave Macmillan, 2005.

Panunzio, Vito. *Fedeltà al sindacato e alla corporazione.* Rome: L'Economia Italiana, 1942.

———. *Il "secondo fascismo," 1936–1943: La reazione della nuova generazione alla crisi del movimento e del regime.* Milan: Mursia, 1988.

Passmore, Kevin. "The Essence of Fascism." In *Fascism Past and Present, West and East: An International Debate on Concepts and Cases in the Comparative Study of the Extreme Right,* ed. Roger Griffin, Werner Loh, and Andreas Umland. Stuttgart: Ibidem, 2006, 352–59.

———. *Fascism: A Very Short Introduction.* Oxford: Oxford University Press, 2002.

———. *From Liberalism to Fascism: The Right in a French Province, 1928–1939.* Cambridge: Cambridge University Press, 1997.

———. "Theories of Fascism: A Critique from the Perspective of Women's and Gender History." In *Rethinking the Nature of Fascism: Comparative Perspectives,* ed. António Costa Pinto. Basingstoke: Palgrave Macmillan, 2011, 119–40.

———, ed. *Women, Gender and Fascism in Europe, 1919–1945.* New Brunswick, NJ: Rutgers University Press, 2003.

Paxton, Robert O. *The Anatomy of Fascism.* New York: Random House (Vintage): 2005.

———. "Jews: How Vichy Made It Worse." *New York Review of Books,* 6 March 2014, 40–43.

Payne, Stanley G. Comment on Gilbert Allardyce, "What Fascism Is Not: Thoughts on the Deflation of a Concept." *American Historical Review* 84, no. 2 (April 1979): 389–91.

———. *A History of Fascism, 1914–1945.* Madison: University of Wisconsin Press, 1995.

Pellizzi, Camillo. *Problemi e realtà del fascismo.* Florence: Vallecchi, 1924.

Pelt, Mogens. "Stages in the Development of the 'Fourth of August' Regime in Greece." In *Rethinking Fascism and Dictatorship in Interwar Europe,* ed. António Costa Pinto and Aristotle Kallis. Basingstoke: Palgrave Macmillan, 2014, 198–218.

Peniston-Bird, Corinna. "Austria." In *The Oxford Handbook of Fascism,* ed. R.J.B. Bosworth. Oxford: Oxford University Press, 2009, 434–52.

Peukert, Detlev J.K. *The Weimar Republic: The Crisis of Classical Modernity.* Trans. Richard Deveson. New York: Hill and Wang, 1993.

Pinto, António Costa. "Elites, Single Parties and Political Decision-Making in Fascist Era Dictatorships." *Contemporary European History* 11, no. 3 (2002): 429–54.

———. *The Nature of Fascism Revisited.* Boulder, CO: Social Science Monographs, 2012.

———. "Reply: State, Dictators and Single Parties—Where Are the Fascist Regimes?" *Contemporary European History* 11, no. 3 (2002): 462–66.

————. "Single Party, Cabinet and Political Decision-Making in Fascist Era Dictatorships: Comparative Perspectives." In *Ruling Elites and Decision-Making*, ed. António Costa Pinto. Boulder, CO: Social Science Monographs, 2009, 215–51.

————, ed. *Rethinking the Nature of Fascism: Comparative Perspectives*. Basingstoke: Palgrave Macmillan, 2011.

————, ed. *Ruling Elites and Decision-Making in Fascist-Era Dictatorships*. Boulder, CO: Social Science Monographs, 2009.

————, ed. *Salazar's Dictatorship and European Fascism: Problems of Interpretation*. Boulder, CO: Social Science Monographs, 2009.

Pinto, António Costa, and Aristotle Kallis, eds. *Rethinking Fascism and Dictatorship in Interwar Europe*. Basingstoke: Palgrave Macmillan, 2014.

Pittaway, Mark. "Hungary." In *The Oxford Handbook of Fascism*, ed. R.J.B. Bosworth. Oxford: Oxford University Press, 2009, 380–97.

Pollard, J.F. "Fascism and Catholicism." In *The Oxford Handbook of Fascism*, ed. R.J.B. Bosworth. Oxford: Oxford University Press, 2009, 166–84.

Proctor, Robert. *The Nazi War on Cancer*. Princeton, NJ: Princeton University Press, 1999.

————. *Racial Hygiene: Medicine under the Nazis*. Cambridge, CA: Harvard University Press, 1988.

Promitzer, Christian, Sevastri Trubeta, and Marius Turda, eds. *Health, Hygiene, and Eugenics in Southeastern Europe to 1945*. Budapest: Central European University Press, 2011.

Pugh, Martin. *"Hurrah for the Blackshirts!": Fascists and Fascism in Britain between the Wars*. London: Jonathan Cape, 2005.

Reichardt, Sven, and Armin Nolzen, eds. *Faschismus in Italien und Deutschland: Studien zu Transfer und Vergleich*. Göttingen: Wallstein Verlag, 2005.

Reynolds, E. Bruce. "Peculiar Characteristics: The Japanese Political System in the Fascist Era." In *Japan in the Fascist Era*, ed. E. Bruce Reynolds. New York: Palgrave Macmillan, 2004, 155–97.

————, ed. *Japan in the Fascist Era*. New York: Palgrave Macmillan, 2004.

Roberts, David D. "Comment: Fascism, Single-Party Dictatorships, and the Search for a Comparative Framework." *Contemporary European History* 11, no. 3 (2002): 455–61.

————. "Fascism, Marxism, and the Question of Modern Revolution." *European Journal of Political Theory* 9, no. 2 (April 2010): 183–201.

————. "Fascism, Modernism, and the Quest for an Alternative Modernity." *Patterns of Prejudice* 43, no. 1 (February 2009): 91–102.

————. "Fascism, Para-fascism, and the Framework for Interactive Political Innovation during the Era of the Two World Wars." In *Rethinking Fascism and Dictatorship in Interwar Europe*, ed. António Costa Pinto and Aristotle Kallis. Basingstoke: Palgrave Macmillan, 2014, 42–66.

————. "'Political Religion' and the Totalitarian Departures of Interwar Europe: On the Uses and Disadvantages of an Analytical Category." *Contemporary European History* 18, no. 4 (November 2009): 381–414.

————. "Reconsidering Gramsci's Interpretation of Fascism." *Journal of Modern Italian Studies* 16, no. 2 (March 2011): 239–55.

————. "Roger Griffin, Ernst Nolte, and the Historical Place of Fascism." In *Fascism Past and Present, West and East: An International Debate on Concepts and Cases in the Comparative Study of the Extreme Right*, ed. Roger Griffin, Werner Loh, and Andreas Umland. Stuttgart: Ibidem, 2006, 376–80.

————. *The Syndicalist Tradition and Italian Fascism*. Chapel Hill: University of North Carolina Press, 1979.

————. *The Totalitarian Experiment in Twentieth-Century Europe: Understanding the Poverty of Great Politics*. London and New York: Routledge, 2006.

————. "Understanding Fascism as Historically Specific." In *Fascism Past and Present, West and East: An International Debate on Concepts and Cases in the Comparative Study of the Extreme Right*, ed. Roger Griffin, Werner Loh, and Andreas Umland. Stuttgart: Ibidem, 2006, 202–4.

Rocco, Alfredo. "Crisi dello Stato e sindacati." In *Scritti e discorsi politici*. 3 vols. Milan: A. Giuffré, 1938, 2:631–45.

————. "The *Politica* Manifesto, December 15th, 1918." In *Italian Fascisms from Pareto to Gentile*, ed. Adrian Lyttelton. New York, Harper & Row (Torchbooks), 1975, 249–68.

————. *Scritti e discorsi politici*. 3 vols. Milan: A. Giuffré, 1938.

Rodogno, Davide. *Fascism's European Empire: Italian Occupation during the Second World War*. Trans. Adrian Belton. Cambridge: Cambridge University Press, 2006.

Romsics, Ignác. "The Hungarian Aristocracy and Its Politics." In *European Aristocracies and the Radical Right, 1919–1939*, ed. Karina Urbach. Oxford: Oxford University Press, 2007, 187–200.

Rorty, Richard. *Contingency, Irony, and Solidarity*. Cambridge: Cambridge University Press, 1989.

Roseman, Mark. "National Socialism and Modernization." In *Fascist Italy and Nazi Germany: Comparisons and Contrasts*, ed. Richard Bessel. Cambridge: Cambridge University Press, 1996, 197–229.

Sakmyster, Thomas L. *Hungary's Admiral on Horseback: Miklos Horthy, 1918–1944*. Boulder, CO: East European Monographs, 1994.

Santomassimo, Gianpasquale. *La terza via fascista: Il mito del corporativismo*. Rome: Carocci, 2006.

Schnapp, Jeffrey T. *Building Fascism, Communism, Liberal Democracy: Gaetano Ciocca—Architect, Inventor, Farmer, Writer, Engineer*. Stanford, CA: Stanford University Press, 2004.

————. *Staging Fascism: 18 BL and the Theater of Masses for Masses*. Stanford, CA: Stanford University Press, 1996.

Sherrill, Charles H. *Kamal Roosevelt Mussolini*. Bologna: Nicola Zanichelli, 1936.

Shorten, Richard. *Modernism and Totalitarianism: Rethinking the Intellectual Sources of Nazism and Stalinism, 1945 to the Present*. Basingstoke: Palgrave Macmillan, 2012.

Snowden, Frank M. *The Conquest of Malaria: Italy, 1900–1962.* New Haven, CT: Yale University Press, 2006.

Snyder, Timothy. *Bloodlands: Europe between Hitler and Stalin.* New York: Basic Books, 2010.

Solonari, Vladimir. *Purifying the Nation: Population Exchange and Ethnic Cleansing in Nazi-Allied Romania.* Washington, DC: Woodrow Wilson Center Press; Baltimore: Johns Hopkins University Press, 2010.

Sottile, Joseph P. "The Fascist Era: Imperial Japan and the Axis Alliance in Historical Perspective." In *Japan in the Fascist Era,* ed. E. Bruce Reynolds. New York: Palgrave Macmillan, 2004, 1–48.

Spirito, Ugo. *Il corporativismo.* Florence: Sansoni, 1970.

Steigmann-Gall, Richard. *The Holy Reich: Nazi Conceptions of Christianity, 1919–1945.* Cambridge: Cambridge University Press, 2003.

Sternhell, Zeev. *The Anti-Enlightenment Tradition.* Trans. David Maisel. New Haven, CT: Yale University Press, 2010.

———. *Neither Right nor Left: Fascist Ideology in France.* Trans. David Maisel. Berkeley: University of California Press, 1986.

Stone, Dan. *Responses to Nazism in Britain, 1933–1939: Before War and Holocaust.* Basingstoke: Palgrave Macmillan, 2003.

Suckert, Curzio. "La conquista dello Stato nella concezione organica di Sergio Panunzio." *Corriere Padano* (Ferrara), 16 December 1925, 1.

Sugar, Peter F. "Conclusion." In *Native Fascism in the Successor States, 1918–1945,* ed. Peter F. Sugar. Santa Barbara, CA: ABC-Clio, 1971, 145–56.

———, ed. *Native Fascism in the Successor States, 1918–1945.* Santa Barbara, CA: ABC-Clio, 1971.

Talbot, George. *Censorship in Fascist Italy, 1922–1943: Policies, Procedures and Protagonists.* Basingstoke: Palgrave Macmillan, 2007.

Talmon, J.L. *The Origins of Totalitarian Democracy.* New York: W.W. Norton, 1970 (first pub. 1952).

Tarquini, Alessandra. *Il Gentile dei fascisti: Gentiliani e antigentiliani nel regime fascista.* Bologna: Il Mulino, 2009.

Taruskin, Richard. *On Russian Music.* Berkeley: University of California Press, 2009.

Tooze, Adam. *The Wages of Destruction: The Making and Breaking of the Nazi Economy.* New York: Penguin, 2006.

Turda, Marius. "Controlling the National Body: Ideas of Racial Purification in Romania, 1918–1944." In *Health, Hygiene, and Eugenics in Southeastern Europe to 1945,* ed. Christian Promitzer, Sevastri Trubeta, and Marius Turda. Budapest: Central European University Press, 2011, 325–50.

———. "The First Debates on Eugenics in Hungary, 1910–1918." In *"Blood and Homeland": Eugenics and Racial Nationalism in Central and Southeast Europe, 1900–1940,* ed. Marius Turda and Paul J. Weindling. Budapest: Central European University Press, 2007, 185–221.

Turda, Marius, and Paul J. Weindling, eds. *"Blood and Homeland": Eugenics and*

Racial Nationalism in Central and Southeast Europe, 1900–1940. Budapest: Central European University Press, 2007.

Turner, Henry Ashby, ed. *Reappraisals of Fascism*. New York: Franklin Watts (New Viewpoints), 1975.

Turner, Stephen P., and Dirk Käsler, eds. *Sociology Responds to Fascism*. London: Routledge, 1992.

Ungari, Paolo. *Alfredo Rocco e l'ideologia giuridica del fascismo*. Brescia: Morcelliana, 1963.

Urbach, Karina, ed. *European Aristocracies and the Radical Right, 1919–1939*. Oxford: Oxford University Press, 2007.

Vincent, Mary. "Spain." In *The Oxford Handbook of Fascism*, ed. R.J.B. Bosworth. Oxford: Oxford University Press, 2009, 362–79.

Werner, Michael, and Bénédicte Zimmermann. "Beyond Comparison: *Histoire Croisée* and the Challenge of Reflexivity." *History and Theory* 45, no. 1 (February 2006): 30–50.

———, eds. *De la comparaison à l'histoire croisée*. Paris: Editions du Seuil, 2004.

Williams, Manuela A. *Mussolini's Propaganda Abroad: Subversion in the Mediterranean and the Middle East, 1935–1940*. London and New York: Routledge, 2006.

Wippermann, Wolfgang. *Faschismus: Eine Weltgeschichte vom 19. Jahrhundert bis Heute*. Darmstadt: Primus, 2009.

INDEX

www.ingramcontent.com/pod-product-compliance
Lightning Source LLC
Chambersburg PA
CBHW070907030426
42336CB00014BA/2328